ASTRA

LOST IN SPACE

4

[REVELATION]

KENTA SHINOHARA

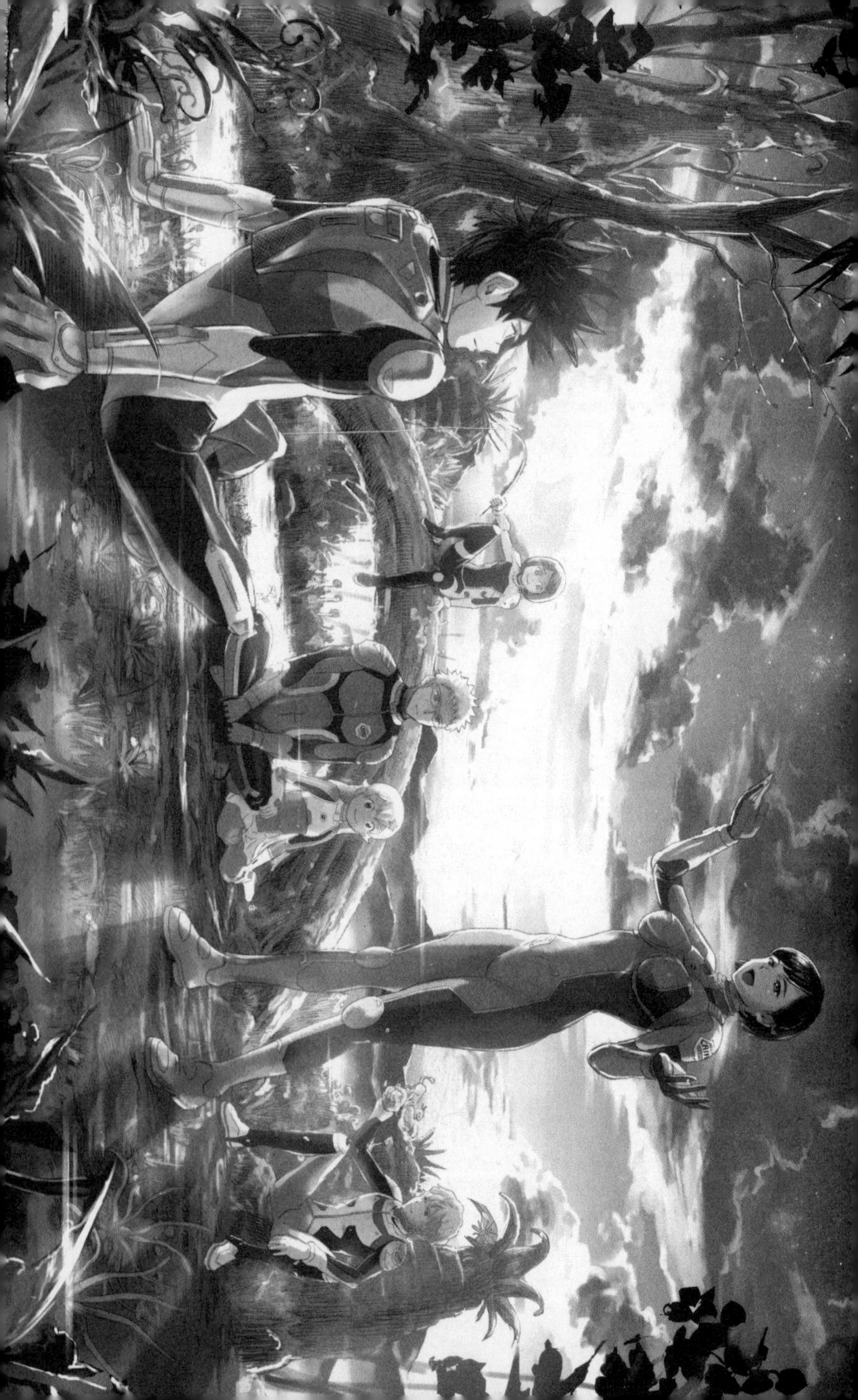

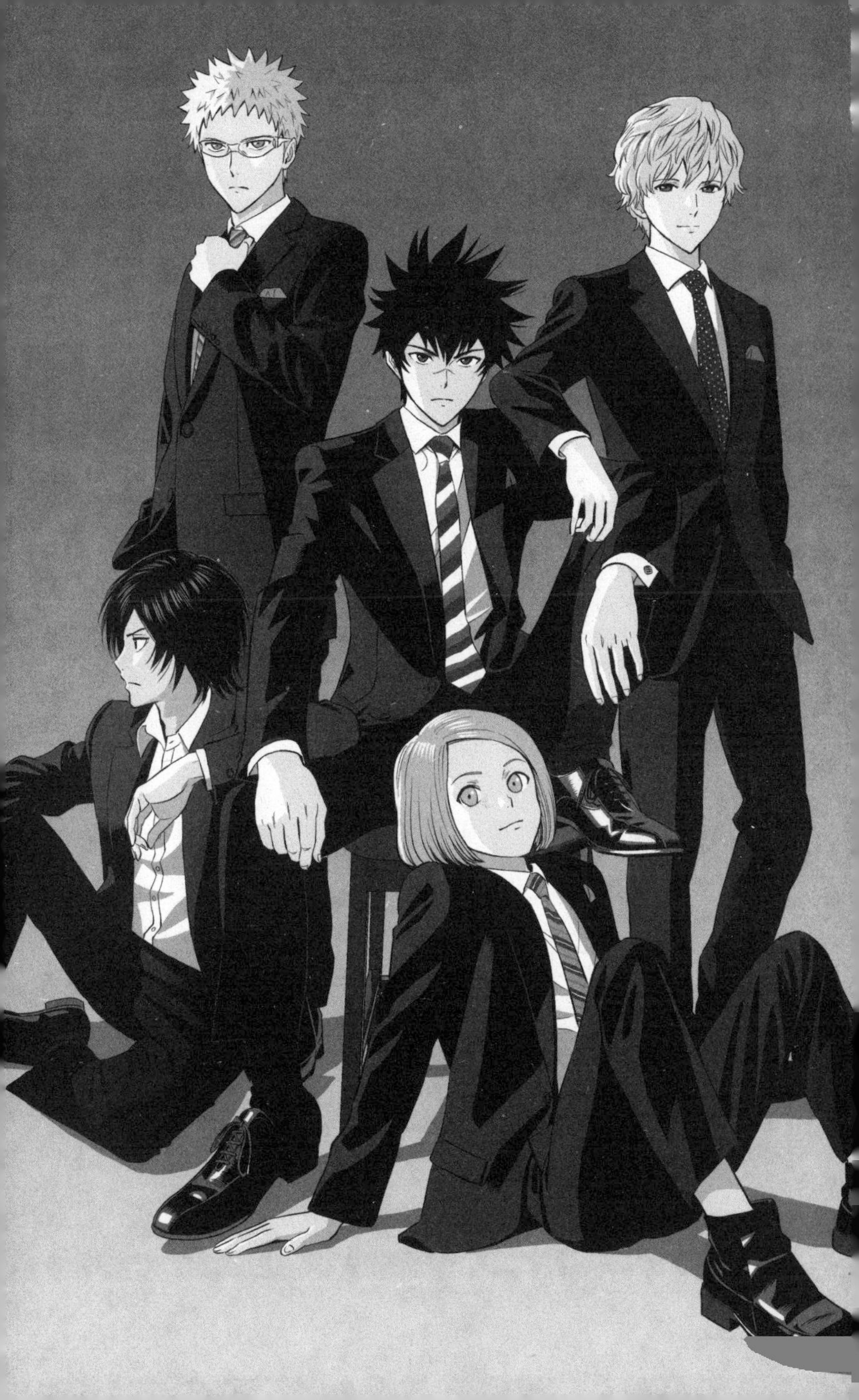

CHARACTERS&STORY

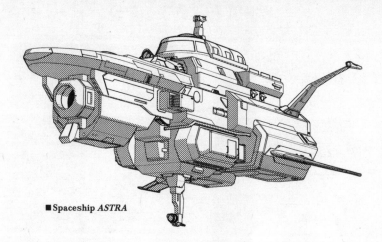

■Spaceship *ASTRA*

STORY

It's the year 2063, and interstellar space travel has become the norm. A group of students from Caird High School is set to take off for a five-day camp on Planet McPa at the Mousanish Spaceport. However, shortly after arriving, the group encounters a mysterious glowing orb that swallows them up and spits them out into the depths of space. By a stroke of good luck, they find an abandoned spaceship where they can take shelter, but its long-range communications system is offline. Not only that, they quickly discover they weren't spat out above McPa as they initially thought, but were instead transported 5,000 light-years away! Critically short on both food and water, the group manages to piece together a string of five planets where they can forage for supplies while making their way home one planet at a time. But just as things barely get under way, they find out one of the crew may be a killer sent on a suicide mission to murder all of them!

The crew of the *Astra* makes it to Icriss, the fourth planet on their journey home. But before they can land, they are attacked by a giant creature, and their panicked escape leads to a disastrous crash-landing. The *Astra* is heavily damaged and can no longer manage spaceflight. With no means of repairing the ship, the crew faces a harsh reality—their journey is over. But while exploring their new home planet, they stumble across...another *Astra*?!

ASTRA
LOST IN SPACE

CHARACTERS

Zack Walker

Aries Spring

Kanata Hoshijima

Luca Esposito

Funicia Raffaeli

Quitterie Raffaeli

Charce Lacroix

Yun-hua Lu

Ulgar Zweig

ASTRA
LOST IN SPACE
CONTENTS

4

[REVELATION]

#29 ——————— 7

#30 ——————— 25

#31 ——————— 45

#32 ——————— 67

#33 ——————— 87

#34 ——————— 107

#35 ——————— 127

#36 ——————— 149

#37 ——————— 169

ASTRA LOST IN SPACE

#29

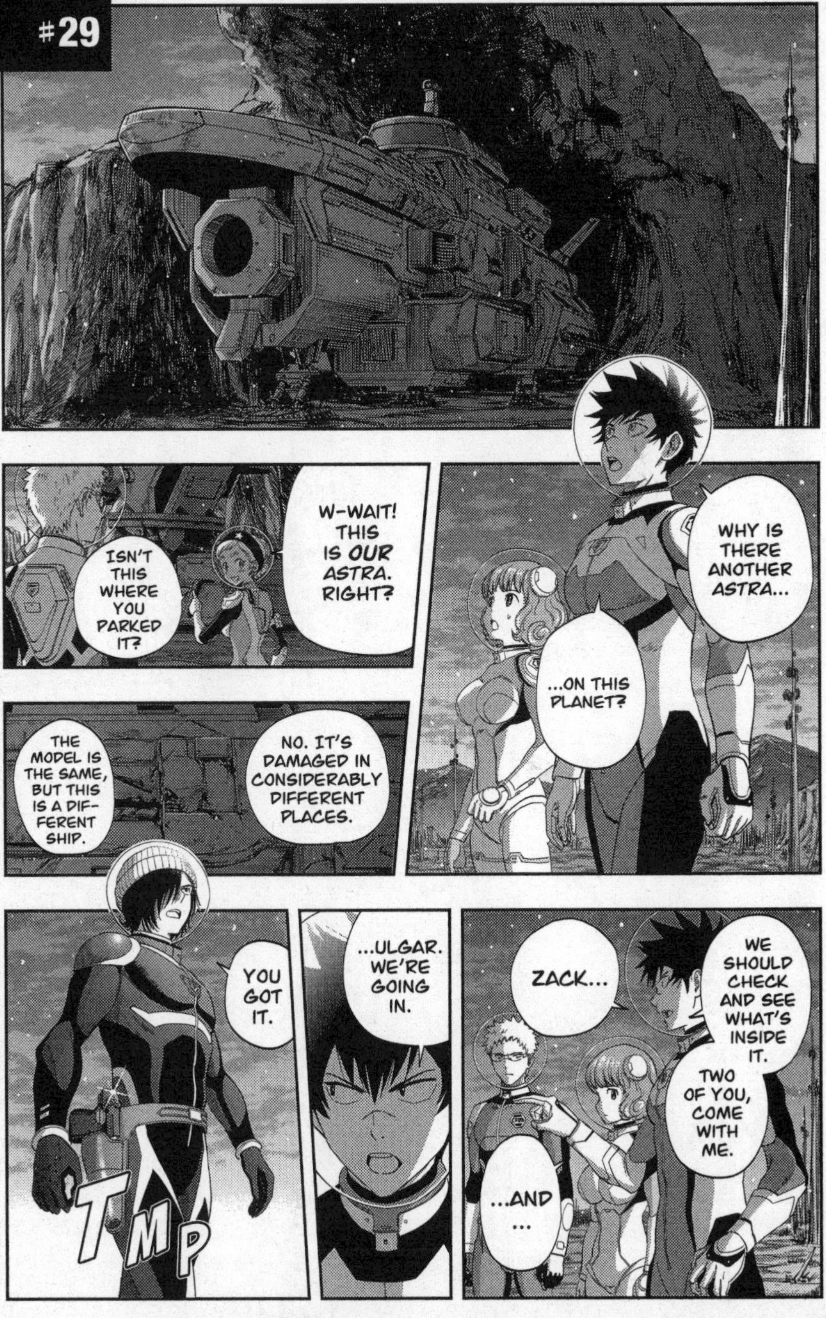
WHY IS THERE ANOTHER ASTRA...
...ON THIS PLANET?
W-WAIT! THIS IS *OUR* ASTRA. RIGHT?
ISN'T THIS WHERE YOU PARKED IT?
NO. IT'S DAMAGED IN CONSIDERABLY DIFFERENT PLACES.
THE MODEL IS THE SAME, BUT THIS IS A DIF-FERENT SHIP.
WE SHOULD CHECK AND SEE WHAT'S INSIDE IT.
ZACK...
TWO OF YOU, COME WITH ME.
...AND ...
...ULGAR. WE'RE GOING IN.
YOU GOT IT.
TMP

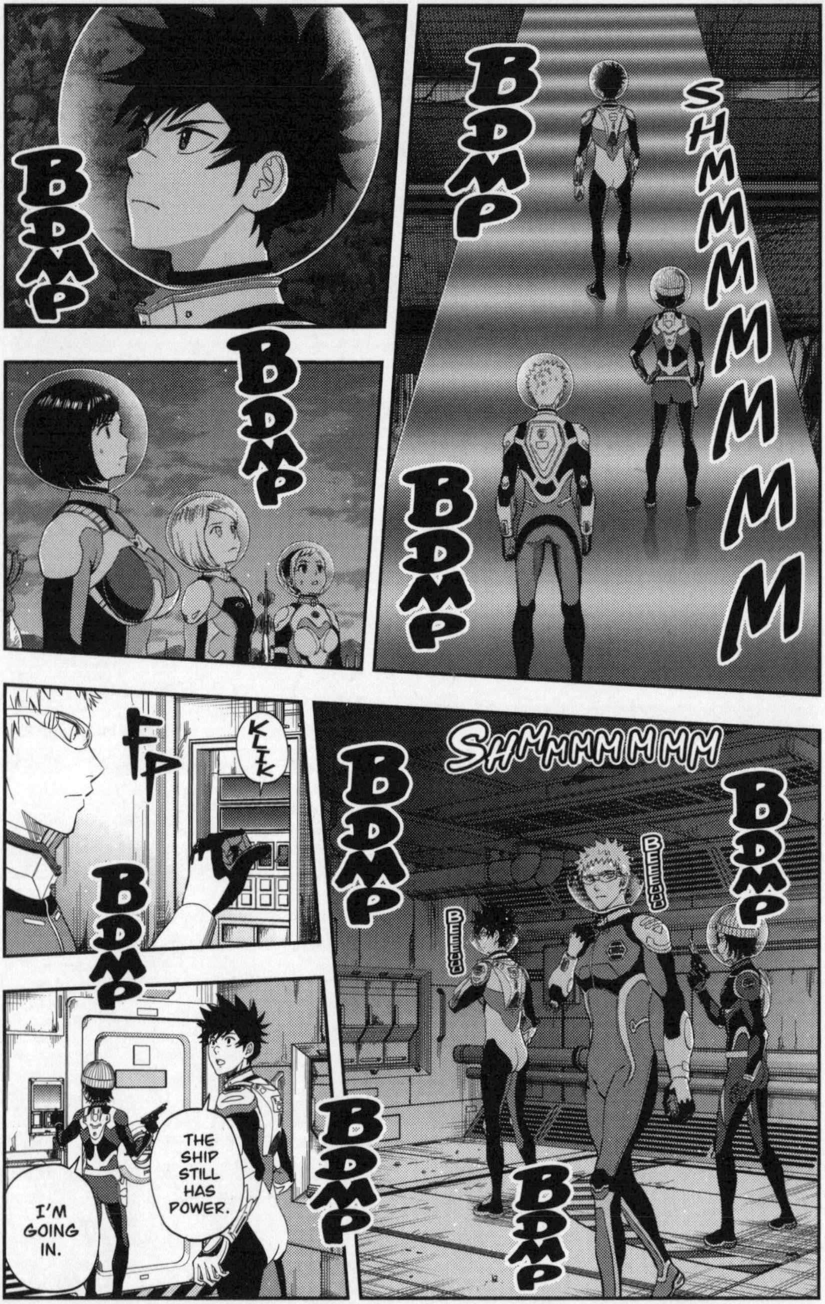
SHMMMMMMMM
BDMP
BDMP
BDMP
BDMP
SHMMMMMMMM
BDMP
BDMP
BDMP
KLIK
FP
BDMP
THE SHIP STILL HAS POWER.
I'M GOING IN.
BDMP

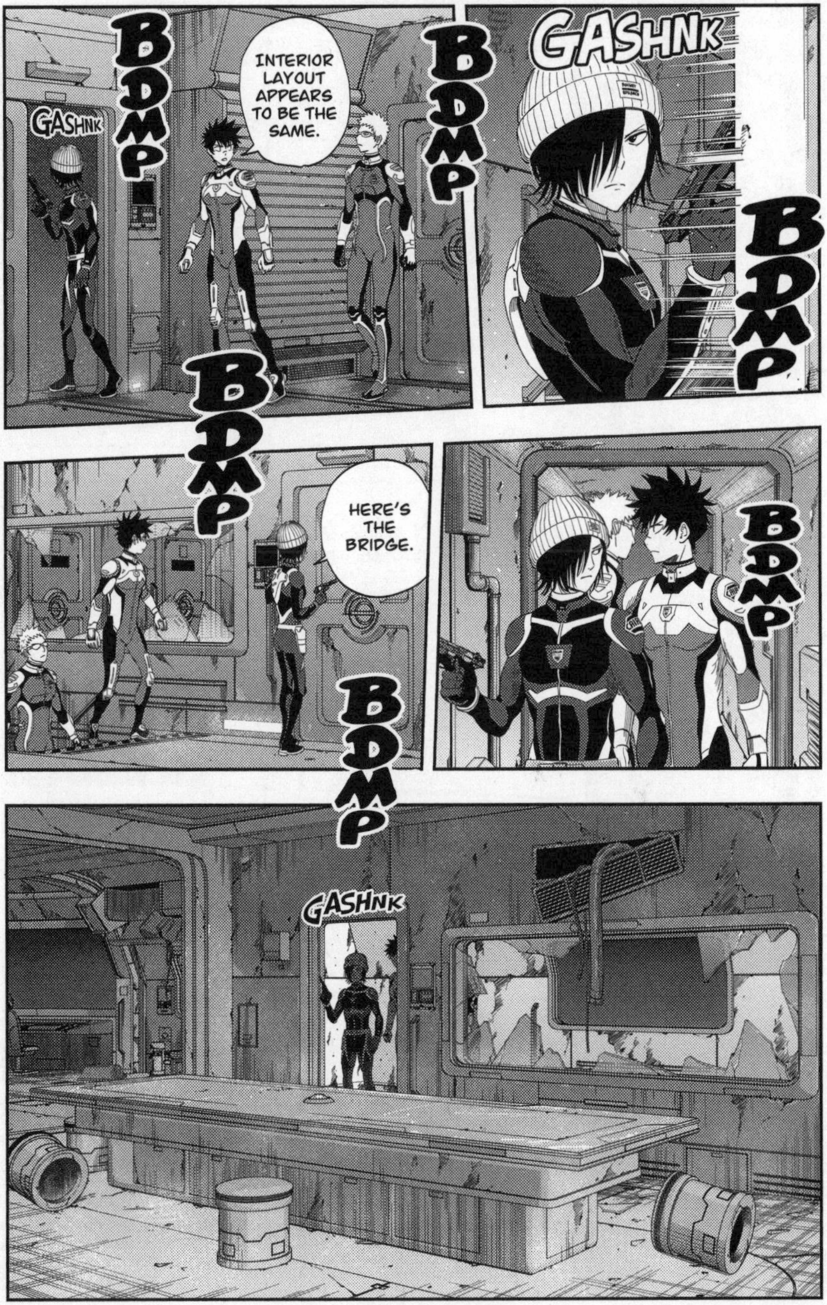
GASHNK
BDMP
BDMP
INTERIOR LAYOUT APPEARS TO BE THE SAME.
GASHNK
BDMP
BDMP
BDMP
HERE'S THE BRIDGE.
BDMP
GASHNK

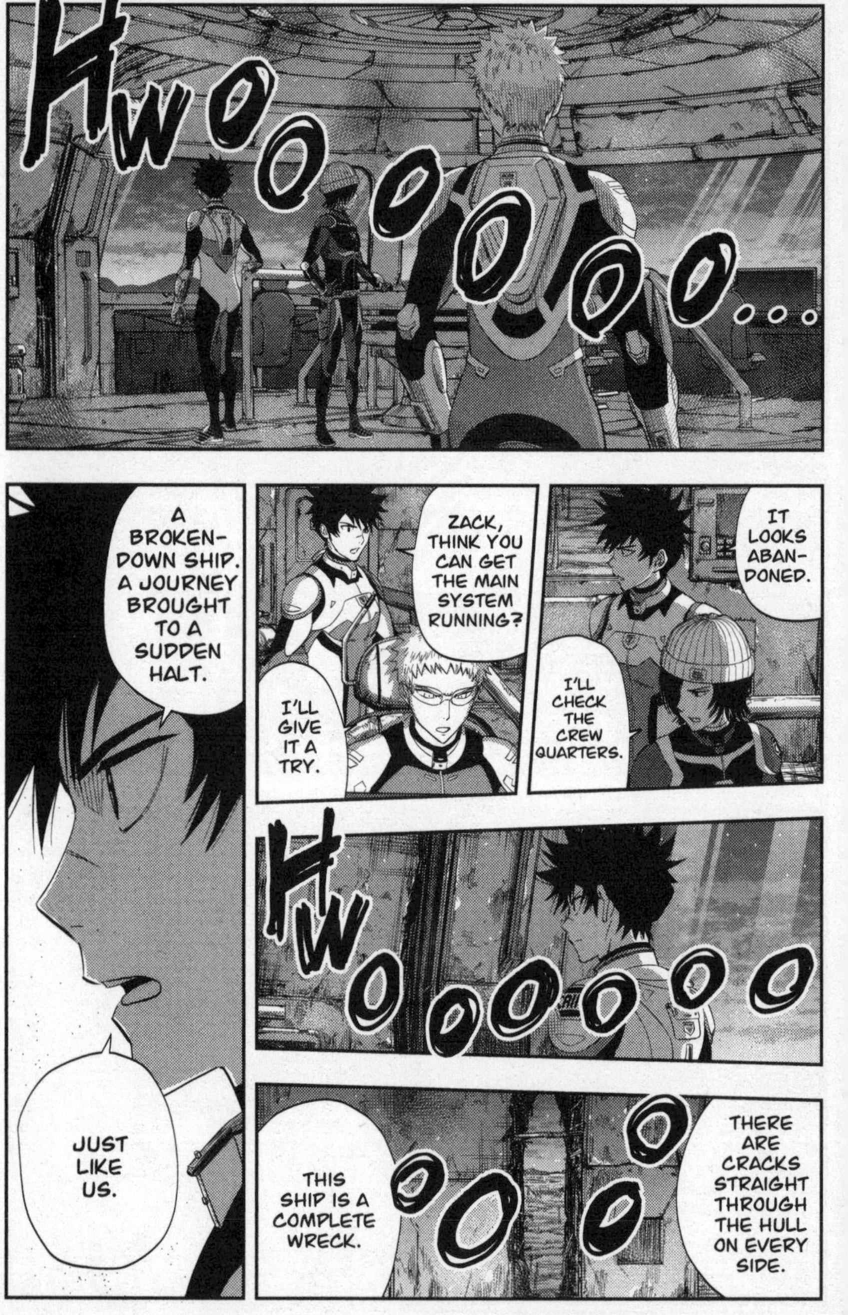
HWOOOOOOOOO...
IT LOOKS ABANDONED.
I'LL CHECK THE CREW QUARTERS.
ZACK, THINK YOU CAN GET THE MAIN SYSTEM RUNNING?
I'LL GIVE IT A TRY.
HWOOOOOOOO
THERE ARE CRACKS STRAIGHT THROUGH THE HULL ON EVERY SIDE.
OOOO
THIS SHIP IS A COMPLETE WRECK.
A BROKEN-DOWN SHIP. A JOURNEY BROUGHT TO A SUDDEN HALT.
JUST LIKE US.

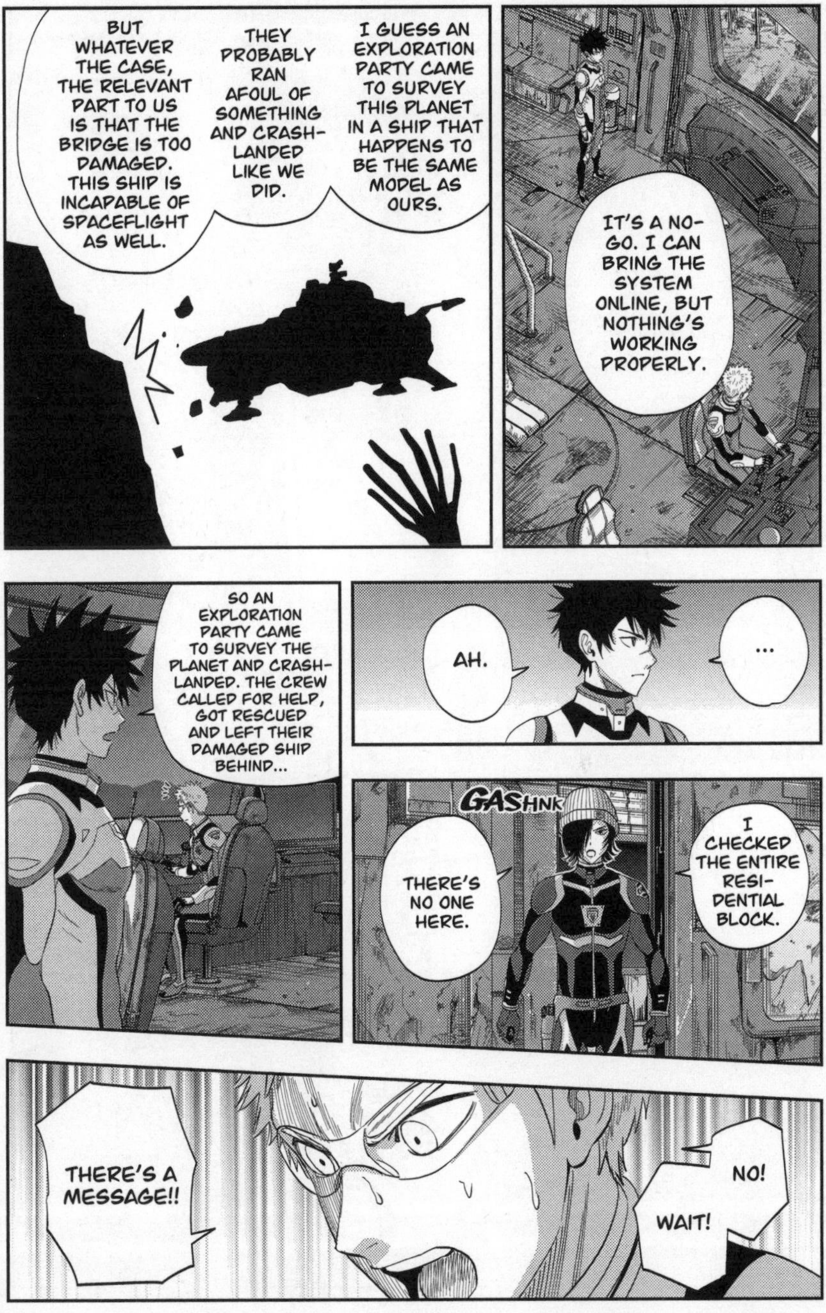
IT'S A NO-GO. I CAN BRING THE SYSTEM ONLINE, BUT NOTHING'S WORKING PROPERLY.
I GUESS AN EXPLORATION PARTY CAME TO SURVEY THIS PLANET IN A SHIP THAT HAPPENS TO BE THE SAME MODEL AS OURS.
THEY PROBABLY RAN AFOUL OF SOMETHING AND CRASH-LANDED LIKE WE DID.
BUT WHATEVER THE CASE, THE RELEVANT PART TO US IS THAT THE BRIDGE IS TOO DAMAGED. THIS SHIP IS INCAPABLE OF SPACEFLIGHT AS WELL.
...
AH.
GASHNK
I CHECKED THE ENTIRE RESI-DENTIAL BLOCK.
THERE'S NO ONE HERE.
SO AN EXPLORATION PARTY CAME TO SURVEY THE PLANET AND CRASH-LANDED. THE CREW CALLED FOR HELP, GOT RESCUED AND LEFT THEIR DAMAGED SHIP BEHIND...
NO!
WAIT!
THERE'S A MESSAGE!!

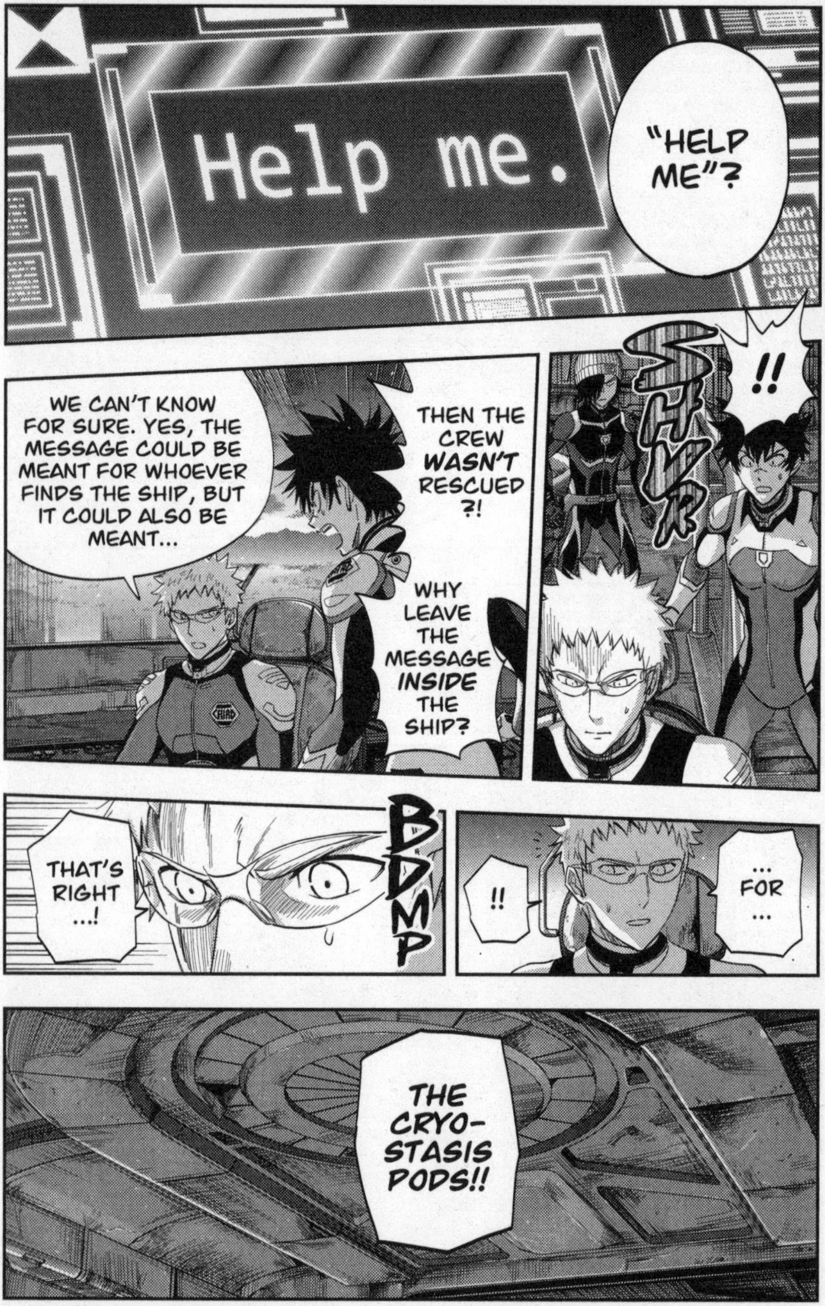
Help me.
"HELP ME"?
!!
THEN THE CREW WASN'T RESCUED?!
WHY LEAVE THE MESSAGE INSIDE THE SHIP?
WE CAN'T KNOW FOR SURE. YES, THE MESSAGE COULD BE MEANT FOR WHOEVER FINDS THE SHIP, BUT IT COULD ALSO BE MEANT...
... FOR ...
!!
BDMP
THAT'S RIGHT ...!
THE CRYO-STASIS PODS!!

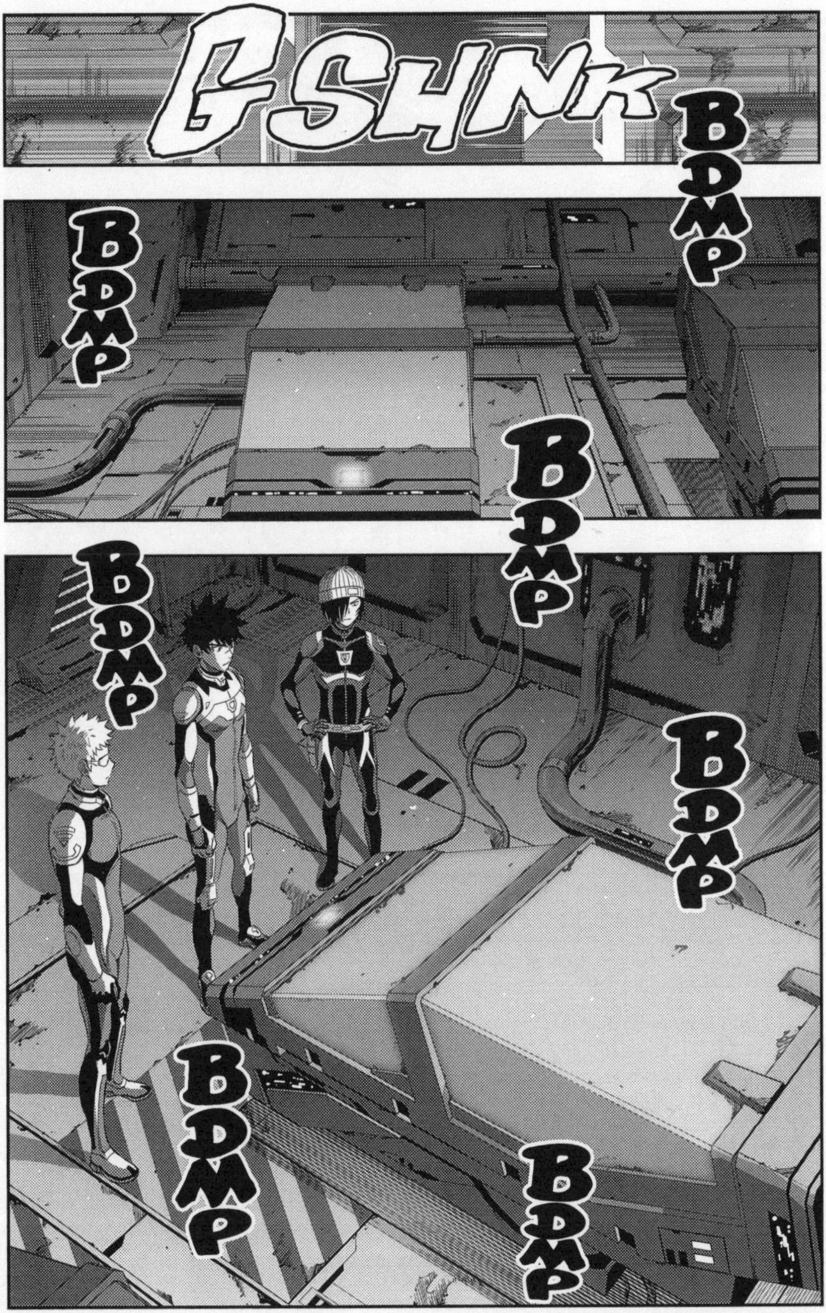
GSHNK
BDMP
BDMP
BDMP
BDMP
BDMP
BDMP
BDMP

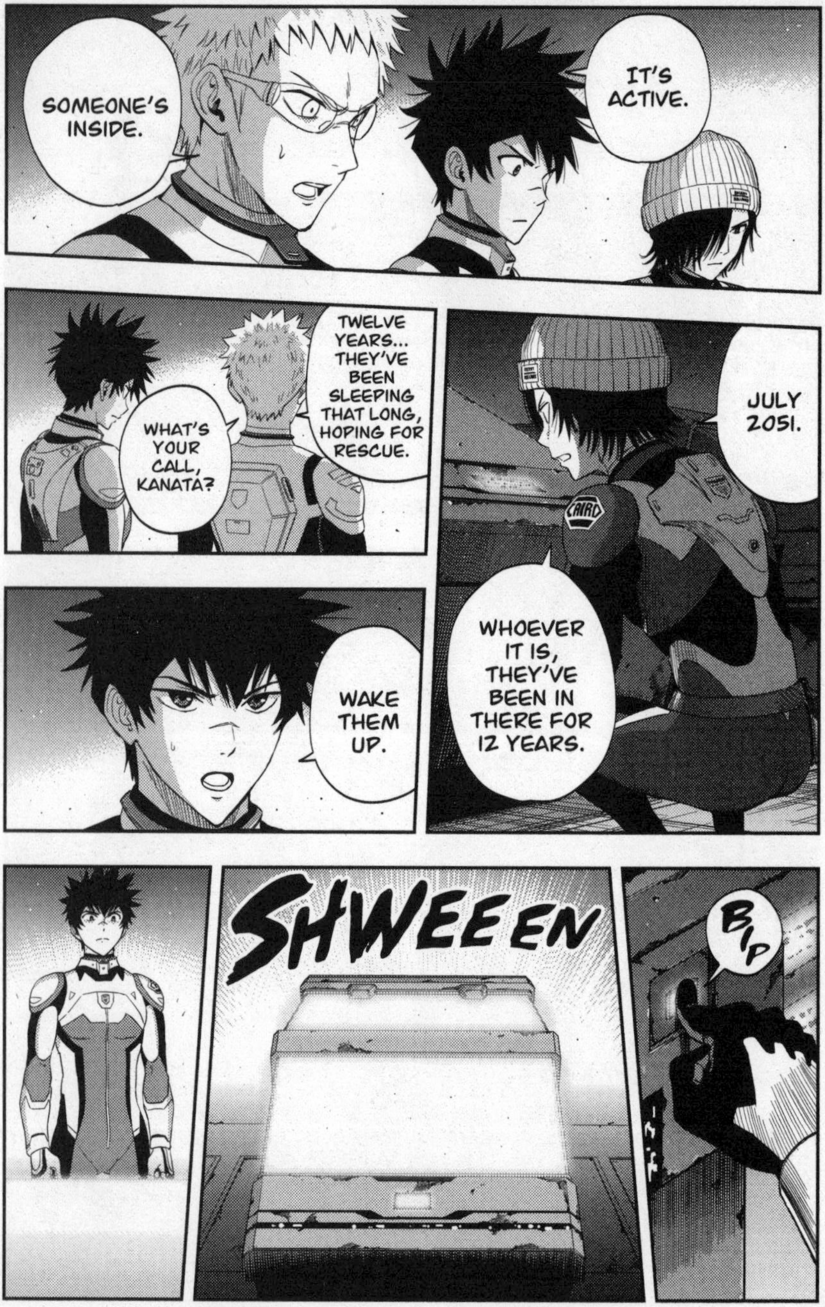
IT'S ACTIVE.
SOMEONE'S INSIDE.
JULY 2051.
WHOEVER IT IS, THEY'VE BEEN IN THERE FOR 12 YEARS.
TWELVE YEARS... THEY'VE BEEN SLEEPING THAT LONG, HOPING FOR RESCUE.
WHAT'S YOUR CALL, KANATA?
WAKE THEM UP.
BIP
SHWEEEN

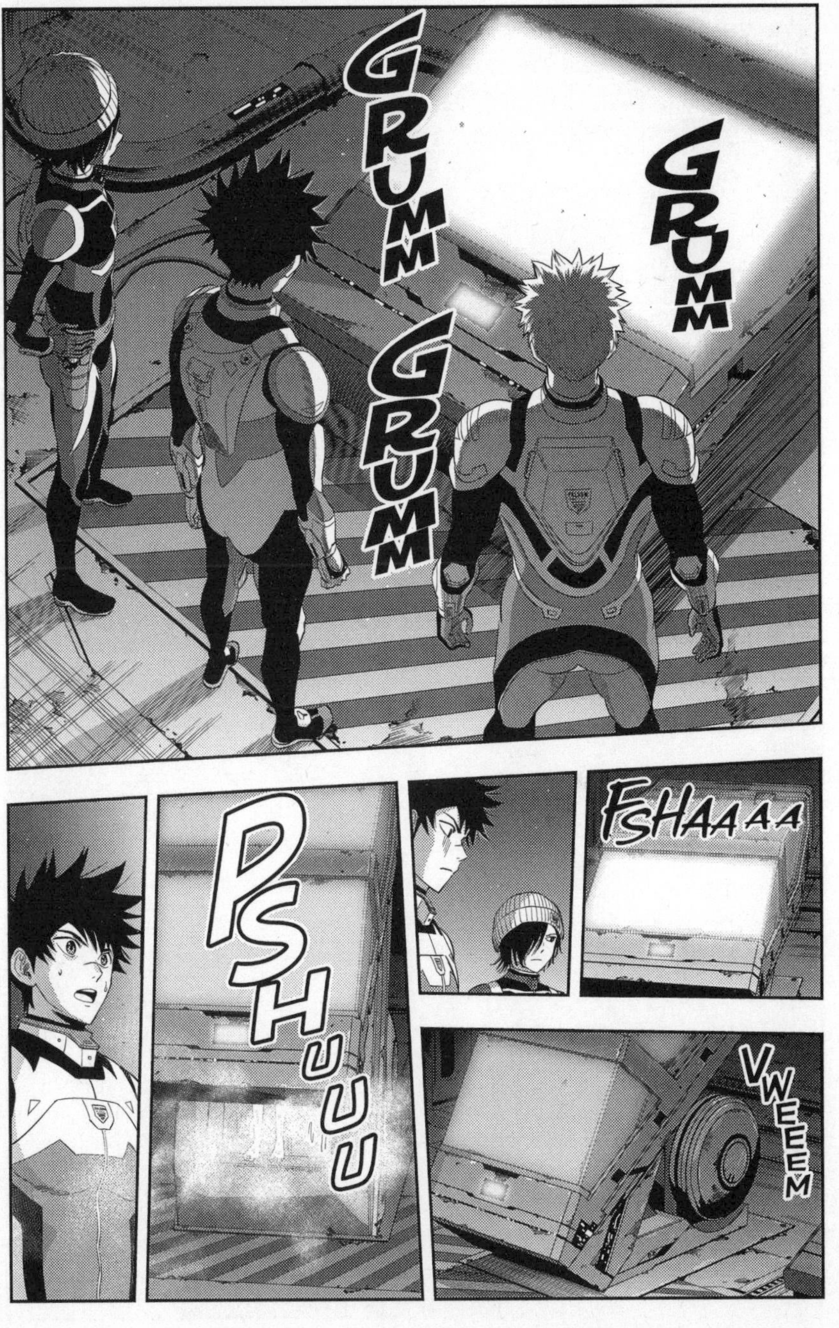
GRUMM
GRUMM
GRUMM
FSHAAAAA
VWEEEM
PSHUUUU

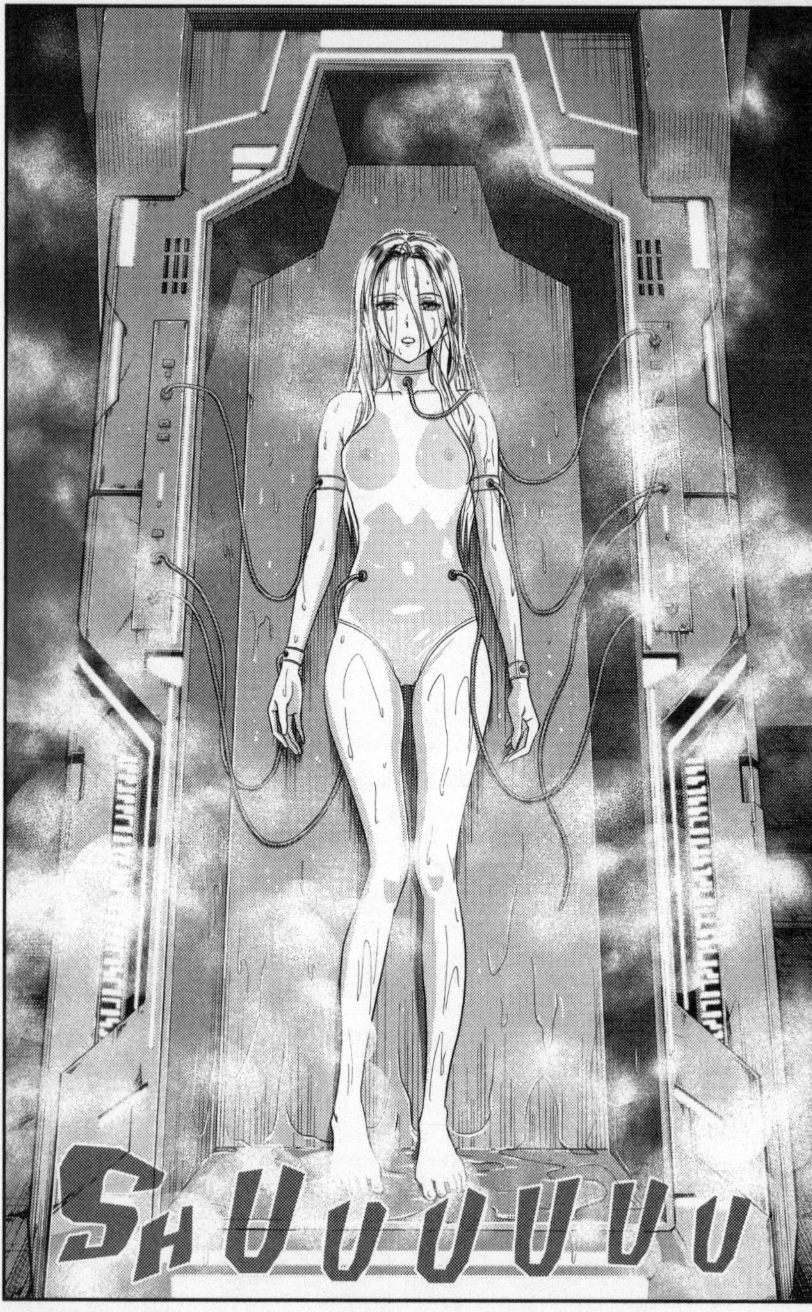
SHUUUUUUU

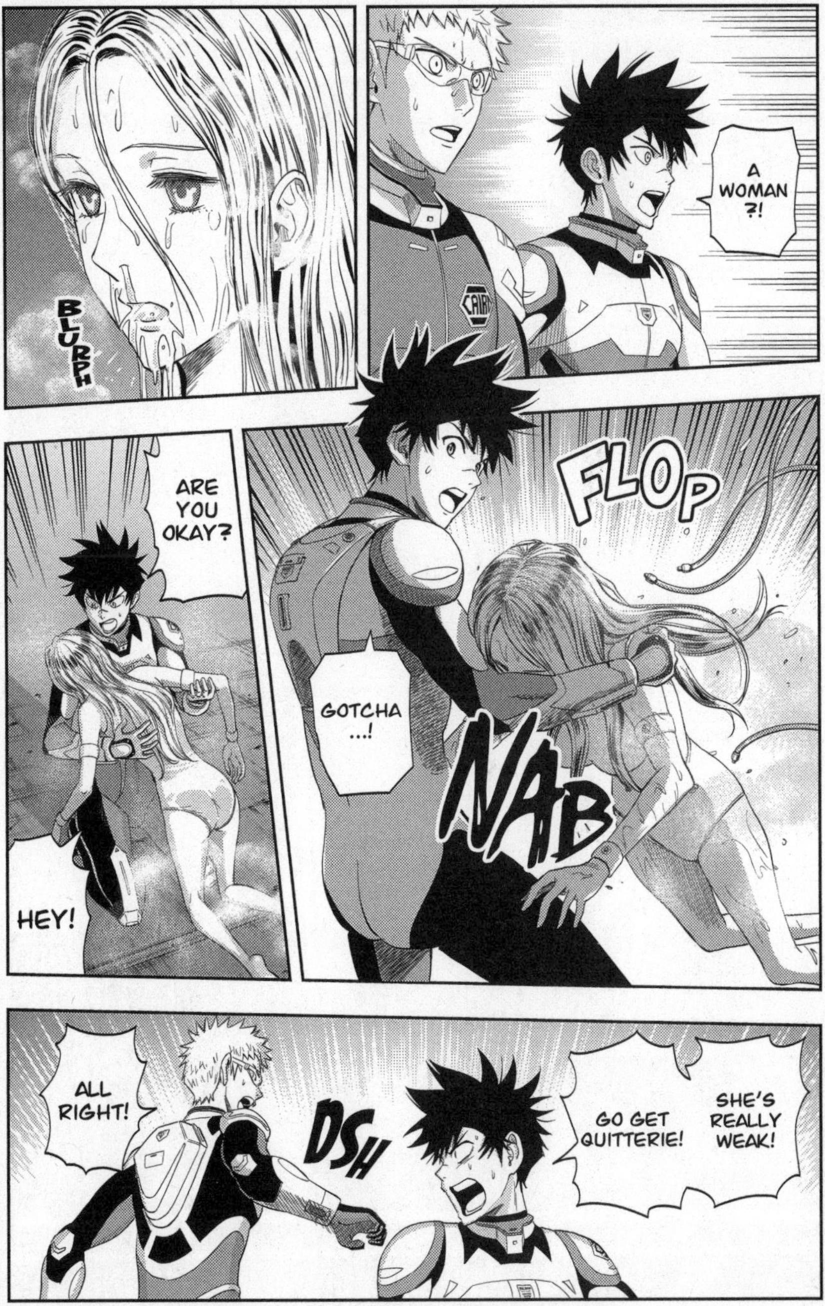
A WOMAN ?!
BLURPH
FLOP
GOTCHA ...!
NAB
ARE YOU OKAY?
HEY!
SHE'S REALLY WEAK!
GO GET QUITTERIE!
DSH
ALL RIGHT!

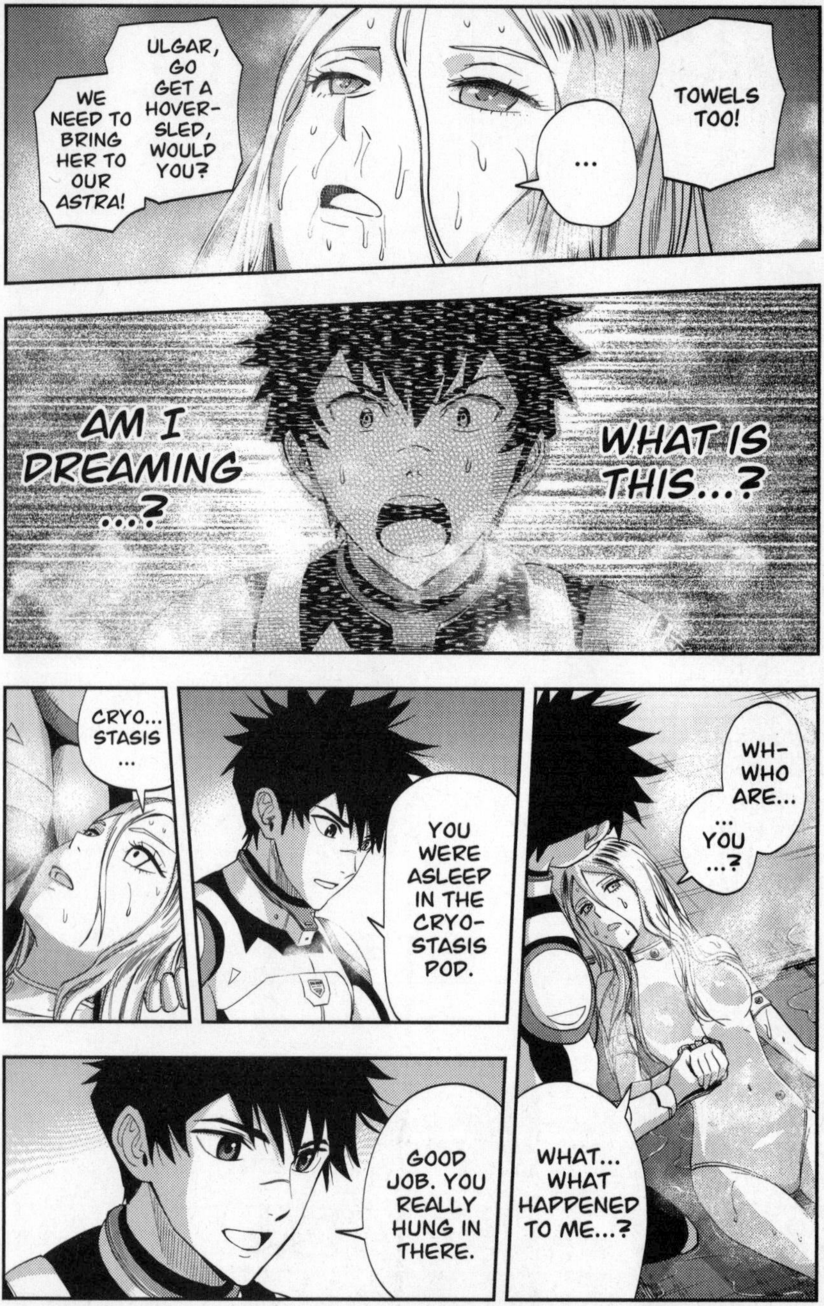
TOWELS TOO!
...
ULGAR, GO GET A HOVER-SLED, WOULD YOU?
WE NEED TO BRING HER TO OUR ASTRA!
WHAT IS THIS...?
AM I DREAMING ...?
WH- WHO ARE... ... YOU ...?
WHAT... WHAT HAPPENED TO ME...?
YOU WERE ASLEEP IN THE CRYO-STASIS POD.
CRYO... STASIS ...
GOOD JOB. YOU REALLY HUNG IN THERE.

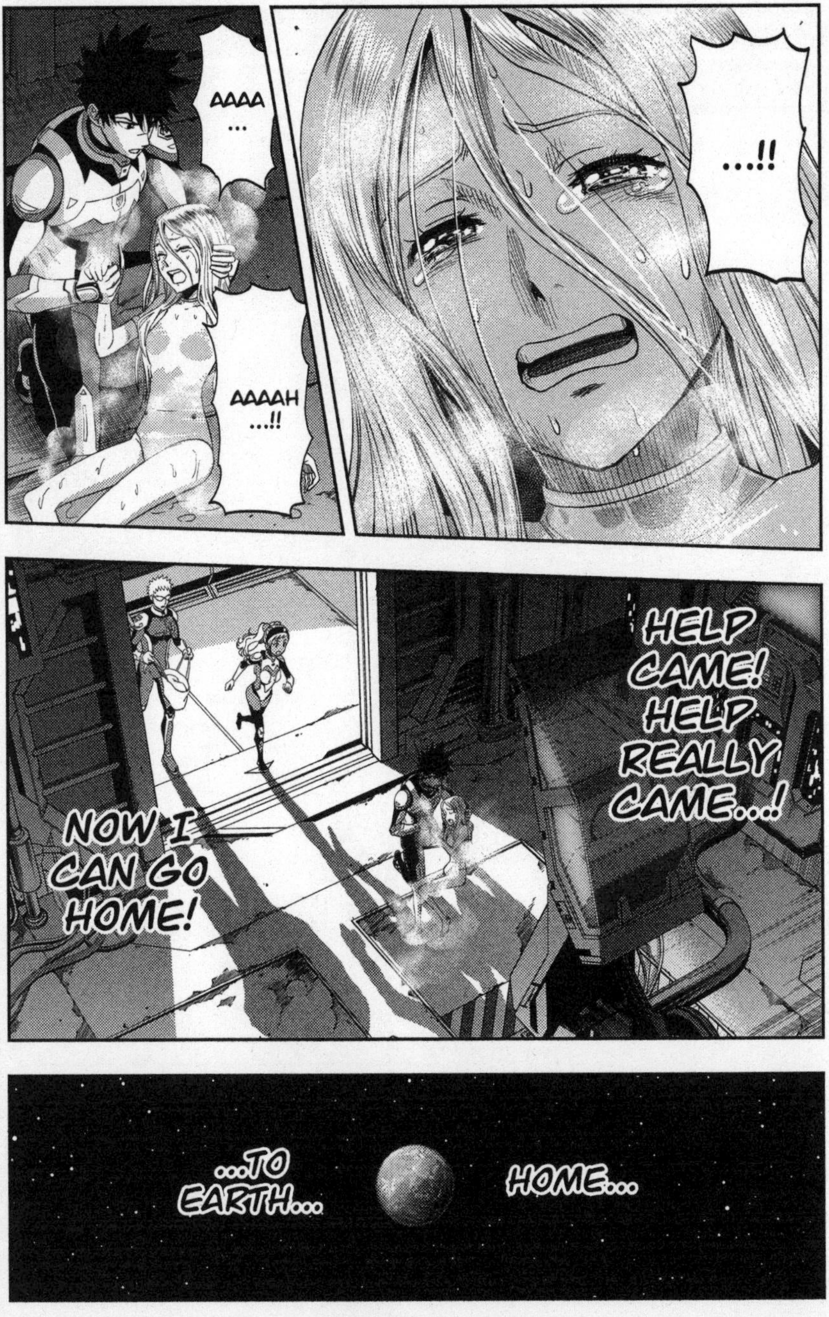
...!!
AAAA ...
AAAAH ...!!
HELP CAME! HELP REALLY CAME...!
NOW I CAN GO HOME!
HOME...
...TO EARTH...

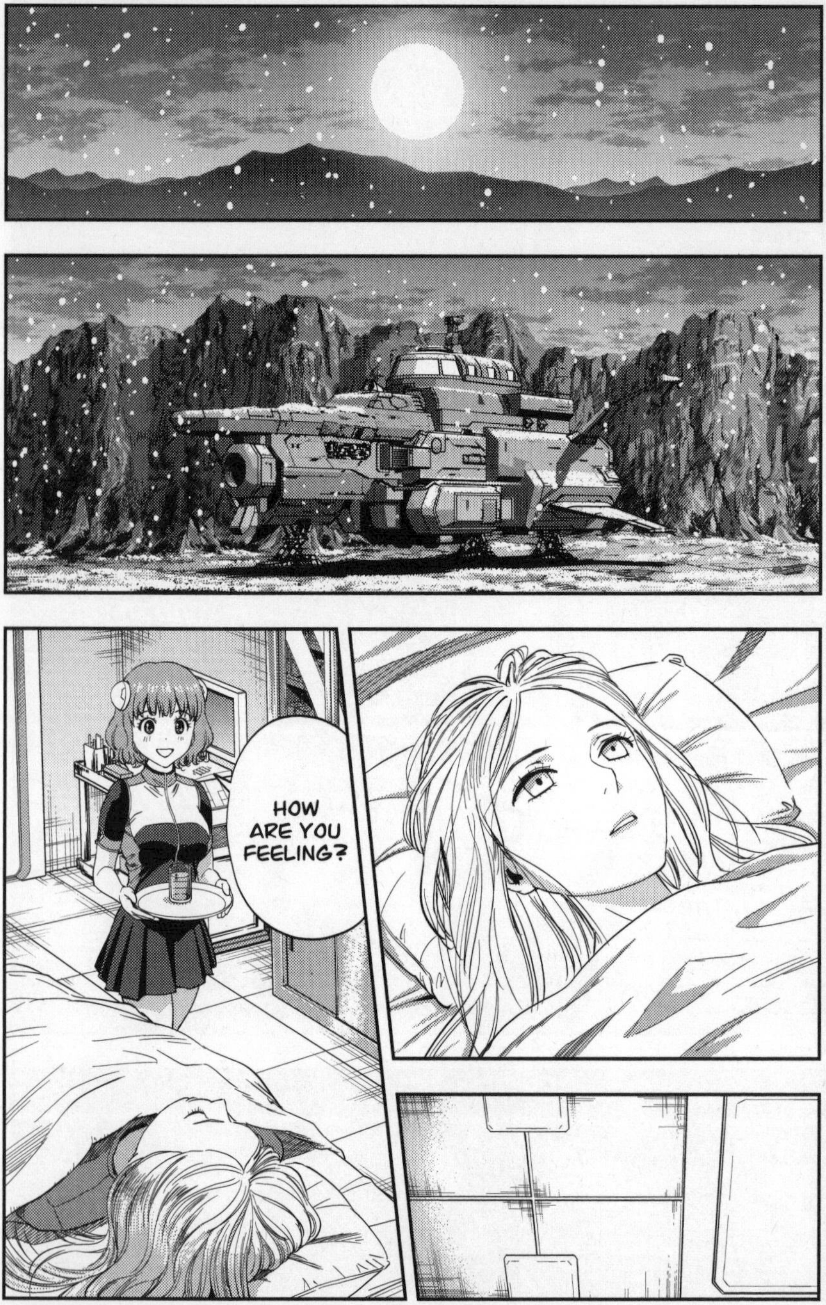
HOW ARE YOU FEELING?

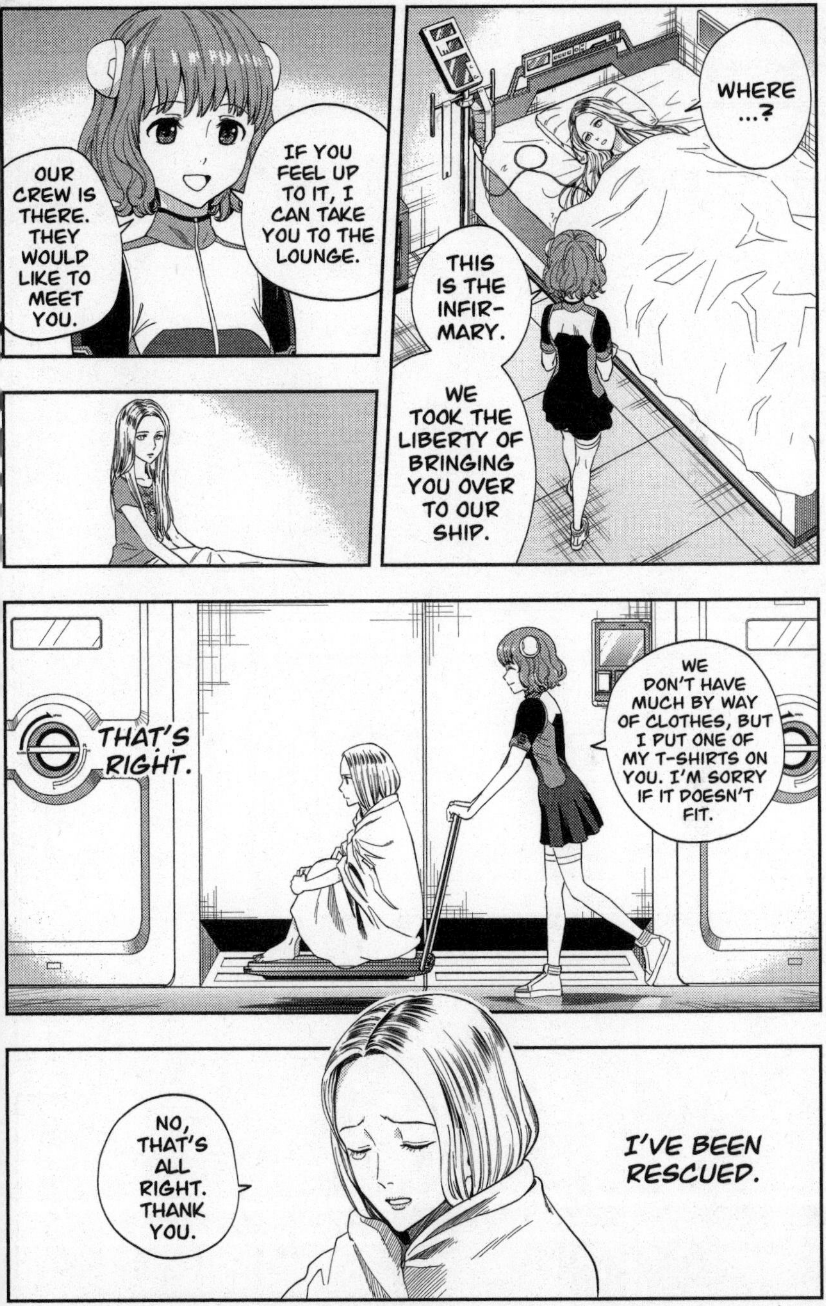
WHERE ...?
THIS IS THE INFIRMARY.
WE TOOK THE LIBERTY OF BRINGING YOU OVER TO OUR SHIP.
IF YOU FEEL UP TO IT, I CAN TAKE YOU TO THE LOUNGE.
OUR CREW IS THERE. THEY WOULD LIKE TO MEET YOU.
WE DON'T HAVE MUCH BY WAY OF CLOTHES, BUT I PUT ONE OF MY T-SHIRTS ON YOU. I'M SORRY IF IT DOESN'T FIT.
THAT'S RIGHT.
I'VE BEEN RESCUED.
NO, THAT'S ALL RIGHT. THANK YOU.

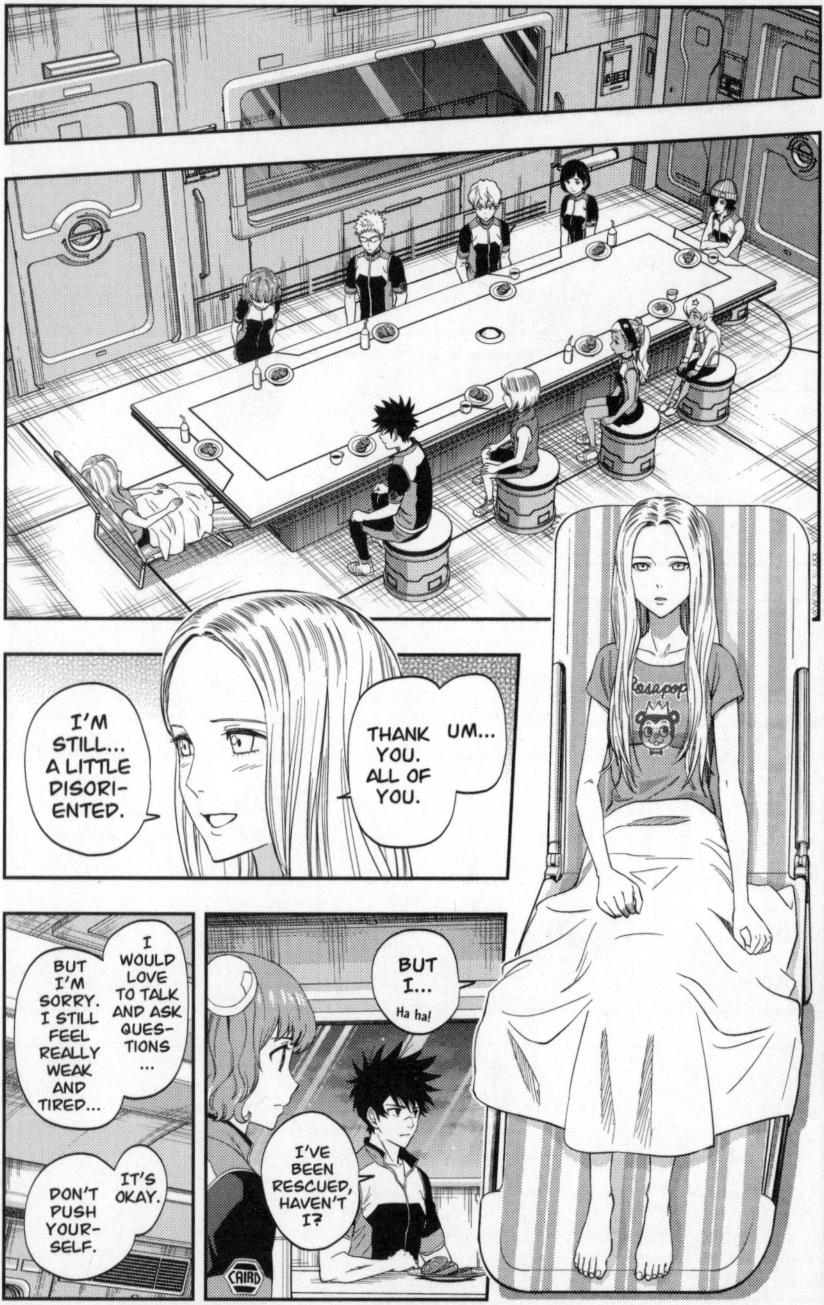
UM...
THANK YOU. ALL OF YOU.
I'M STILL... A LITTLE DISORIENTED.
BUT I...
Ha ha!
I'VE BEEN RESCUED, HAVEN'T I?
I WOULD LOVE TO TALK AND ASK QUESTIONS...
BUT I'M SORRY. I STILL FEEL REALLY WEAK AND TIRED...
IT'S OKAY.
DON'T PUSH YOURSELF.

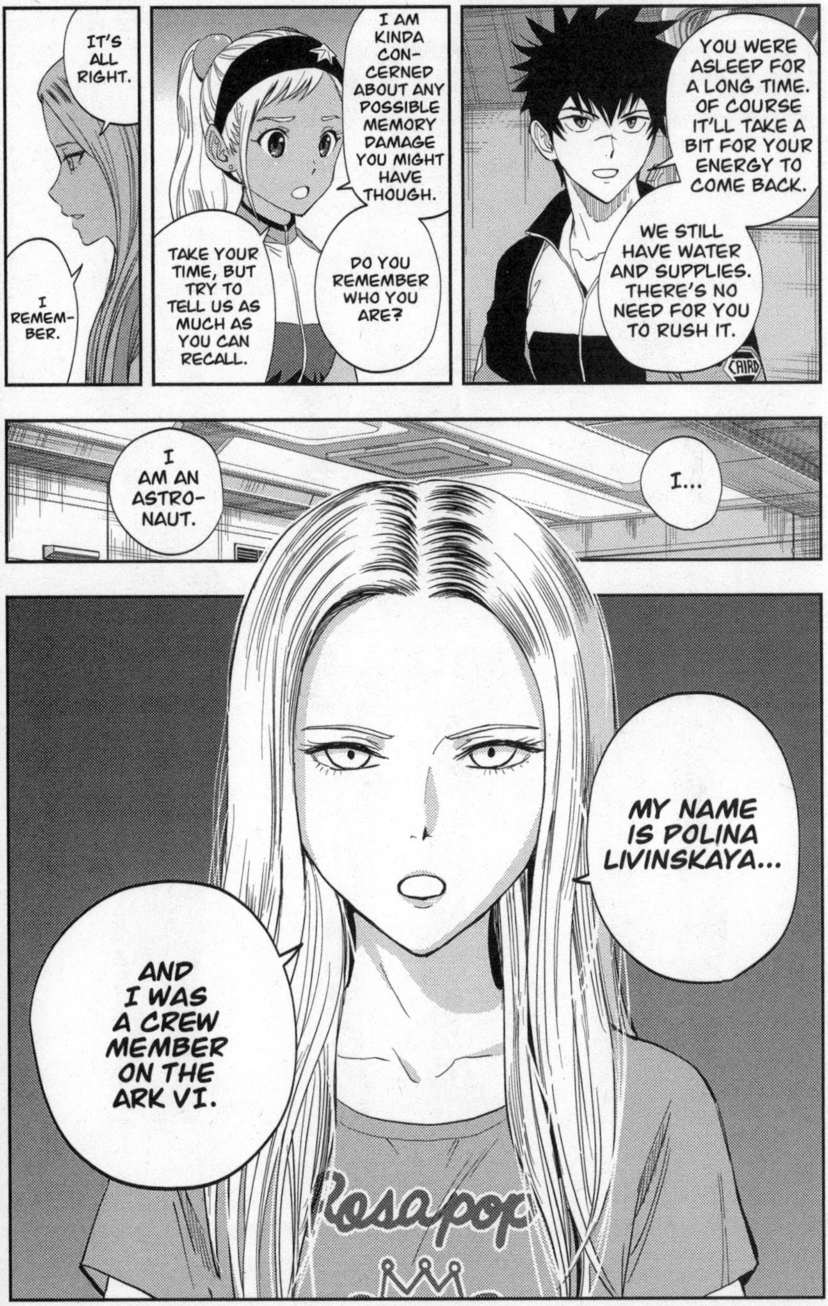
YOU WERE ASLEEP FOR A LONG TIME. OF COURSE IT'LL TAKE A BIT FOR YOUR ENERGY TO COME BACK.
WE STILL HAVE WATER AND SUPPLIES. THERE'S NO NEED FOR YOU TO RUSH IT.
I AM KINDA CONCERNED ABOUT ANY POSSIBLE MEMORY DAMAGE YOU MIGHT HAVE THOUGH.
DO YOU REMEMBER WHO YOU ARE?
TAKE YOUR TIME, BUT TRY TO TELL US AS MUCH AS YOU CAN RECALL.
IT'S ALL RIGHT.
I REMEMBER.
I...
I AM AN ASTRONAUT.
MY NAME IS POLINA LIVINSKAYA...
AND I WAS A CREW MEMBER ON THE ARK VI.

Material Collection Costume Design

ULGAR'S CRUST SUIT

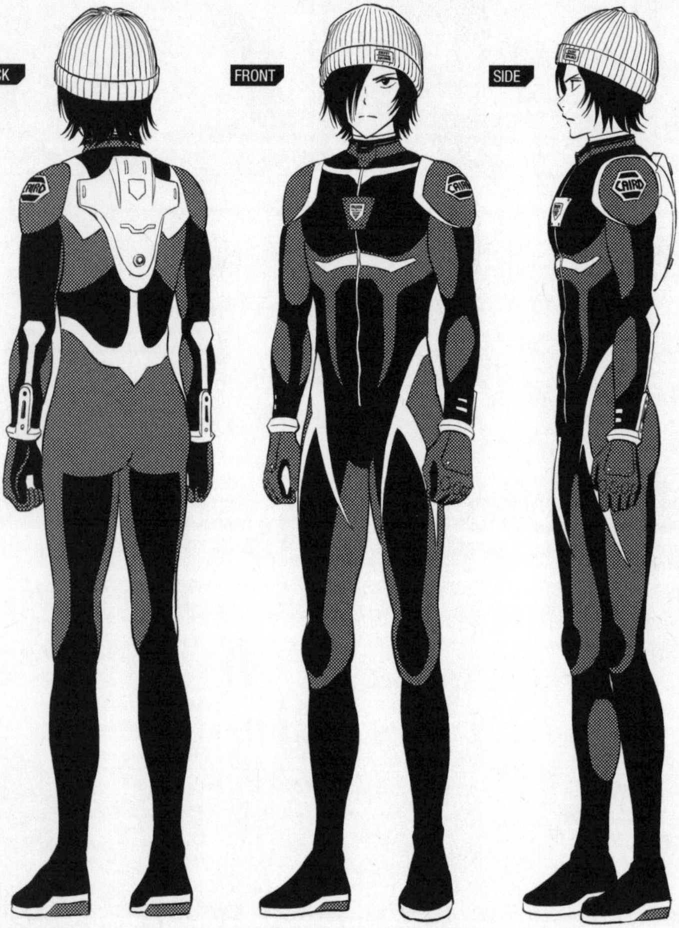
BACK
FRONT
SIDE
CAIRD
CAIRD
CAIRD

A Falken men's crust suit.

Black.

The black base color scheme is rare for crust suits.

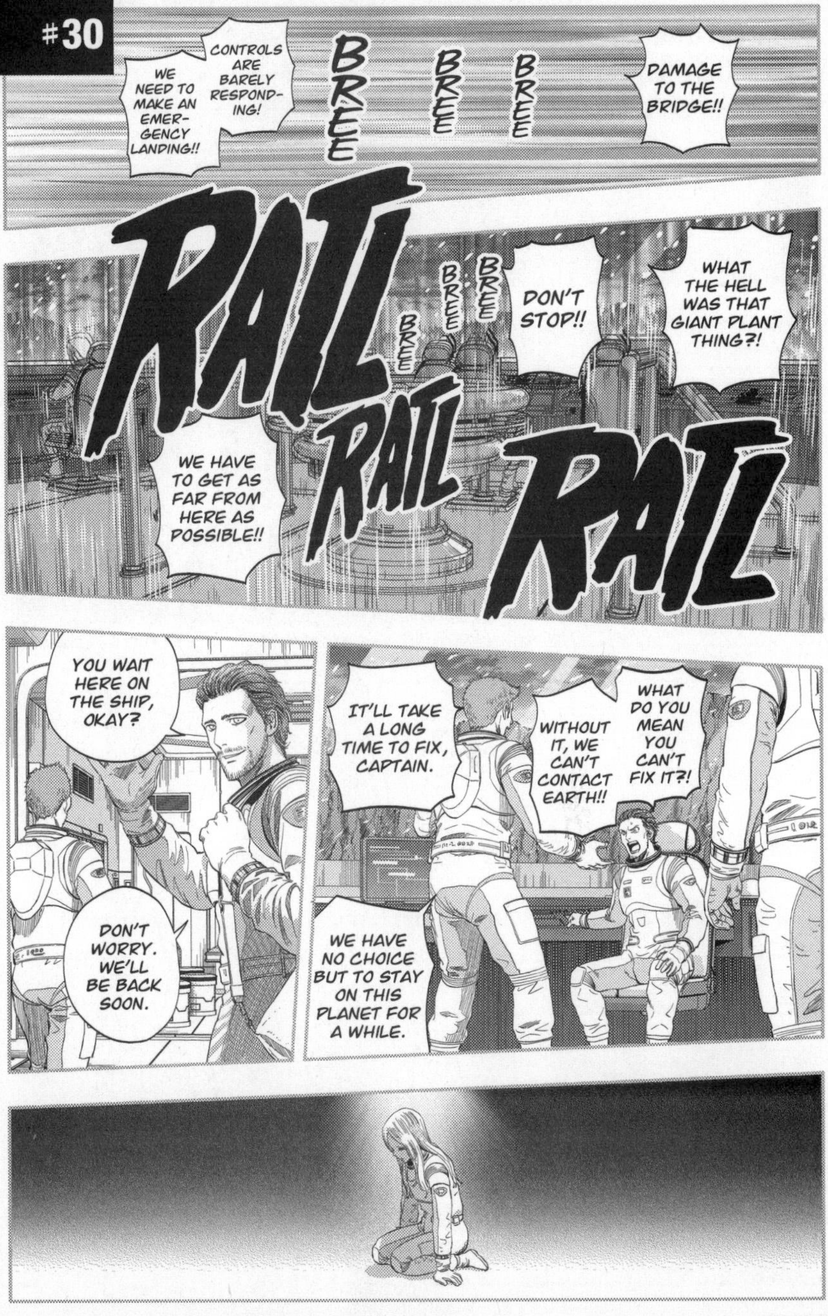
DAMAGE TO THE BRIDGE!!
BREE
BREE
BREE
CONTROLS ARE BARELY RESPOND-ING!
WE NEED TO MAKE AN EMER-GENCY LANDING!!
WHAT THE HELL WAS THAT GIANT PLANT THING?!
DON'T STOP!!
BREE
BREE
BREE
RATL
RATL
RATL
WE HAVE TO GET AS FAR FROM HERE AS POSSIBLE!!
WHAT DO YOU MEAN YOU CAN'T FIX IT?!
WITHOUT IT, WE CAN'T CONTACT EARTH!!
IT'LL TAKE A LONG TIME TO FIX, CAPTAIN.
WE HAVE NO CHOICE BUT TO STAY ON THIS PLANET FOR A WHILE.
YOU WAIT HERE ON THE SHIP, OKAY?
DON'T WORRY. WE'LL BE BACK SOON.

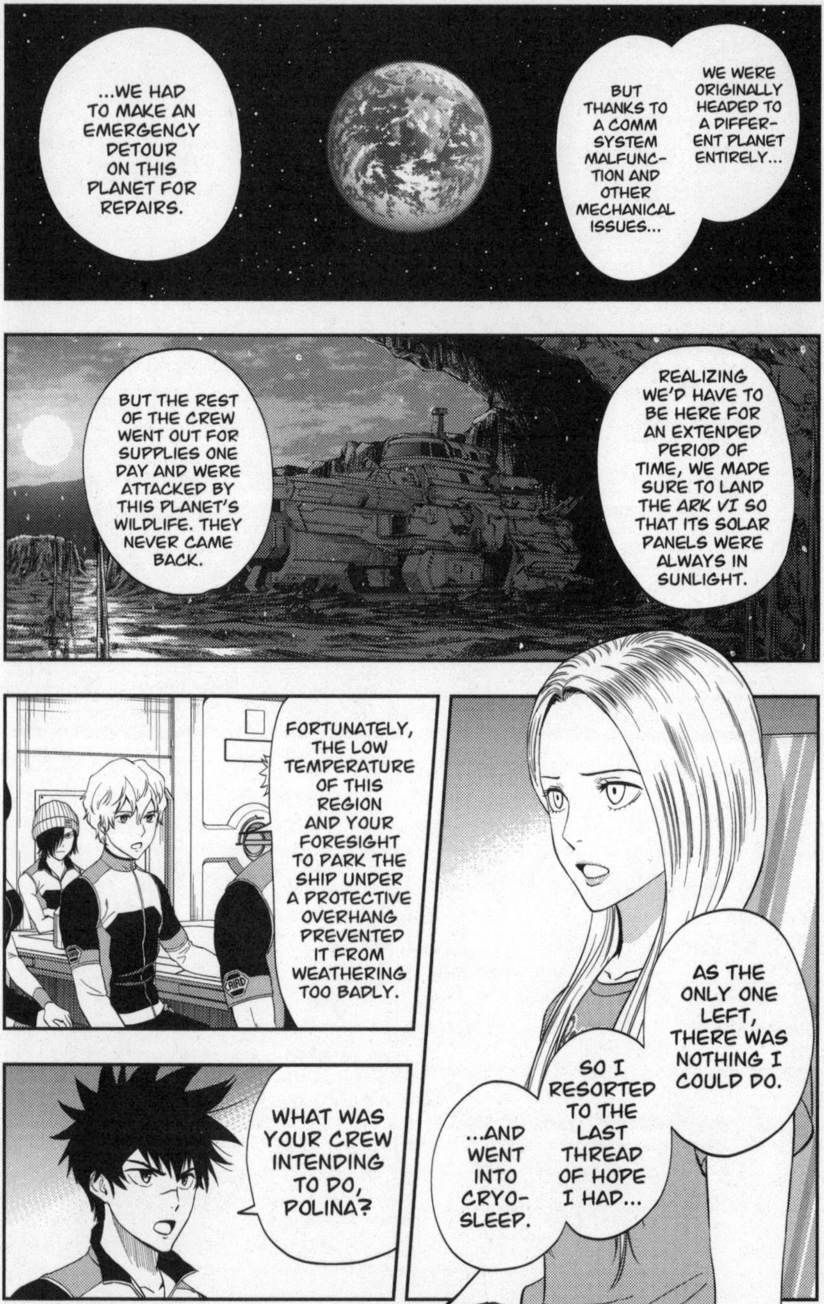
WE WERE ORIGINALLY HEADED TO A DIFFERENT PLANET ENTIRELY...
BUT THANKS TO A COMM SYSTEM MALFUNCTION AND OTHER MECHANICAL ISSUES...
...WE HAD TO MAKE AN EMERGENCY DETOUR ON THIS PLANET FOR REPAIRS.
REALIZING WE'D HAVE TO BE HERE FOR AN EXTENDED PERIOD OF TIME, WE MADE SURE TO LAND THE ARK VI SO THAT ITS SOLAR PANELS WERE ALWAYS IN SUNLIGHT.
BUT THE REST OF THE CREW WENT OUT FOR SUPPLIES ONE DAY AND WERE ATTACKED BY THIS PLANET'S WILDLIFE. THEY NEVER CAME BACK.
AS THE ONLY ONE LEFT, THERE WAS NOTHING I COULD DO.
SO I RESORTED TO THE LAST THREAD OF HOPE I HAD...
...AND WENT INTO CRYO-SLEEP.
FORTUNATELY, THE LOW TEMPERATURE OF THIS REGION AND YOUR FORESIGHT TO PARK THE SHIP UNDER A PROTECTIVE OVERHANG PREVENTED IT FROM WEATHERING TOO BADLY.
WHAT WAS YOUR CREW INTENDING TO DO, POLINA?

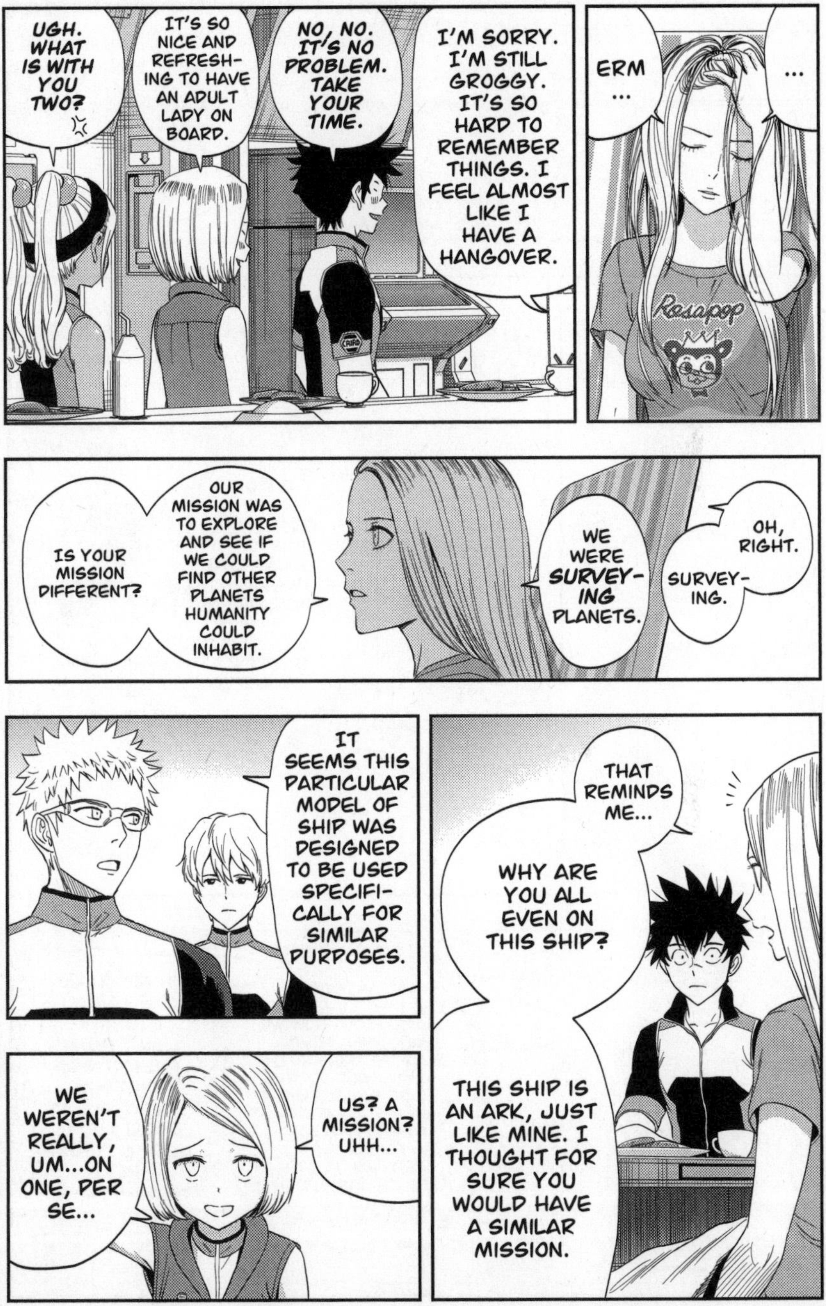
...
ERM ...
I'M SORRY. I'M STILL GROGGY. IT'S SO HARD TO REMEMBER THINGS. I FEEL ALMOST LIKE I HAVE A HANGOVER.
NO, NO. IT'S NO PROBLEM. TAKE YOUR TIME.
IT'S SO NICE AND REFRESHING TO HAVE AN ADULT LADY ON BOARD.
UGH. WHAT IS WITH YOU TWO?
OH, RIGHT.
SURVEYING.
WE WERE SURVEYING PLANETS.
OUR MISSION WAS TO EXPLORE AND SEE IF WE COULD FIND OTHER PLANETS HUMANITY COULD INHABIT.
IS YOUR MISSION DIFFERENT?
THAT REMINDS ME...
WHY ARE YOU ALL EVEN ON THIS SHIP?
THIS SHIP IS AN ARK, JUST LIKE MINE. I THOUGHT FOR SURE YOU WOULD HAVE A SIMILAR MISSION.
IT SEEMS THIS PARTICULAR MODEL OF SHIP WAS DESIGNED TO BE USED SPECIFICALLY FOR SIMILAR PURPOSES.
US? A MISSION? UHH...
WE WEREN'T REALLY, UM...ON ONE, PER SE...

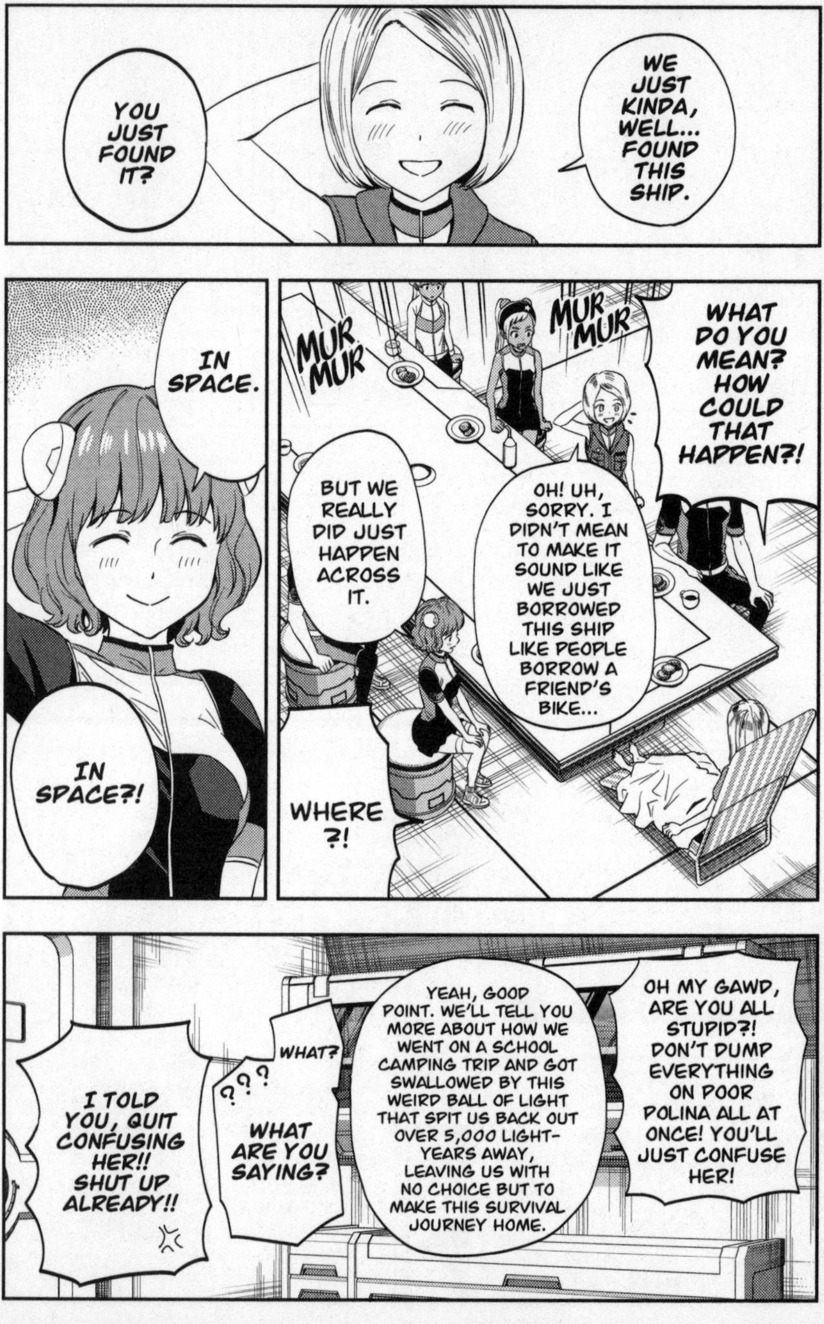
WE JUST KINDA, WELL... FOUND THIS SHIP.
YOU JUST FOUND IT?
WHAT DO YOU MEAN? HOW COULD THAT HAPPEN?!
MUR MUR
MUR MUR
OH! UH, SORRY. I DIDN'T MEAN TO MAKE IT SOUND LIKE WE JUST BORROWED THIS SHIP LIKE PEOPLE BORROW A FRIEND'S BIKE...
BUT WE REALLY DID JUST HAPPEN ACROSS IT.
WHERE ?!
IN SPACE.
IN SPACE?!
OH MY GAWD, ARE YOU ALL STUPID?! DON'T DUMP EVERYTHING ON POOR POLINA ALL AT ONCE! YOU'LL JUST CONFUSE HER!
YEAH, GOOD POINT. WE'LL TELL YOU MORE ABOUT HOW WE WENT ON A SCHOOL CAMPING TRIP AND GOT SWALLOWED BY THIS WEIRD BALL OF LIGHT THAT SPIT US BACK OUT OVER 5,000 LIGHT-YEARS AWAY, LEAVING US WITH NO CHOICE BUT TO MAKE THIS SURVIVAL JOURNEY HOME.
WHAT?
???
WHAT ARE YOU SAYING?
I TOLD YOU, QUIT CONFUSING HER!! SHUT UP ALREADY!!

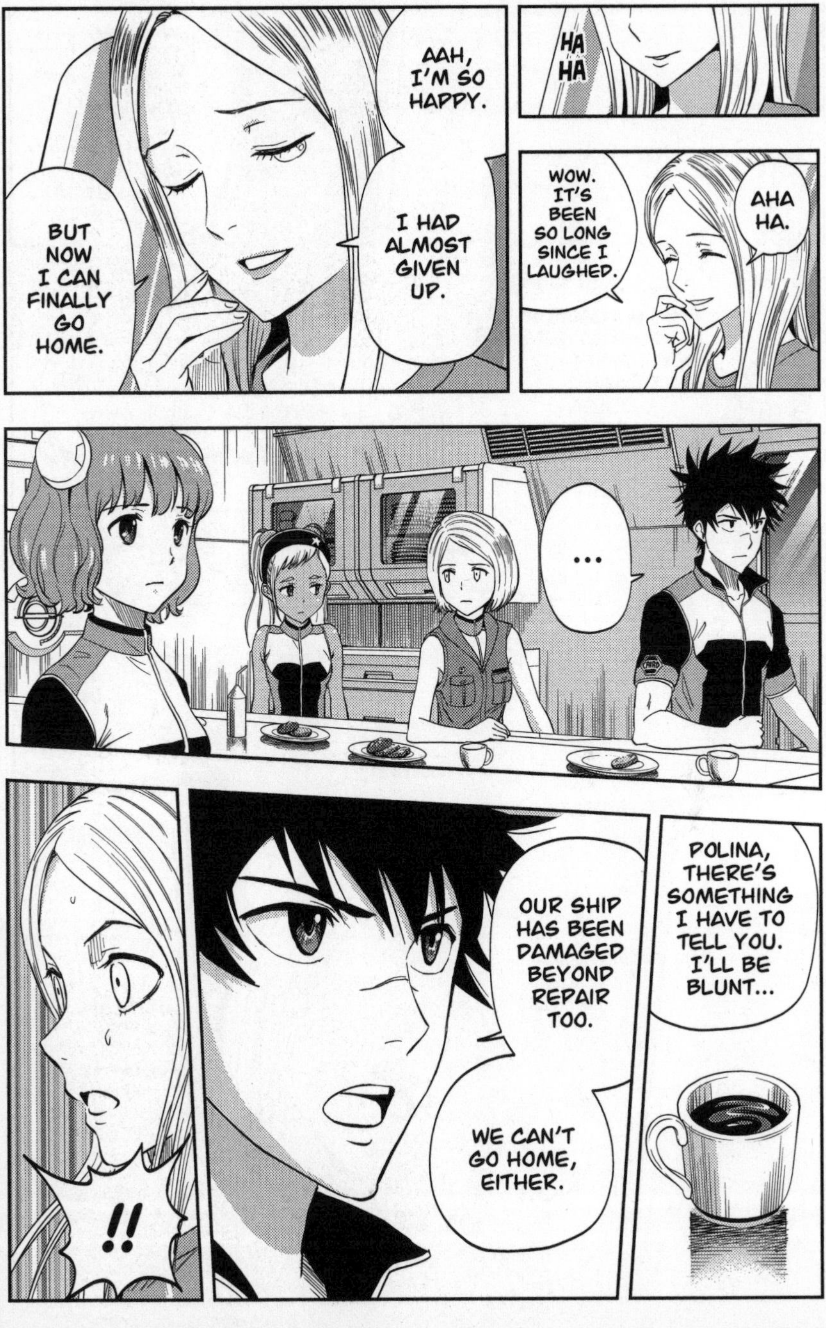
HA HA
AHA HA.
WOW. IT'S BEEN SO LONG SINCE I LAUGHED.
AAH, I'M SO HAPPY.
I HAD ALMOST GIVEN UP.
BUT NOW I CAN FINALLY GO HOME.
...
POLINA, THERE'S SOMETHING I HAVE TO TELL YOU. I'LL BE BLUNT...
OUR SHIP HAS BEEN DAMAGED BEYOND REPAIR TOO.
WE CAN'T GO HOME, EITHER.
!!

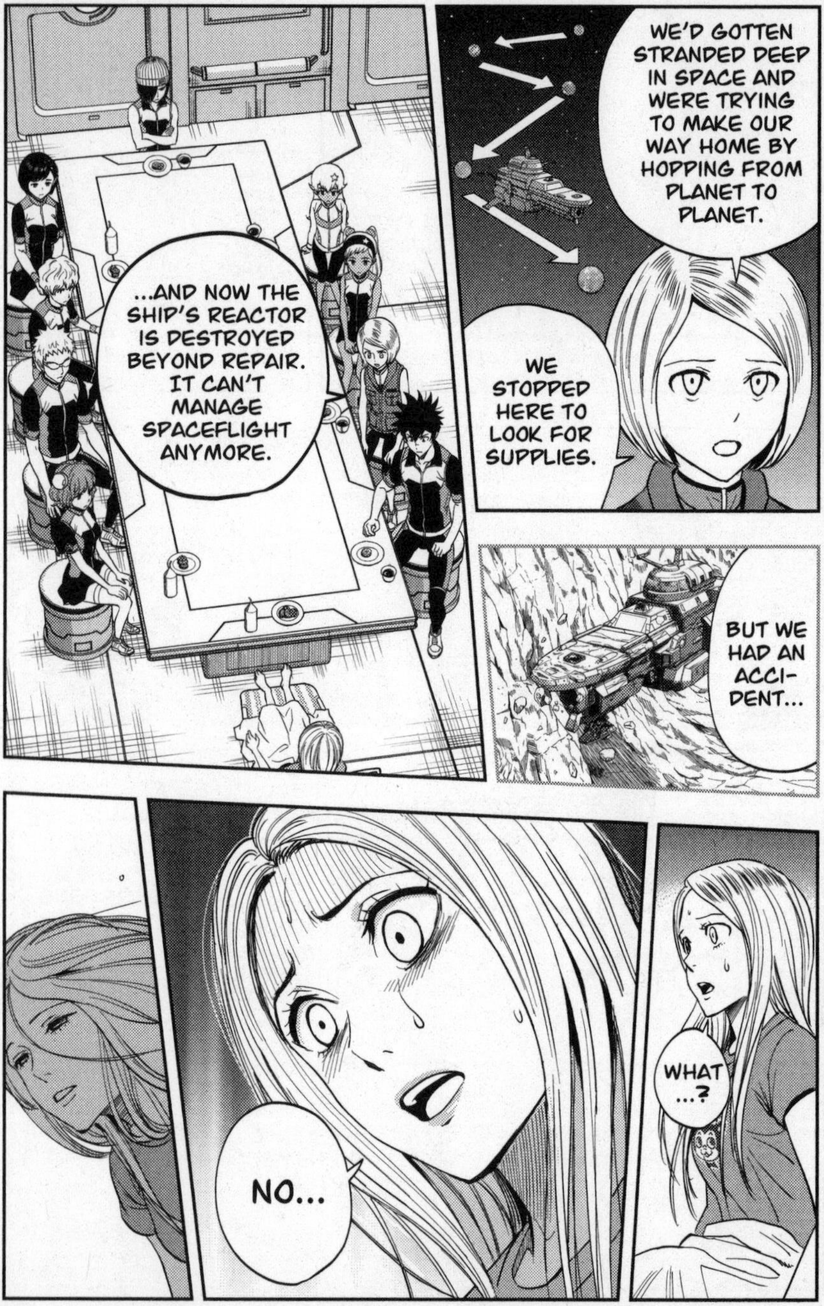
WE'D GOTTEN STRANDED DEEP IN SPACE AND WERE TRYING TO MAKE OUR WAY HOME BY HOPPING FROM PLANET TO PLANET.
WE STOPPED HERE TO LOOK FOR SUPPLIES.
BUT WE HAD AN ACCI-DENT...
...AND NOW THE SHIP'S REACTOR IS DESTROYED BEYOND REPAIR. IT CAN'T MANAGE SPACEFLIGHT ANYMORE.
WHAT ...?
NO...

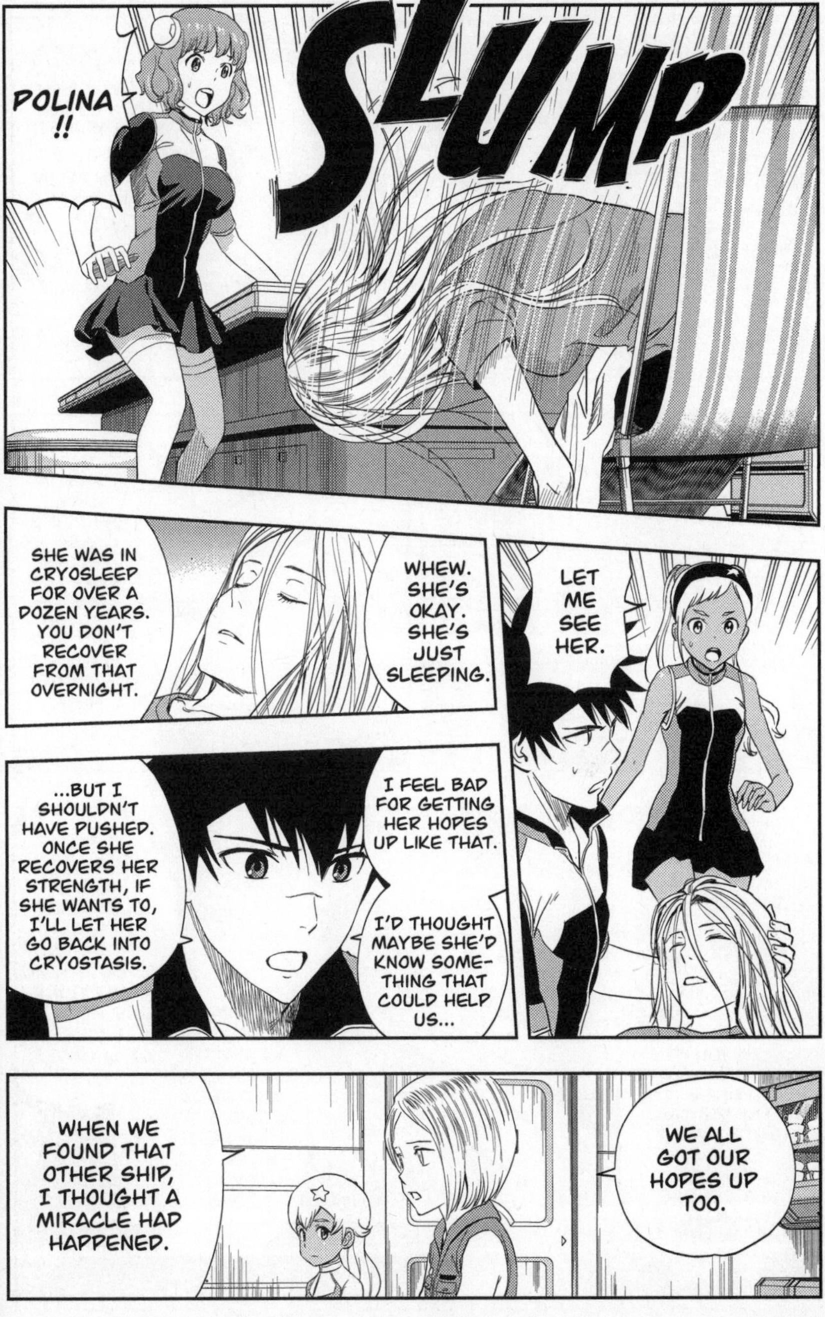
SLUMP
POLINA!!
LET ME SEE HER.
WHEW. SHE'S OKAY. SHE'S JUST SLEEPING.
SHE WAS IN CRYOSLEEP FOR OVER A DOZEN YEARS. YOU DON'T RECOVER FROM THAT OVERNIGHT.
I FEEL BAD FOR GETTING HER HOPES UP LIKE THAT.
I'D THOUGHT MAYBE SHE'D KNOW SOME-THING THAT COULD HELP US...
...BUT I SHOULDN'T HAVE PUSHED. ONCE SHE RECOVERS HER STRENGTH, IF SHE WANTS TO, I'LL LET HER GO BACK INTO CRYOSTASIS.
WE ALL GOT OUR HOPES UP TOO.
WHEN WE FOUND THAT OTHER SHIP, I THOUGHT A MIRACLE HAD HAPPENED.

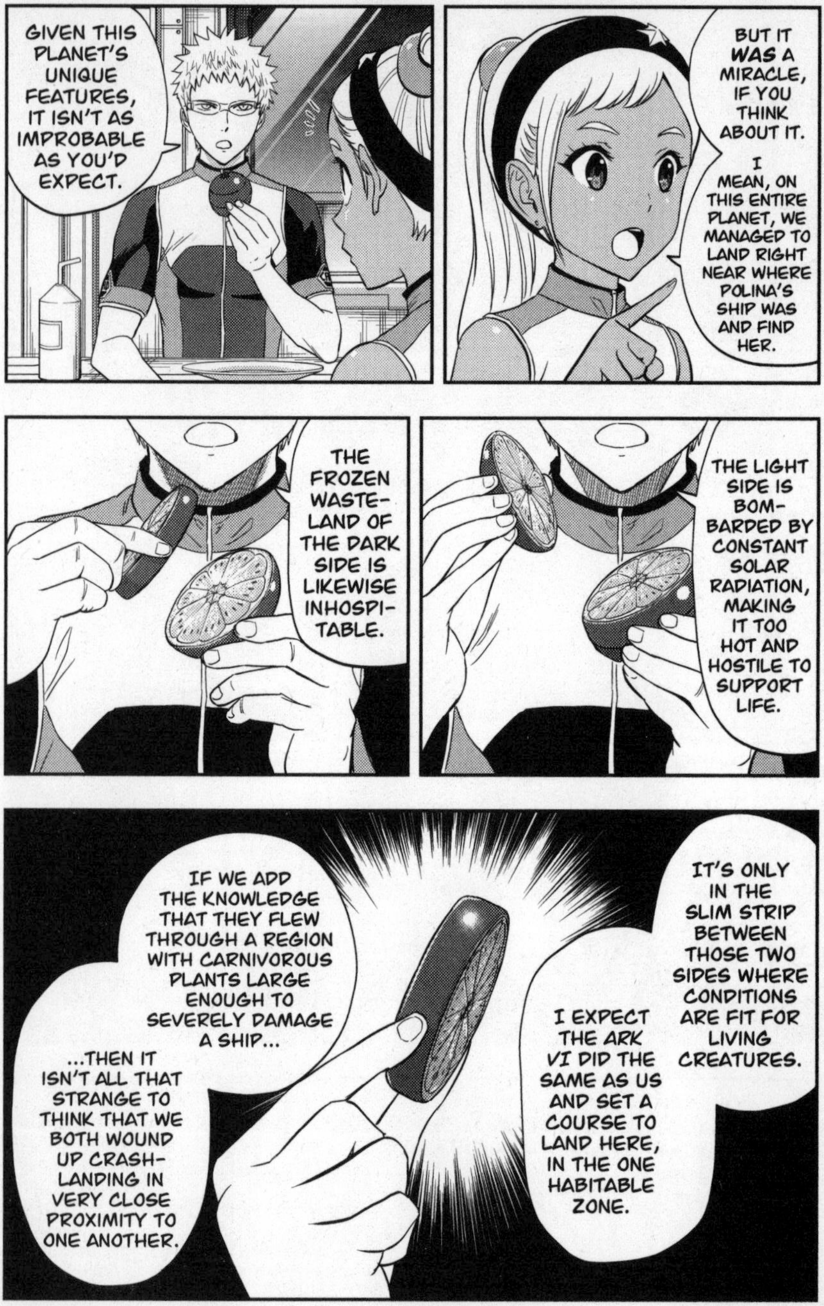
BUT IT WAS A MIRACLE, IF YOU THINK ABOUT IT.
I MEAN, ON THIS ENTIRE PLANET, WE MANAGED TO LAND RIGHT NEAR WHERE POLINA'S SHIP WAS AND FIND HER.
GIVEN THIS PLANET'S UNIQUE FEATURES, IT ISN'T AS IMPROBABLE AS YOU'D EXPECT.
THE LIGHT SIDE IS BOMBARDED BY CONSTANT SOLAR RADIATION, MAKING IT TOO HOT AND HOSTILE TO SUPPORT LIFE.
THE FROZEN WASTELAND OF THE DARK SIDE IS LIKEWISE INHOSPITABLE.
IT'S ONLY IN THE SLIM STRIP BETWEEN THOSE TWO SIDES WHERE CONDITIONS ARE FIT FOR LIVING CREATURES.
I EXPECT THE ARK VI DID THE SAME AS US AND SET A COURSE TO LAND HERE, IN THE ONE HABITABLE ZONE.
IF WE ADD THE KNOWLEDGE THAT THEY FLEW THROUGH A REGION WITH CARNIVOROUS PLANTS LARGE ENOUGH TO SEVERELY DAMAGE A SHIP...
...THEN IT ISN'T ALL THAT STRANGE TO THINK THAT WE BOTH WOUND UP CRASH-LANDING IN VERY CLOSE PROXIMITY TO ONE ANOTHER.

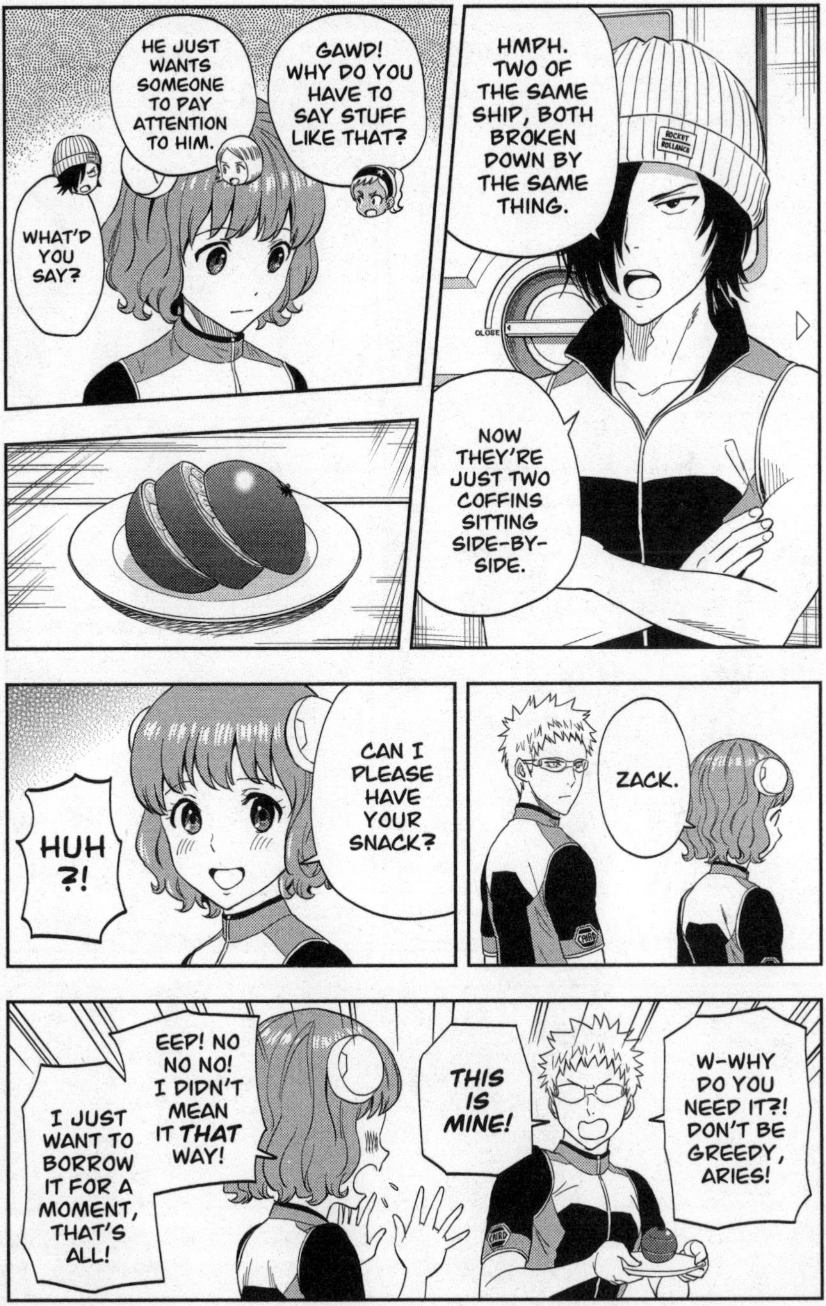
HMPH. TWO OF THE SAME SHIP, BOTH BROKEN DOWN BY THE SAME THING.
NOW THEY'RE JUST TWO COFFINS SITTING SIDE-BY-SIDE.
GAWD! WHY DO YOU HAVE TO SAY STUFF LIKE THAT?
HE JUST WANTS SOMEONE TO PAY ATTENTION TO HIM.
WHAT'D YOU SAY?
ZACK.
CAN I PLEASE HAVE YOUR SNACK?
HUH ?!
W-WHY DO YOU NEED IT?! DON'T BE GREEDY, ARIES!
THIS IS MINE!
EEP! NO NO NO! I DIDN'T MEAN IT THAT WAY!
I JUST WANT TO BORROW IT FOR A MOMENT, THAT'S ALL!

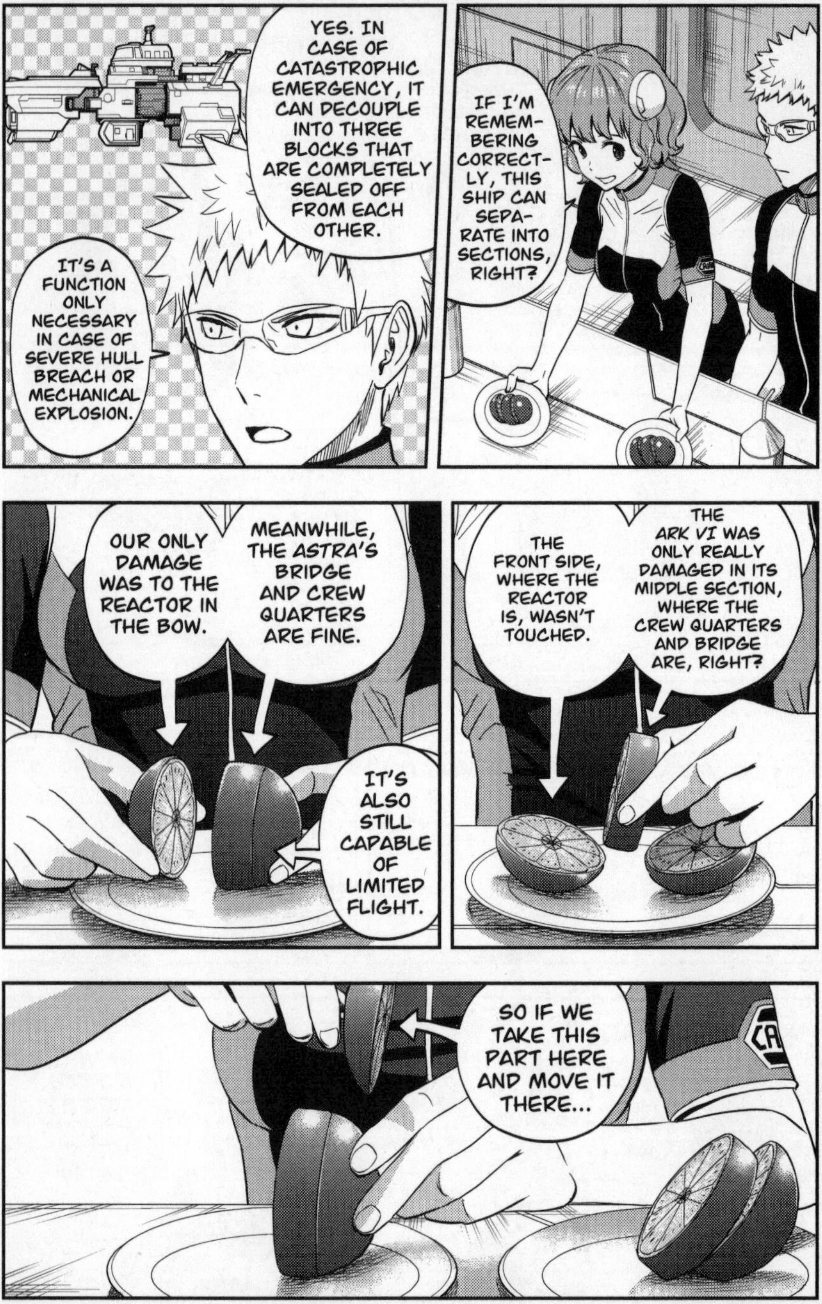
IF I'M REMEMBERING CORRECTLY, THIS SHIP CAN SEPARATE INTO SECTIONS, RIGHT?
YES. IN CASE OF CATASTROPHIC EMERGENCY, IT CAN DECOUPLE INTO THREE BLOCKS THAT ARE COMPLETELY SEALED OFF FROM EACH OTHER.
IT'S A FUNCTION ONLY NECESSARY IN CASE OF SEVERE HULL BREACH OR MECHANICAL EXPLOSION.
THE ARK VI WAS ONLY REALLY DAMAGED IN ITS MIDDLE SECTION, WHERE THE CREW QUARTERS AND BRIDGE ARE, RIGHT?
THE FRONT SIDE, WHERE THE REACTOR IS, WASN'T TOUCHED.
MEANWHILE, THE ASTRA'S BRIDGE AND CREW QUARTERS ARE FINE.
OUR ONLY DAMAGE WAS TO THE REACTOR IN THE BOW.
IT'S ALSO STILL CAPABLE OF LIMITED FLIGHT.
SO IF WE TAKE THIS PART HERE AND MOVE IT THERE...

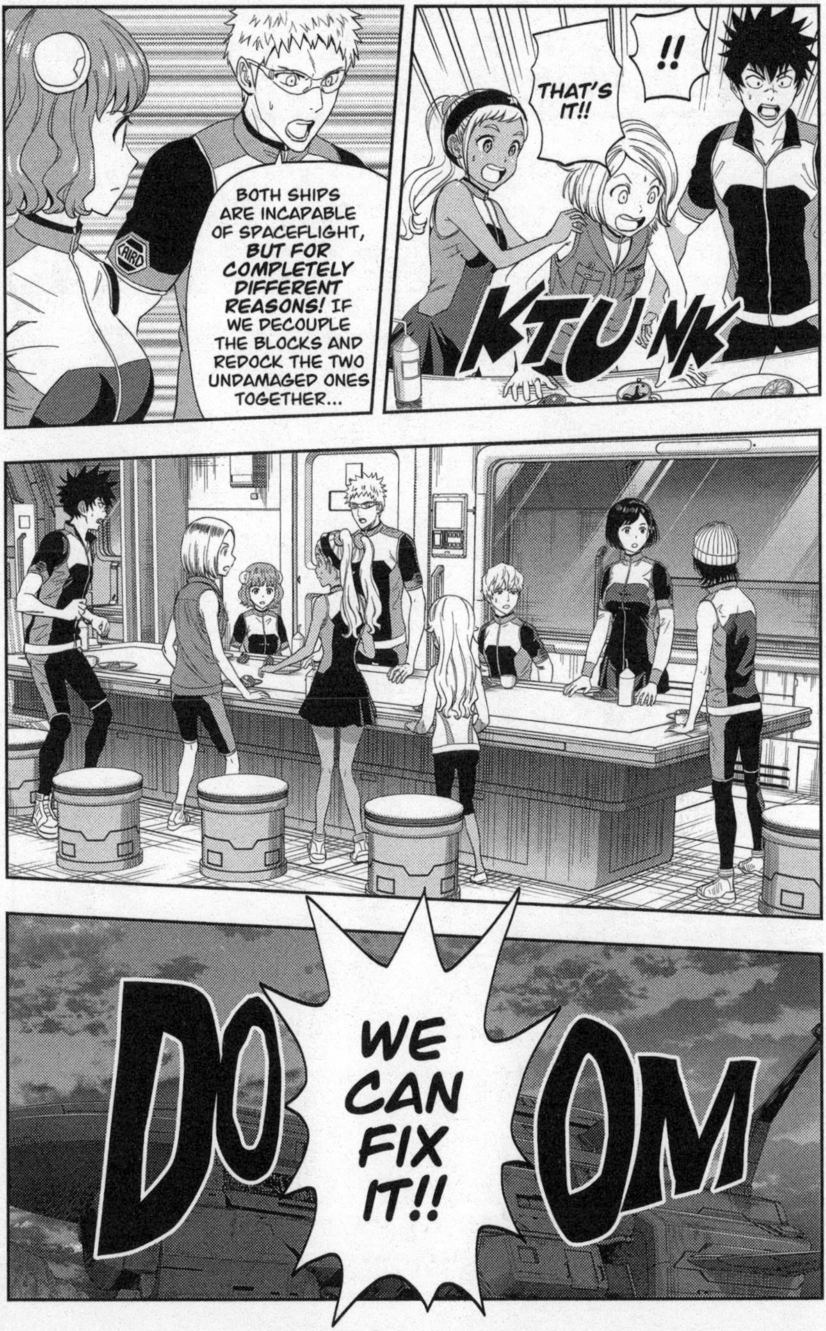
!!
THAT'S IT!!
KTUNK
BOTH SHIPS ARE INCAPABLE OF SPACEFLIGHT, BUT FOR COMPLETELY DIFFERENT REASONS! IF WE DECOUPLE THE BLOCKS AND REDOCK THE TWO UNDAMAGED ONES TOGETHER...
DO
WE CAN FIX IT!!
OM

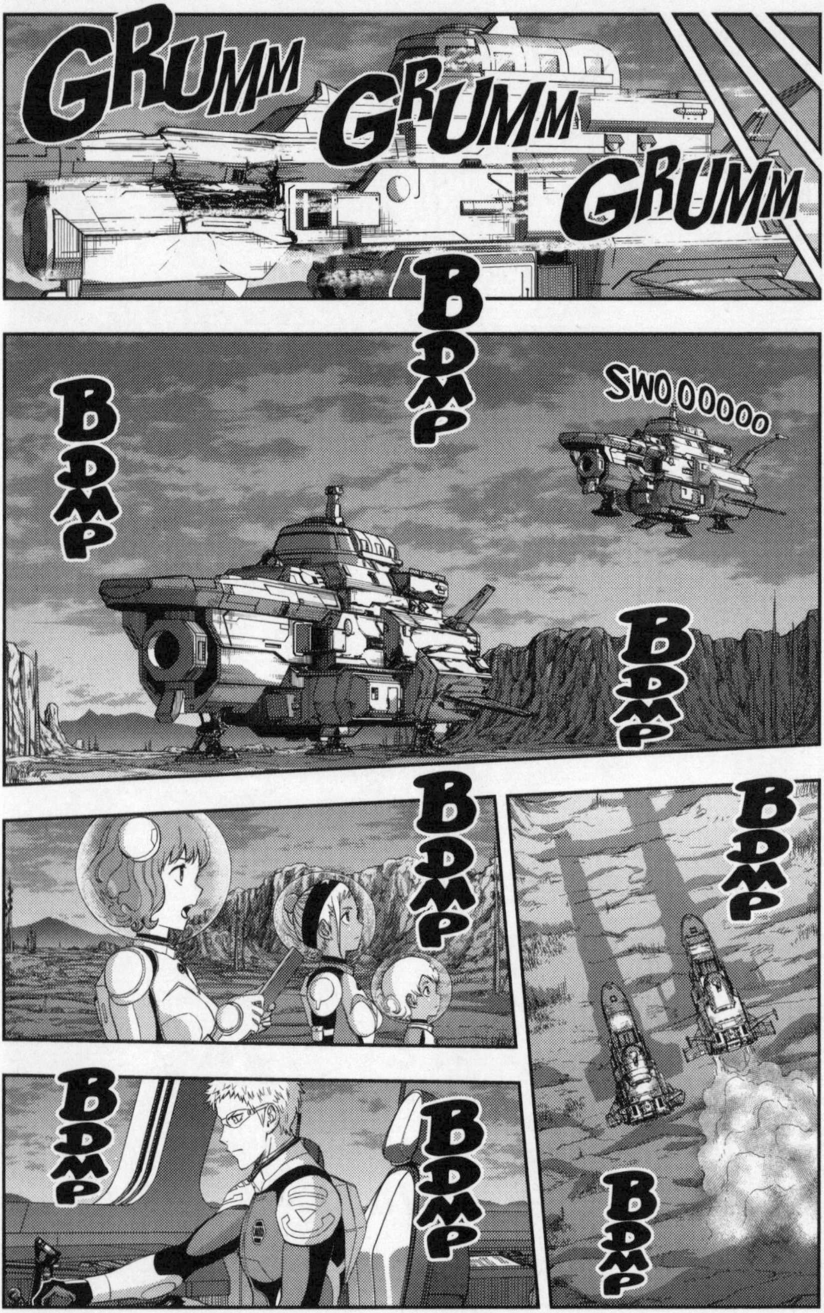
GRUMM
GRUMM
GRUMM
SWOOOOOO
BDMP
BDMP
BDMP
BDMP
BDMP
BDMP
BDMP
BDMP

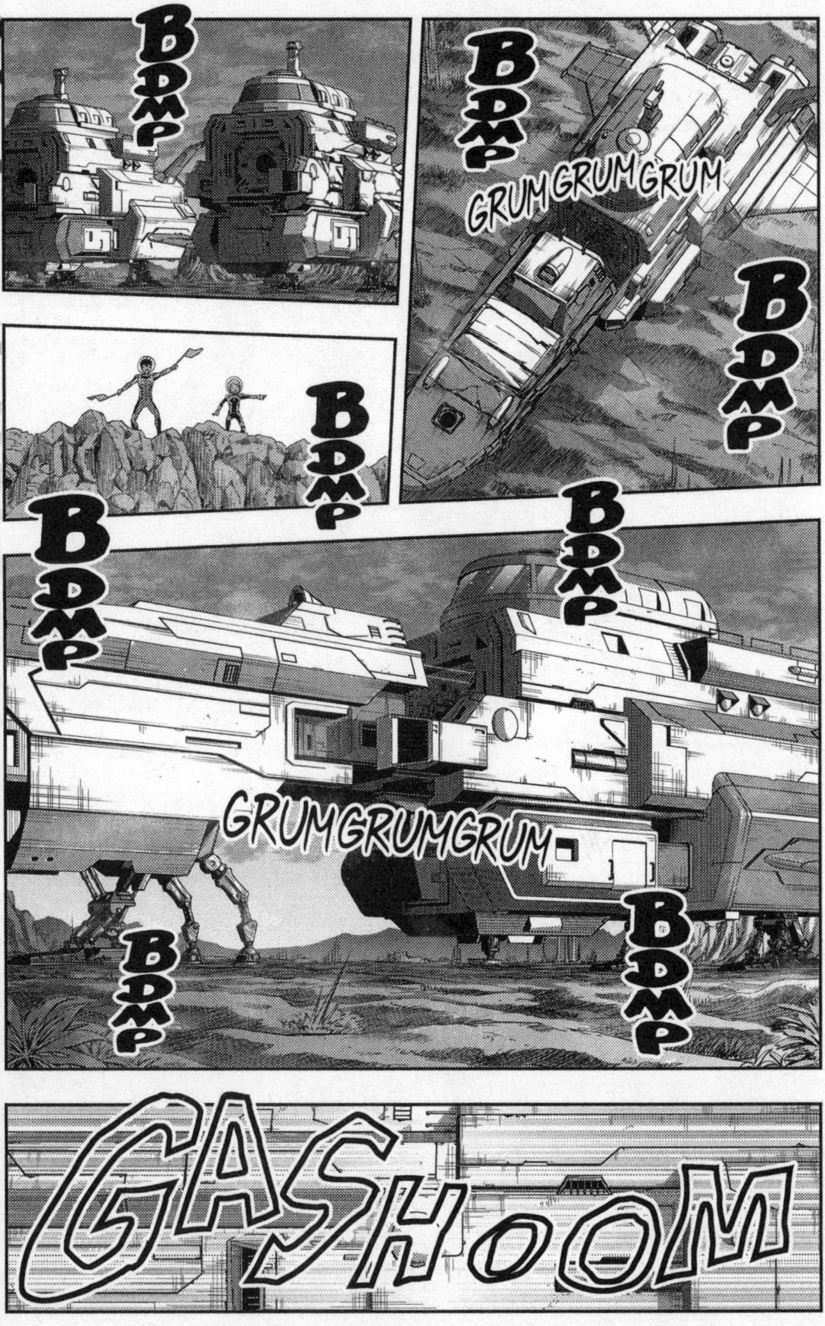
BDMP
GRUM GRUM GRUM
BDMP
BDMP
BDMP
BDMP
BDMP
GRUMGRUMGRUM
BDMP
BDMP
GASHOOM

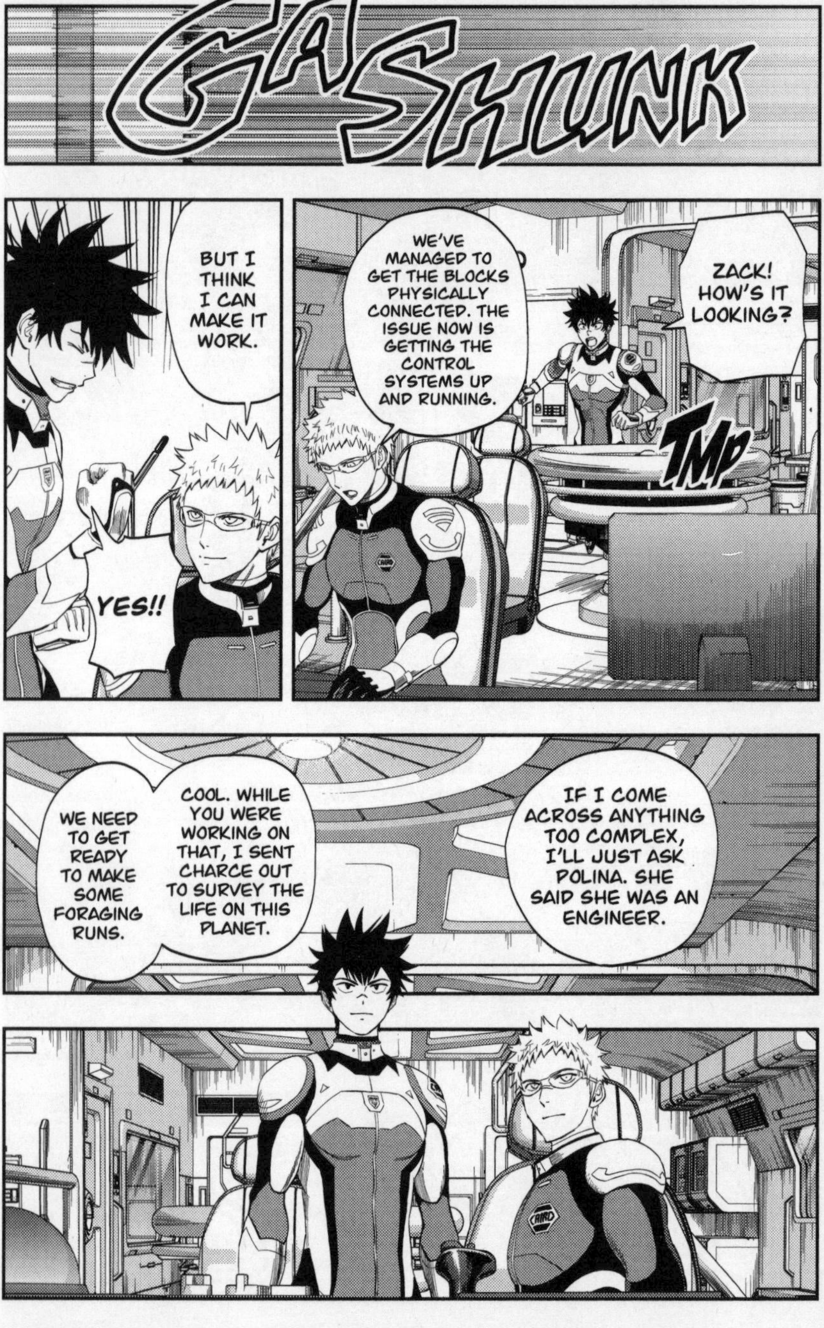
GASHUNK
ZACK! HOW'S IT LOOKING?
TMP
WE'VE MANAGED TO GET THE BLOCKS PHYSICALLY CONNECTED. THE ISSUE NOW IS GETTING THE CONTROL SYSTEMS UP AND RUNNING.
BUT I THINK I CAN MAKE IT WORK.
YES!!
IF I COME ACROSS ANYTHING TOO COMPLEX, I'LL JUST ASK POLINA. SHE SAID SHE WAS AN ENGINEER.
COOL. WHILE YOU WERE WORKING ON THAT, I SENT CHARCE OUT TO SURVEY THE LIFE ON THIS PLANET.
WE NEED TO GET READY TO MAKE SOME FORAGING RUNS.

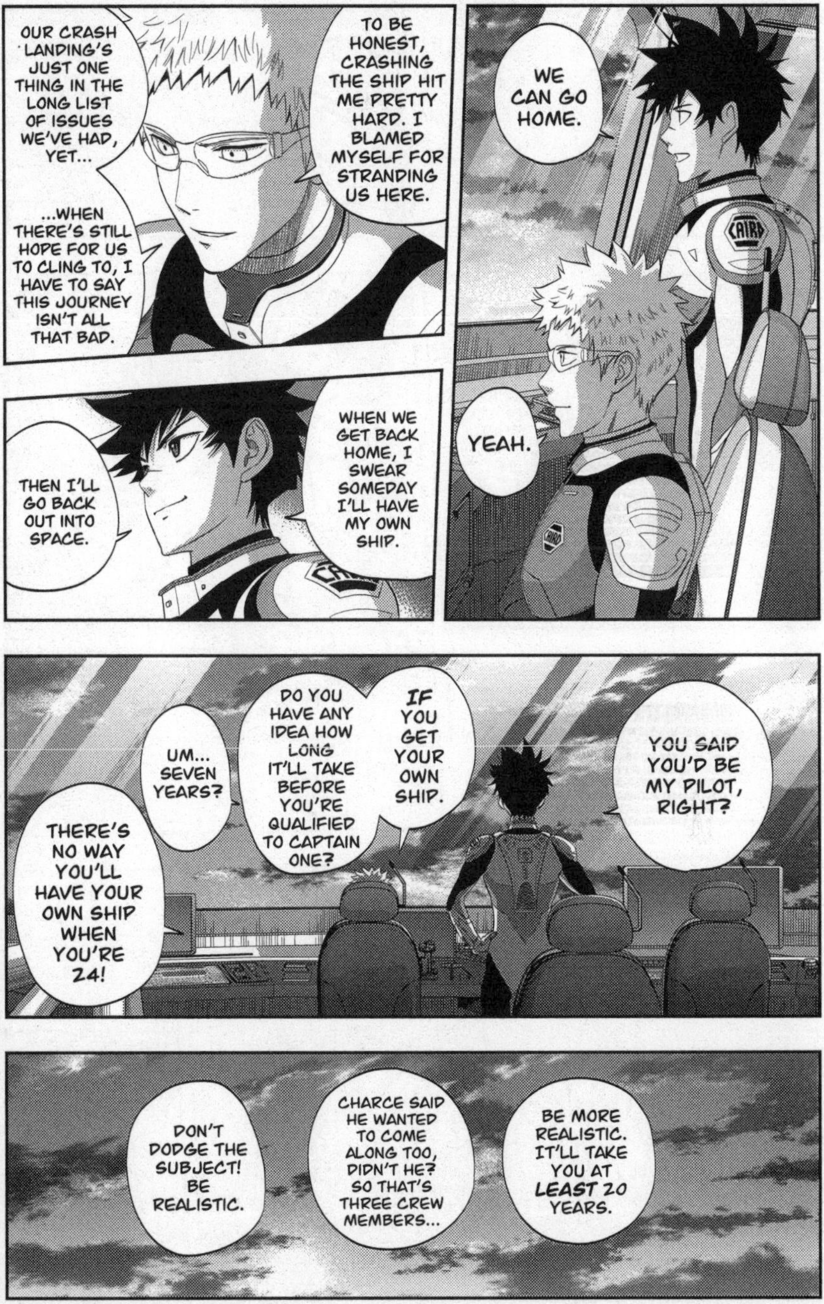
WE CAN GO HOME.
YEAH.
TO BE HONEST, CRASHING THE SHIP HIT ME PRETTY HARD. I BLAMED MYSELF FOR STRANDING US HERE.
OUR CRASH LANDING'S JUST ONE THING IN THE LONG LIST OF ISSUES WE'VE HAD, YET...
...WHEN THERE'S STILL HOPE FOR US TO CLING TO, I HAVE TO SAY THIS JOURNEY ISN'T ALL THAT BAD.
WHEN WE GET BACK HOME, I SWEAR SOMEDAY I'LL HAVE MY OWN SHIP.
THEN I'LL GO BACK OUT INTO SPACE.
YOU SAID YOU'D BE MY PILOT, RIGHT?
IF YOU GET YOUR OWN SHIP.
DO YOU HAVE ANY IDEA HOW LONG IT'LL TAKE BEFORE YOU'RE QUALIFIED TO CAPTAIN ONE?
UM... SEVEN YEARS?
THERE'S NO WAY YOU'LL HAVE YOUR OWN SHIP WHEN YOU'RE 24!
BE MORE REALISTIC. IT'LL TAKE YOU AT LEAST 20 YEARS.
CHARCE SAID HE WANTED TO COME ALONG TOO, DIDN'T HE? SO THAT'S THREE CREW MEMBERS...
DON'T DODGE THE SUBJECT! BE REALISTIC.

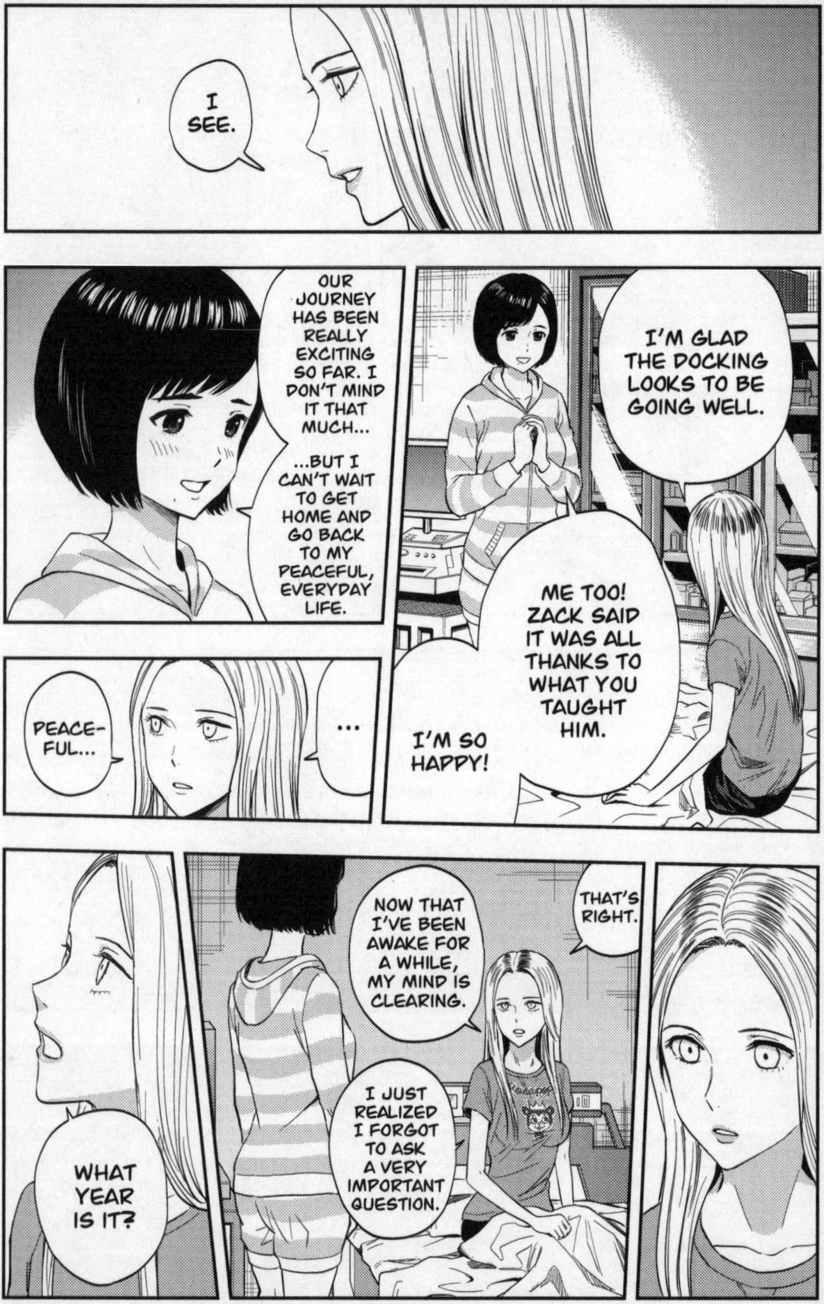
I SEE.
I'M GLAD THE DOCKING LOOKS TO BE GOING WELL.
ME TOO! ZACK SAID IT WAS ALL THANKS TO WHAT YOU TAUGHT HIM.
I'M SO HAPPY!
OUR JOURNEY HAS BEEN REALLY EXCITING SO FAR. I DON'T MIND IT THAT MUCH...
...BUT I CAN'T WAIT TO GET HOME AND GO BACK TO MY PEACEFUL, EVERYDAY LIFE.
...
PEACE-FUL...
THAT'S RIGHT.
NOW THAT I'VE BEEN AWAKE FOR A WHILE, MY MIND IS CLEARING.
I JUST REALIZED I FORGOT TO ASK A VERY IMPORTANT QUESTION.
WHAT YEAR IS IT?

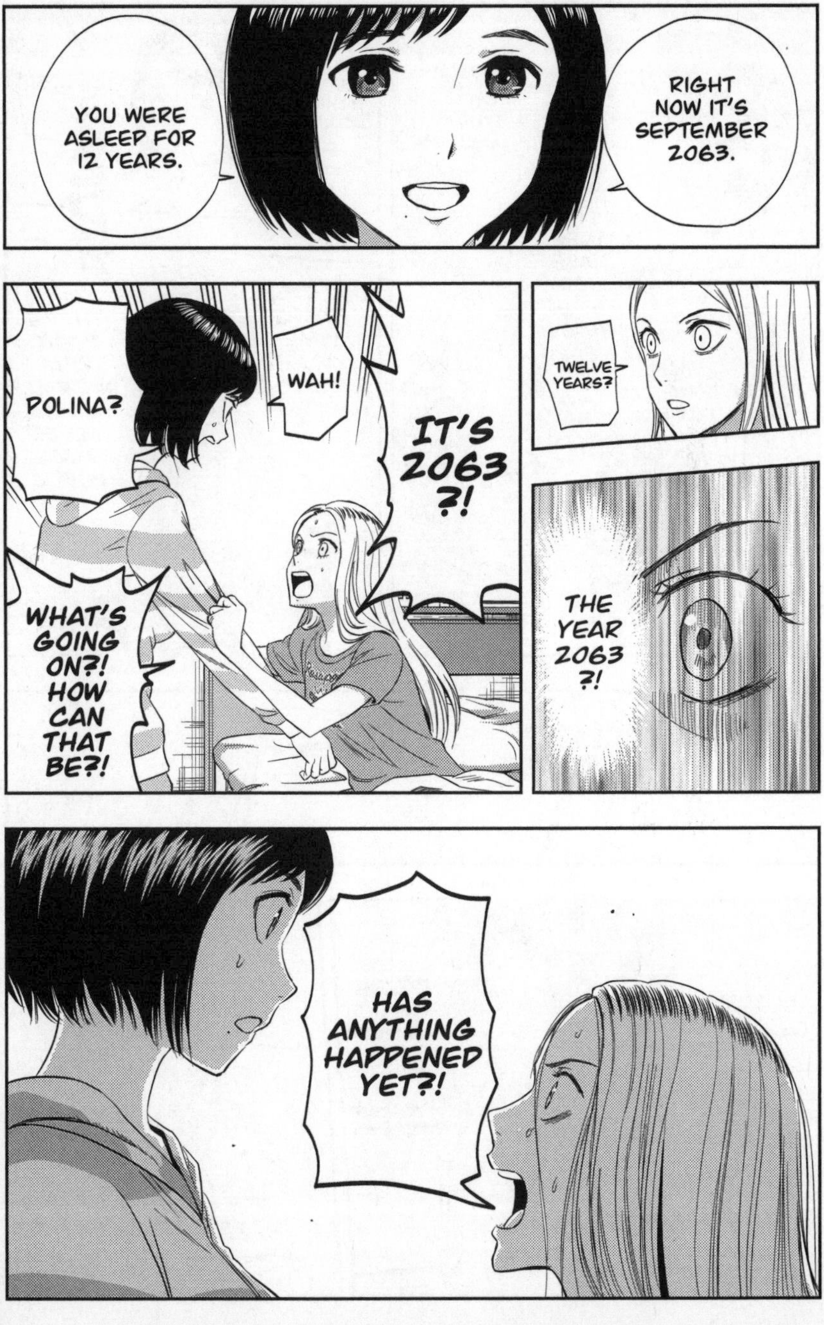
RIGHT NOW IT'S SEPTEMBER 2063.
YOU WERE ASLEEP FOR 12 YEARS.
TWELVE YEARS?
THE YEAR 2063?!
WAH!
IT'S 2063?!
POLINA?
WHAT'S GOING ON?! HOW CAN THAT BE?!
HAS ANYTHING HAPPENED YET?!

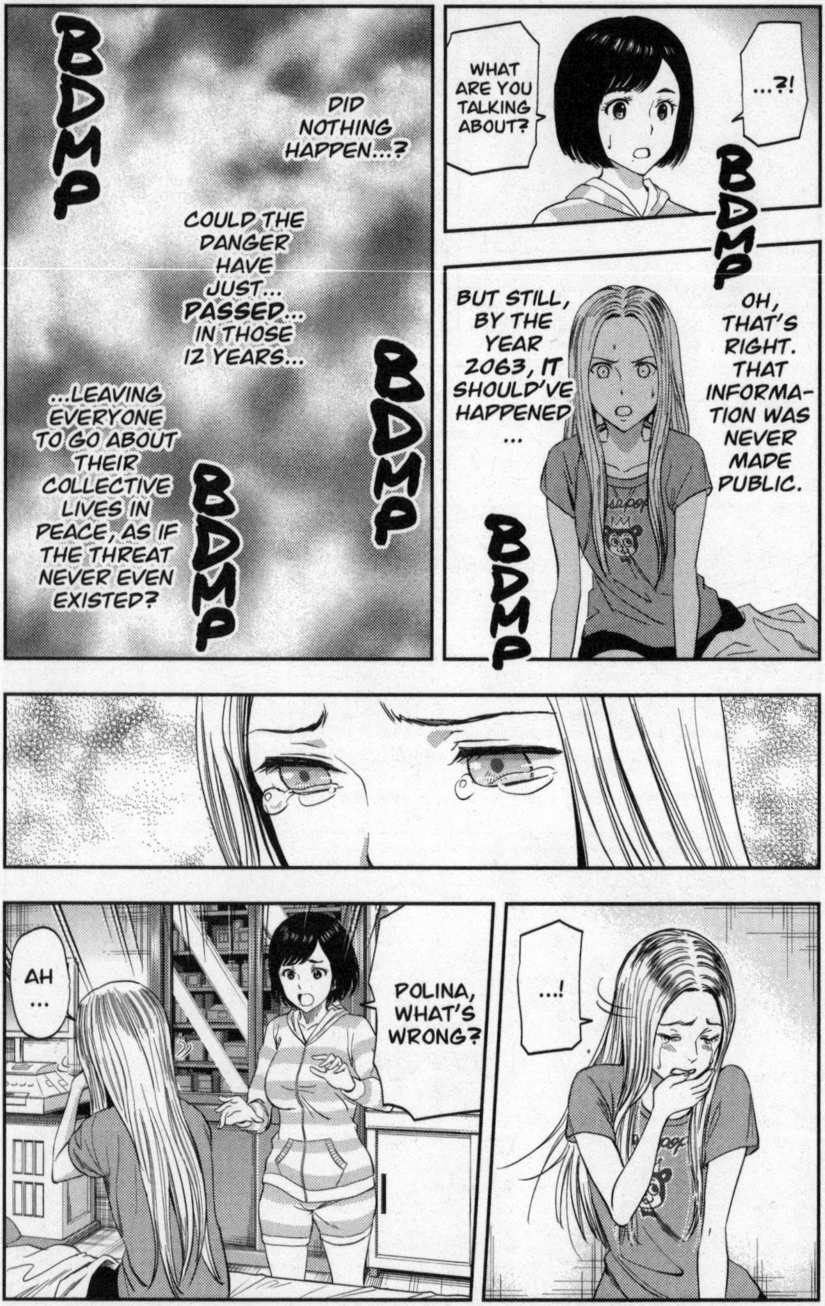
...?!
WHAT ARE YOU TALKING ABOUT?
BDMP
OH, THAT'S RIGHT. THAT INFORMATION WAS NEVER MADE PUBLIC.
BUT STILL, BY THE YEAR 2063, IT SHOULD'VE HAPPENED ...
BDMP
BDMP
DID NOTHING HAPPEN...?
COULD THE DANGER HAVE JUST... PASSED... IN THOSE 12 YEARS...
BDMP
...LEAVING EVERYONE TO GO ABOUT THEIR COLLECTIVE LIVES IN PEACE, AS IF THE THREAT NEVER EVEN EXISTED?
BDMP
...!
POLINA, WHAT'S WRONG?
AH ...

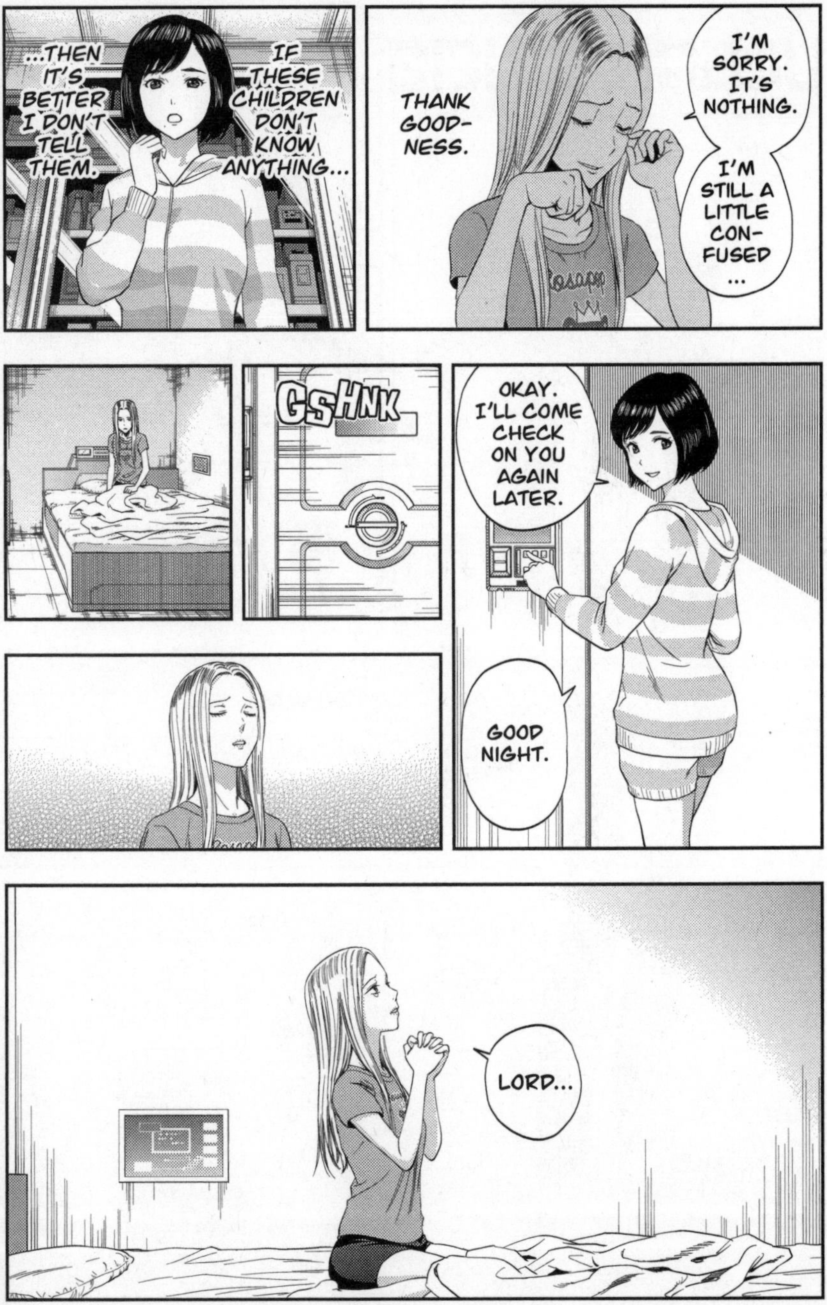
I'M SORRY. IT'S NOTHING.
I'M STILL A LITTLE CON-FUSED ...
THANK GOOD-NESS.
IF THESE CHILDREN DON'T KNOW ANYTHING...
...THEN IT'S BETTER I DON'T TELL THEM.
OKAY. I'LL COME CHECK ON YOU AGAIN LATER.
GOOD NIGHT.
GSHNK
LORD...

ULGAR ZWEIG

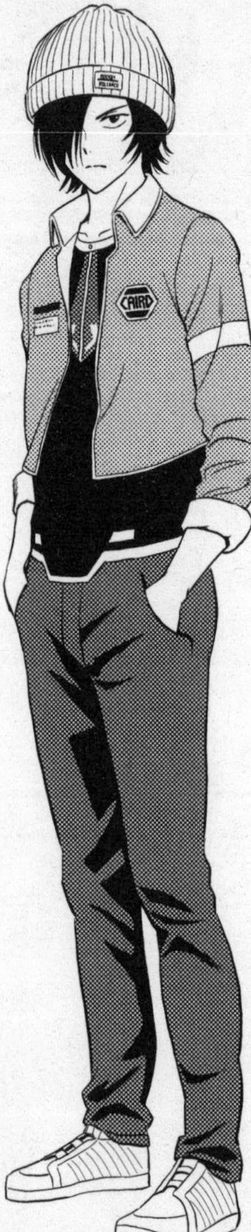
CAIRD

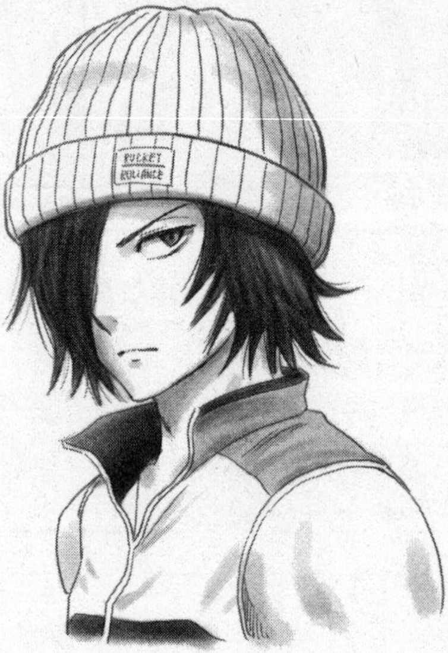
ROCKET
ROLLANCE

DATA

Name: **Ulgar Zweig**

Age: **17**

Birthday: **August 23**

Height: **5'5"**

Weight: **124 lbs.**

Blood Type: **B**

Eye Color: **Amber**

Hometown: **Mousanish District**

After losing his brother, the only person who had ever cared for him, Ulgar swore he'd get revenge. He began honing his marksmanship skills to kill the man who'd killed his brother. His favorite knit cap is from the popular Rocket Rollance fashion brand.

ASTRA
LOST IN
SPACE
#31

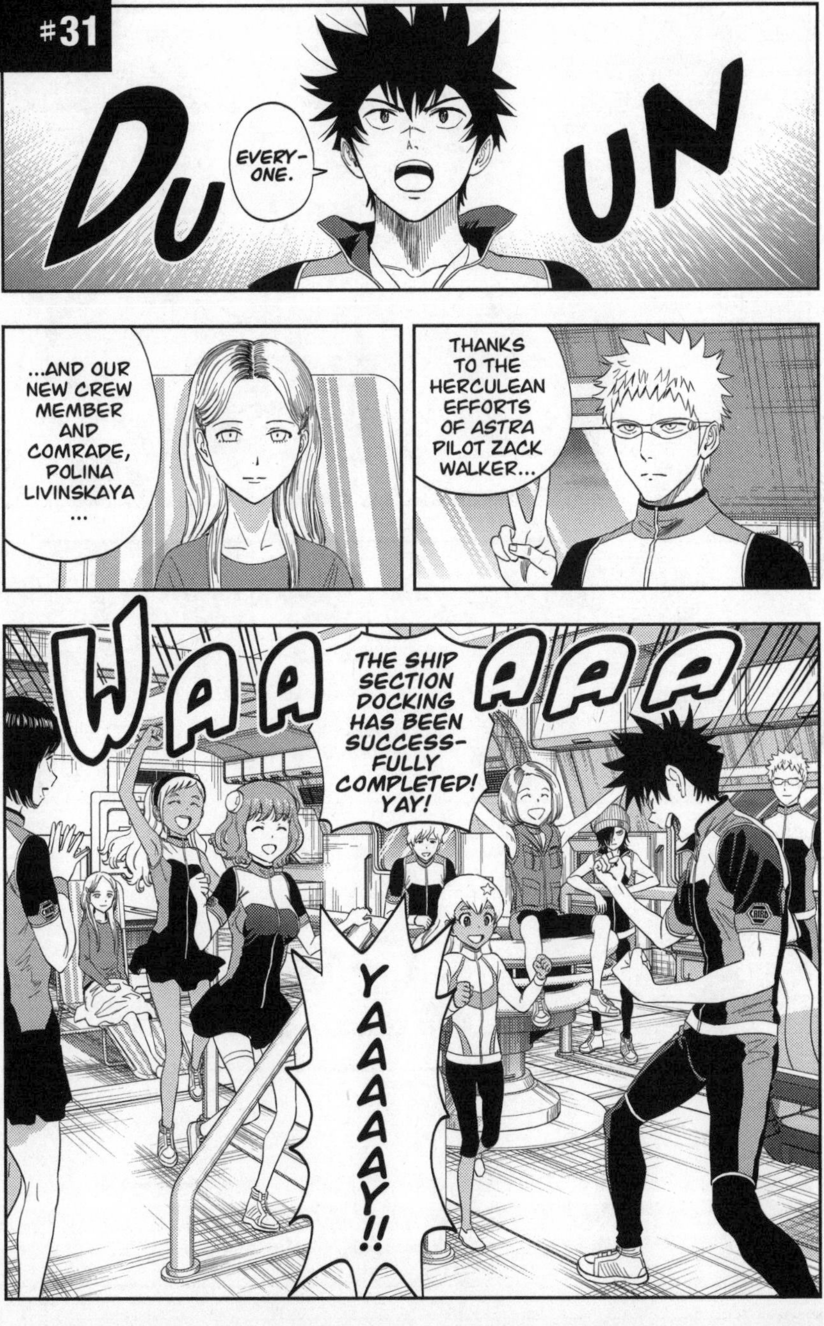
DU UN
EVERY-ONE.
THANKS TO THE HERCULEAN EFFORTS OF ASTRA PILOT ZACK WALKER...
...AND OUR NEW CREW MEMBER AND COMRADE, POLINA LIVINSKAYA ...
WAA AAA
THE SHIP SECTION DOCKING HAS BEEN SUCCESS-FULLY COMPLETED! YAY!
YAAAAAY!!

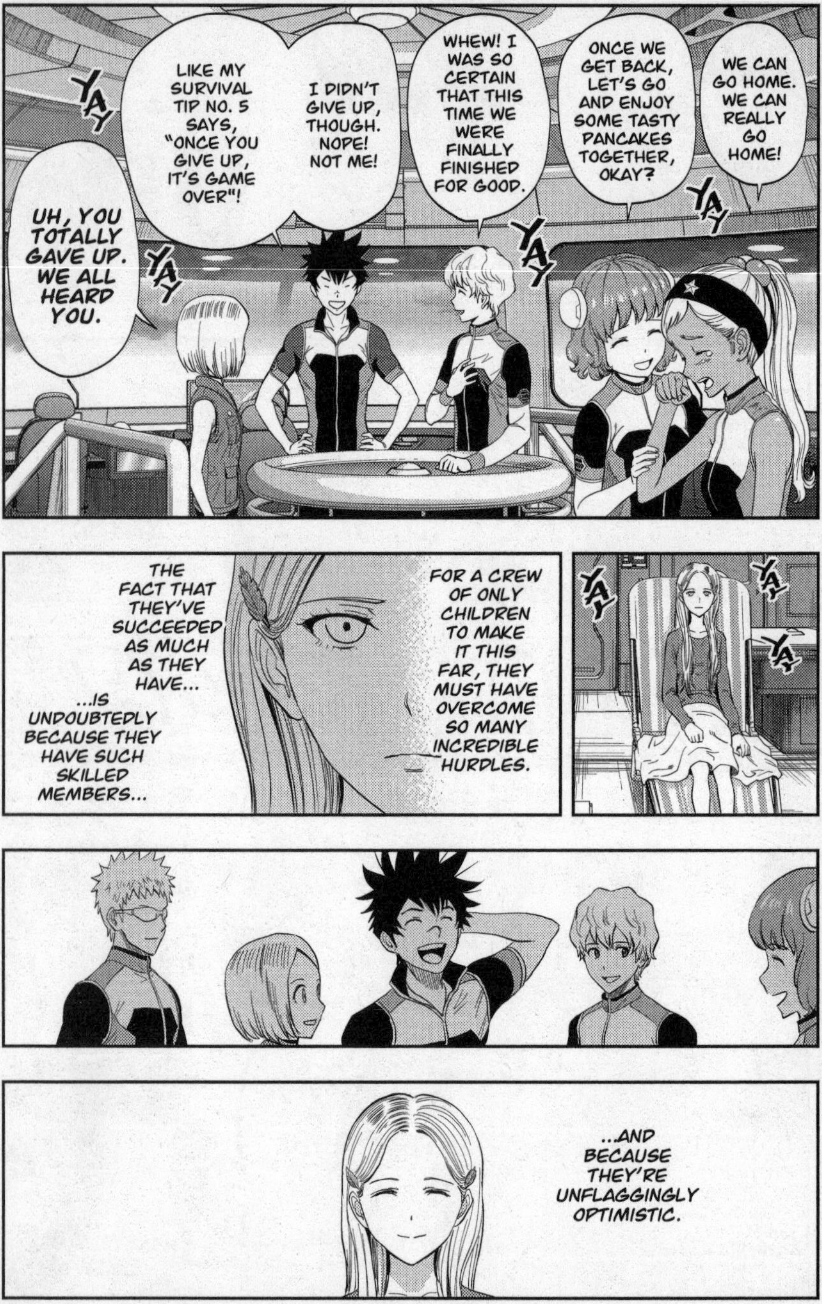
YAY
WE CAN GO HOME. WE CAN REALLY GO HOME!
ONCE WE GET BACK, LET'S GO AND ENJOY SOME TASTY PANCAKES TOGETHER, OKAY?
YAY
WHEW! I WAS SO CERTAIN THAT THIS TIME WE WERE FINALLY FINISHED FOR GOOD.
I DIDN'T GIVE UP, THOUGH. NOPE! NOT ME!
LIKE MY SURVIVAL TIP NO. 5 SAYS, "ONCE YOU GIVE UP, IT'S GAME OVER"!
YAY
YAY
UH, YOU TOTALLY GAVE UP. WE ALL HEARD YOU.
YAY
YAY
YAY
FOR A CREW OF ONLY CHILDREN TO MAKE IT THIS FAR, THEY MUST HAVE OVERCOME SO MANY INCREDIBLE HURDLES.
THE FACT THAT THEY'VE SUCCEEDED AS MUCH AS THEY HAVE...
...IS UNDOUBTEDLY BECAUSE THEY HAVE SUCH SKILLED MEMBERS...
...AND BECAUSE THEY'RE UNFLAGGINGLY OPTIMISTIC.

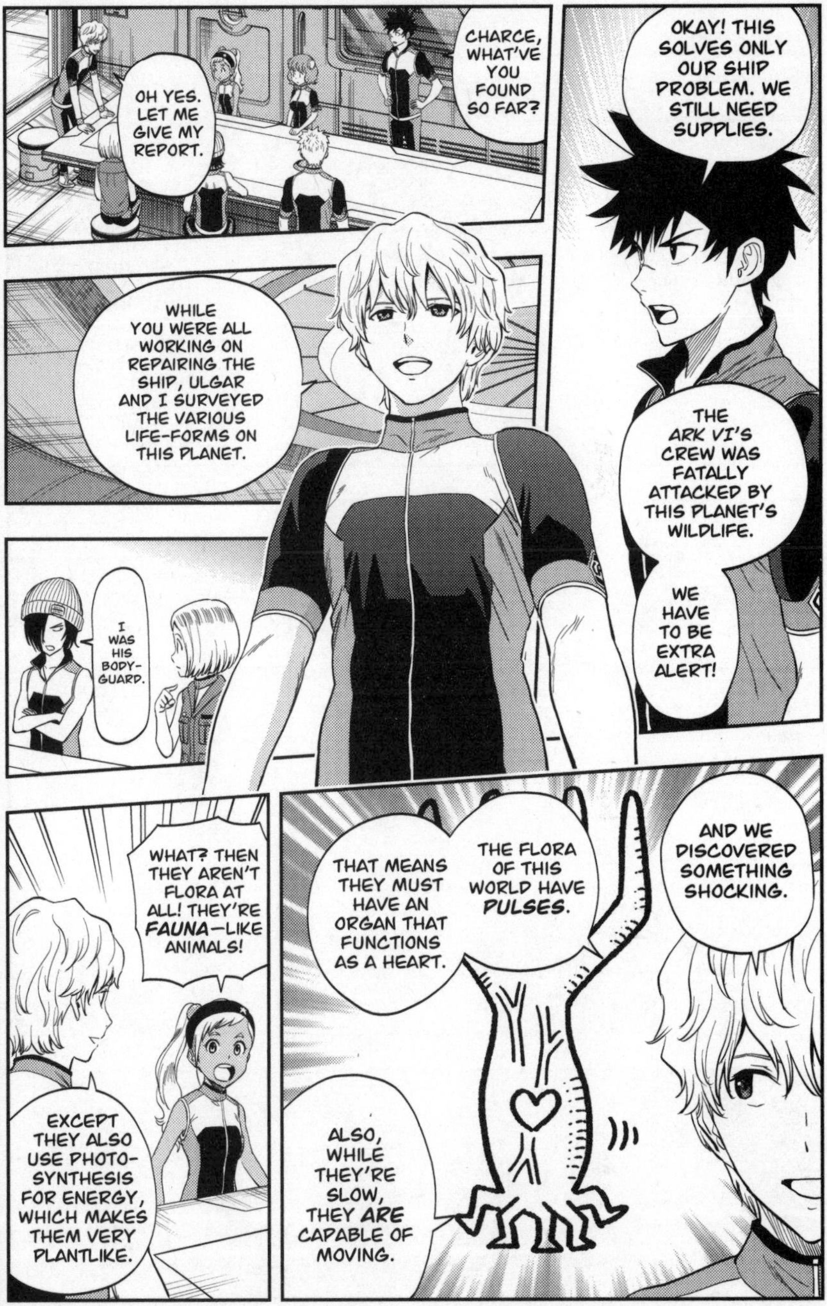
OKAY! THIS SOLVES ONLY OUR SHIP PROBLEM. WE STILL NEED SUPPLIES.
THE ARK VI'S CREW WAS FATALLY ATTACKED BY THIS PLANET'S WILDLIFE.
WE HAVE TO BE EXTRA ALERT!
CHARCE, WHAT'VE YOU FOUND SO FAR?
OH YES. LET ME GIVE MY REPORT.
WHILE YOU WERE ALL WORKING ON REPAIRING THE SHIP, ULGAR AND I SURVEYED THE VARIOUS LIFE-FORMS ON THIS PLANET.
I WAS HIS BODY-GUARD.
AND WE DISCOVERED SOMETHING SHOCKING.
THE FLORA OF THIS WORLD HAVE *PULSES*.
THAT MEANS THEY MUST HAVE AN ORGAN THAT FUNCTIONS AS A HEART.
ALSO, WHILE THEY'RE SLOW, THEY *ARE* CAPABLE OF MOVING.
WHAT? THEN THEY AREN'T FLORA AT ALL! THEY'RE *FAUNA*—LIKE ANIMALS!
EXCEPT THEY ALSO USE PHOTO-SYNTHESIS FOR ENERGY, WHICH MAKES THEM VERY PLANTLIKE.

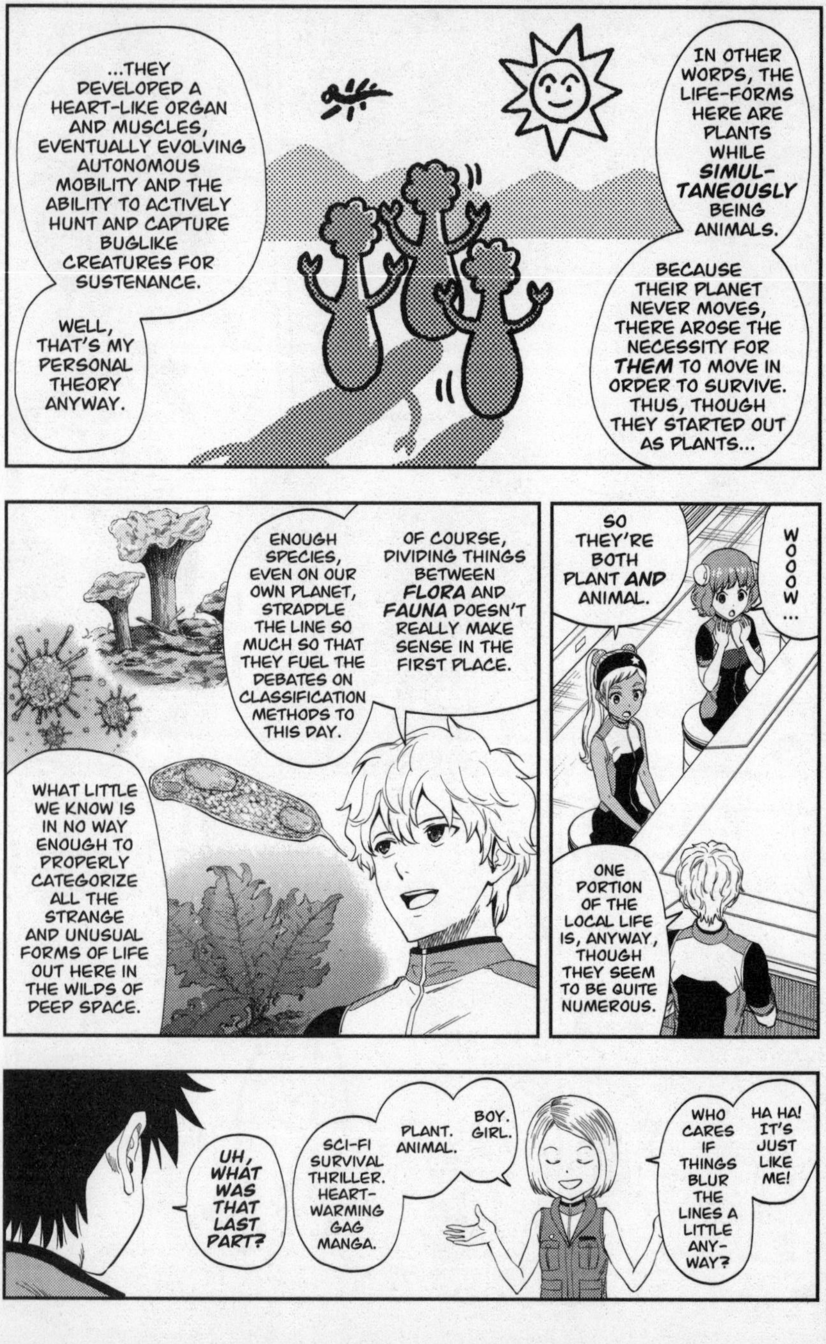
IN OTHER WORDS, THE LIFE-FORMS HERE ARE PLANTS WHILE SIMUL-TANEOUSLY BEING ANIMALS.
BECAUSE THEIR PLANET NEVER MOVES, THERE AROSE THE NECESSITY FOR THEM TO MOVE IN ORDER TO SURVIVE. THUS, THOUGH THEY STARTED OUT AS PLANTS...
...THEY DEVELOPED A HEART-LIKE ORGAN AND MUSCLES, EVENTUALLY EVOLVING AUTONOMOUS MOBILITY AND THE ABILITY TO ACTIVELY HUNT AND CAPTURE BUGLIKE CREATURES FOR SUSTENANCE.
WELL, THAT'S MY PERSONAL THEORY ANYWAY.
WOOOW...
SO THEY'RE BOTH PLANT AND ANIMAL.
ONE PORTION OF THE LOCAL LIFE IS, ANYWAY, THOUGH THEY SEEM TO BE QUITE NUMEROUS.
OF COURSE, DIVIDING THINGS BETWEEN FLORA AND FAUNA DOESN'T REALLY MAKE SENSE IN THE FIRST PLACE.
ENOUGH SPECIES, EVEN ON OUR OWN PLANET, STRADDLE THE LINE SO MUCH SO THAT THEY FUEL THE DEBATES ON CLASSIFICATION METHODS TO THIS DAY.
WHAT LITTLE WE KNOW IS IN NO WAY ENOUGH TO PROPERLY CATEGORIZE ALL THE STRANGE AND UNUSUAL FORMS OF LIFE OUT HERE IN THE WILDS OF DEEP SPACE.
HA HA! IT'S JUST LIKE ME!
WHO CARES IF THINGS BLUR THE LINES A LITTLE ANYWAY?
BOY. GIRL.
PLANT. ANIMAL.
SCI-FI SURVIVAL THRILLER. HEART-WARMING GAG MANGA.
UH, WHAT WAS THAT LAST PART?

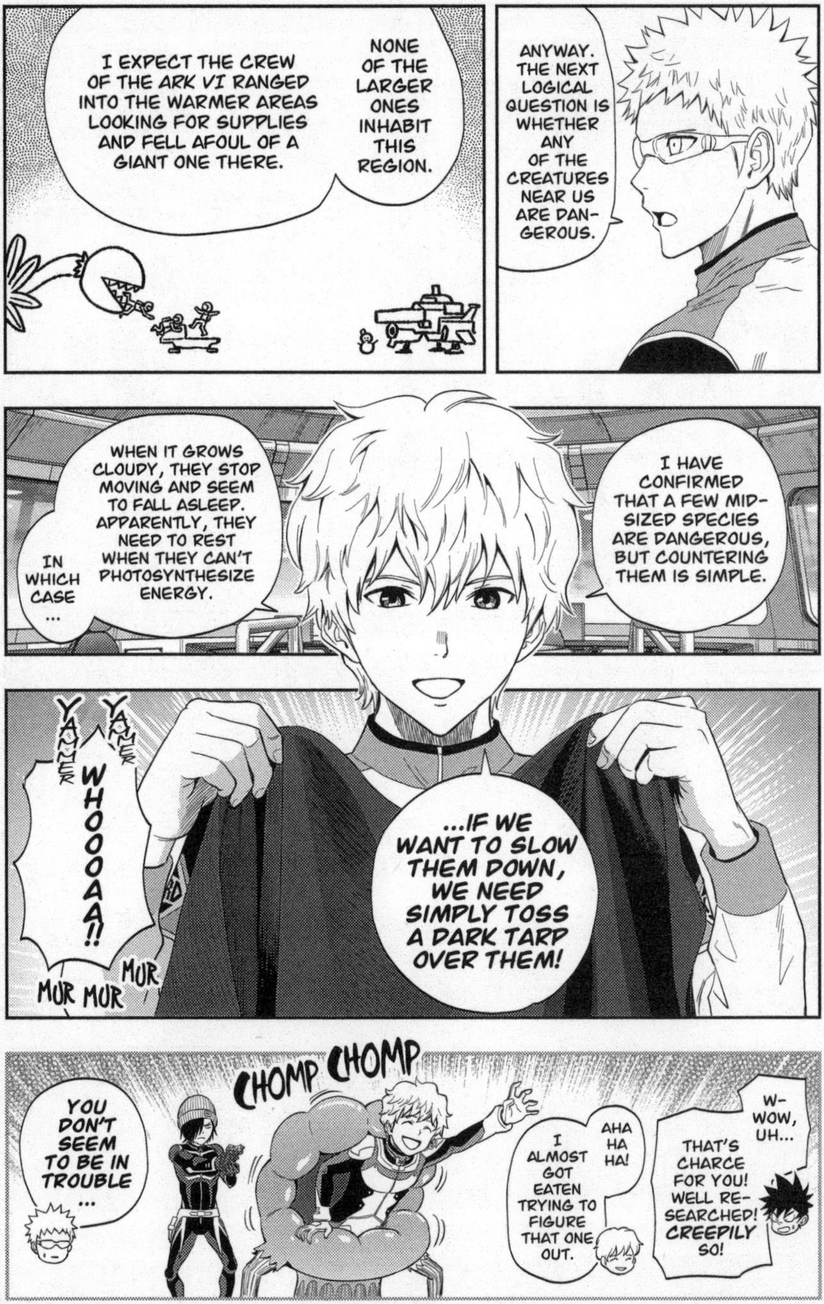
ANYWAY. THE NEXT LOGICAL QUESTION IS WHETHER ANY OF THE CREATURES NEAR US ARE DANGEROUS.
NONE OF THE LARGER ONES INHABIT THIS REGION.
I EXPECT THE CREW OF THE ARK VI RANGED INTO THE WARMER AREAS LOOKING FOR SUPPLIES AND FELL AFOUL OF A GIANT ONE THERE.
I HAVE CONFIRMED THAT A FEW MID-SIZED SPECIES ARE DANGEROUS, BUT COUNTERING THEM IS SIMPLE.
WHEN IT GROWS CLOUDY, THEY STOP MOVING AND SEEM TO FALL ASLEEP. APPARENTLY, THEY NEED TO REST WHEN THEY CAN'T PHOTOSYNTHESIZE ENERGY.
IN WHICH CASE ...
...IF WE WANT TO SLOW THEM DOWN, WE NEED SIMPLY TOSS A DARK TARP OVER THEM!
YAMMER YAMMER
WHOOOOAA!!
MUR MUR MUR
W-WOW, UH...
THAT'S CHARCE FOR YOU! WELL RE-SEARCHED! CREEPILY SO!
AHA HA HA!
I ALMOST GOT EATEN TRYING TO FIGURE THAT ONE OUT.
CHOMP CHOMP
YOU DON'T SEEM TO BE IN TROUBLE ...

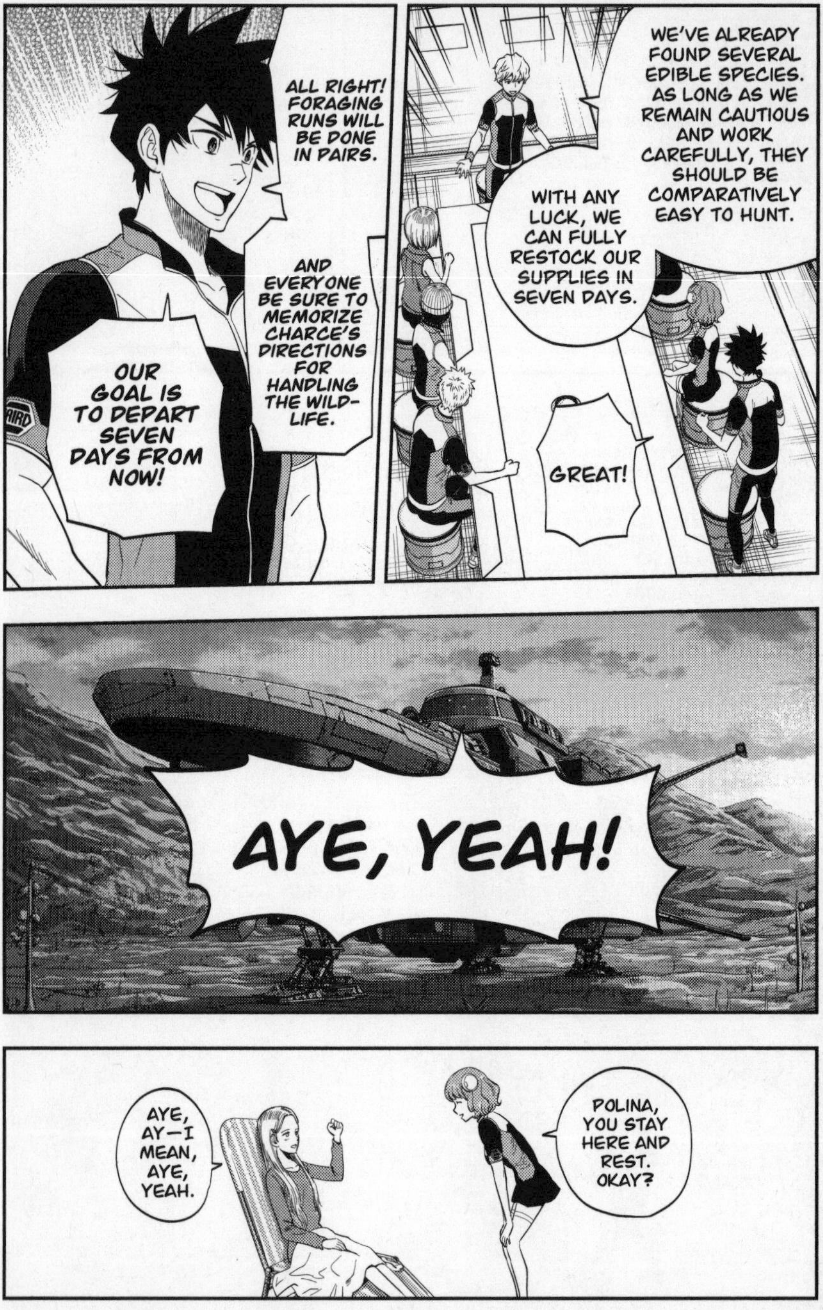
WE'VE ALREADY FOUND SEVERAL EDIBLE SPECIES. AS LONG AS WE REMAIN CAUTIOUS AND WORK CAREFULLY, THEY SHOULD BE COMPARATIVELY EASY TO HUNT.
WITH ANY LUCK, WE CAN FULLY RESTOCK OUR SUPPLIES IN SEVEN DAYS.
GREAT!
ALL RIGHT! FORAGING RUNS WILL BE DONE IN PAIRS.
AND EVERYONE BE SURE TO MEMORIZE CHARCE'S DIRECTIONS FOR HANDLING THE WILD-LIFE.
OUR GOAL IS TO DEPART SEVEN DAYS FROM NOW!
AYE, YEAH!
POLINA, YOU STAY HERE AND REST. OKAY?
AYE, AY—I MEAN, AYE, YEAH.

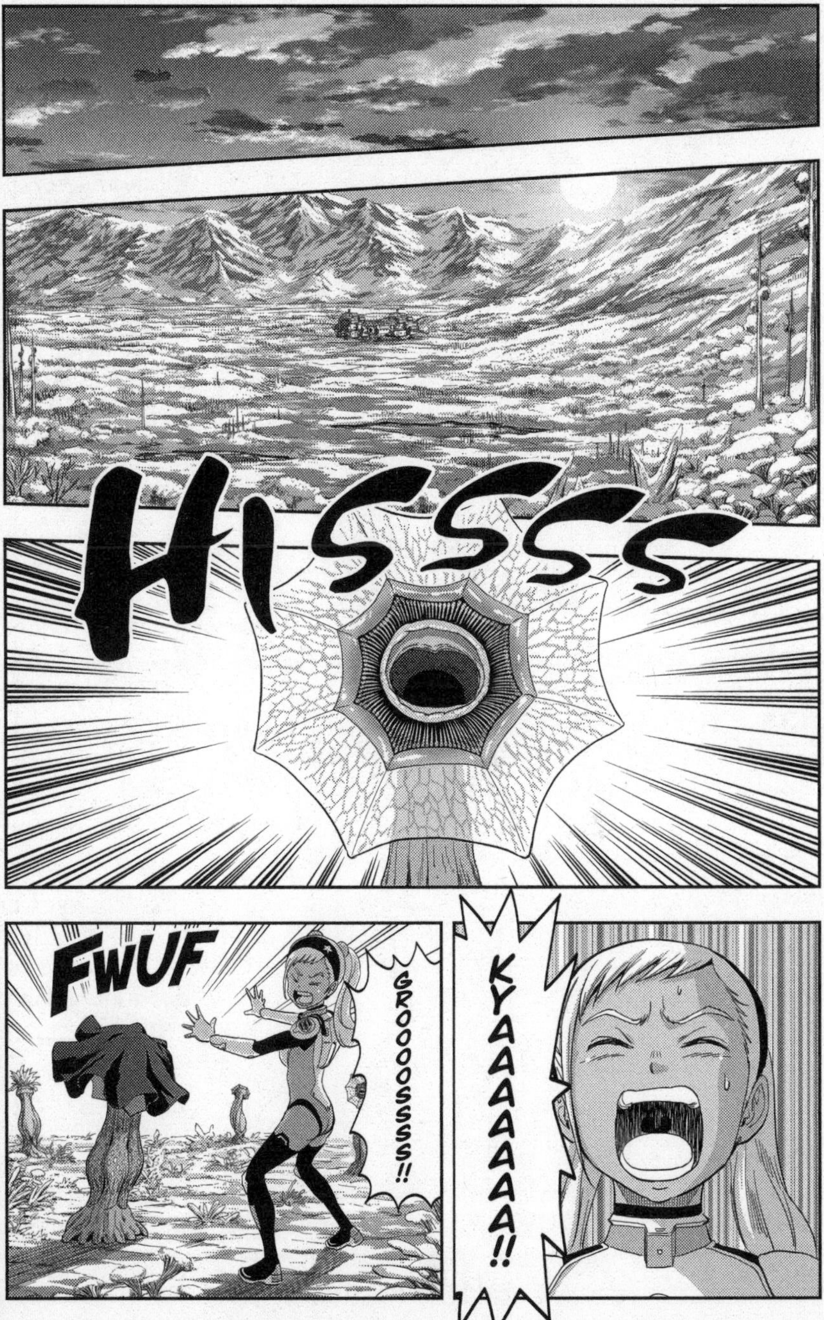
HISSSS
KYAAAAAAAAA!!
FWUF
GROOOOSSSSS!!

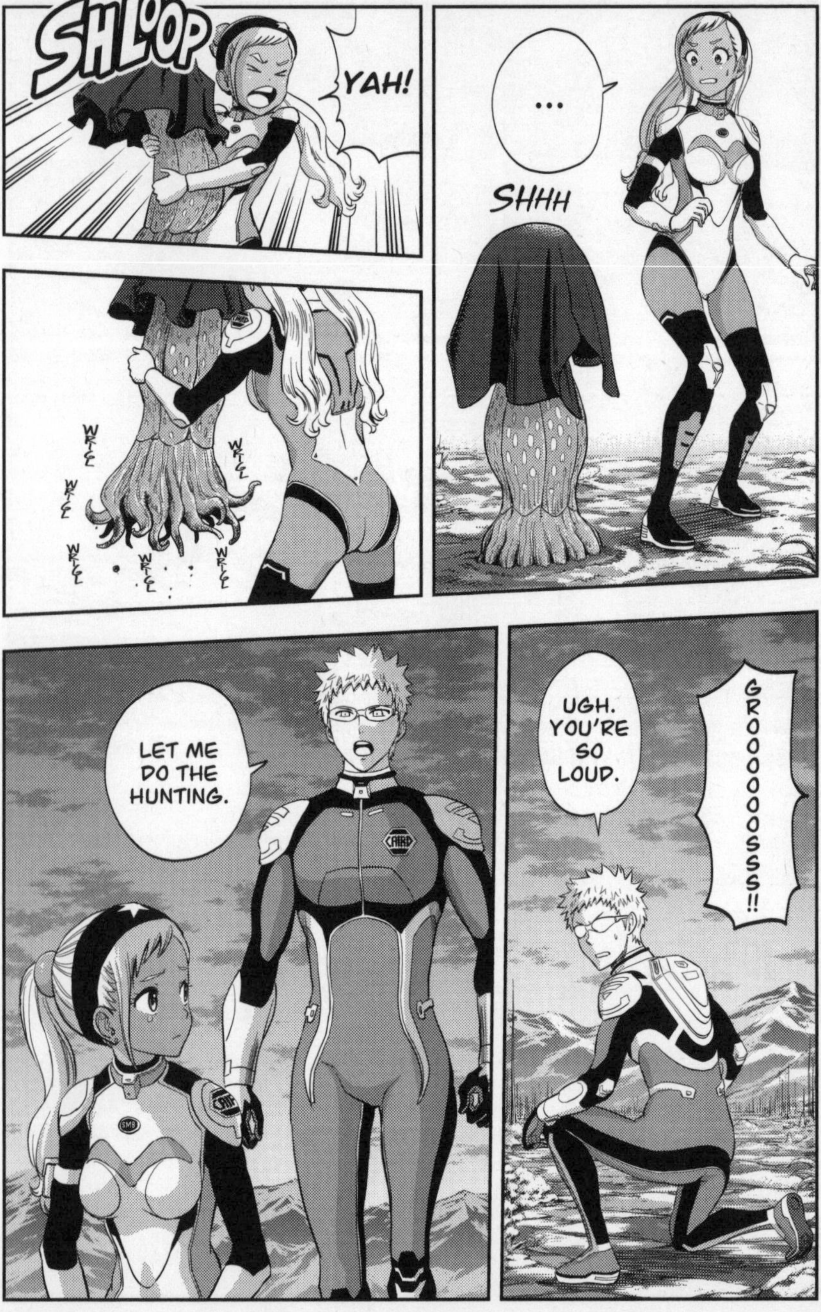
...
SHHH
SHLOOP
YAH!
WRIGL
WRIGL
WRIGL
WRIGL
WRIGL
WRIGL
GROOOOOOSSS!!
UGH. YOU'RE SO LOUD.
LET ME DO THE HUNTING.

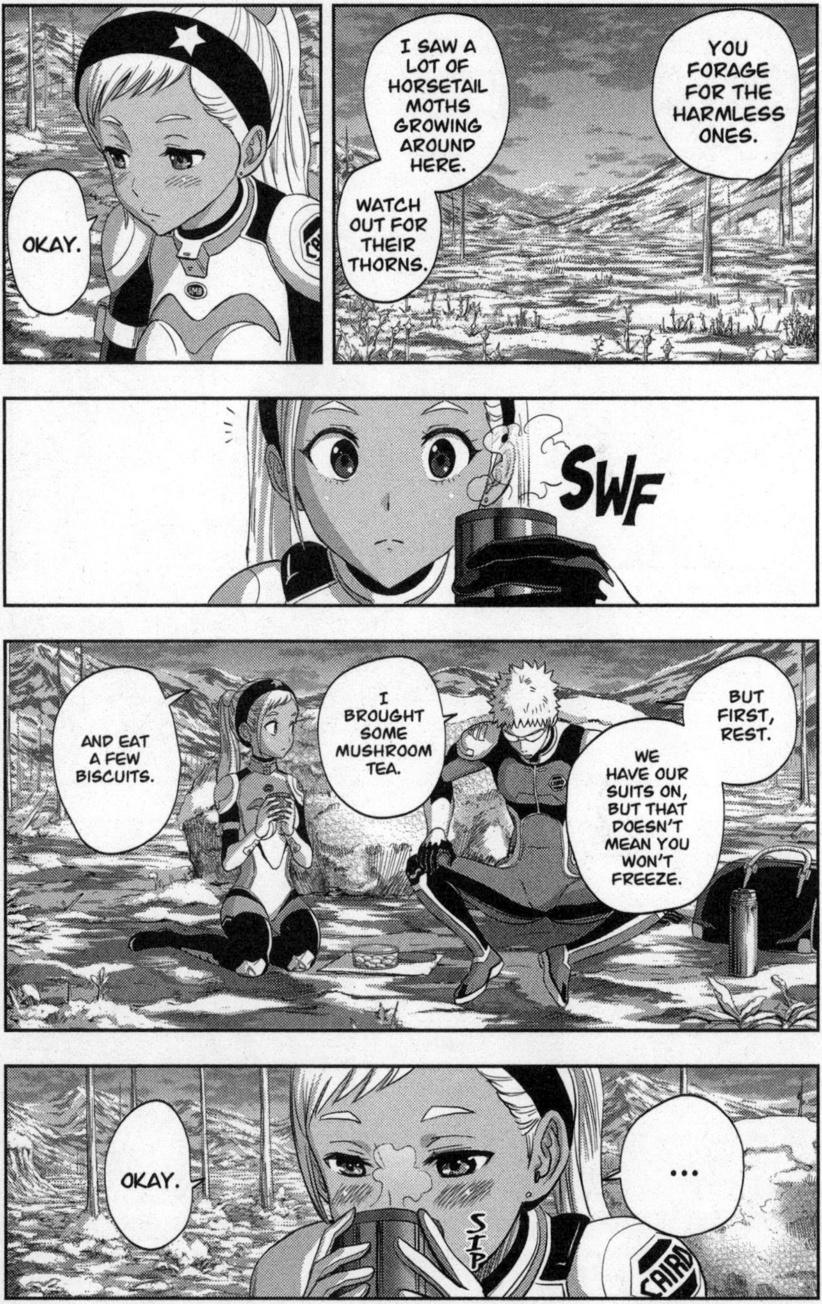
YOU FORAGE FOR THE HARMLESS ONES.
I SAW A LOT OF HORSETAIL MOTHS GROWING AROUND HERE.
WATCH OUT FOR THEIR THORNS.
OKAY.
SWF
BUT FIRST, REST.
WE HAVE OUR SUITS ON, BUT THAT DOESN'T MEAN YOU WON'T FREEZE.
I BROUGHT SOME MUSHROOM TEA.
AND EAT A FEW BISCUITS.
...
SIP
OKAY.

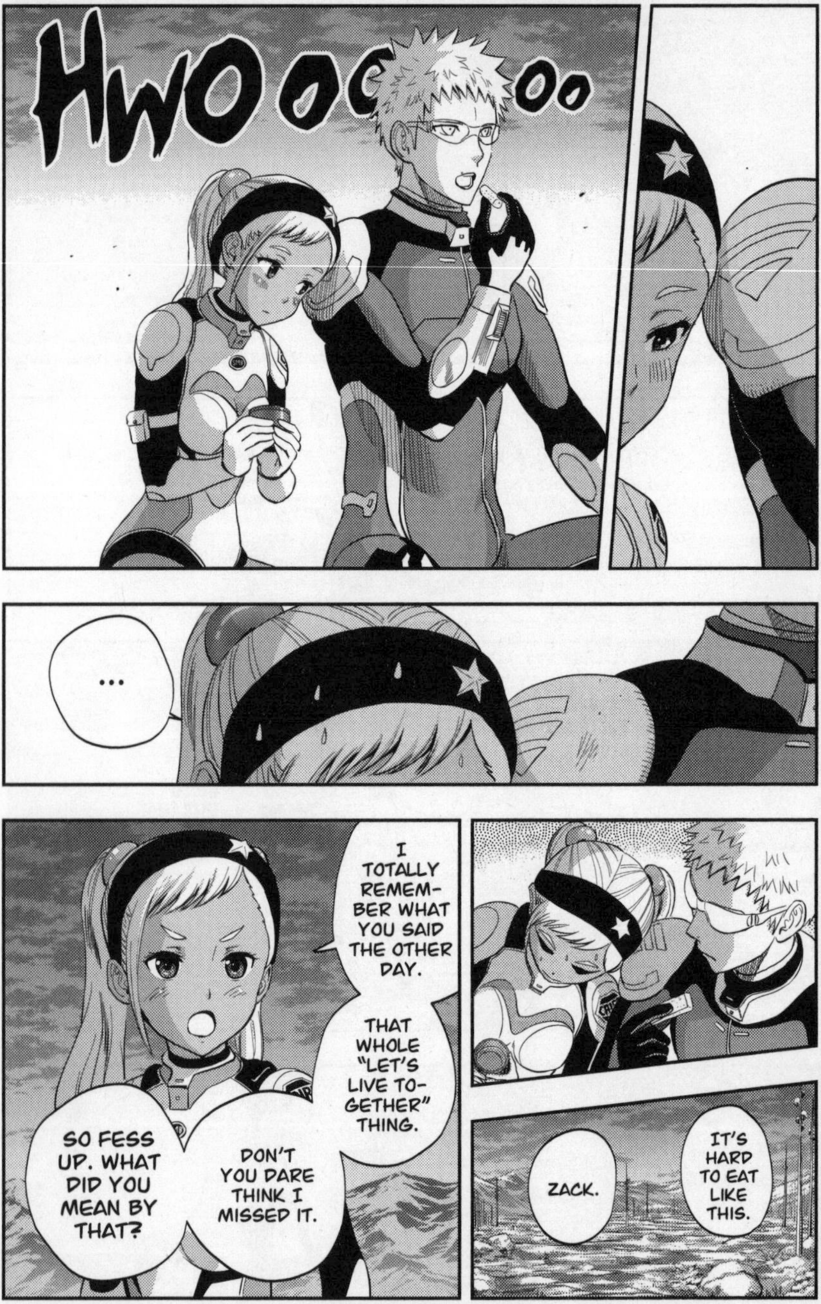
HWOOOOO
...
IT'S HARD TO EAT LIKE THIS.
ZACK.
I TOTALLY REMEMBER WHAT YOU SAID THE OTHER DAY.
THAT WHOLE "LET'S LIVE TOGETHER" THING.
DON'T YOU DARE THINK I MISSED IT.
SO FESS UP. WHAT DID YOU MEAN BY THAT?

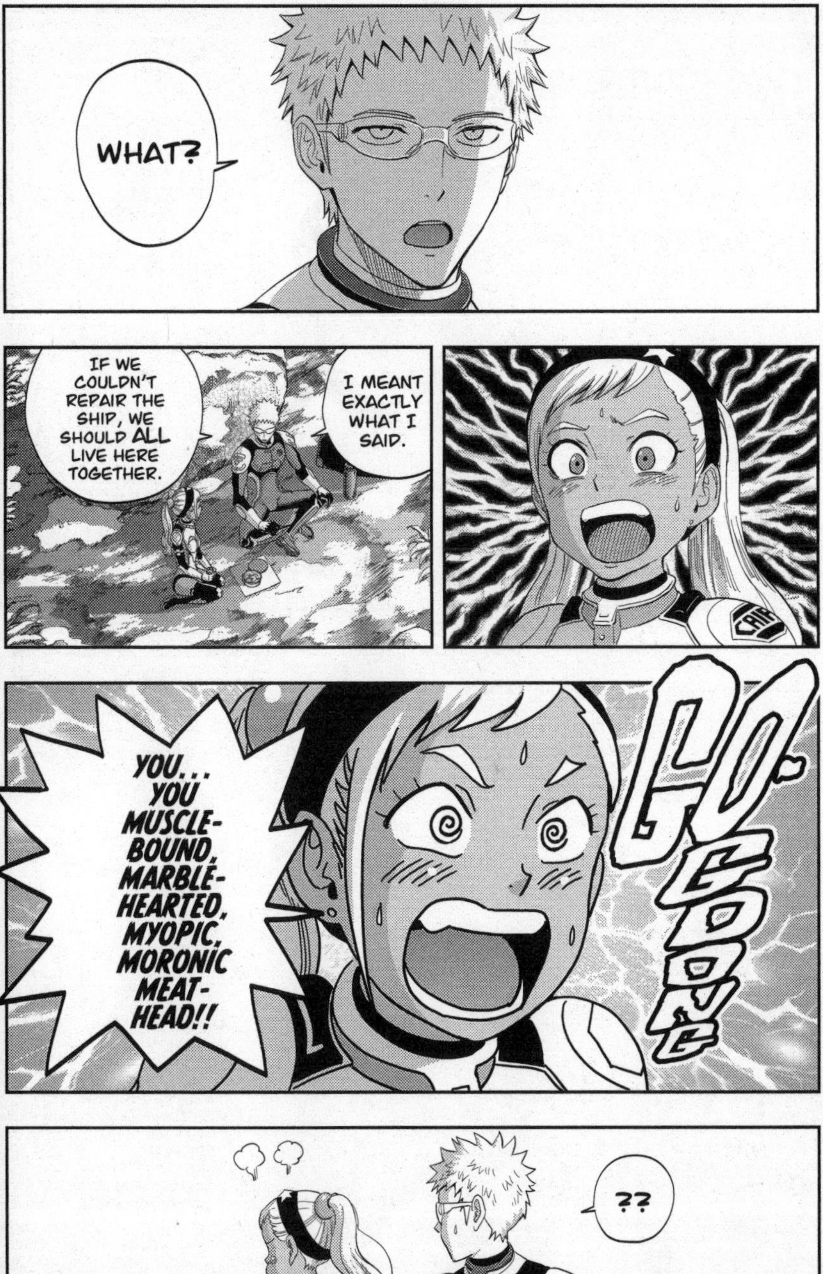
WHAT?
I MEANT EXACTLY WHAT I SAID.
IF WE COULDN'T REPAIR THE SHIP, WE SHOULD ALL LIVE HERE TOGETHER.
GOGOONG
YOU... YOU MUSCLE-BOUND, MARBLE-HEARTED, MYOPIC, MORONIC MEAT-HEAD!!
??

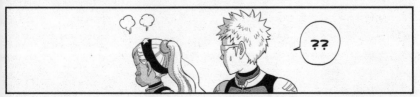

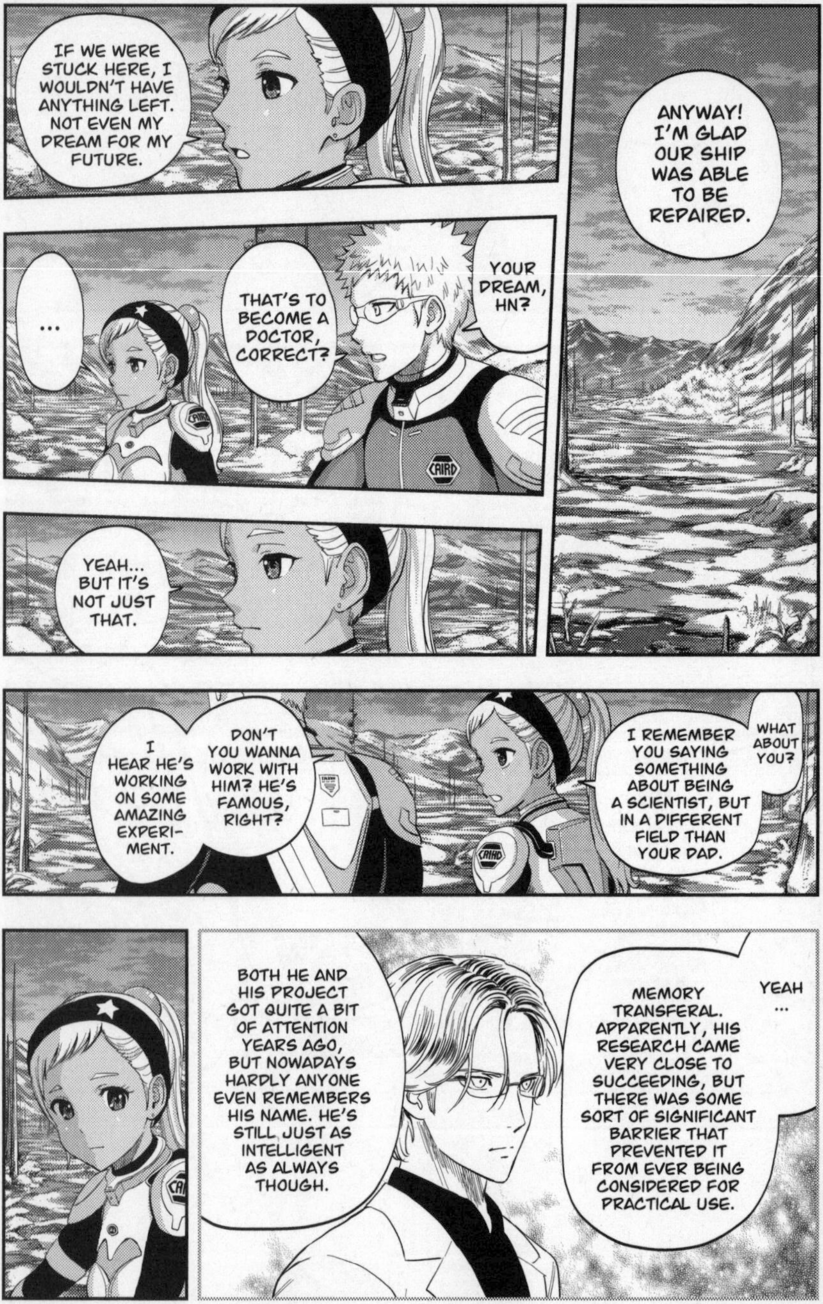
ANYWAY! I'M GLAD OUR SHIP WAS ABLE TO BE REPAIRED.
IF WE WERE STUCK HERE, I WOULDN'T HAVE ANYTHING LEFT. NOT EVEN MY DREAM FOR MY FUTURE.
YOUR DREAM, HN?
THAT'S TO BECOME A DOCTOR, CORRECT?
...
YEAH... BUT IT'S NOT JUST THAT.
WHAT ABOUT YOU?
I REMEMBER YOU SAYING SOMETHING ABOUT BEING A SCIENTIST, BUT IN A DIFFERENT FIELD THAN YOUR DAD.
DON'T YOU WANNA WORK WITH HIM? HE'S FAMOUS, RIGHT?
I HEAR HE'S WORKING ON SOME AMAZING EXPERI-MENT.
YEAH...
MEMORY TRANSFERAL. APPARENTLY, HIS RESEARCH CAME VERY CLOSE TO SUCCEEDING, BUT THERE WAS SOME SORT OF SIGNIFICANT BARRIER THAT PREVENTED IT FROM EVER BEING CONSIDERED FOR PRACTICAL USE.
BOTH HE AND HIS PROJECT GOT QUITE A BIT OF ATTENTION YEARS AGO, BUT NOWADAYS HARDLY ANYONE EVEN REMEMBERS HIS NAME. HE'S STILL JUST AS INTELLIGENT AS ALWAYS THOUGH.

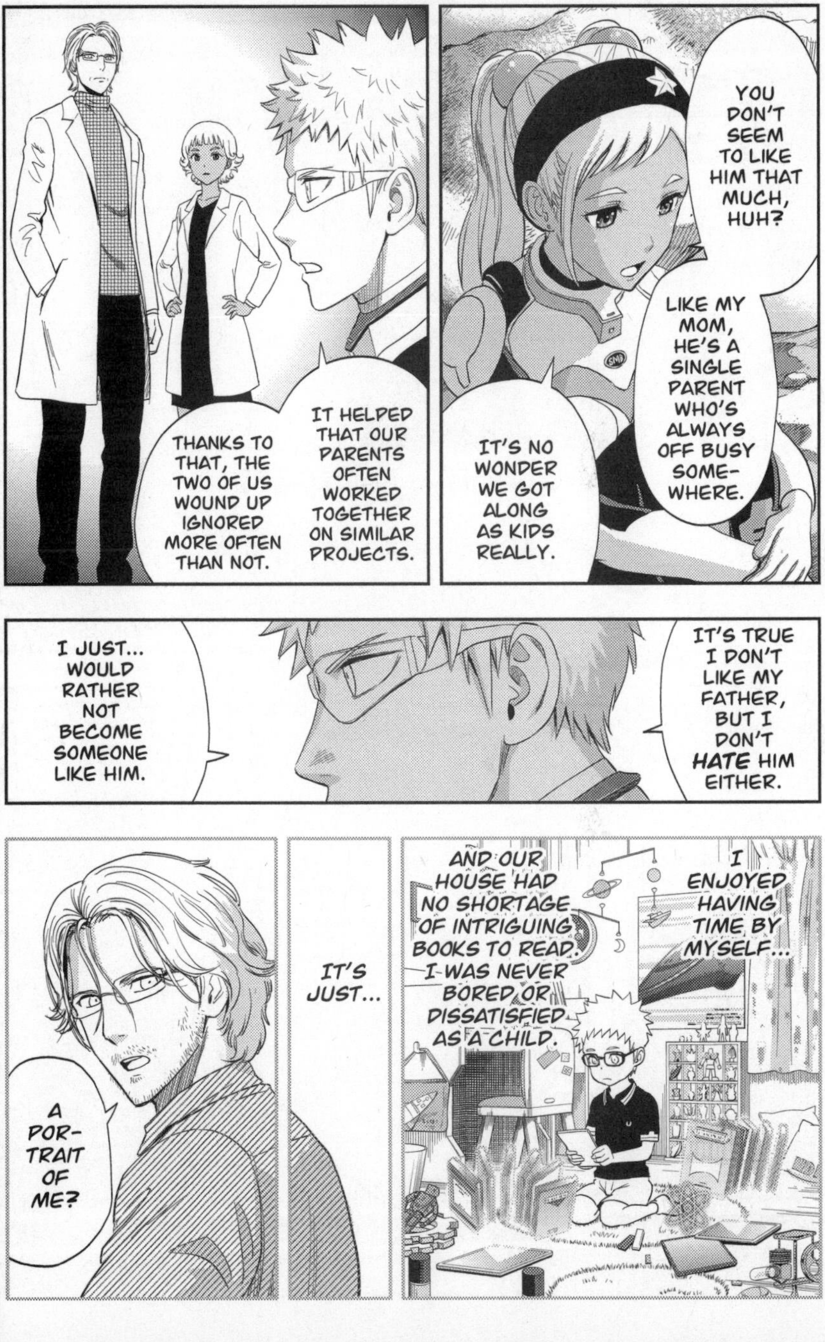
YOU DON'T SEEM TO LIKE HIM THAT MUCH, HUH?
LIKE MY MOM, HE'S A SINGLE PARENT WHO'S ALWAYS OFF BUSY SOMEWHERE.
IT'S NO WONDER WE GOT ALONG AS KIDS REALLY.
IT HELPED THAT OUR PARENTS OFTEN WORKED TOGETHER ON SIMILAR PROJECTS.
THANKS TO THAT, THE TWO OF US WOUND UP IGNORED MORE OFTEN THAN NOT.
IT'S TRUE I DON'T LIKE MY FATHER, BUT I DON'T **HATE** HIM EITHER.
I JUST... WOULD RATHER NOT BECOME SOMEONE LIKE HIM.
I ENJOYED HAVING TIME BY MYSELF...
AND OUR HOUSE HAD NO SHORTAGE OF INTRIGUING BOOKS TO READ. I WAS NEVER BORED OR DISSATISFIED AS A CHILD.
IT'S JUST...
A PORTRAIT OF ME?

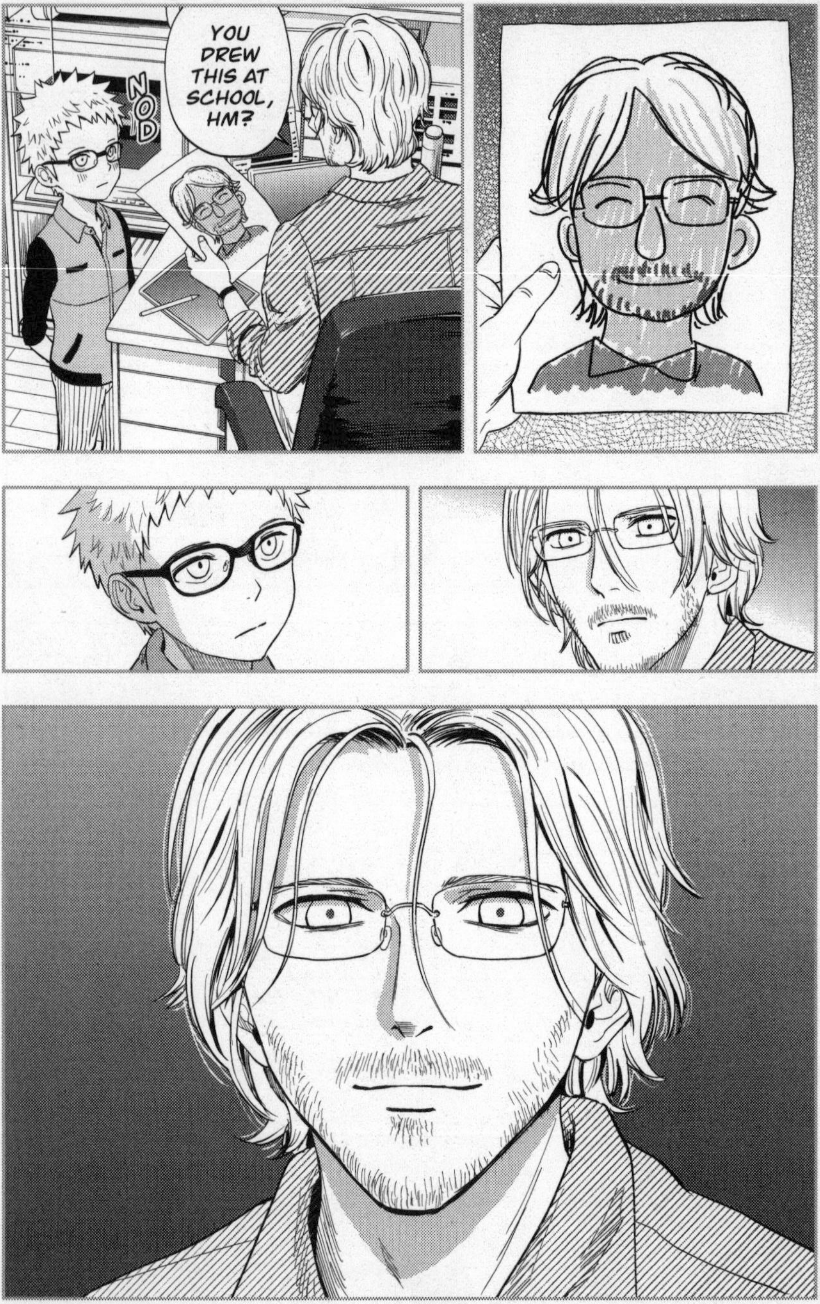
YOU DREW THIS AT SCHOOL, HM?
NOD

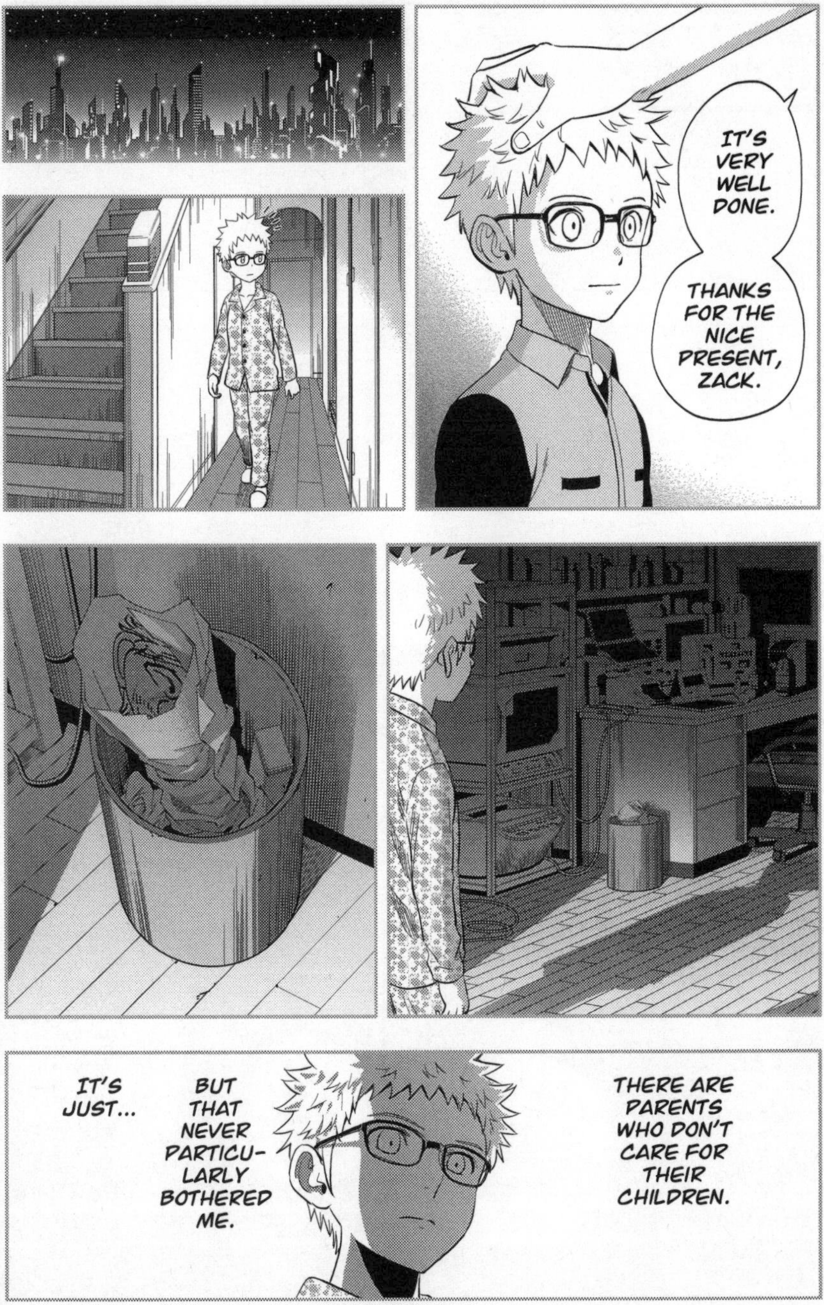
IT'S VERY WELL DONE.
THANKS FOR THE NICE PRESENT, ZACK.
THERE ARE PARENTS WHO DON'T CARE FOR THEIR CHILDREN.
BUT THAT NEVER PARTICULARLY BOTHERED ME.
IT'S JUST...

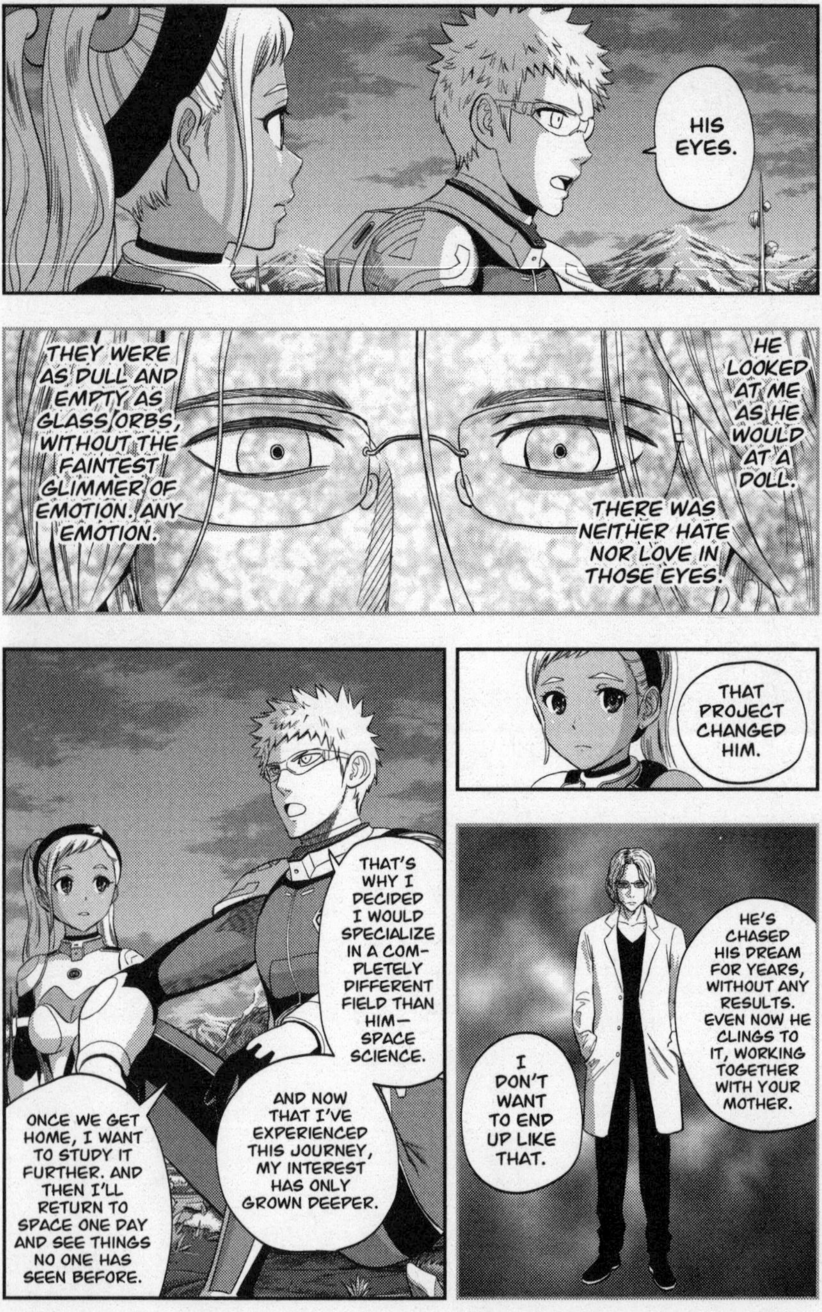
HIS EYES.
HE LOOKED AT ME AS HE WOULD AT A DOLL.
THEY WERE AS DULL AND EMPTY AS GLASS ORBS, WITHOUT THE FAINTEST GLIMMER OF EMOTION. ANY EMOTION.
THERE WAS NEITHER HATE NOR LOVE IN THOSE EYES.
THAT PROJECT CHANGED HIM.
HE'S CHASED HIS DREAM FOR YEARS, WITHOUT ANY RESULTS. EVEN NOW HE CLINGS TO IT, WORKING TOGETHER WITH YOUR MOTHER.
I DON'T WANT TO END UP LIKE THAT.
THAT'S WHY I DECIDED I WOULD SPECIALIZE IN A COM-PLETELY DIFFERENT FIELD THAN HIM—SPACE SCIENCE.
AND NOW THAT I'VE EXPERIENCED THIS JOURNEY, MY INTEREST HAS ONLY GROWN DEEPER.
ONCE WE GET HOME, I WANT TO STUDY IT FURTHER. AND THEN I'LL RETURN TO SPACE ONE DAY AND SEE THINGS NO ONE HAS SEEN BEFORE.

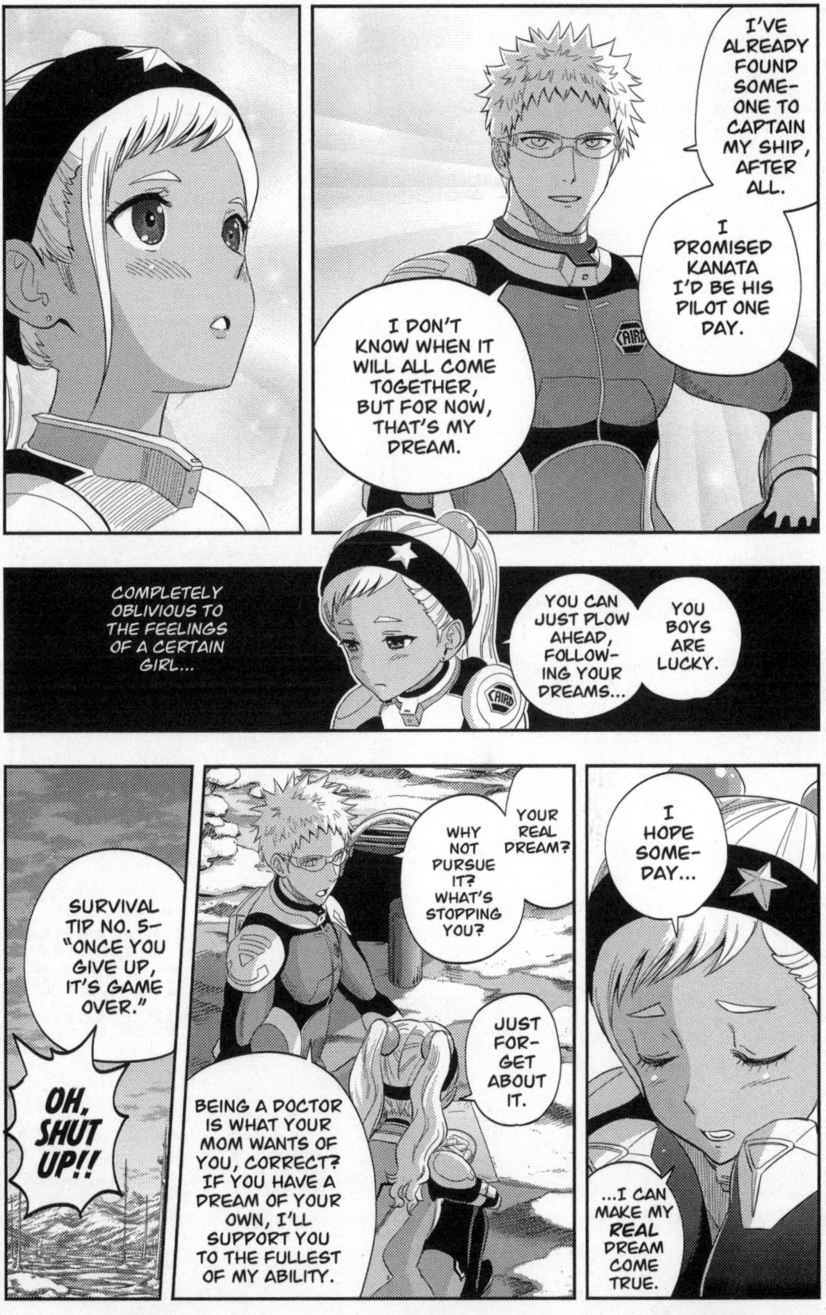

I'VE ALREADY FOUND SOMEONE TO CAPTAIN MY SHIP, AFTER ALL.
I PROMISED KANATA I'D BE HIS PILOT ONE DAY.
I DON'T KNOW WHEN IT WILL ALL COME TOGETHER, BUT FOR NOW, THAT'S MY DREAM.
YOU BOYS ARE LUCKY.
YOU CAN JUST PLOW AHEAD, FOLLOWING YOUR DREAMS...
COMPLETELY OBLIVIOUS TO THE FEELINGS OF A CERTAIN GIRL...
I HOPE SOMEDAY...
...I CAN MAKE MY *REAL* DREAM COME TRUE.
YOUR REAL DREAM?
WHY NOT PURSUE IT? WHAT'S STOPPING YOU?
JUST FORGET ABOUT IT.
BEING A DOCTOR IS WHAT YOUR MOM WANTS OF YOU, CORRECT? IF YOU HAVE A DREAM OF YOUR OWN, I'LL SUPPORT YOU TO THE FULLEST OF MY ABILITY.
SURVIVAL TIP NO. 5— "ONCE YOU GIVE UP, IT'S GAME OVER."
OH, SHUT UP!!

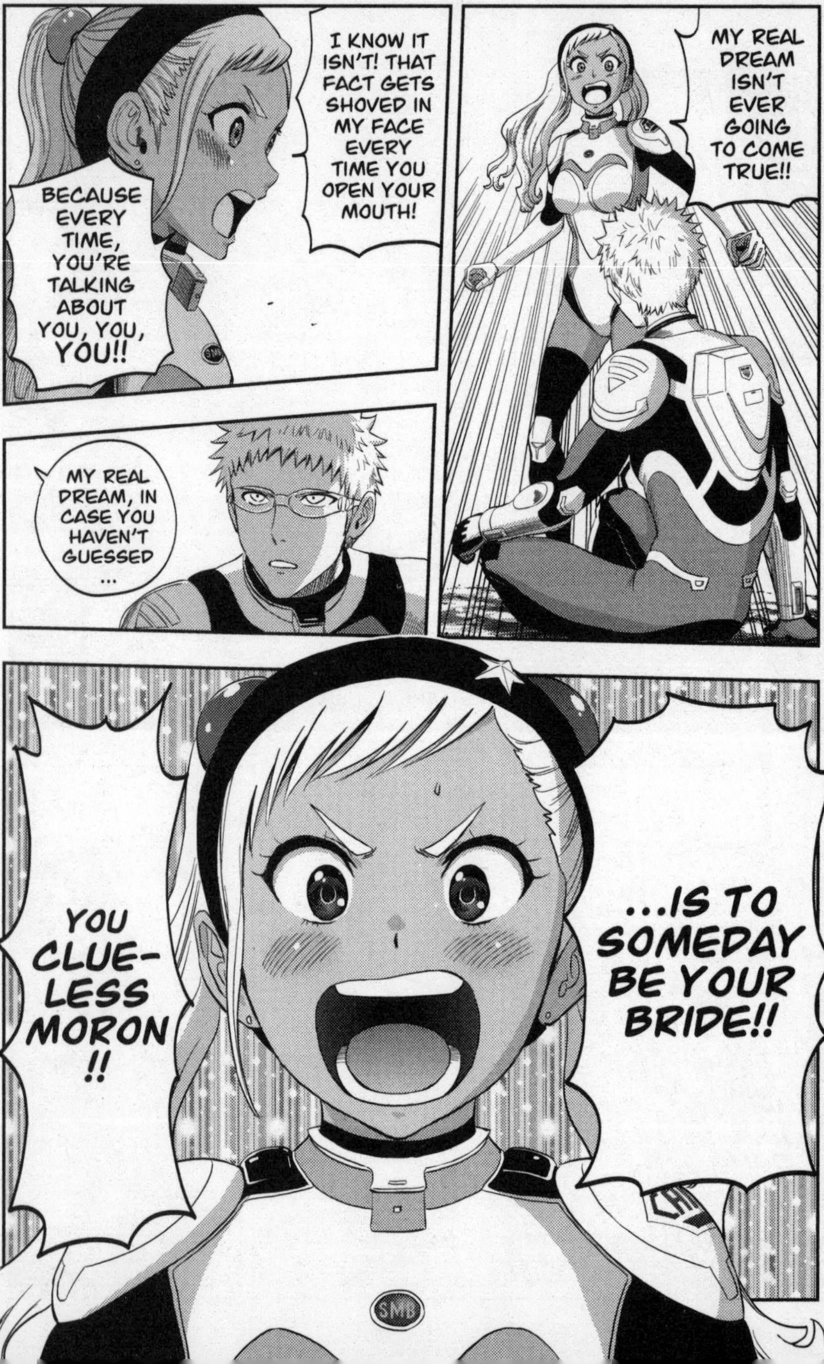
MY REAL DREAM ISN'T EVER GOING TO COME TRUE!!
I KNOW IT ISN'T! THAT FACT GETS SHOVED IN MY FACE EVERY TIME YOU OPEN YOUR MOUTH!
BECAUSE EVERY TIME, YOU'RE TALKING ABOUT YOU, YOU, YOU!!
MY REAL DREAM, IN CASE YOU HAVEN'T GUESSED ...
...IS TO SOMEDAY BE YOUR BRIDE!!
YOU CLUELESS MORON !!

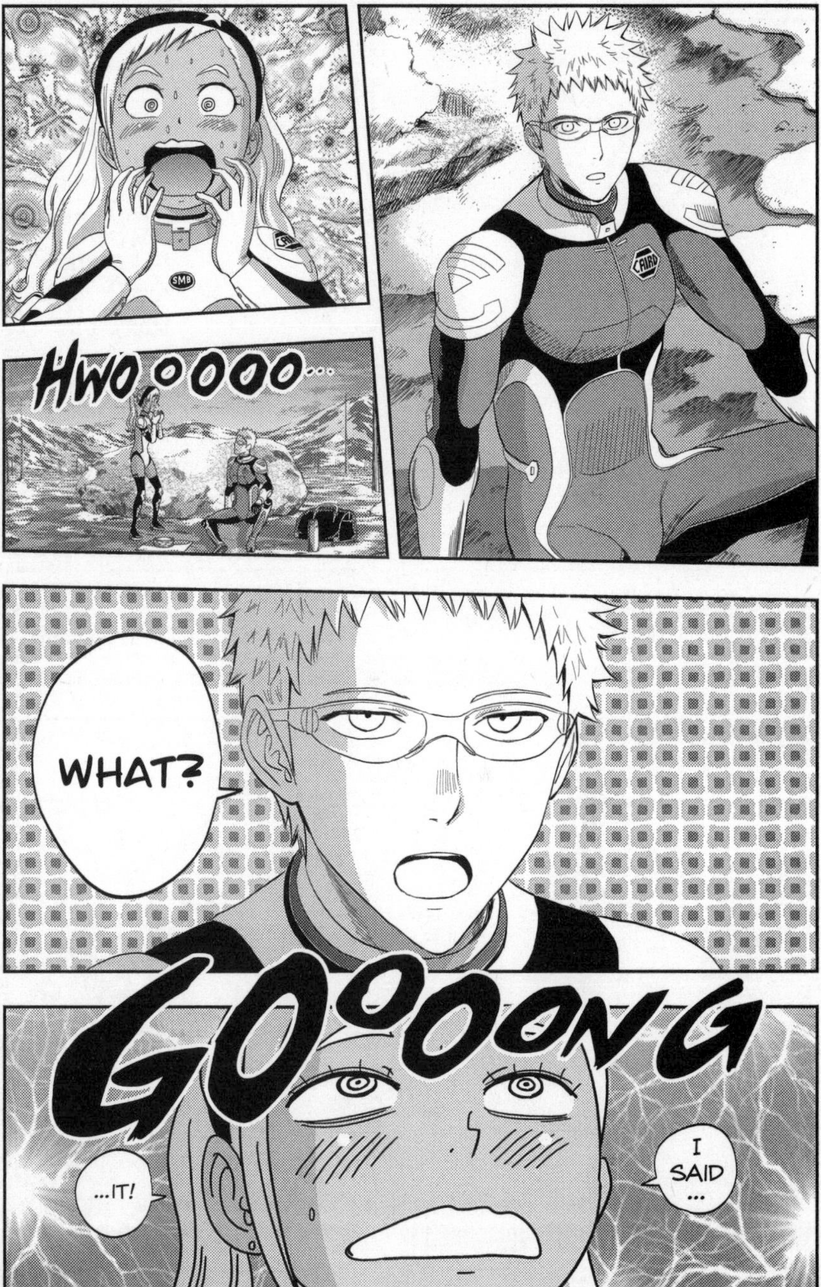
HWO OOOO...
WHAT?
GOOOONG
I SAID ...
...IT!

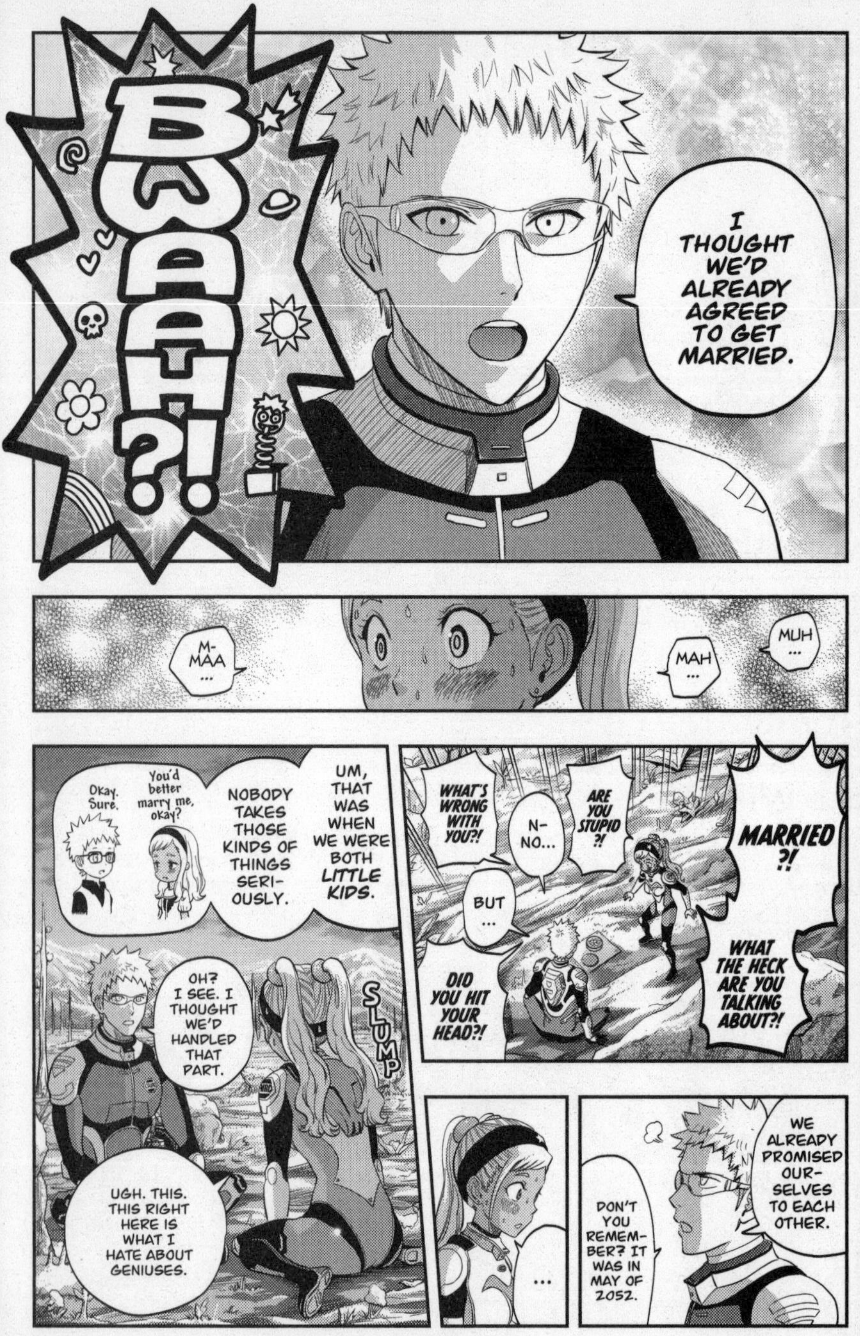
I THOUGHT WE'D ALREADY AGREED TO GET MARRIED.
BWAAAH?!
MUH...
MAH...
M-MAA...
MARRIED?!
WHAT THE HECK ARE YOU TALKING ABOUT?!
ARE YOU STUPID?!
WHAT'S WRONG WITH YOU?!
N-NO...
BUT...
DID YOU HIT YOUR HEAD?!
WE ALREADY PROMISED OUR-SELVES TO EACH OTHER.
DON'T YOU REMEM-BER? IT WAS IN MAY OF 2052.
...
UM, THAT WAS WHEN WE WERE BOTH LITTLE KIDS.
NOBODY TAKES THOSE KINDS OF THINGS SERI-OUSLY.
You'd better marry me, okay?
Okay. Sure.
SLUMP
OH? I SEE. I THOUGHT WE'D HANDLED THAT PART.
UGH. THIS. THIS RIGHT HERE IS WHAT I HATE ABOUT GENIUSES.

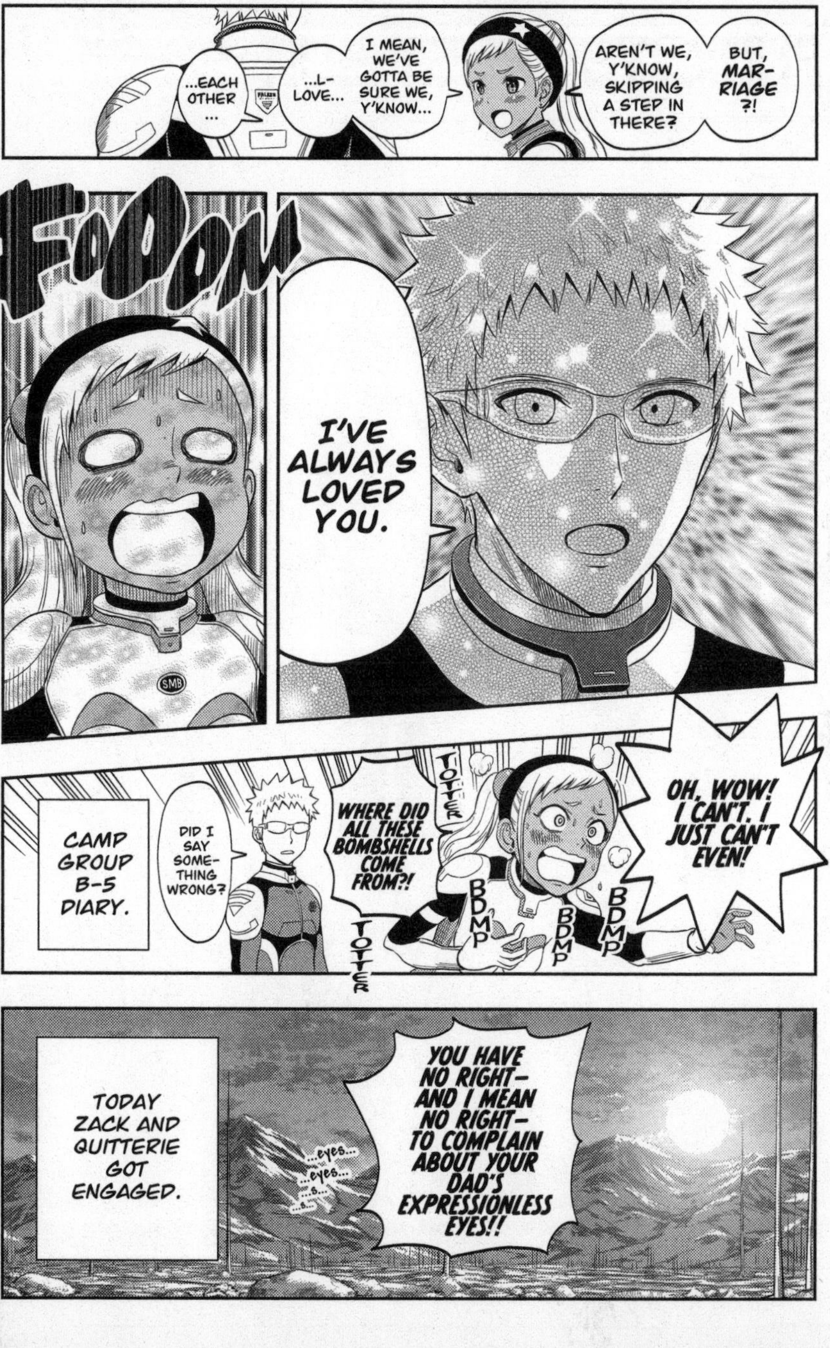
BUT, MARRIAGE?!
AREN'T WE, Y'KNOW, SKIPPING A STEP IN THERE?
I MEAN, WE'VE GOTTA BE SURE WE, Y'KNOW...
...L-LOVE...
...EACH OTHER...
I'VE ALWAYS LOVED YOU.
OH, WOW! I CAN'T. I JUST CAN'T EVEN!
BDMP
BDMP
BDMP
TOTTER
WHERE DID ALL THESE BOMBSHELLS COME FROM?!
TOTTER
DID I SAY SOMETHING WRONG?
CAMP GROUP B-5 DIARY.
YOU HAVE NO RIGHT— AND I MEAN NO RIGHT— TO COMPLAIN ABOUT YOUR DAD'S EXPRESSIONLESS EYES!!
...eyes...
...eyes...
...s...
...s...
TODAY ZACK AND QUITTERIE GOT ENGAGED.

FUNICIA'S CRUST SUIT

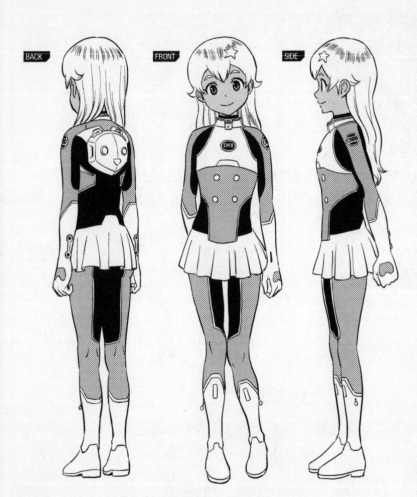

BACK   FRONT   SIDE

A SMB children's crust suit.

Orange.

A popular crust suit design for kids, it has a decorative skirt and its power pack is in the shape of a teddy bear's face.

ASTRA
LOST IN SPACE
#32

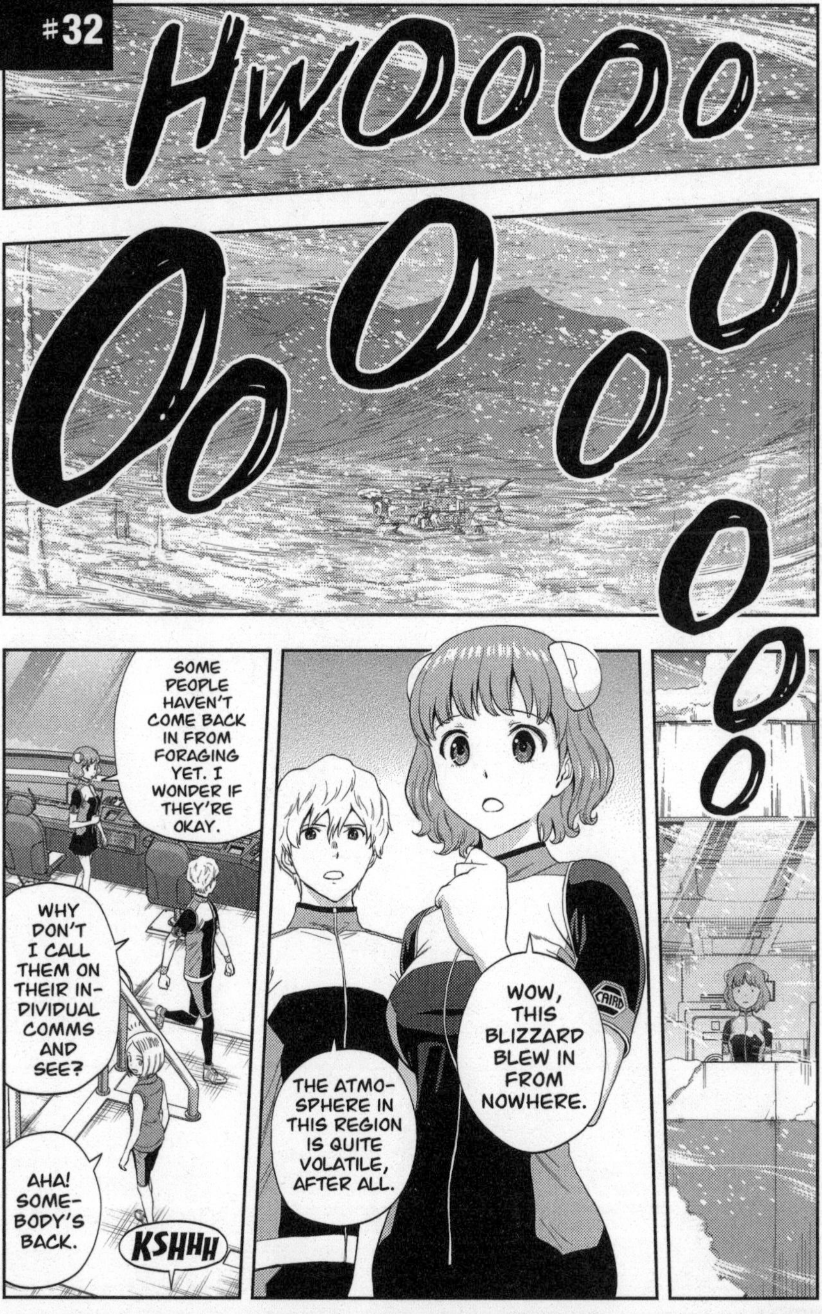
HWOOOOOO
OOOOOOOOOOOO
WOW, THIS BLIZZARD BLEW IN FROM NOWHERE.
THE ATMOSPHERE IN THIS REGION IS QUITE VOLATILE, AFTER ALL.
SOME PEOPLE HAVEN'T COME BACK IN FROM FORAGING YET. I WONDER IF THEY'RE OKAY.
WHY DON'T I CALL THEM ON THEIR INDIVIDUAL COMMS AND SEE?
KSHHH
AHA! SOMEBODY'S BACK.

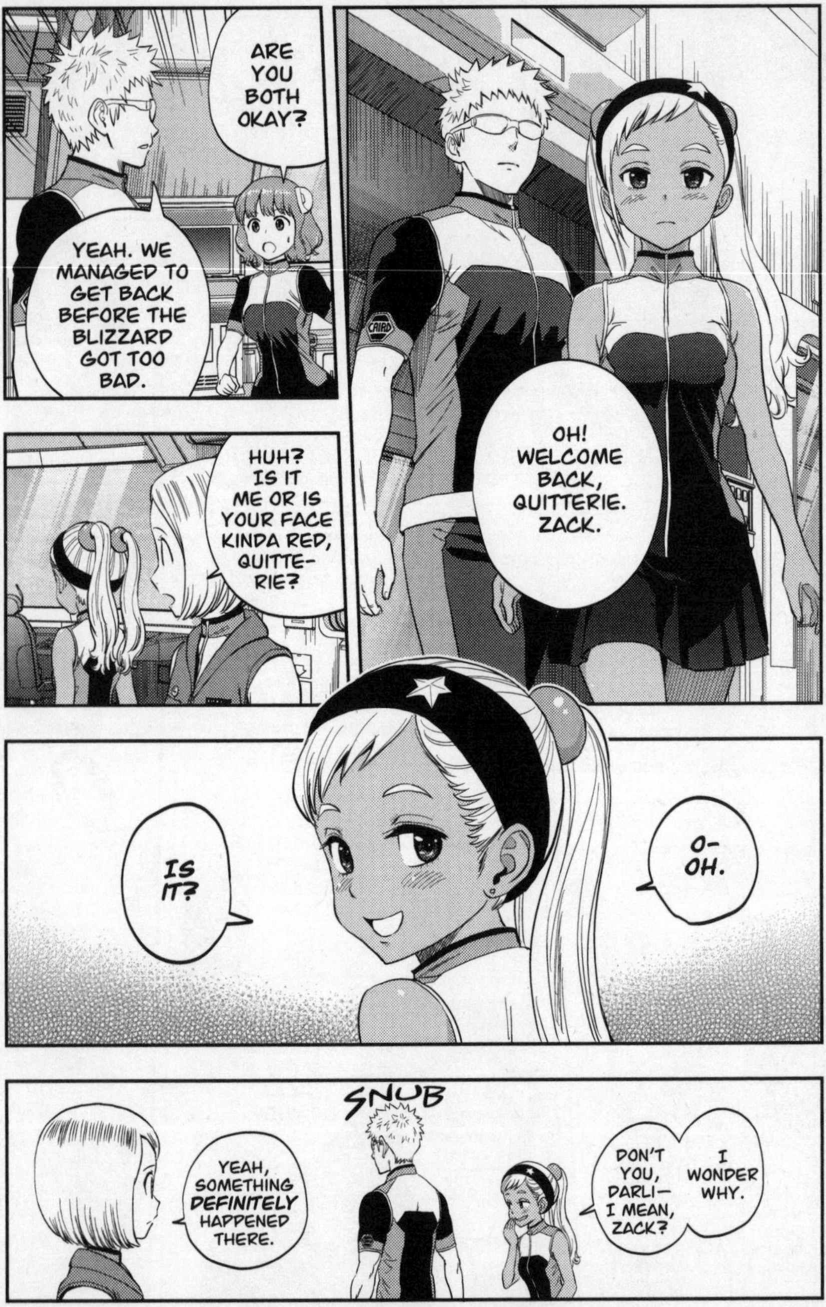
OH! WELCOME BACK, QUITTERIE. ZACK.
ARE YOU BOTH OKAY?
YEAH. WE MANAGED TO GET BACK BEFORE THE BLIZZARD GOT TOO BAD.
HUH? IS IT ME OR IS YOUR FACE KINDA RED, QUITTE-RIE?
O-OH.
IS IT?
SNUB
I WONDER WHY.
DON'T YOU, DARLI— I MEAN, ZACK?
YEAH, SOMETHING **DEFINITELY** HAPPENED THERE.

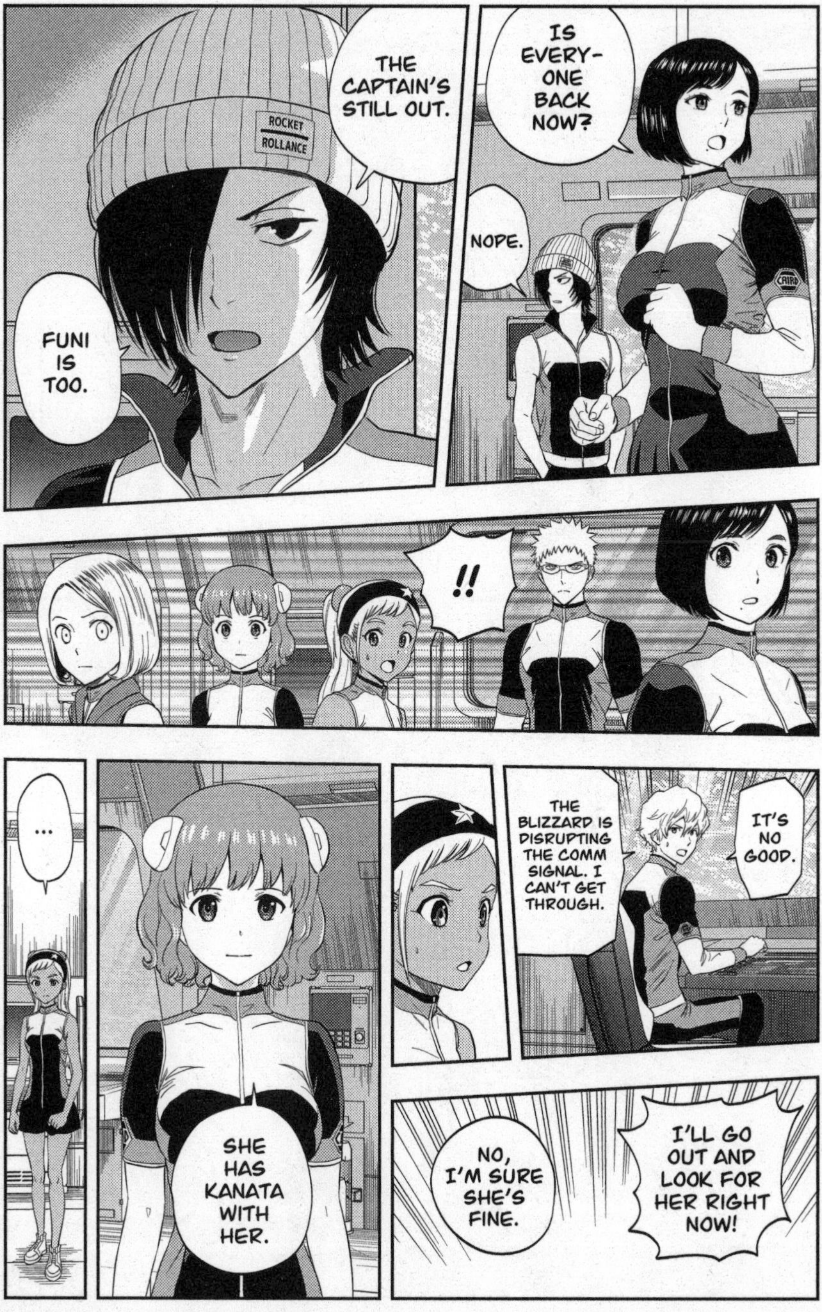
IS EVERY-ONE BACK NOW?
NOPE.
THE CAPTAIN'S STILL OUT.
FUNI IS TOO.
ROCKET ROLLANCE
!!
IT'S NO GOOD.
THE BLIZZARD IS DISRUPTING THE COMM SIGNAL. I CAN'T GET THROUGH.
I'LL GO OUT AND LOOK FOR HER RIGHT NOW!
NO, I'M SURE SHE'S FINE.
SHE HAS KANATA WITH HER.
...

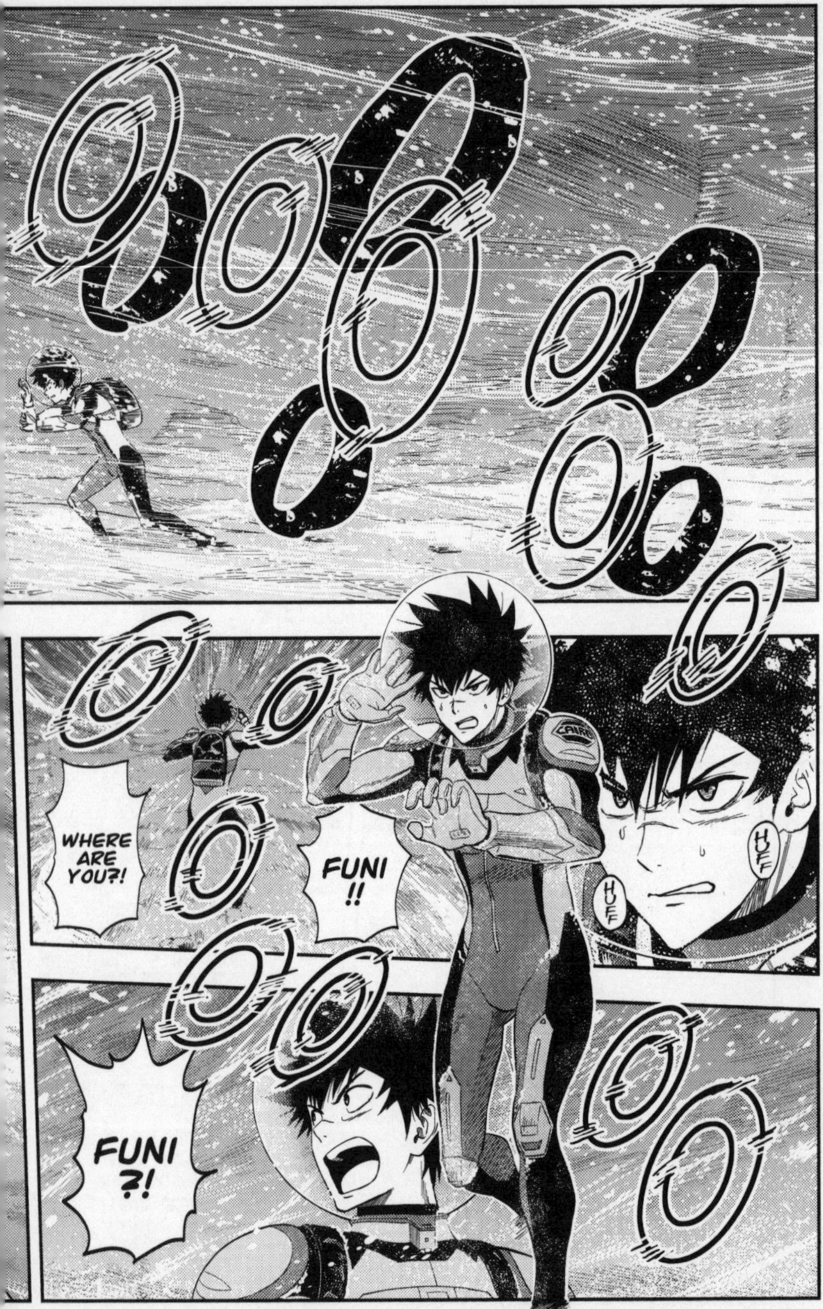
HUFF
HUFF
FUNI !!
WHERE ARE YOU?!
FUNI ?!

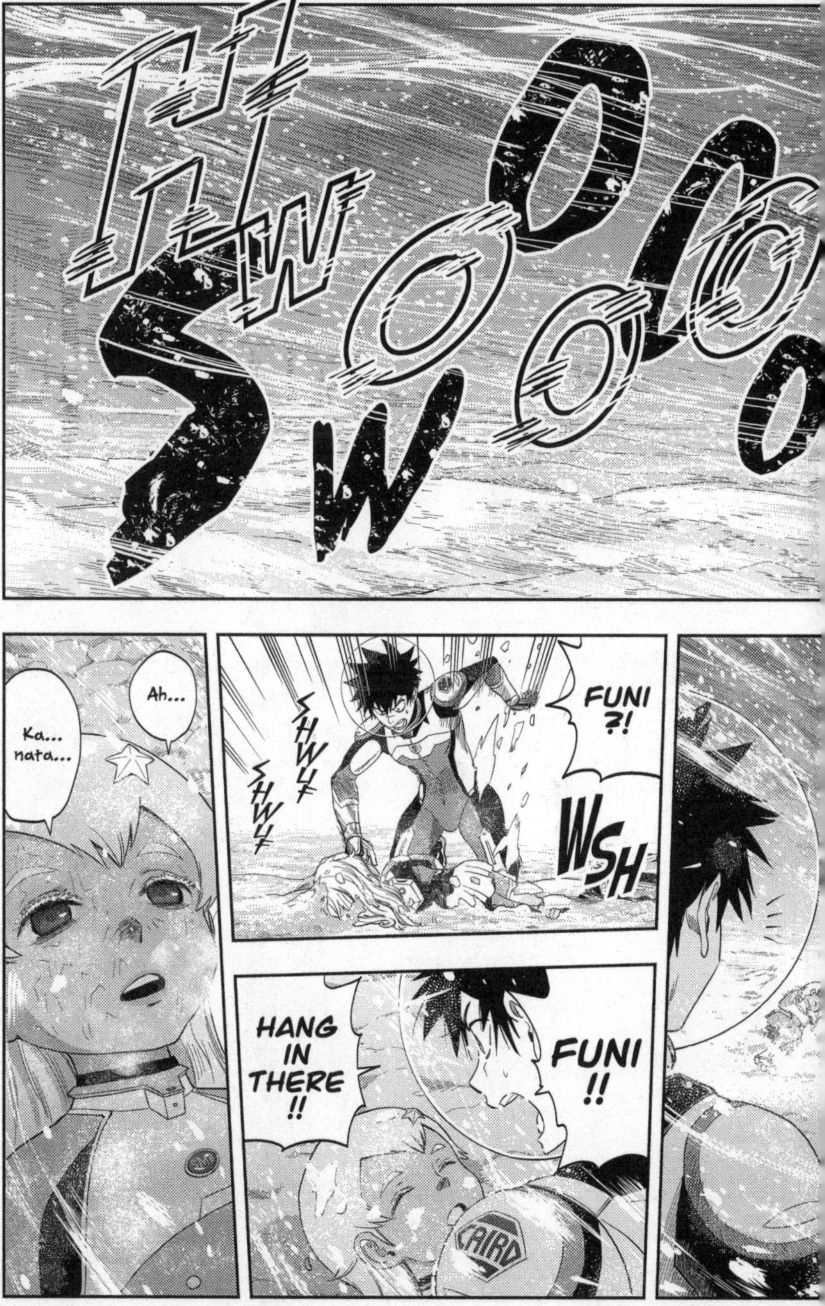
FWUSHWOOOOOO
FUNI ?!
SHWUF
SHWUF
WSH
FUNI !!
HANG IN THERE !!
Ah...
Ka... nata...

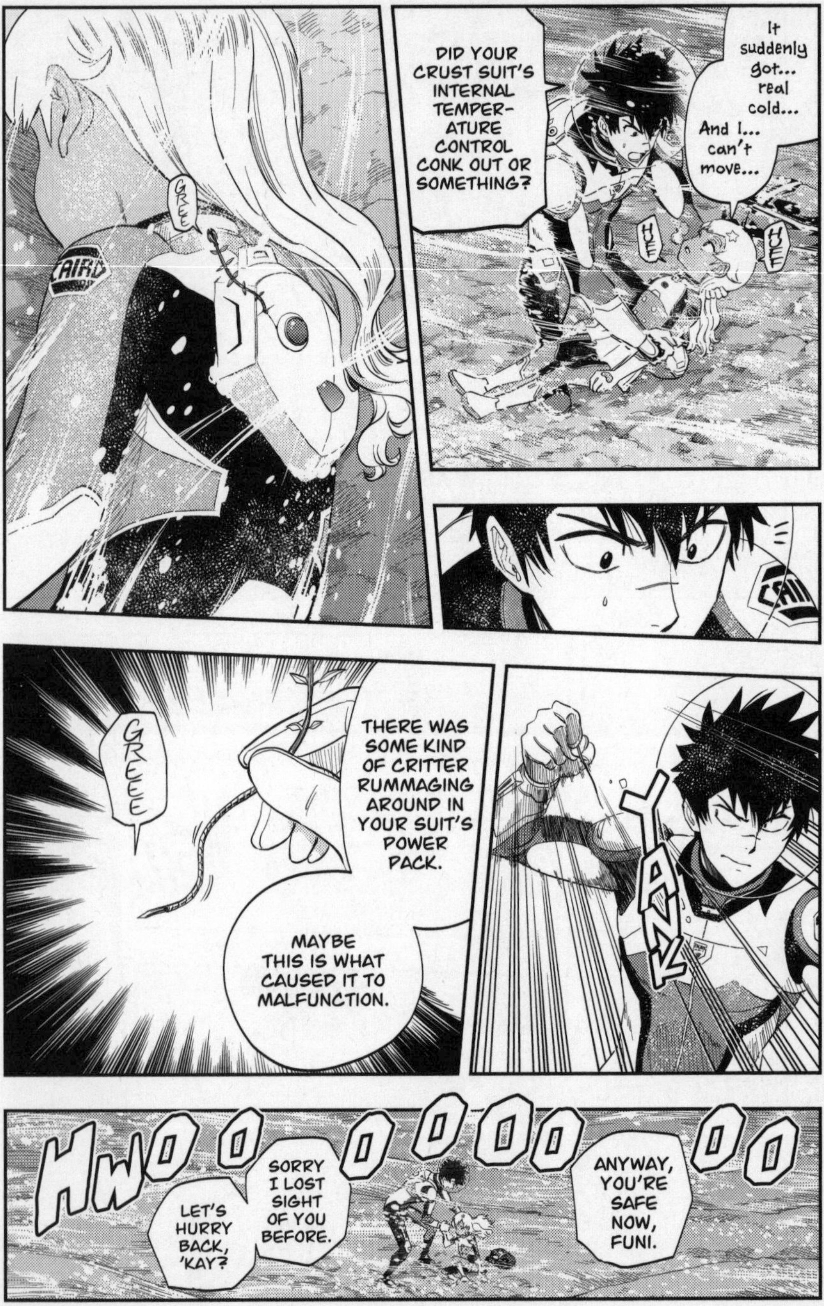
It suddenly got... real cold...
And I... can't move...
DID YOUR CRUST SUIT'S INTERNAL TEMPERATURE CONTROL CONK OUT OR SOMETHING?
HUFF
HUFF
GREE
YANK
GREEEE
THERE WAS SOME KIND OF CRITTER RUMMAGING AROUND IN YOUR SUIT'S POWER PACK.
MAYBE THIS IS WHAT CAUSED IT TO MALFUNCTION.
HWOOOOOOOOO
ANYWAY, YOU'RE SAFE NOW, FUNI.
SORRY I LOST SIGHT OF YOU BEFORE.
LET'S HURRY BACK, 'KAY?

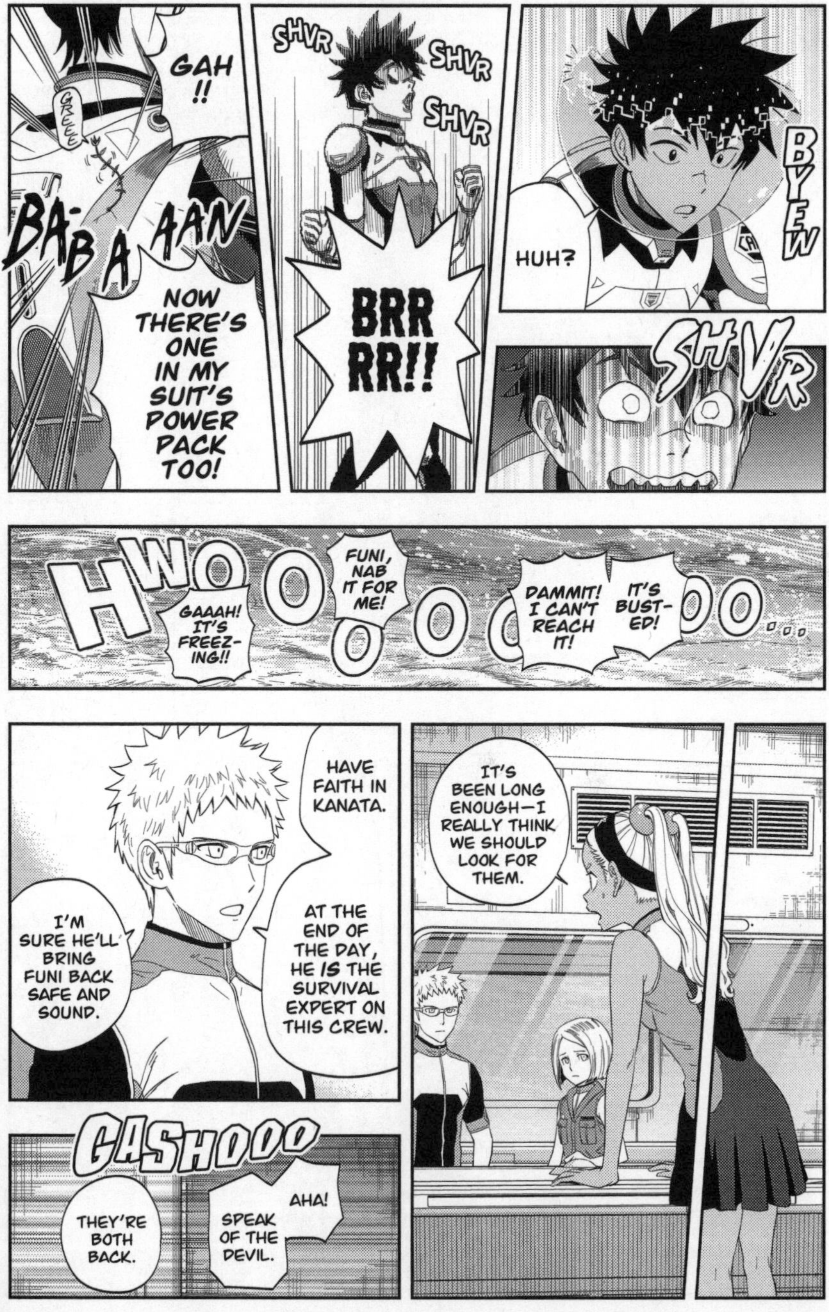
BYEW
HUH?
SHVR
SHVR
SHVR
SHVR
BRRRR!!
GAH!!
GREEE
BA-BA-AAN
NOW THERE'S ONE IN MY SUIT'S POWER PACK TOO!
IT'S BUSTED!
DAMMIT! I CAN'T REACH IT!
FUNI, NAB IT FOR ME!
GAAAH! IT'S FREEZING!!
HWOOOOOOOOO...
IT'S BEEN LONG ENOUGH—I REALLY THINK WE SHOULD LOOK FOR THEM.
HAVE FAITH IN KANATA.
AT THE END OF THE DAY, HE *IS* THE SURVIVAL EXPERT ON THIS CREW.
I'M SURE HE'LL BRING FUNI BACK SAFE AND SOUND.
GASHOOO
AHA!
SPEAK OF THE DEVIL.
THEY'RE BOTH BACK.

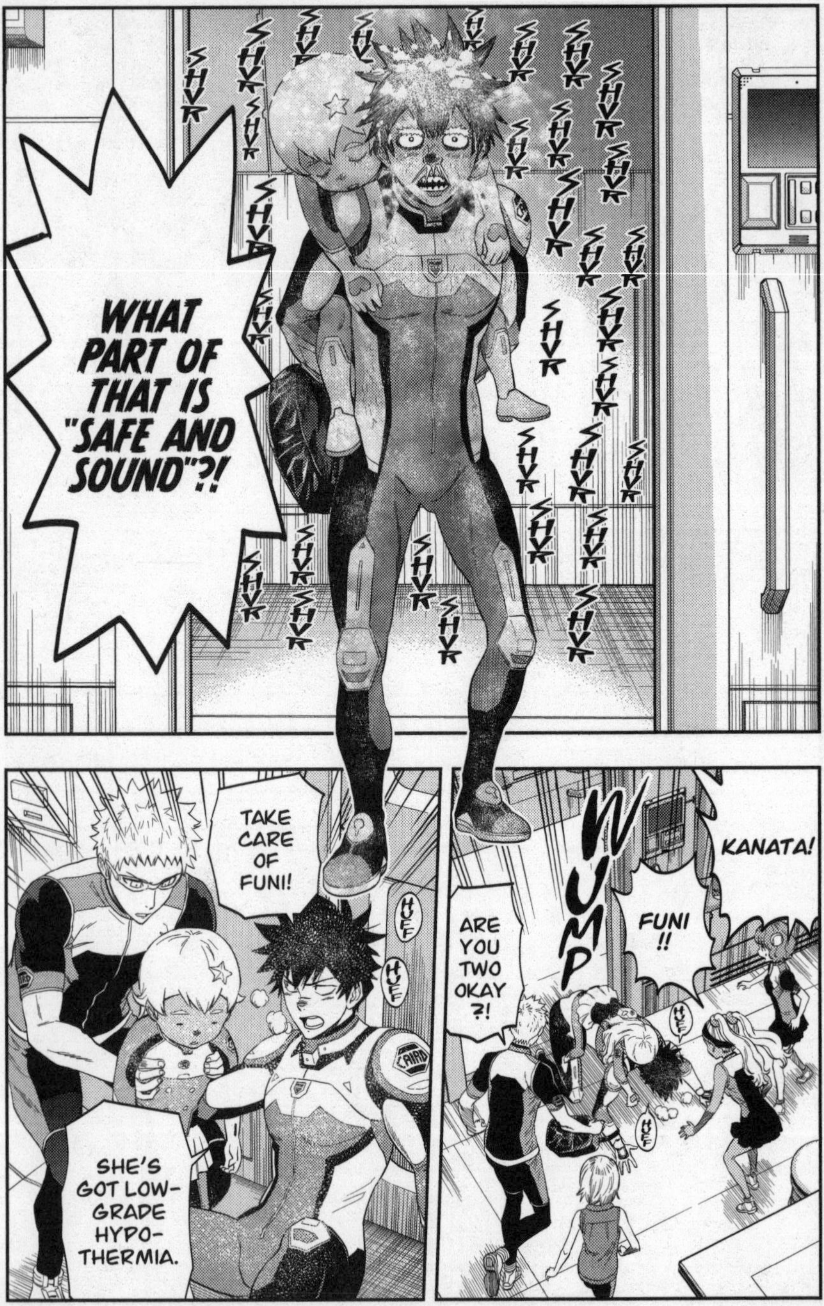
SHVR SHVR SHVR SHVR SHVR
WHAT PART OF THAT IS "SAFE AND SOUND"?!
KANATA!
FUNI !!
WUMP
ARE YOU TWO OKAY ?!
HUFF
HUFF
TAKE CARE OF FUNI!
HUFF
HUFF
SHE'S GOT LOW-GRADE HYPO-THERMIA.

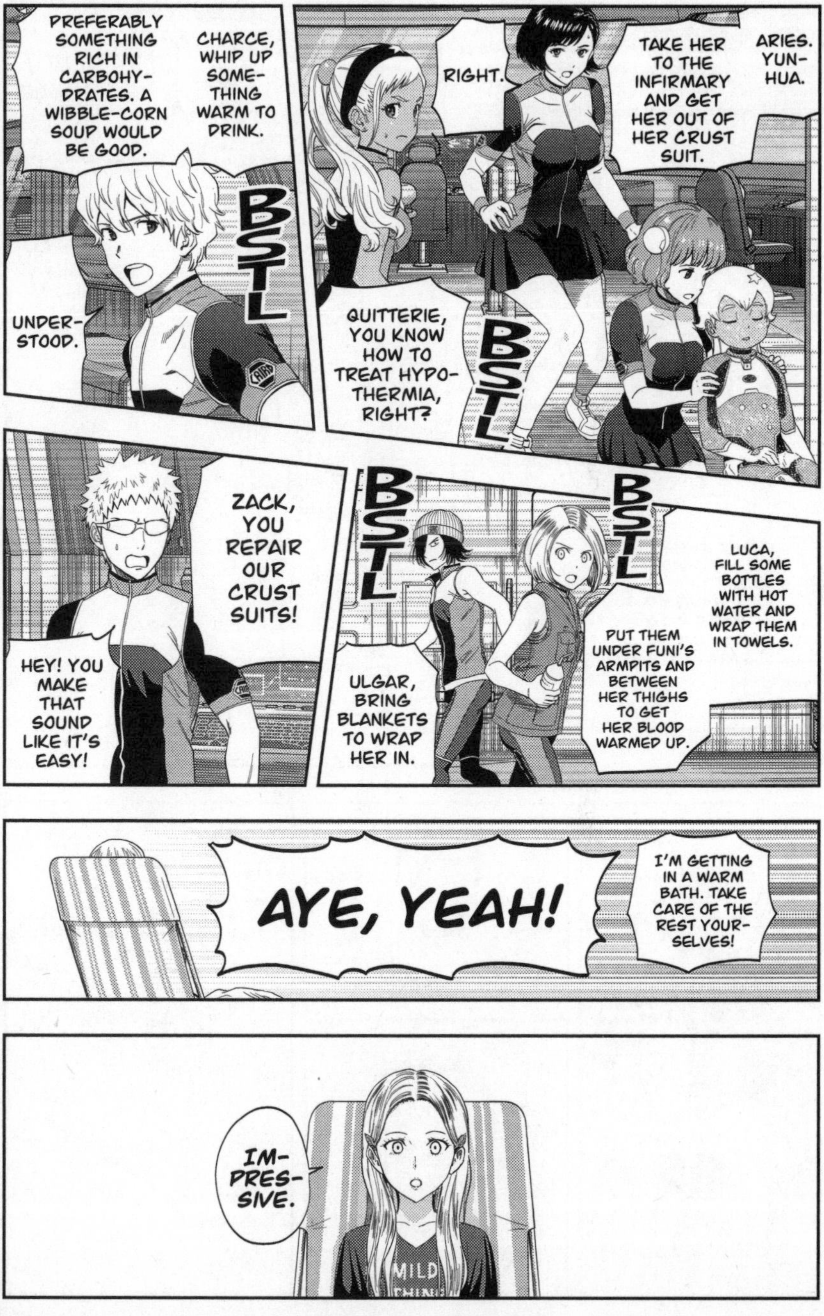
ARIES. YUNHUA.
TAKE HER TO THE INFIRMARY AND GET HER OUT OF HER CRUST SUIT.
RIGHT.
QUITTERIE, YOU KNOW HOW TO TREAT HYPOTHERMIA, RIGHT?
BSTL
BSTL
CHARCE, WHIP UP SOMETHING WARM TO DRINK.
PREFERABLY SOMETHING RICH IN CARBOHYDRATES. A WIBBLE-CORN SOUP WOULD BE GOOD.
BSTL
UNDERSTOOD.
LUCA, FILL SOME BOTTLES WITH HOT WATER AND WRAP THEM IN TOWELS.
PUT THEM UNDER FUNI'S ARMPITS AND BETWEEN HER THIGHS TO GET HER BLOOD WARMED UP.
BSTL
BSTL
ULGAR, BRING BLANKETS TO WRAP HER IN.
ZACK, YOU REPAIR OUR CRUST SUITS!
HEY! YOU MAKE THAT SOUND LIKE IT'S EASY!
I'M GETTING IN A WARM BATH. TAKE CARE OF THE REST YOURSELVES!
AYE, YEAH!
IMPRESSIVE.

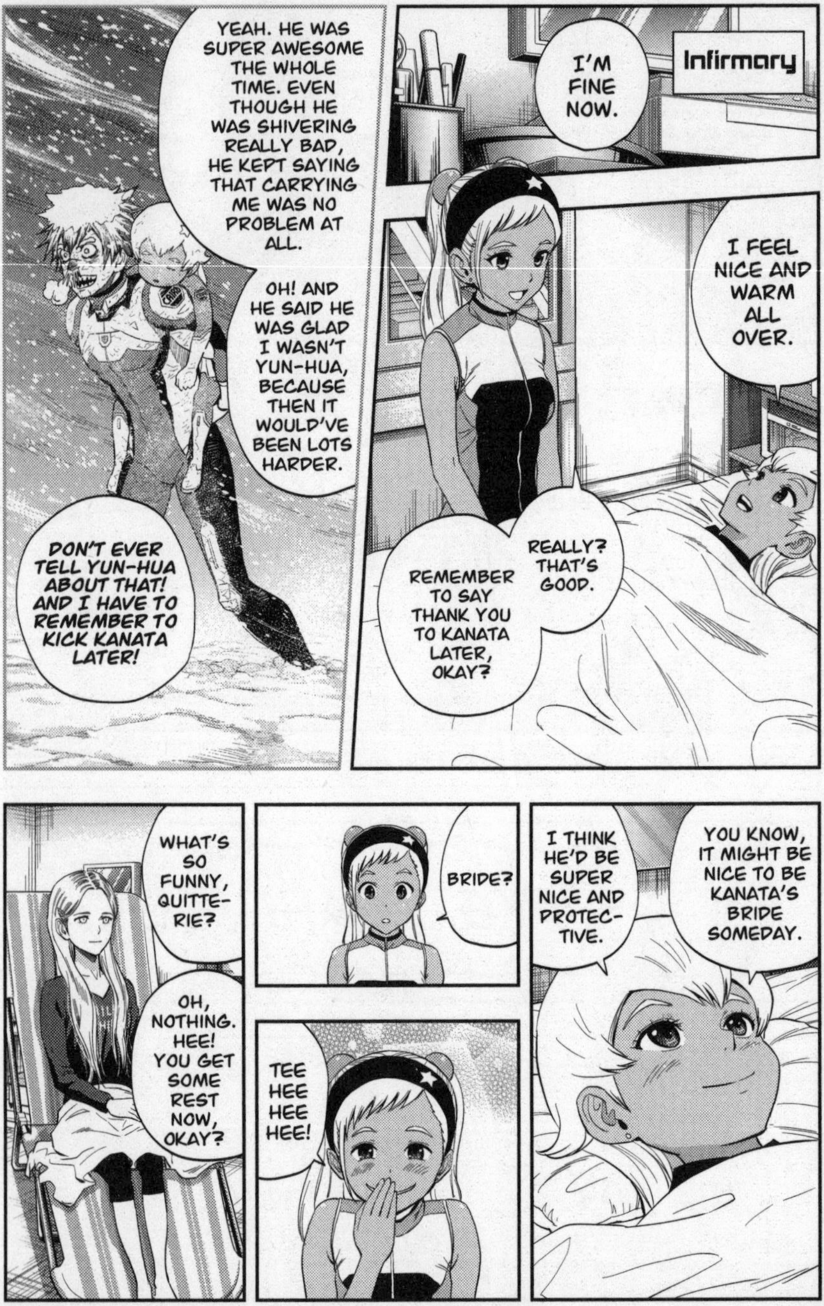
Infirmary
I'M FINE NOW.
I FEEL NICE AND WARM ALL OVER.
REALLY? THAT'S GOOD.
REMEMBER TO SAY THANK YOU TO KANATA LATER, OKAY?
YEAH. HE WAS SUPER AWESOME THE WHOLE TIME. EVEN THOUGH HE WAS SHIVERING REALLY BAD, HE KEPT SAYING THAT CARRYING ME WAS NO PROBLEM AT ALL.
OH! AND HE SAID HE WAS GLAD I WASN'T YUN-HUA, BECAUSE THEN IT WOULD'VE BEEN LOTS HARDER.
DON'T EVER TELL YUN-HUA ABOUT THAT! AND I HAVE TO REMEMBER TO KICK KANATA LATER!
YOU KNOW, IT MIGHT BE NICE TO BE KANATA'S BRIDE SOMEDAY.
I THINK HE'D BE SUPER NICE AND PROTECTIVE.
BRIDE?
TEE HEE HEE HEE!
WHAT'S SO FUNNY, QUITTERIE?
OH, NOTHING. HEE! YOU GET SOME REST NOW, OKAY?

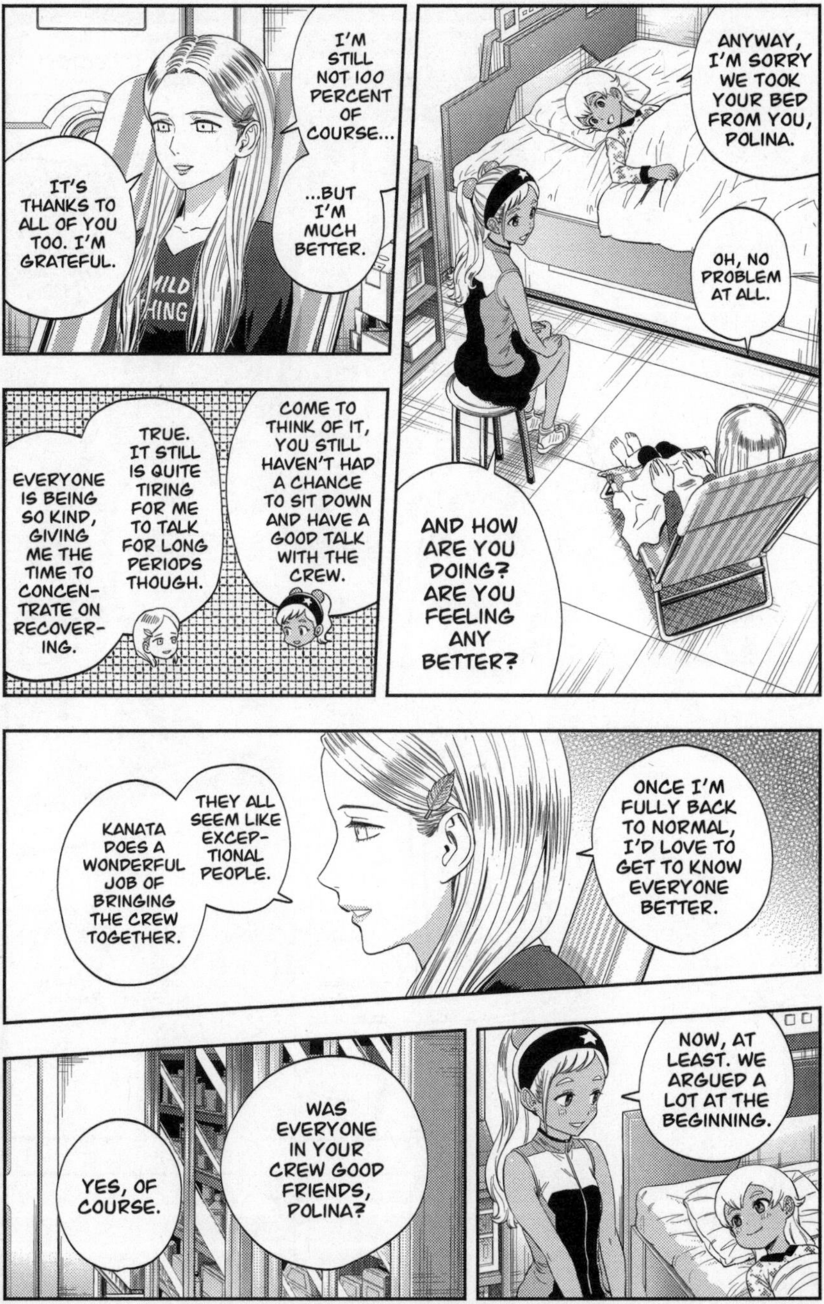
ANYWAY, I'M SORRY WE TOOK YOUR BED FROM YOU, POLINA.
OH, NO PROBLEM AT ALL.
AND HOW ARE YOU DOING? ARE YOU FEELING ANY BETTER?
I'M STILL NOT 100 PERCENT OF COURSE...
...BUT I'M MUCH BETTER.
IT'S THANKS TO ALL OF YOU TOO. I'M GRATEFUL.
COME TO THINK OF IT, YOU STILL HAVEN'T HAD A CHANCE TO SIT DOWN AND HAVE A GOOD TALK WITH THE CREW.
TRUE. IT STILL IS QUITE TIRING FOR ME TO TALK FOR LONG PERIODS THOUGH.
EVERYONE IS BEING SO KIND, GIVING ME THE TIME TO CONCENTRATE ON RECOVERING.
ONCE I'M FULLY BACK TO NORMAL, I'D LOVE TO GET TO KNOW EVERYONE BETTER.
THEY ALL SEEM LIKE EXCEPTIONAL PEOPLE.
KANATA DOES A WONDERFUL JOB OF BRINGING THE CREW TOGETHER.
NOW, AT LEAST. WE ARGUED A LOT AT THE BEGINNING.
WAS EVERYONE IN YOUR CREW GOOD FRIENDS, POLINA?
YES, OF COURSE.

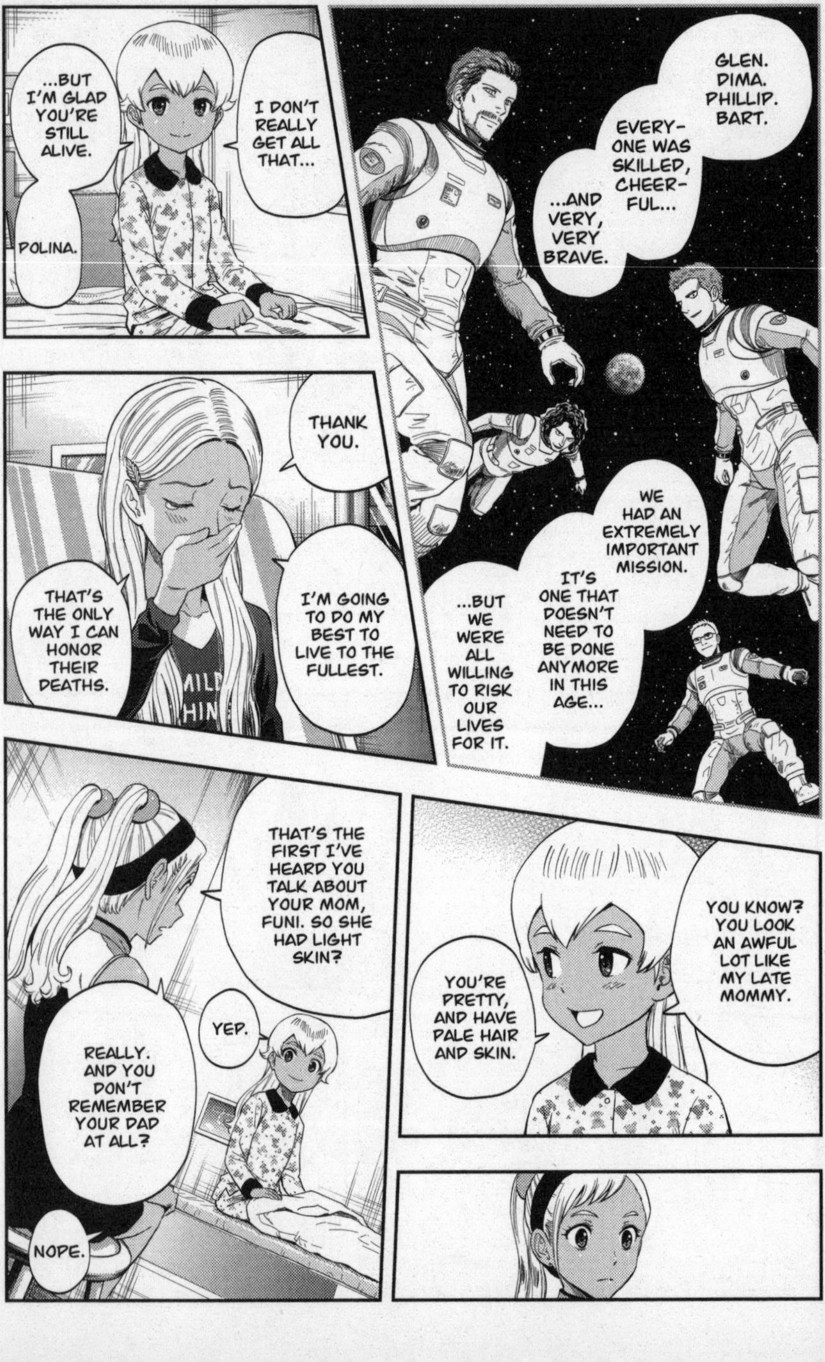
GLEN. DIMA. PHILLIP. BART.
EVERY-ONE WAS SKILLED, CHEER-FUL...
...AND VERY, VERY BRAVE.
WE HAD AN EXTREMELY IMPORTANT MISSION.
IT'S ONE THAT DOESN'T NEED TO BE DONE ANYMORE IN THIS AGE...
...BUT WE WERE ALL WILLING TO RISK OUR LIVES FOR IT.
I DON'T REALLY GET ALL THAT...
...BUT I'M GLAD YOU'RE STILL ALIVE.
POLINA.
THANK YOU.
I'M GOING TO DO MY BEST TO LIVE TO THE FULLEST.
THAT'S THE ONLY WAY I CAN HONOR THEIR DEATHS.
YOU KNOW? YOU LOOK AN AWFUL LOT LIKE MY LATE MOMMY.
YOU'RE PRETTY, AND HAVE PALE HAIR AND SKIN.
THAT'S THE FIRST I'VE HEARD YOU TALK ABOUT YOUR MOM, FUNI. SO SHE HAD LIGHT SKIN?
YEP.
REALLY. AND YOU DON'T REMEMBER YOUR DAD AT ALL?
NOPE.

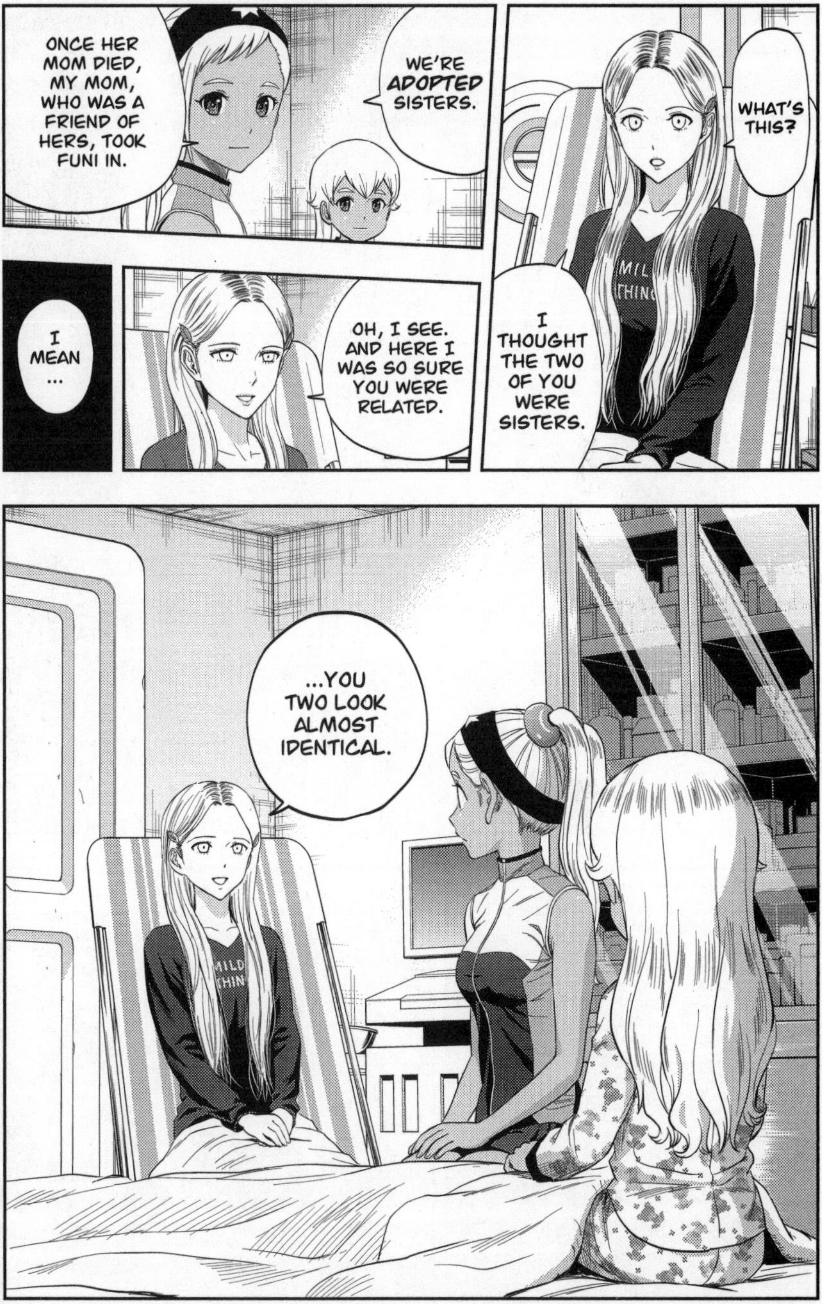
WHAT'S THIS?
I THOUGHT THE TWO OF YOU WERE SISTERS.
WE'RE ADOPTED SISTERS.
ONCE HER MOM DIED, MY MOM, WHO WAS A FRIEND OF HERS, TOOK FUNI IN.
OH, I SEE. AND HERE I WAS SO SURE YOU WERE RELATED.
I MEAN ...
...YOU TWO LOOK ALMOST IDENTICAL.

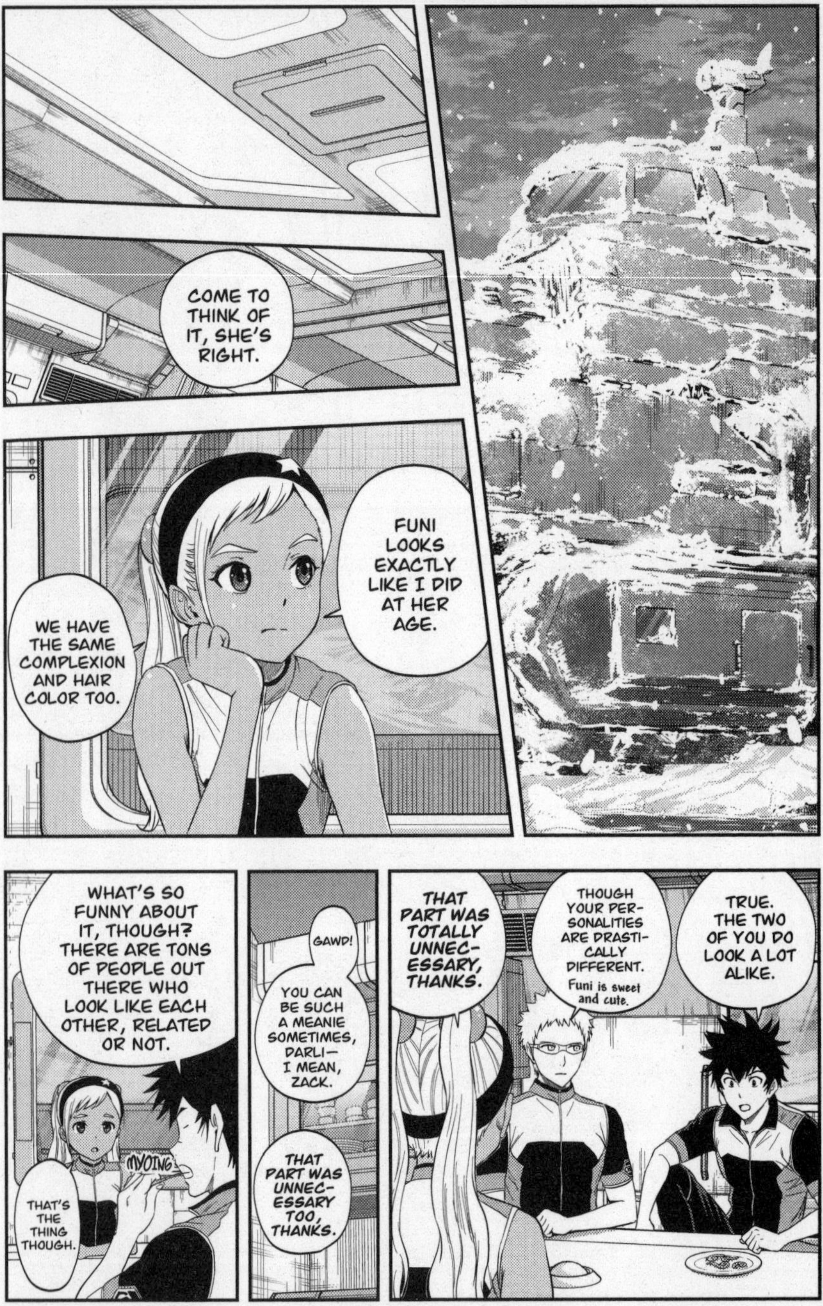

COME TO THINK OF IT, SHE'S RIGHT.
FUNI LOOKS EXACTLY LIKE I DID AT HER AGE.
WE HAVE THE SAME COMPLEXION AND HAIR COLOR TOO.
TRUE. THE TWO OF YOU DO LOOK A LOT ALIKE.
THOUGH YOUR PERSONALITIES ARE DRASTICALLY DIFFERENT.
Funi is sweet and cute.
THAT PART WAS TOTALLY UNNECESSARY, THANKS.
GAWD!
YOU CAN BE SUCH A MEANIE SOMETIMES, DARLI- I MEAN, ZACK.
THAT PART WAS UNNECESSARY TOO, THANKS.
WHAT'S SO FUNNY ABOUT IT, THOUGH? THERE ARE TONS OF PEOPLE OUT THERE WHO LOOK LIKE EACH OTHER, RELATED OR NOT.
MYOING
THAT'S THE THING THOUGH.

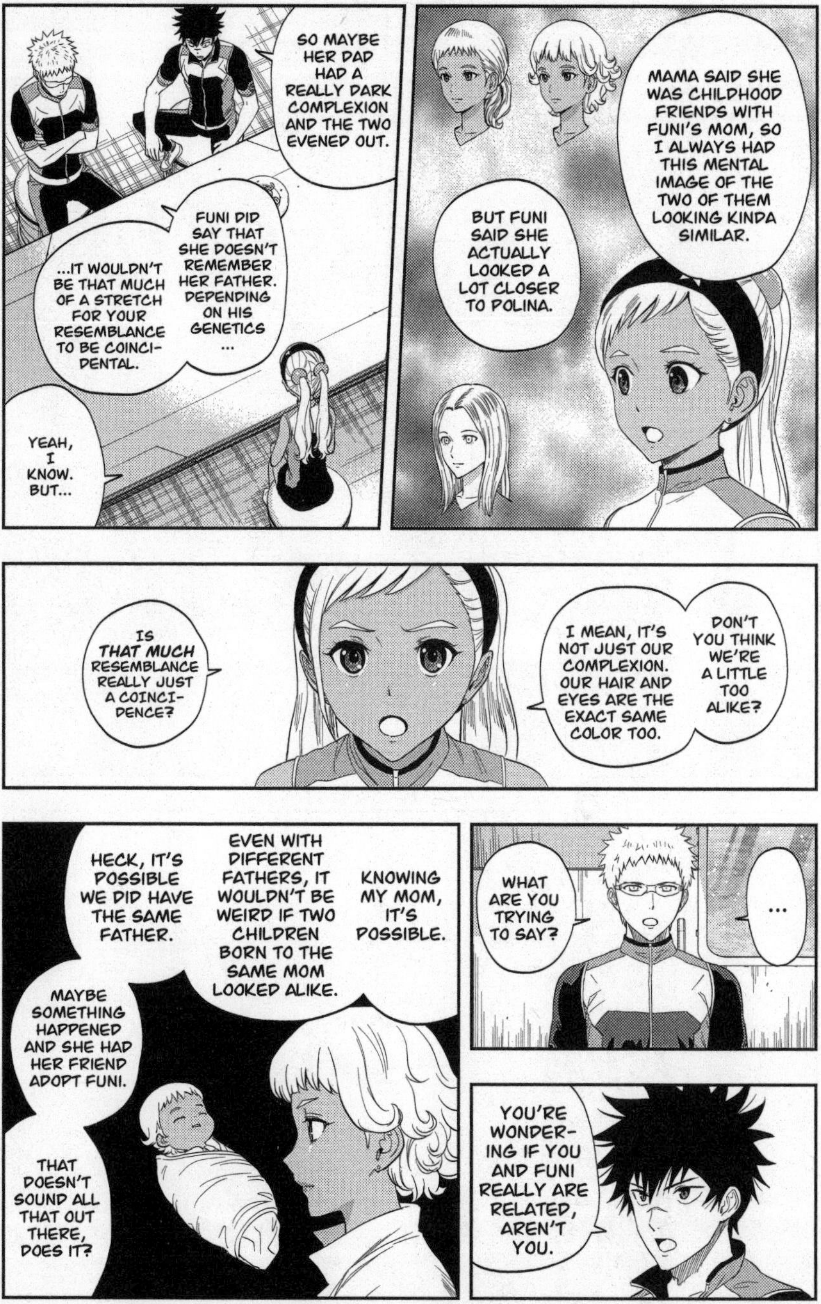
MAMA SAID SHE WAS CHILDHOOD FRIENDS WITH FUNI'S MOM, SO I ALWAYS HAD THIS MENTAL IMAGE OF THE TWO OF THEM LOOKING KINDA SIMILAR.
BUT FUNI SAID SHE ACTUALLY LOOKED A LOT CLOSER TO POLINA.
SO MAYBE HER DAD HAD A REALLY DARK COMPLEXION AND THE TWO EVENED OUT.
FUNI DID SAY THAT SHE DOESN'T REMEMBER HER FATHER. DEPENDING ON HIS GENETICS...
...IT WOULDN'T BE THAT MUCH OF A STRETCH FOR YOUR RESEMBLANCE TO BE COINCI-DENTAL.
YEAH, I KNOW. BUT...
DON'T YOU THINK WE'RE A LITTLE TOO ALIKE?
I MEAN, IT'S NOT JUST OUR COMPLEXION. OUR HAIR AND EYES ARE THE EXACT SAME COLOR TOO.
IS ***THAT MUCH*** RESEMBLANCE REALLY JUST A COINCI-DENCE?
...
WHAT ARE YOU TRYING TO SAY?
YOU'RE WONDER-ING IF YOU AND FUNI REALLY ARE RELATED, AREN'T YOU.
KNOWING MY MOM, IT'S POSSIBLE.
EVEN WITH DIFFERENT FATHERS, IT WOULDN'T BE WEIRD IF TWO CHILDREN BORN TO THE SAME MOM LOOKED ALIKE.
HECK, IT'S POSSIBLE WE DID HAVE THE SAME FATHER.
MAYBE SOMETHING HAPPENED AND SHE HAD HER FRIEND ADOPT FUNI.
THAT DOESN'T SOUND ALL THAT OUT THERE, DOES IT?

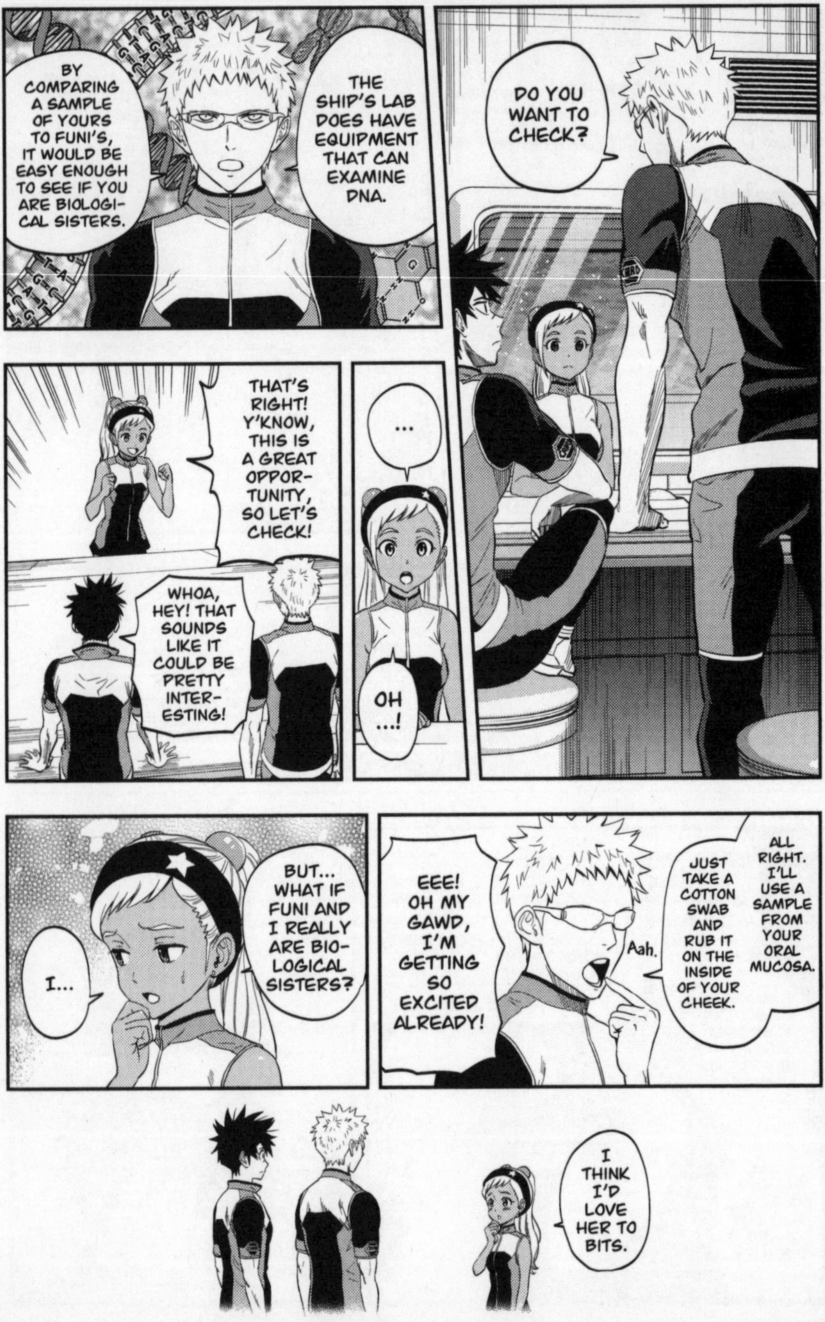
DO YOU WANT TO CHECK?
THE SHIP'S LAB DOES HAVE EQUIPMENT THAT CAN EXAMINE DNA.
BY COMPARING A SAMPLE OF YOURS TO FUNI'S, IT WOULD BE EASY ENOUGH TO SEE IF YOU ARE BIOLOGI-CAL SISTERS.
...
OH ...!
THAT'S RIGHT! Y'KNOW, THIS IS A GREAT OPPOR-TUNITY, SO LET'S CHECK!
WHOA, HEY! THAT SOUNDS LIKE IT COULD BE PRETTY INTER-ESTING!
ALL RIGHT. I'LL USE A SAMPLE FROM YOUR ORAL MUCOSA.
JUST TAKE A COTTON SWAB AND RUB IT ON THE INSIDE OF YOUR CHEEK.
Aah.
EEE! OH MY GAWD, I'M GETTING SO EXCITED ALREADY!
BUT... WHAT IF FUNI AND I REALLY ARE BIO-LOGICAL SISTERS?
I...
I THINK I'D LOVE HER TO BITS.

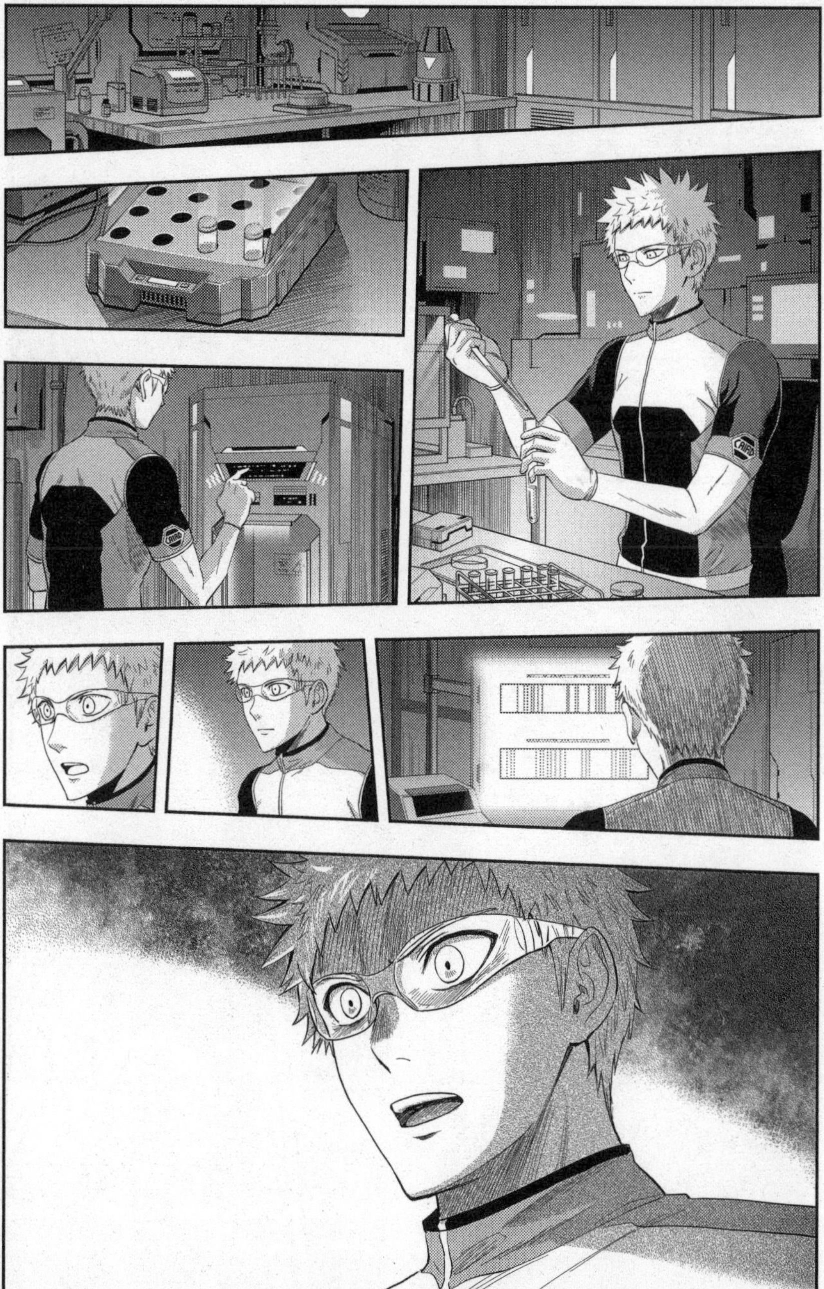

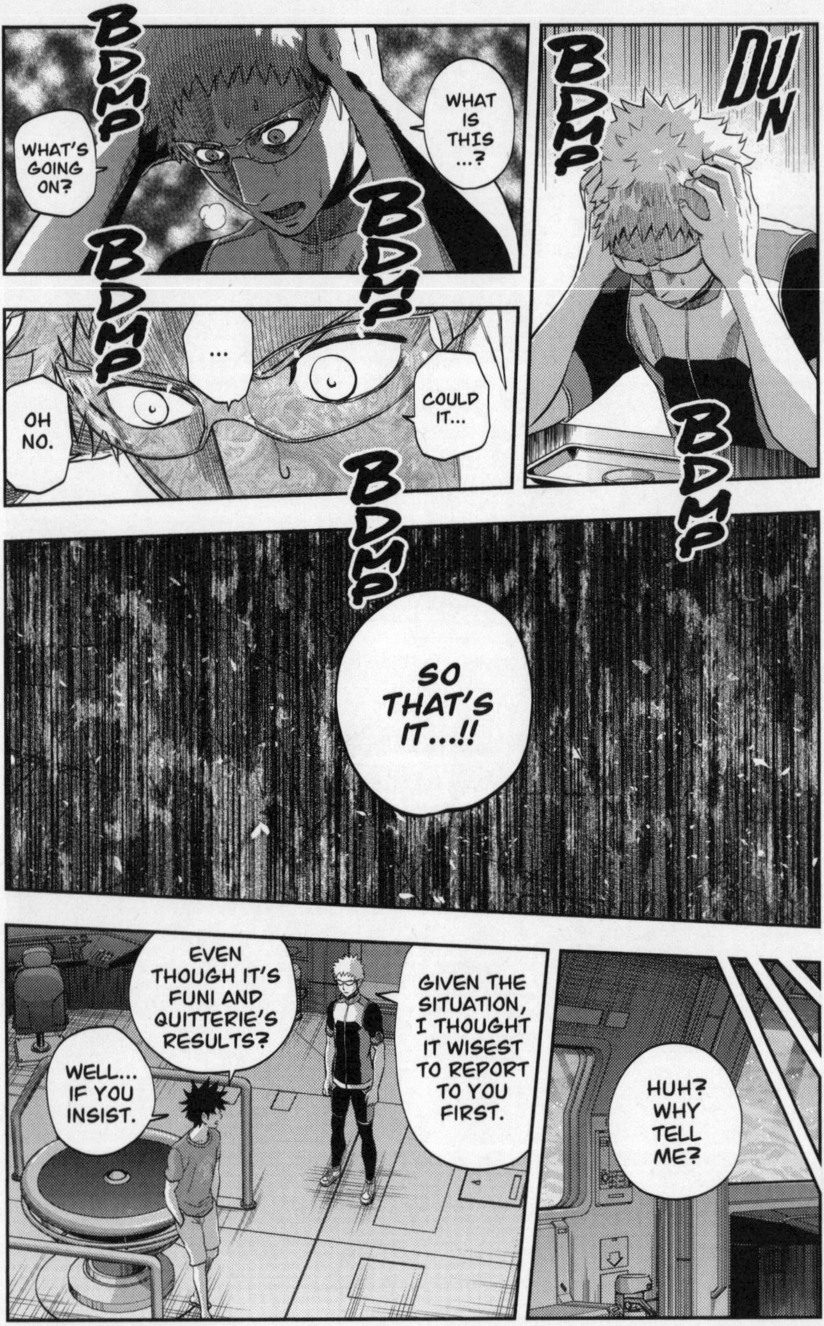
DUN
BDMP
BDMP
WHAT IS THIS ...?
BDMP
WHAT'S GOING ON?
BDMP
COULD IT...
...
BDMP
OH NO.
BDMP
SO THAT'S IT...!!
HUH? WHY TELL ME?
GIVEN THE SITUATION, I THOUGHT IT WISEST TO REPORT TO YOU FIRST.
EVEN THOUGH IT'S FUNI AND QUITTERIE'S RESULTS?
WELL... IF YOU INSIST.

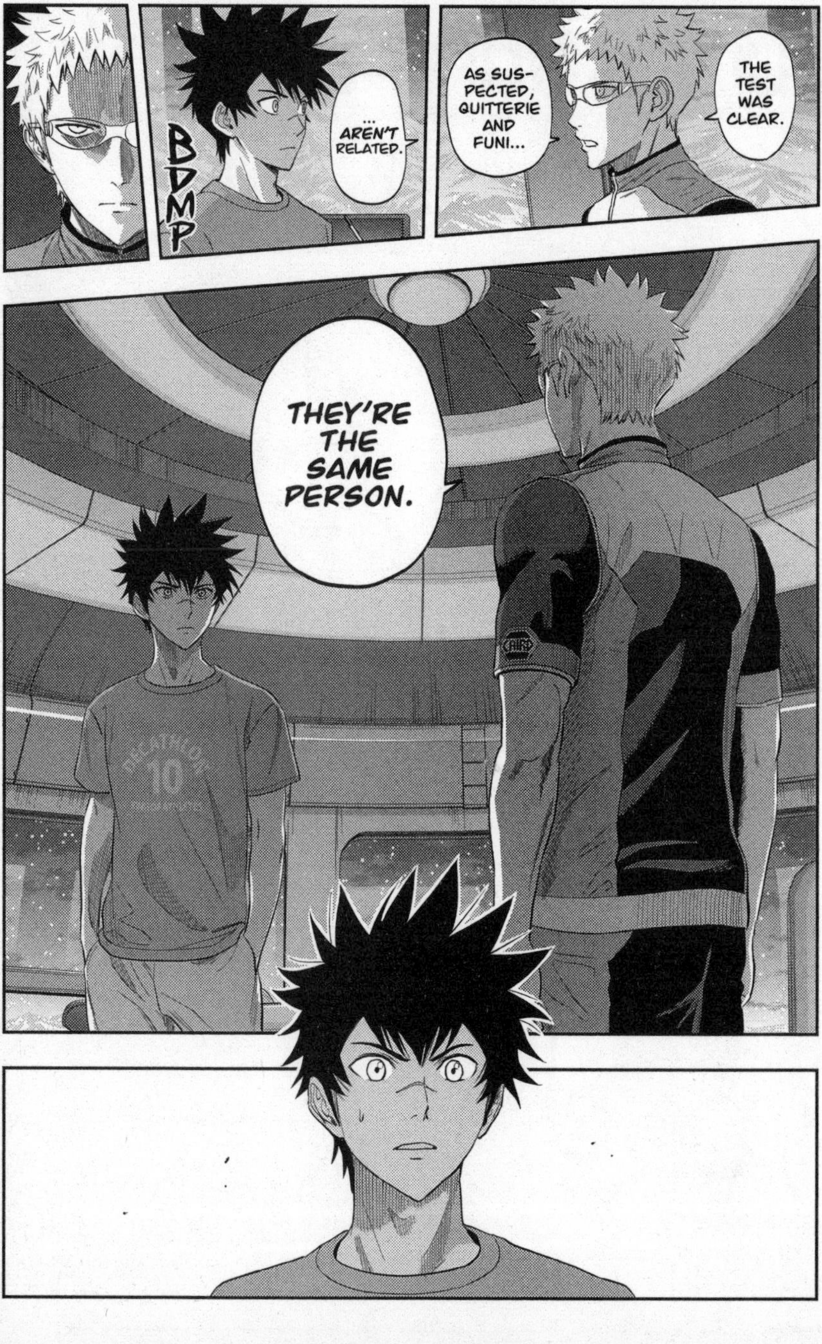
THE TEST WAS CLEAR.
AS SUS-PECTED, QUITTERIE AND FUNI...
...AREN'T RELATED.
BDMP
THEY'RE THE SAME PERSON.

FUNICIA RAFFAELI

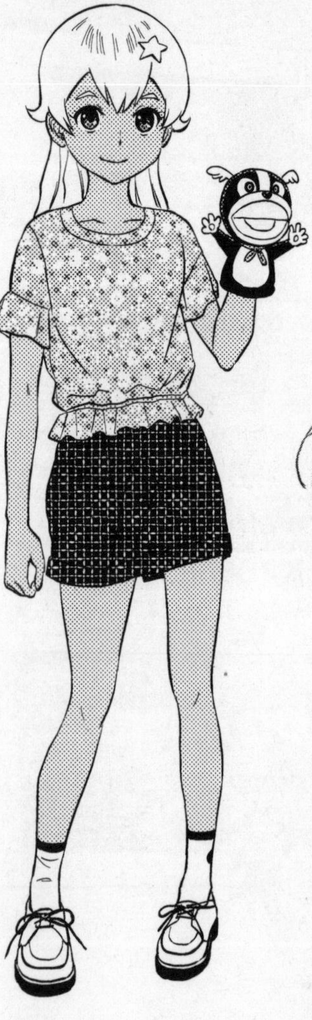

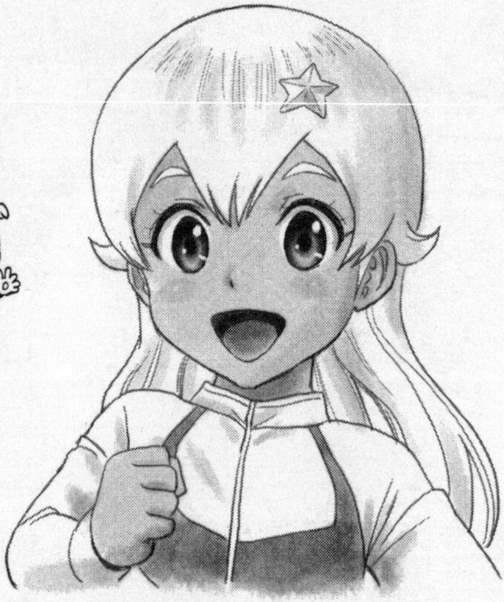

DATA

Name: **Funicia Raffaeli**

Age: **10**

Birthday: **October 19**

Height: **4'6"**

Weight: **68 lbs.**

Blood Type: **A**

Eye Color: **Violet**

Hometown: **Mousanish District**

Her favorite toy is a Beego hand puppet. Beego is the main character of her favorite cartoon show, *Animaroid B5*. When her mother died, she was adopted into the Raffaeli family, making her Quitterie's stepsister.

ASTRA LOST IN SPACE

#33

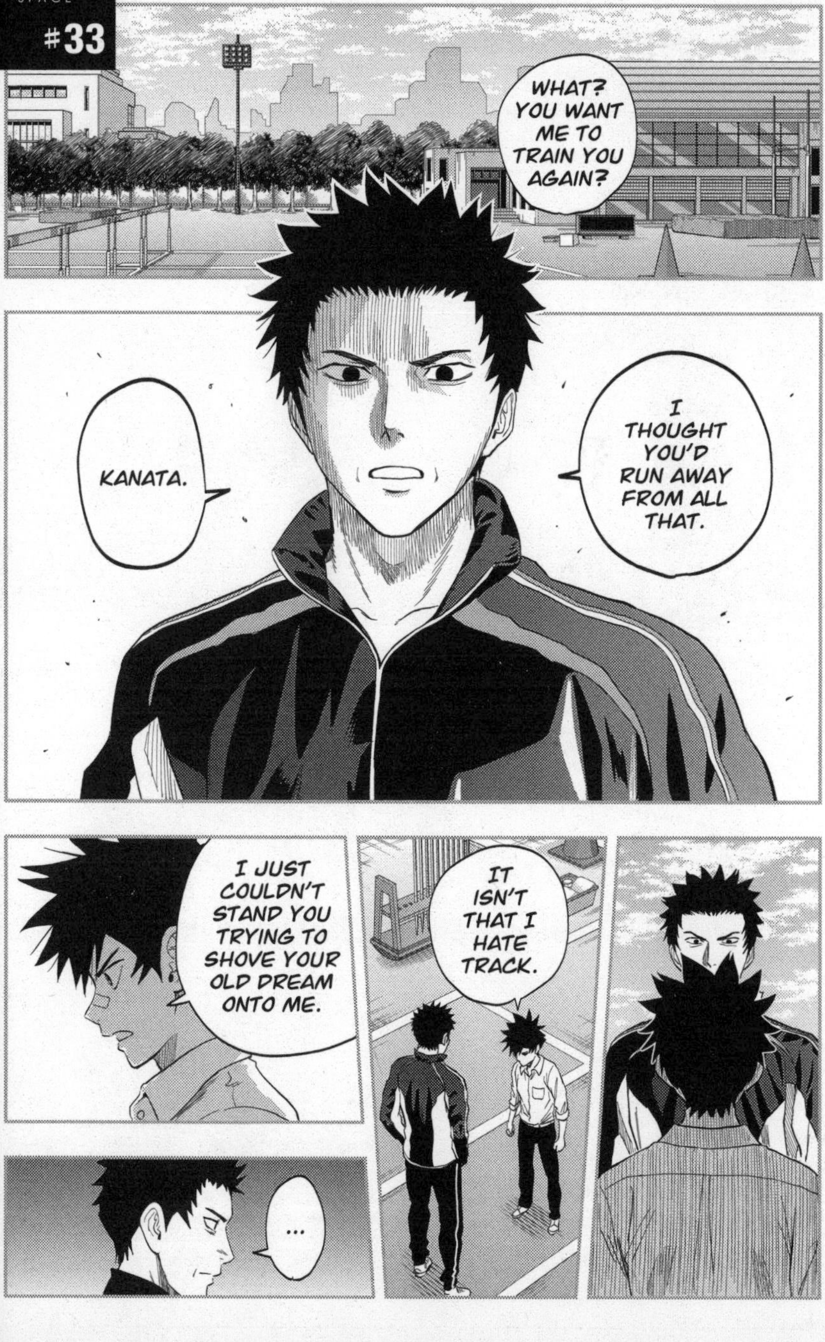
WHAT? YOU WANT ME TO TRAIN YOU AGAIN?
I THOUGHT YOU'D RUN AWAY FROM ALL THAT.
KANATA.
IT ISN'T THAT I HATE TRACK.
I JUST COULDN'T STAND YOU TRYING TO SHOVE YOUR OLD DREAM ONTO ME.
...

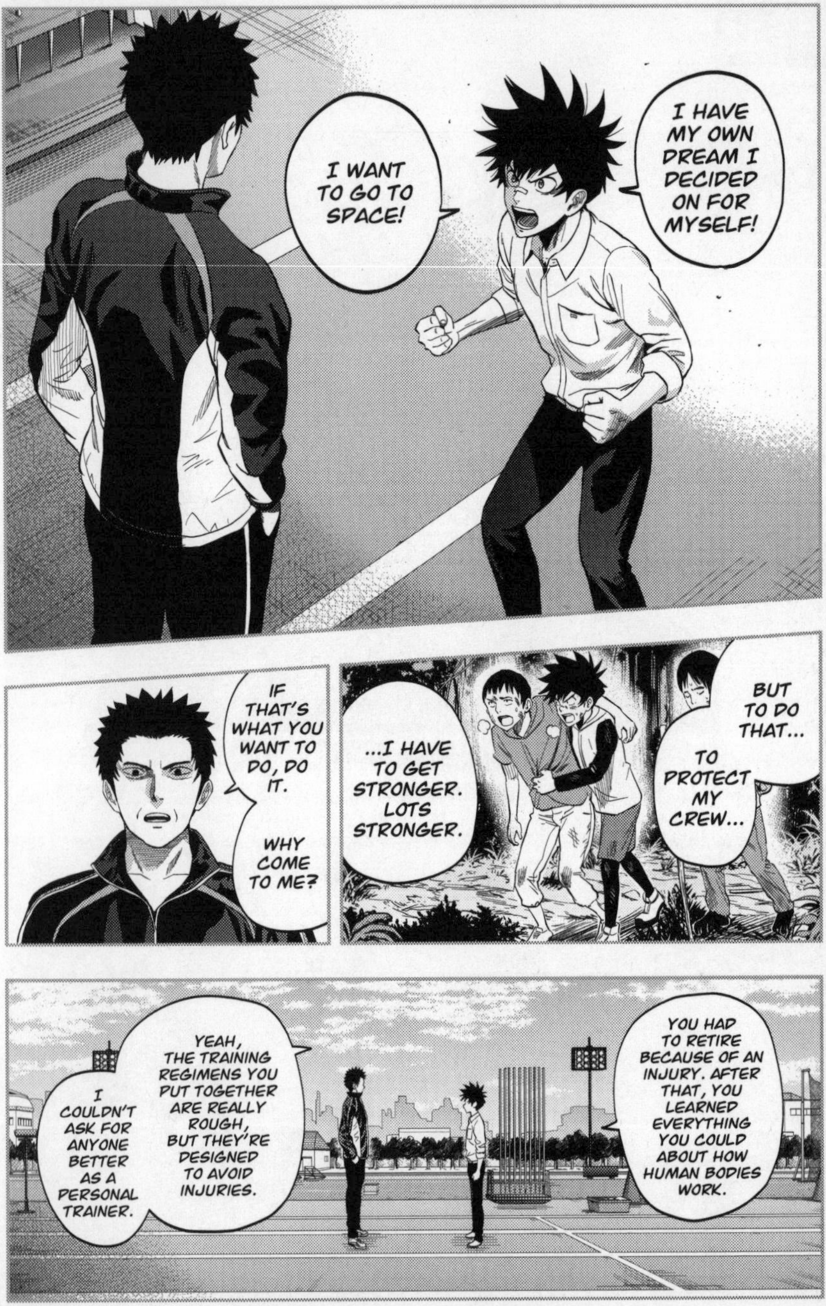
I HAVE MY OWN DREAM I DECIDED ON FOR MYSELF!
I WANT TO GO TO SPACE!
BUT TO DO THAT...
TO PROTECT MY CREW...
...I HAVE TO GET STRONGER. LOTS STRONGER.
IF THAT'S WHAT YOU WANT TO DO, DO IT.
WHY COME TO ME?
YOU HAD TO RETIRE BECAUSE OF AN INJURY. AFTER THAT, YOU LEARNED EVERYTHING YOU COULD ABOUT HOW HUMAN BODIES WORK.
YEAH, THE TRAINING REGIMENS YOU PUT TOGETHER ARE REALLY ROUGH, BUT THEY'RE DESIGNED TO AVOID INJURIES.
I COULDN'T ASK FOR ANYONE BETTER AS A PERSONAL TRAINER.

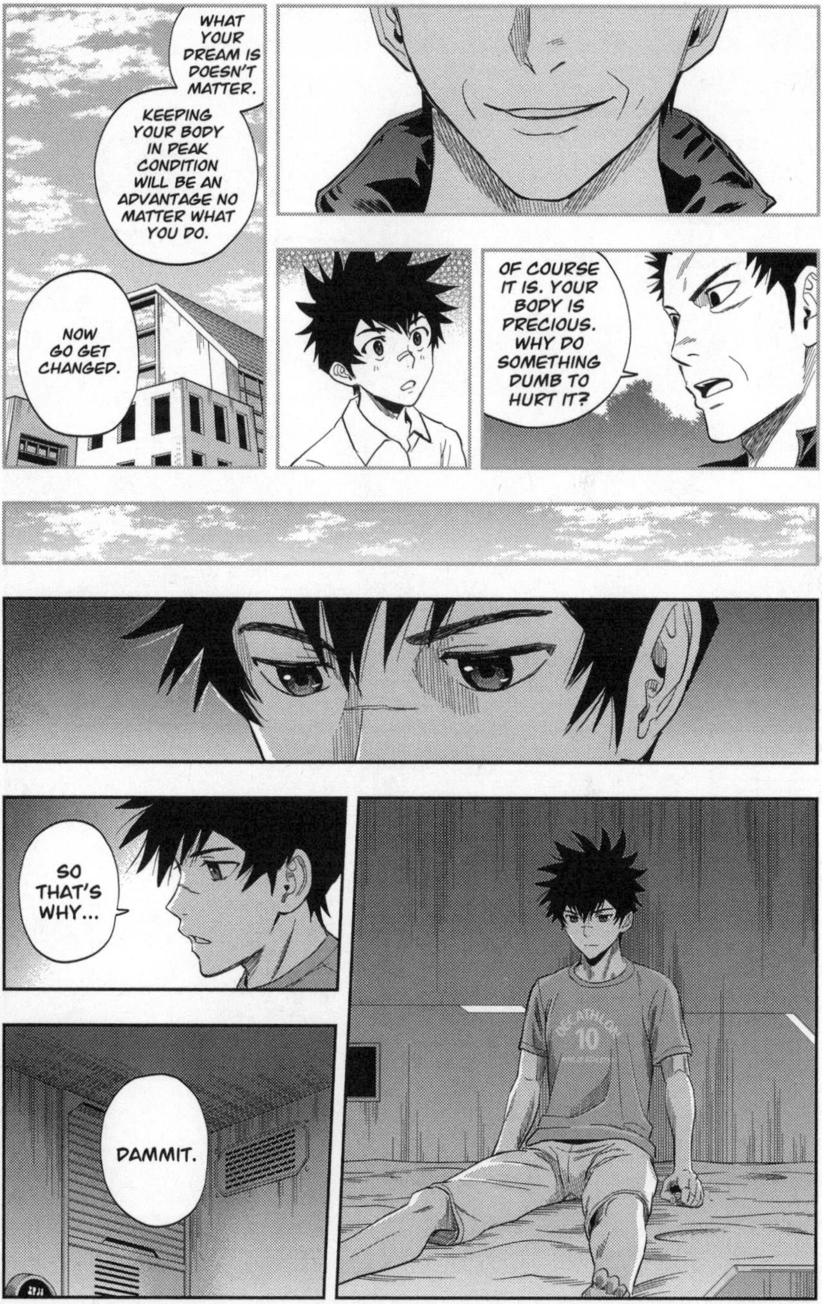
OF COURSE IT IS. YOUR BODY IS PRECIOUS. WHY DO SOMETHING DUMB TO HURT IT?
WHAT YOUR DREAM IS DOESN'T MATTER.
KEEPING YOUR BODY IN PEAK CONDITION WILL BE AN ADVANTAGE NO MATTER WHAT YOU DO.
NOW GO GET CHANGED.
SO THAT'S WHY...
DAMMIT.

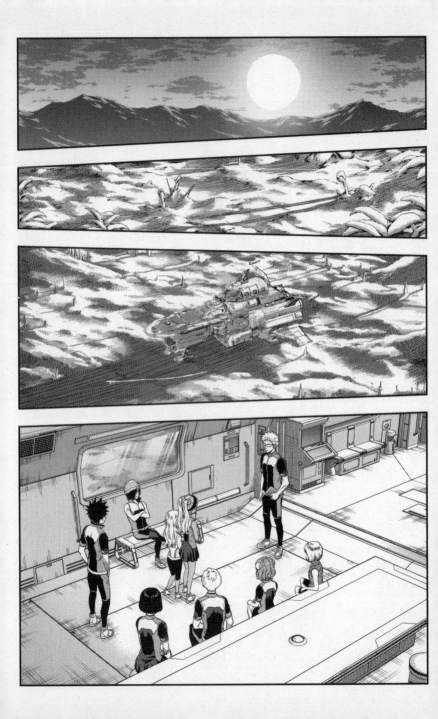

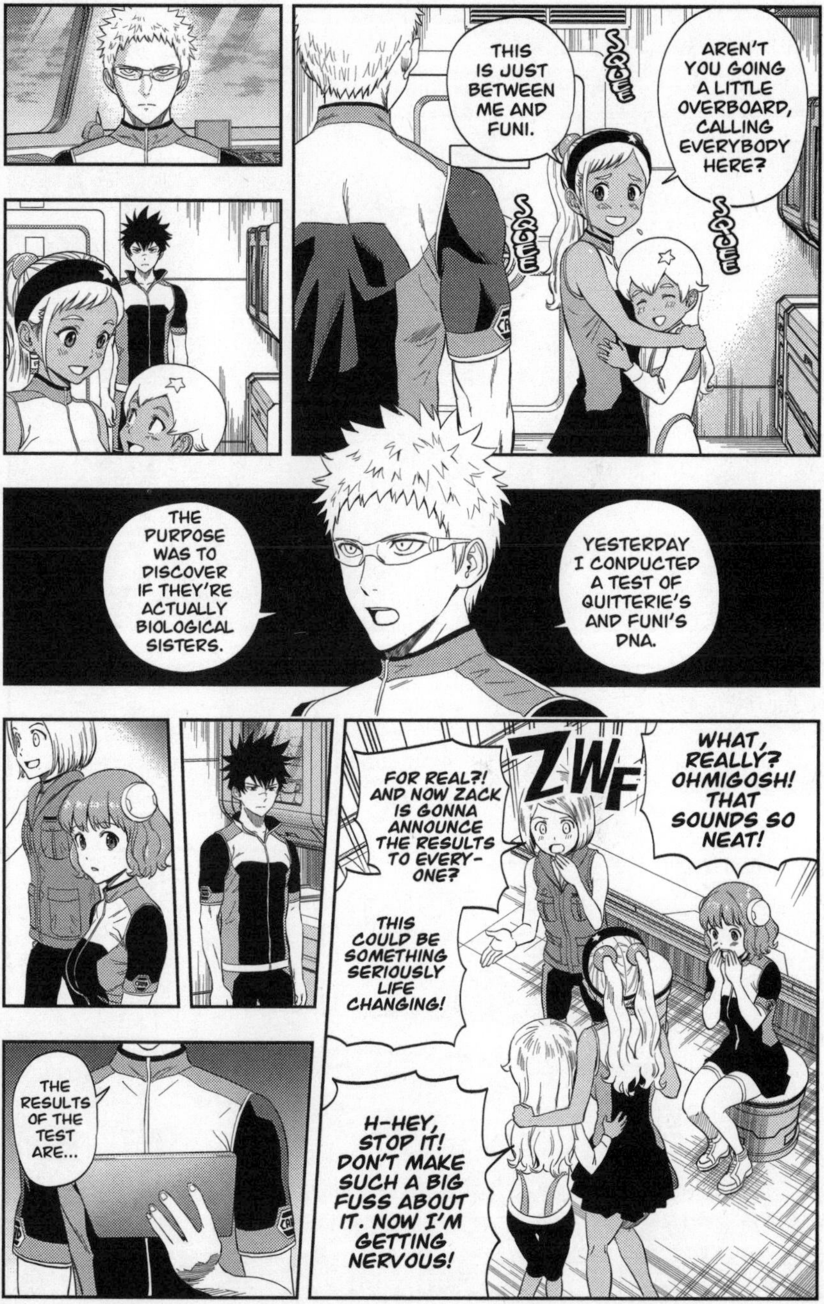
AREN'T YOU GOING A LITTLE OVERBOARD, CALLING EVERYBODY HERE?
SQUEE
SQUEE
SQUEE
THIS IS JUST BETWEEN ME AND FUNI.
YESTERDAY I CONDUCTED A TEST OF QUITTERIE'S AND FUNI'S DNA.
THE PURPOSE WAS TO DISCOVER IF THEY'RE ACTUALLY BIOLOGICAL SISTERS.
WHAT, REALLY? OHMIGOSH! THAT SOUNDS SO NEAT!
ZWF
FOR REAL?! AND NOW ZACK IS GONNA ANNOUNCE THE RESULTS TO EVERY-ONE?
THIS COULD BE SOMETHING SERIOUSLY LIFE CHANGING!
H-HEY, STOP IT! DON'T MAKE SUCH A BIG FUSS ABOUT IT. NOW I'M GETTING NERVOUS!
THE RESULTS OF THE TEST ARE...

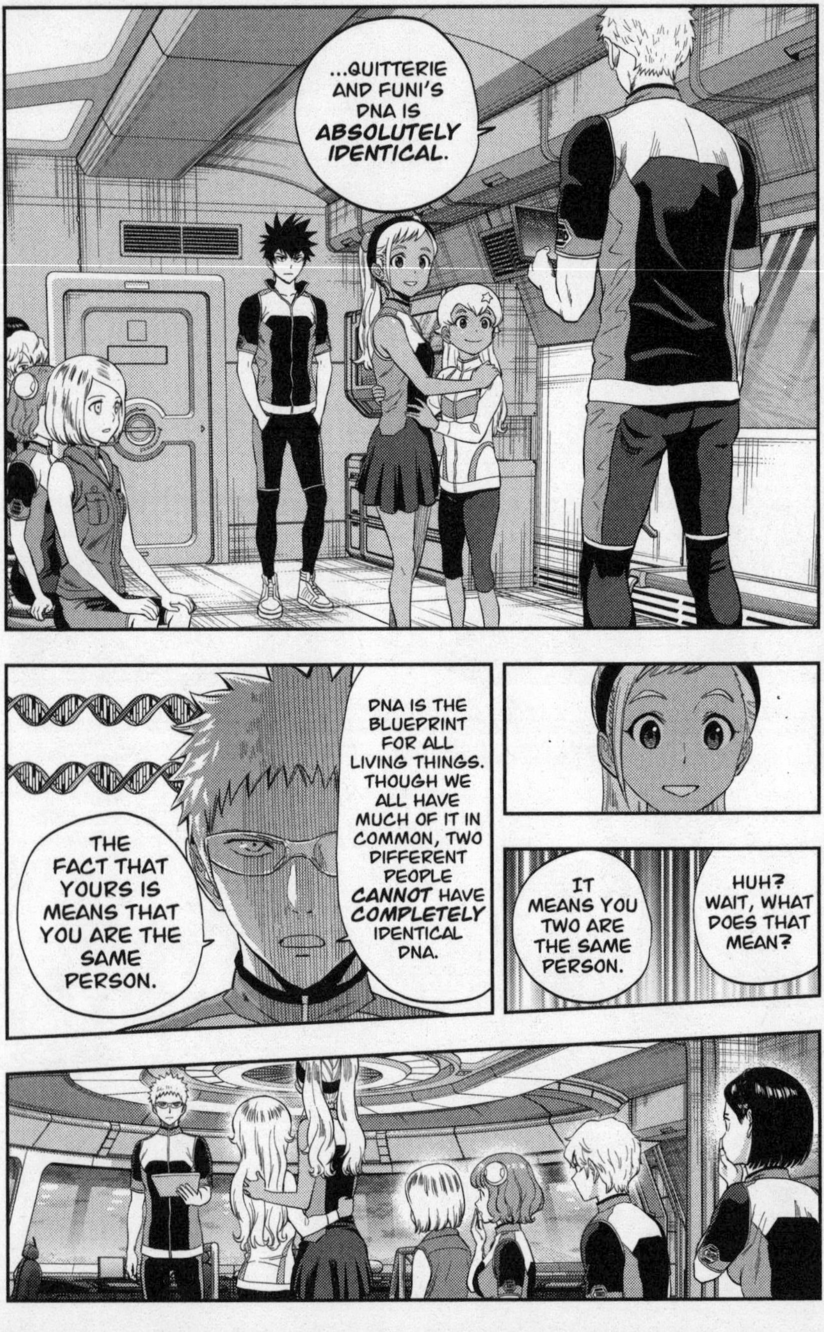
...QUITTERIE AND FUNI'S DNA IS ABSOLUTELY IDENTICAL.
HUH? WAIT, WHAT DOES THAT MEAN?
IT MEANS YOU TWO ARE THE SAME PERSON.
DNA IS THE BLUEPRINT FOR ALL LIVING THINGS. THOUGH WE ALL HAVE MUCH OF IT IN COMMON, TWO DIFFERENT PEOPLE CANNOT HAVE COMPLETELY IDENTICAL DNA.
THE FACT THAT YOURS IS MEANS THAT YOU ARE THE SAME PERSON.

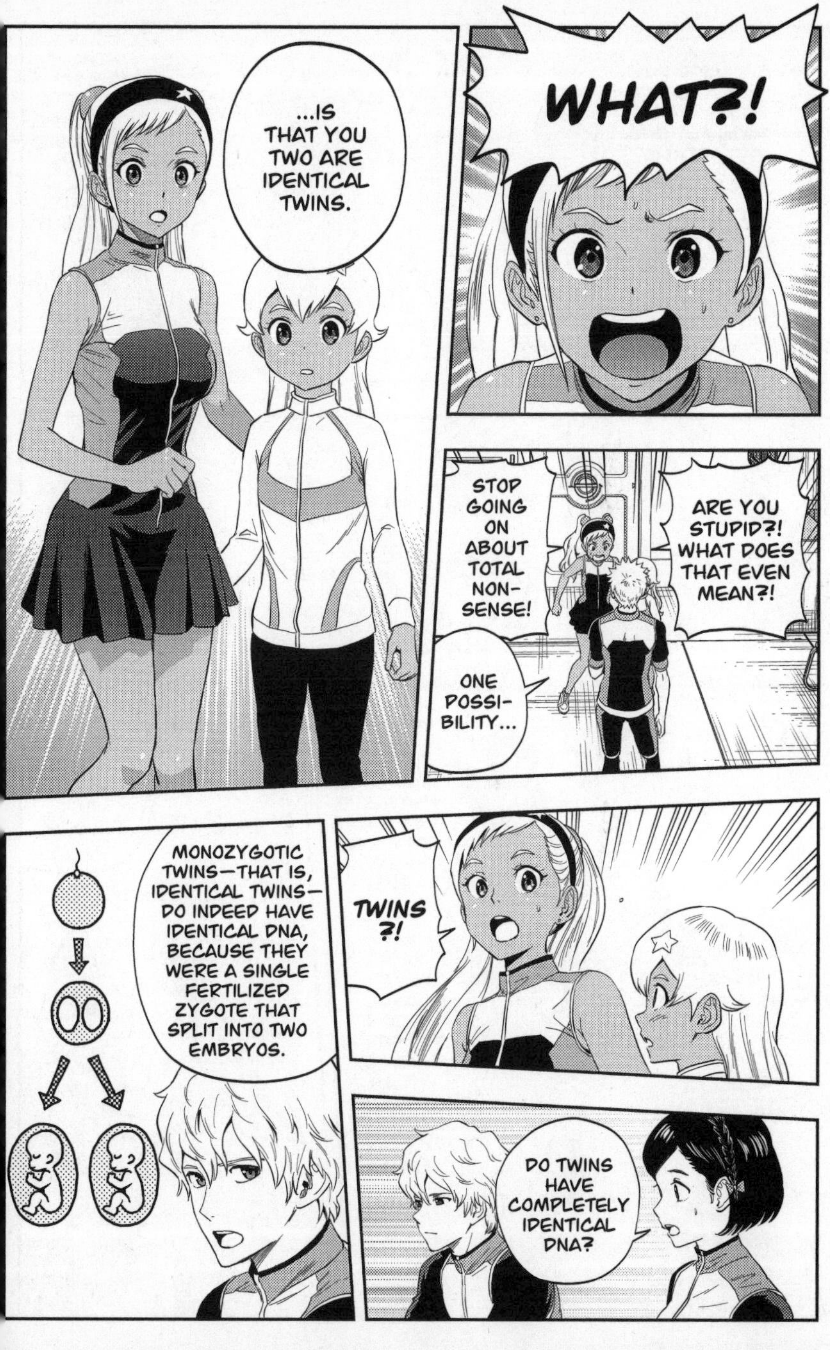
WHAT?!
ARE YOU STUPID?! WHAT DOES THAT EVEN MEAN?!
STOP GOING ON ABOUT TOTAL NON-SENSE!
ONE POSSI-BILITY...
...IS THAT YOU TWO ARE IDENTICAL TWINS.
TWINS?!
DO TWINS HAVE COMPLETELY IDENTICAL DNA?
MONOZYGOTIC TWINS—THAT IS, IDENTICAL TWINS—DO INDEED HAVE IDENTICAL DNA, BECAUSE THEY WERE A SINGLE FERTILIZED ZYGOTE THAT SPLIT INTO TWO EMBRYOS.

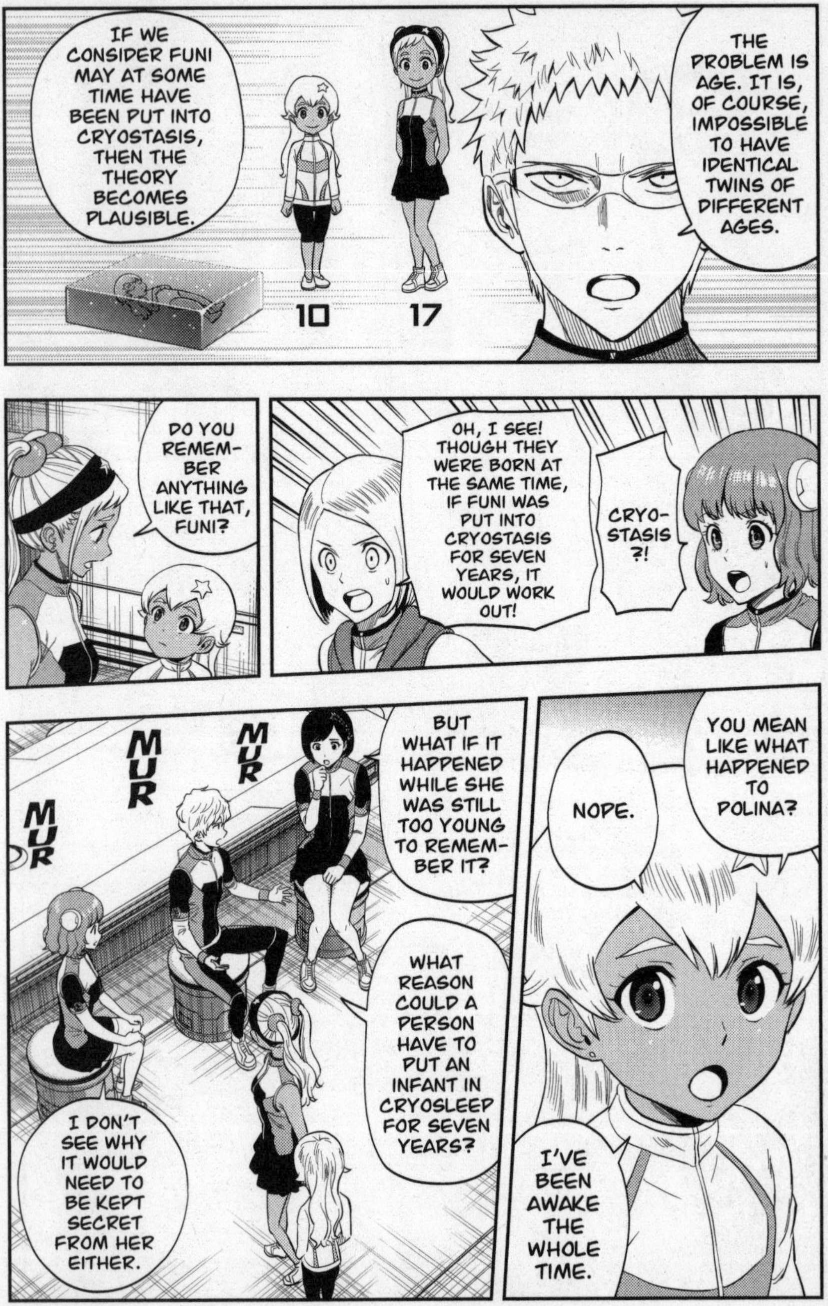
THE PROBLEM IS AGE. IT IS, OF COURSE, IMPOSSIBLE TO HAVE IDENTICAL TWINS OF DIFFERENT AGES.
IF WE CONSIDER FUNI MAY AT SOME TIME HAVE BEEN PUT INTO CRYOSTASIS, THEN THE THEORY BECOMES PLAUSIBLE.
17
10
CRYO-STASIS?!
OH, I SEE! THOUGH THEY WERE BORN AT THE SAME TIME, IF FUNI WAS PUT INTO CRYOSTASIS FOR SEVEN YEARS, IT WOULD WORK OUT!
DO YOU REMEMBER ANYTHING LIKE THAT, FUNI?
YOU MEAN LIKE WHAT HAPPENED TO POLINA?
NOPE.
I'VE BEEN AWAKE THE WHOLE TIME.
BUT WHAT IF IT HAPPENED WHILE SHE WAS STILL TOO YOUNG TO REMEMBER IT?
MUR MUR
MUR MUR
MUR MUR
WHAT REASON COULD A PERSON HAVE TO PUT AN INFANT IN CRYOSLEEP FOR SEVEN YEARS?
I DON'T SEE WHY IT WOULD NEED TO BE KEPT SECRET FROM HER EITHER.

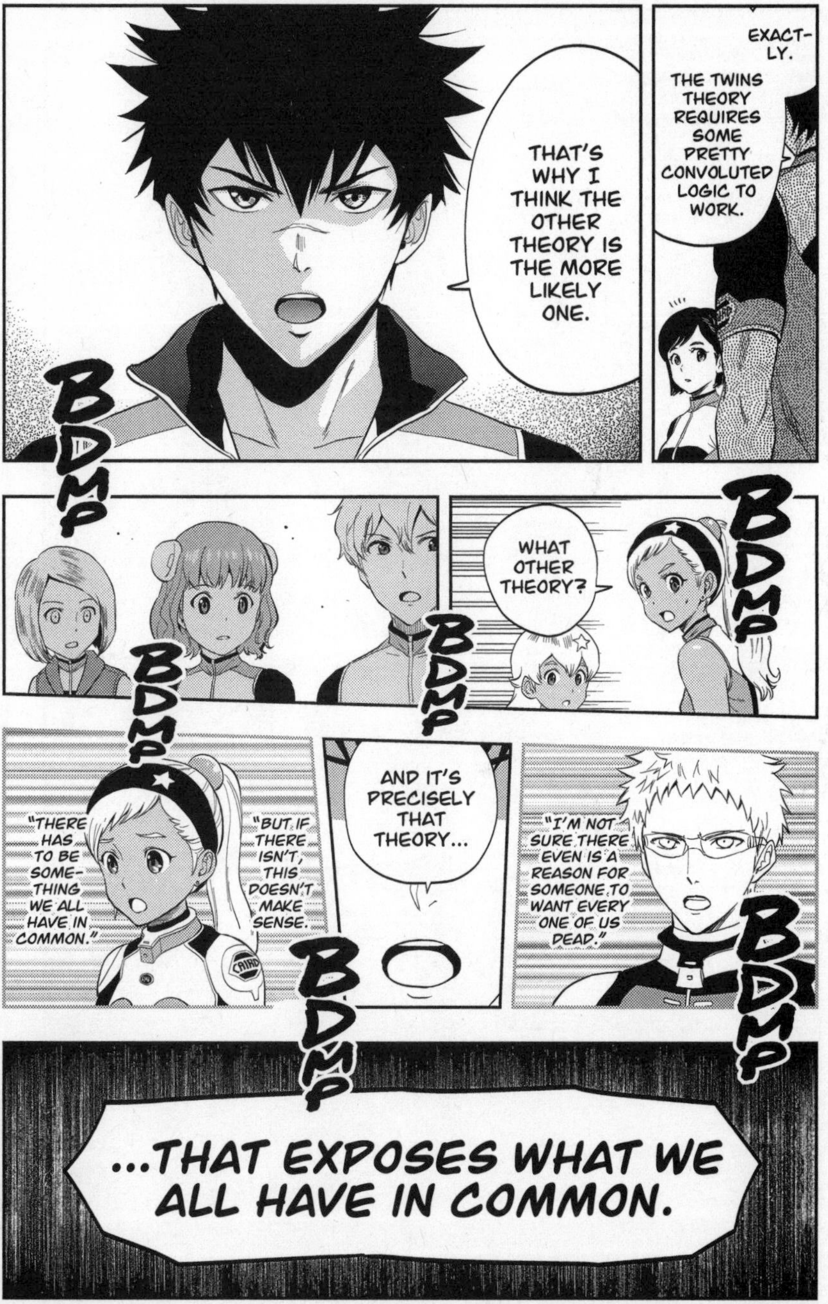
EXACT-LY.
THE TWINS THEORY REQUIRES SOME PRETTY CONVOLUTED LOGIC TO WORK.
THAT'S WHY I THINK THE OTHER THEORY IS THE MORE LIKELY ONE.
BDMP
BDMP
WHAT OTHER THEORY?
BDMP
BDMP
"I'M NOT SURE THERE EVEN IS A REASON FOR SOMEONE TO WANT EVERY ONE OF US DEAD."
BDMP
AND IT'S PRECISELY THAT THEORY...
BDMP
"BUT IF THERE ISN'T, THIS DOESN'T MAKE SENSE.
"THERE HAS TO BE SOME-THING WE ALL HAVE IN COMMON."
BDMP
...THAT EXPOSES WHAT WE ALL HAVE IN COMMON.

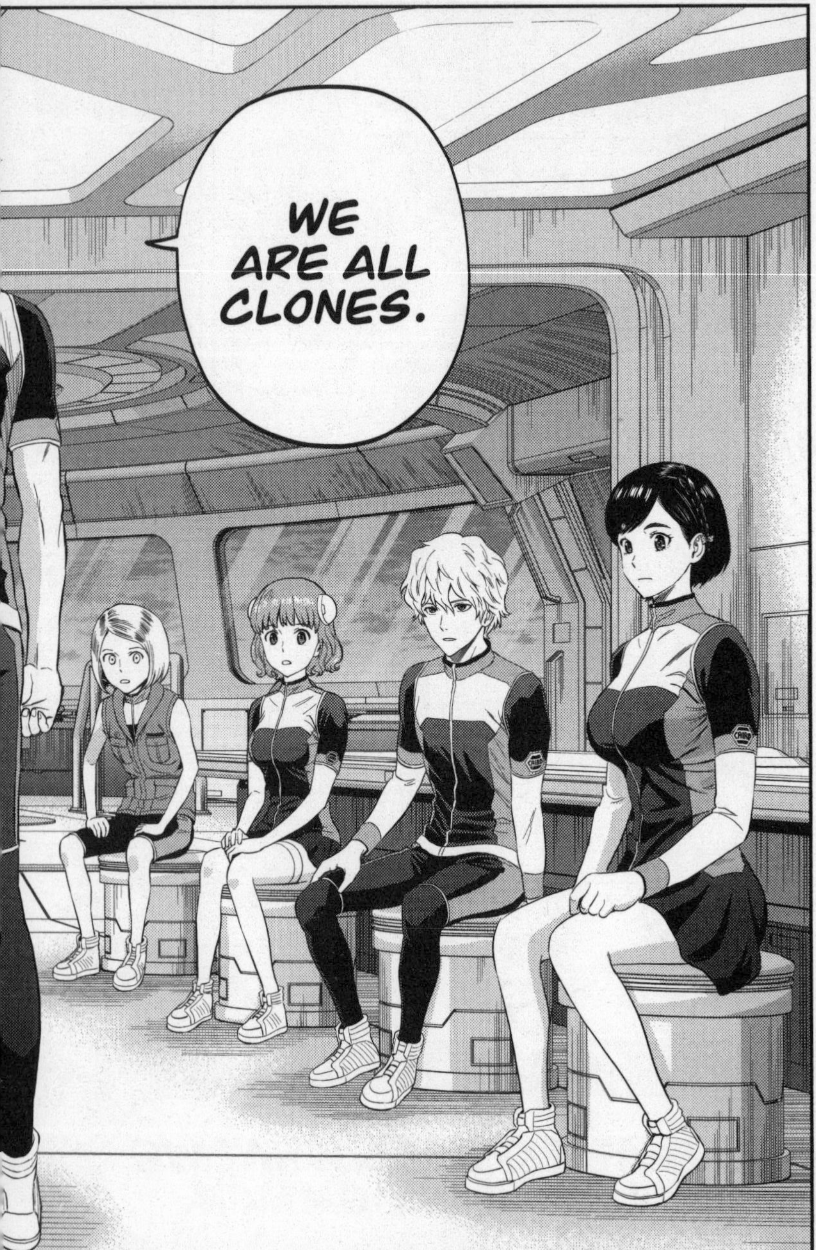
WE ARE ALL CLONES.

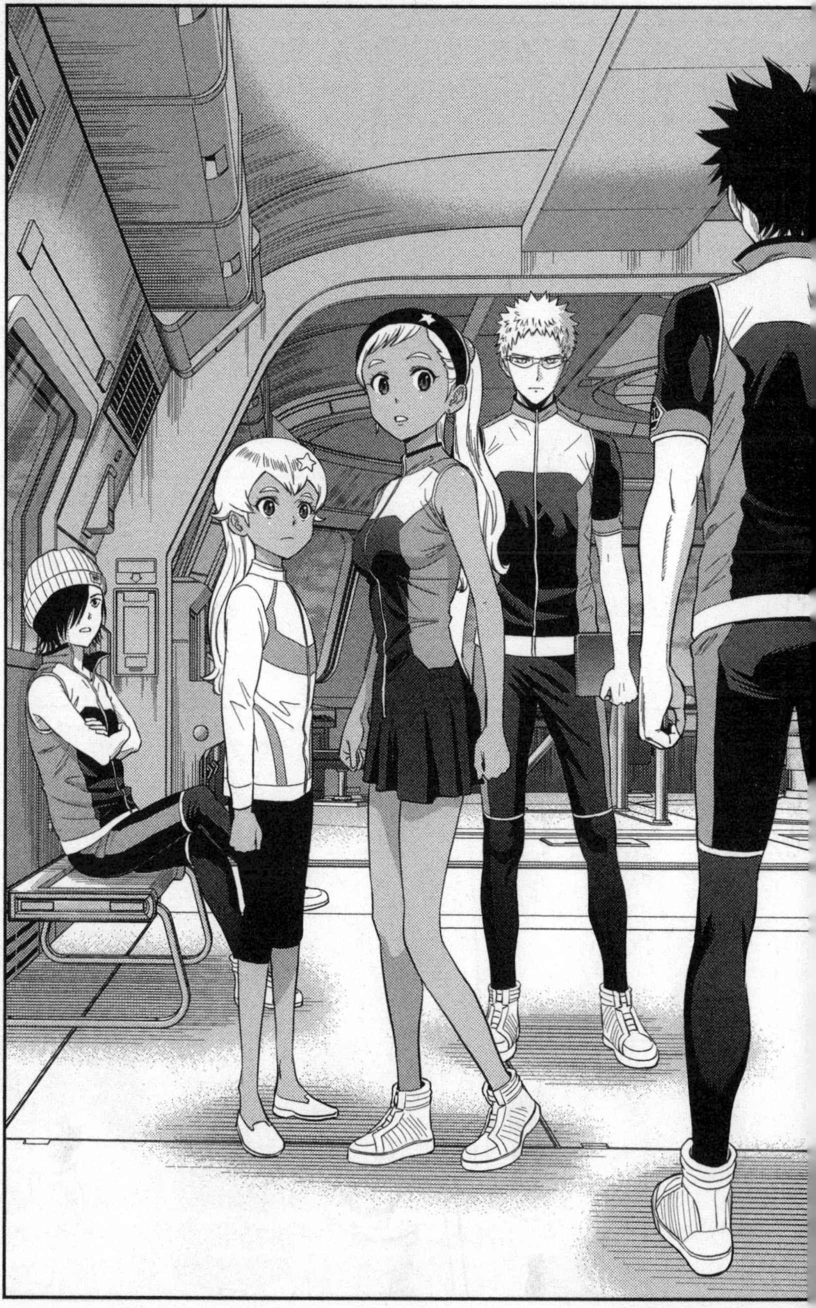

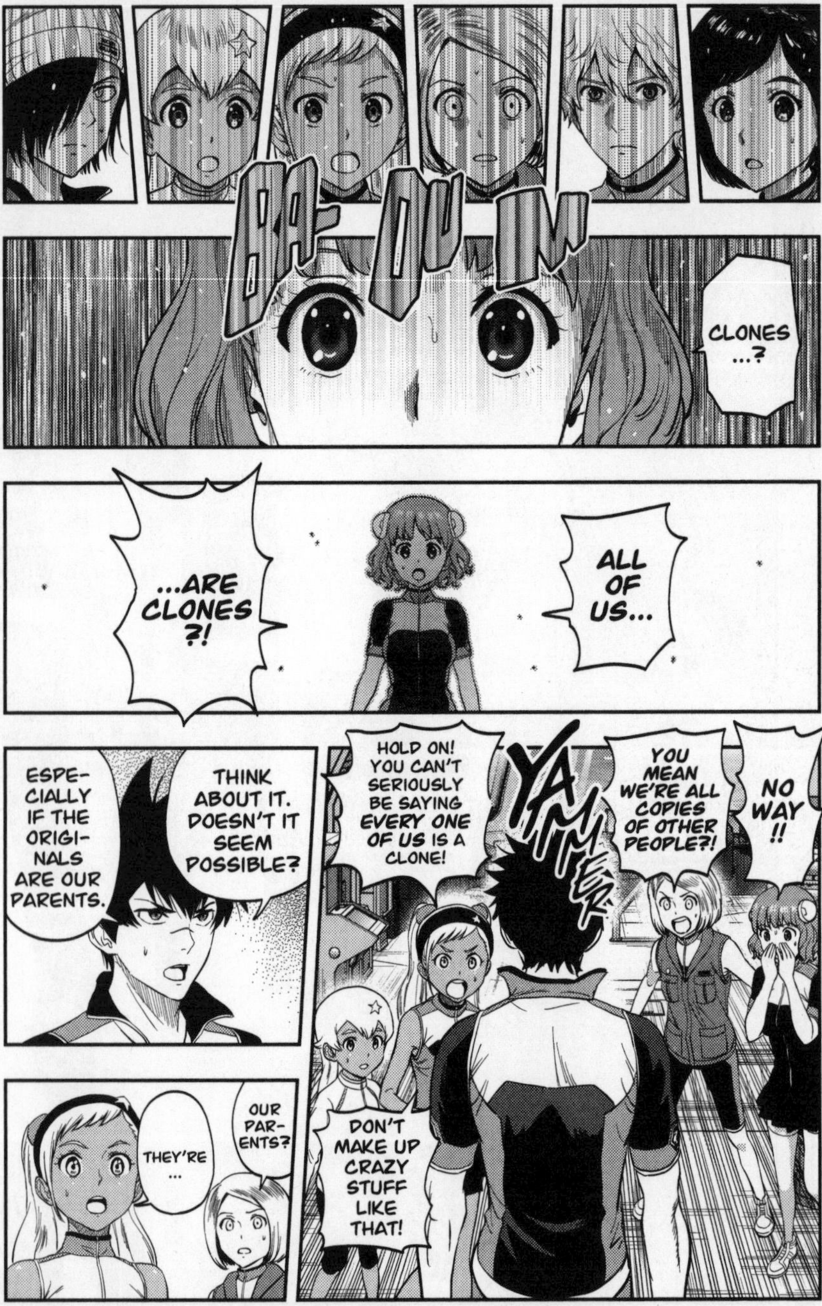
BA-DU-UM
CLONES ...?
ALL OF US...
...ARE CLONES?!
NO WAY!!
YOU MEAN WE'RE ALL COPIES OF OTHER PEOPLE?!
YAMMER
HOLD ON! YOU CAN'T SERIOUSLY BE SAYING EVERY ONE OF US IS A CLONE!
DON'T MAKE UP CRAZY STUFF LIKE THAT!
THINK ABOUT IT. DOESN'T IT SEEM POSSIBLE?
ESPE-CIALLY IF THE ORIGI-NALS ARE OUR PARENTS.
OUR PAR-ENTS?
THEY'RE ...

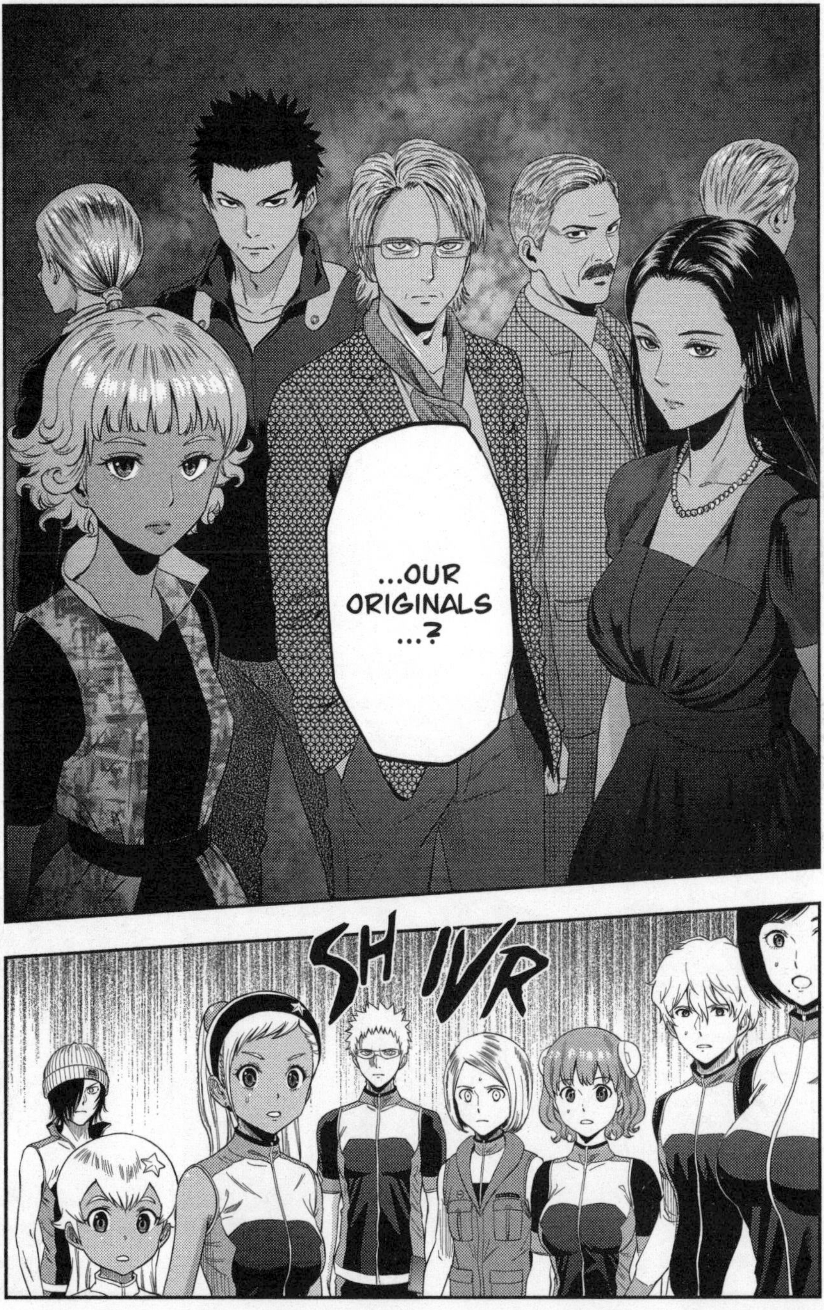
...OUR ORIGINALS ...?
SHIVR

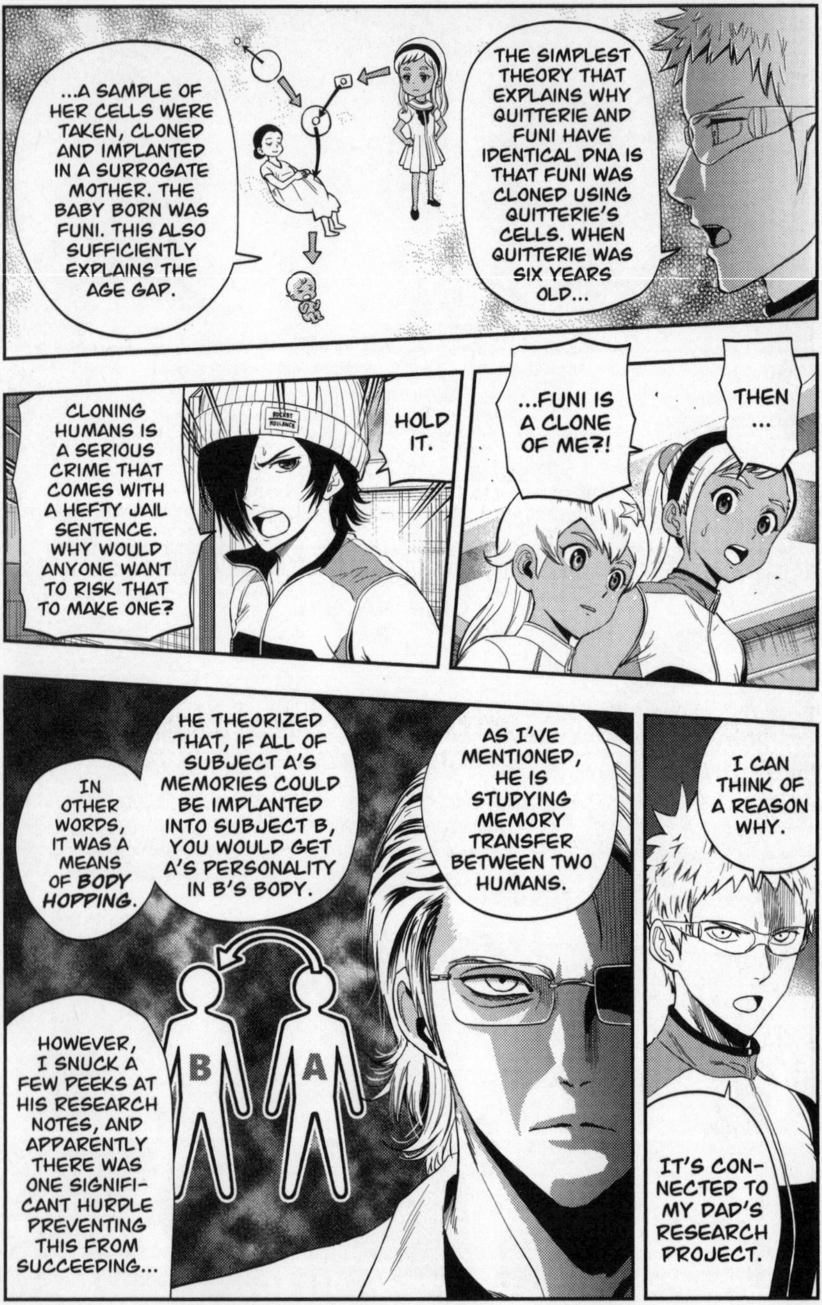
THE SIMPLEST THEORY THAT EXPLAINS WHY QUITTERIE AND FUNI HAVE IDENTICAL DNA IS THAT FUNI WAS CLONED USING QUITTERIE'S CELLS. WHEN QUITTERIE WAS SIX YEARS OLD...
...A SAMPLE OF HER CELLS WERE TAKEN, CLONED AND IMPLANTED IN A SURROGATE MOTHER. THE BABY BORN WAS FUNI. THIS ALSO SUFFICIENTLY EXPLAINS THE AGE GAP.
THEN ...
...FUNI IS A CLONE OF ME?!
HOLD IT.
CLONING HUMANS IS A SERIOUS CRIME THAT COMES WITH A HEFTY JAIL SENTENCE. WHY WOULD ANYONE WANT TO RISK THAT TO MAKE ONE?
I CAN THINK OF A REASON WHY.
IT'S CONNECTED TO MY DAD'S RESEARCH PROJECT.
AS I'VE MENTIONED, HE IS STUDYING MEMORY TRANSFER BETWEEN TWO HUMANS.
HE THEORIZED THAT, IF ALL OF SUBJECT A'S MEMORIES COULD BE IMPLANTED INTO SUBJECT B, YOU WOULD GET A'S PERSONALITY IN B'S BODY.
IN OTHER WORDS, IT WAS A MEANS OF BODY HOPPING.
B
A
HOWEVER, I SNUCK A FEW PEEKS AT HIS RESEARCH NOTES, AND APPARENTLY THERE WAS ONE SIGNIFICANT HURDLE PREVENTING THIS FROM SUCCEEDING...

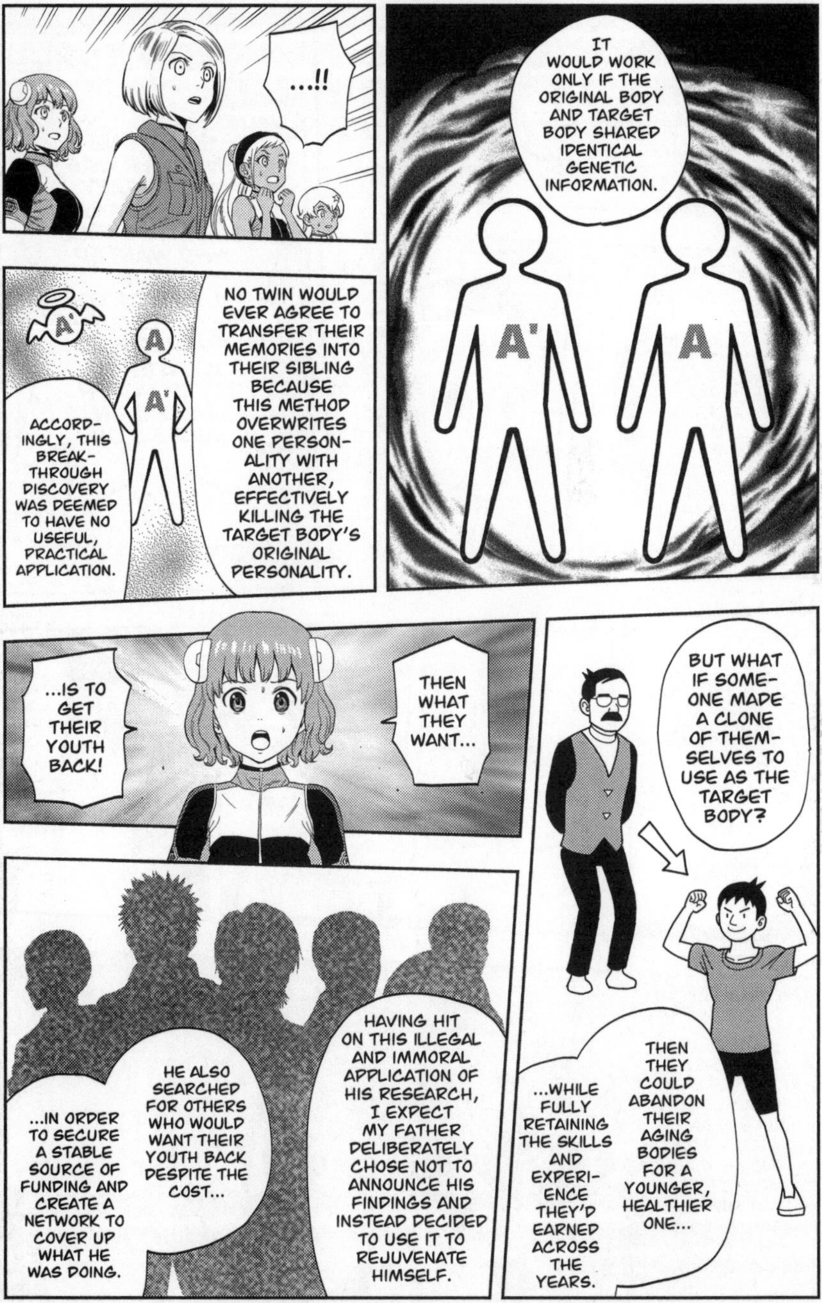
IT WOULD WORK ONLY IF THE ORIGINAL BODY AND TARGET BODY SHARED IDENTICAL GENETIC INFORMATION.
A'
A
...!!
NO TWIN WOULD EVER AGREE TO TRANSFER THEIR MEMORIES INTO THEIR SIBLING BECAUSE THIS METHOD OVERWRITES ONE PERSONALITY WITH ANOTHER, EFFECTIVELY KILLING THE TARGET BODY'S ORIGINAL PERSONALITY.
A
A'
A'
ACCORDINGLY, THIS BREAKTHROUGH DISCOVERY WAS DEEMED TO HAVE NO USEFUL, PRACTICAL APPLICATION.
BUT WHAT IF SOMEONE MADE A CLONE OF THEMSELVES TO USE AS THE TARGET BODY?
THEN THEY COULD ABANDON THEIR AGING BODIES FOR A YOUNGER, HEALTHIER ONE...
...WHILE FULLY RETAINING THE SKILLS AND EXPERIENCE THEY'D EARNED ACROSS THE YEARS.
THEN WHAT THEY WANT...
...IS TO GET THEIR YOUTH BACK!
HAVING HIT ON THIS ILLEGAL AND IMMORAL APPLICATION OF HIS RESEARCH, I EXPECT MY FATHER DELIBERATELY CHOSE NOT TO ANNOUNCE HIS FINDINGS AND INSTEAD DECIDED TO USE IT TO REJUVENATE HIMSELF.
HE ALSO SEARCHED FOR OTHERS WHO WOULD WANT THEIR YOUTH BACK DESPITE THE COST...
...IN ORDER TO SECURE A STABLE SOURCE OF FUNDING AND CREATE A NETWORK TO COVER UP WHAT HE WAS DOING.

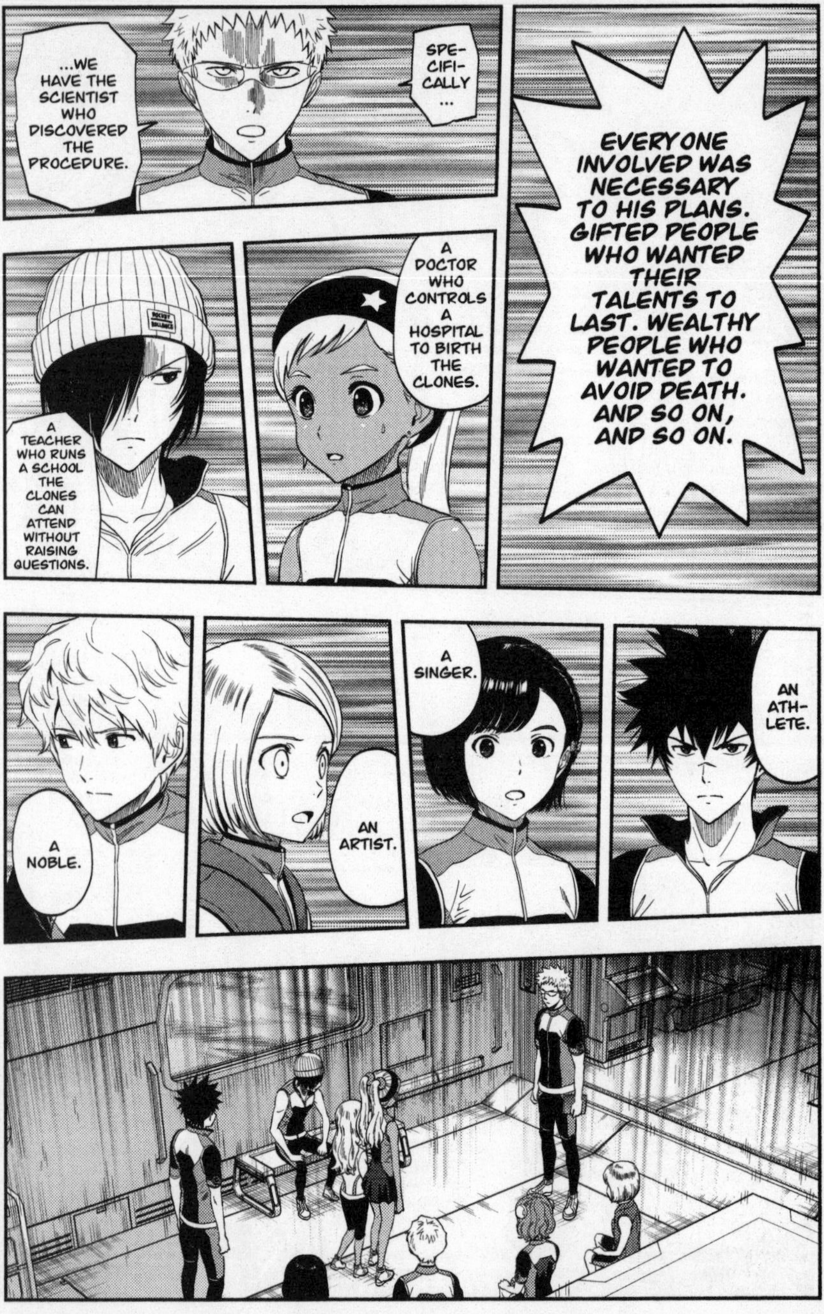
EVERYONE INVOLVED WAS NECESSARY TO HIS PLANS. GIFTED PEOPLE WHO WANTED THEIR TALENTS TO LAST. WEALTHY PEOPLE WHO WANTED TO AVOID DEATH. AND SO ON, AND SO ON.
SPE-CIFI-CALLY...
...WE HAVE THE SCIENTIST WHO DISCOVERED THE PROCEDURE.
A DOCTOR WHO CONTROLS A HOSPITAL TO BIRTH THE CLONES.
A TEACHER WHO RUNS A SCHOOL THE CLONES CAN ATTEND WITHOUT RAISING QUESTIONS.
AN ATH-LETE.
A SINGER.
AN ARTIST.
A NOBLE.

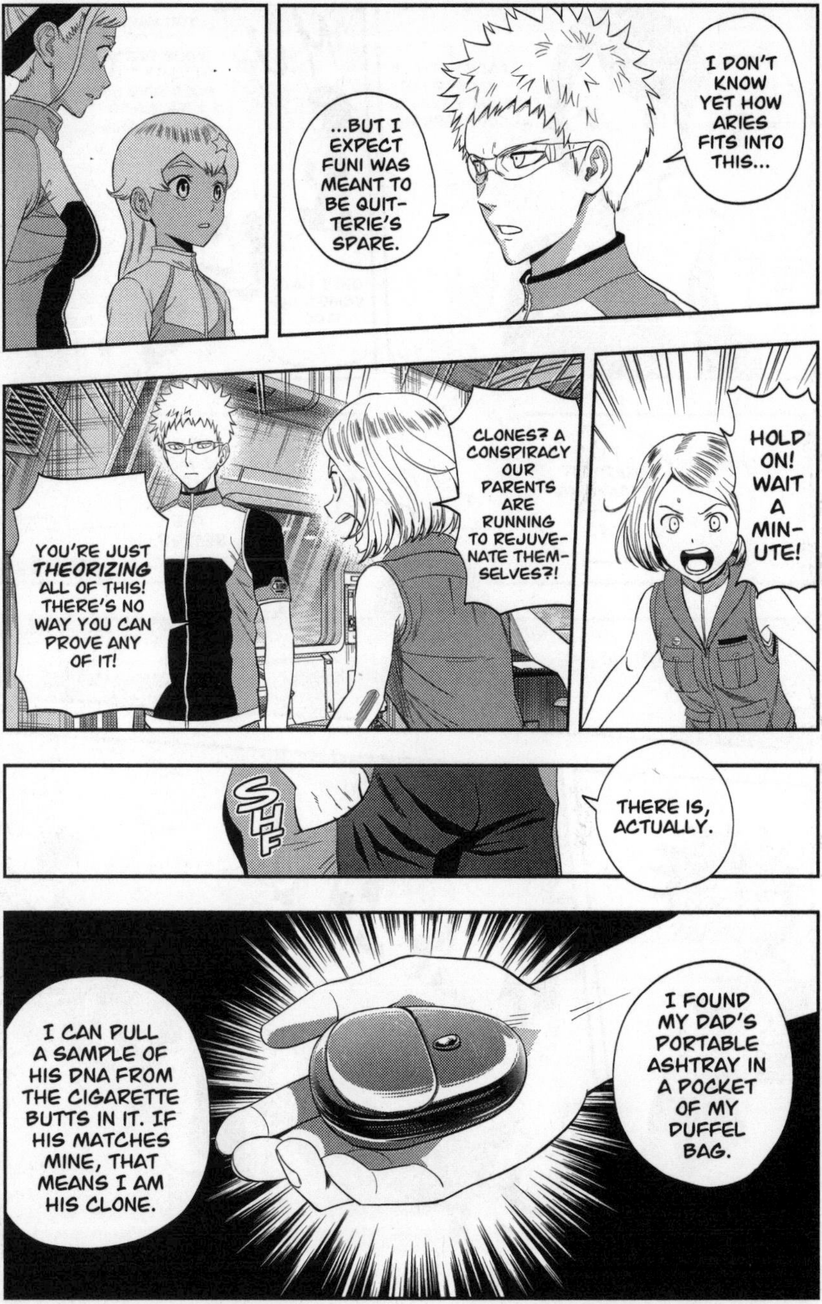
I DON'T KNOW YET HOW ARIES FITS INTO THIS...
...BUT I EXPECT FUNI WAS MEANT TO BE QUITTERIE'S SPARE.
...
HOLD ON! WAIT A MINUTE!
CLONES? A CONSPIRACY OUR PARENTS ARE RUNNING TO REJUVENATE THEMSELVES?!
YOU'RE JUST **THEORIZING** ALL OF THIS! THERE'S NO WAY YOU CAN PROVE ANY OF IT!
SHF
THERE IS, ACTUALLY.
I FOUND MY DAD'S PORTABLE ASHTRAY IN A POCKET OF MY DUFFEL BAG.
I CAN PULL A SAMPLE OF HIS DNA FROM THE CIGARETTE BUTTS IN IT. IF HIS MATCHES MINE, THAT MEANS I AM HIS CLONE.

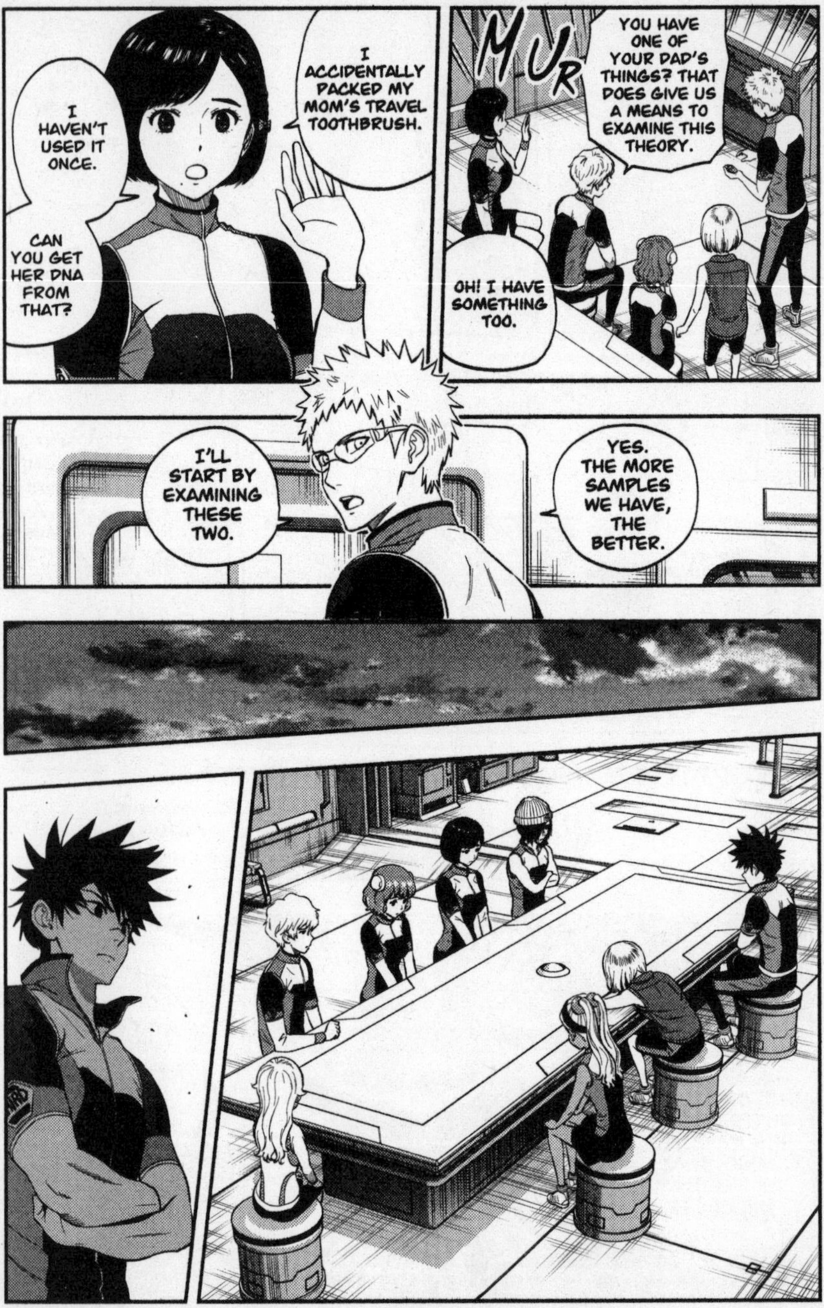
MUR
YOU HAVE ONE OF YOUR DAD'S THINGS? THAT DOES GIVE US A MEANS TO EXAMINE THIS THEORY.
OH! I HAVE SOMETHING TOO.
I ACCIDENTALLY PACKED MY MOM'S TRAVEL TOOTHBRUSH.
I HAVEN'T USED IT ONCE.
CAN YOU GET HER DNA FROM THAT?
YES. THE MORE SAMPLES WE HAVE, THE BETTER.
I'LL START BY EXAMINING THESE TWO.

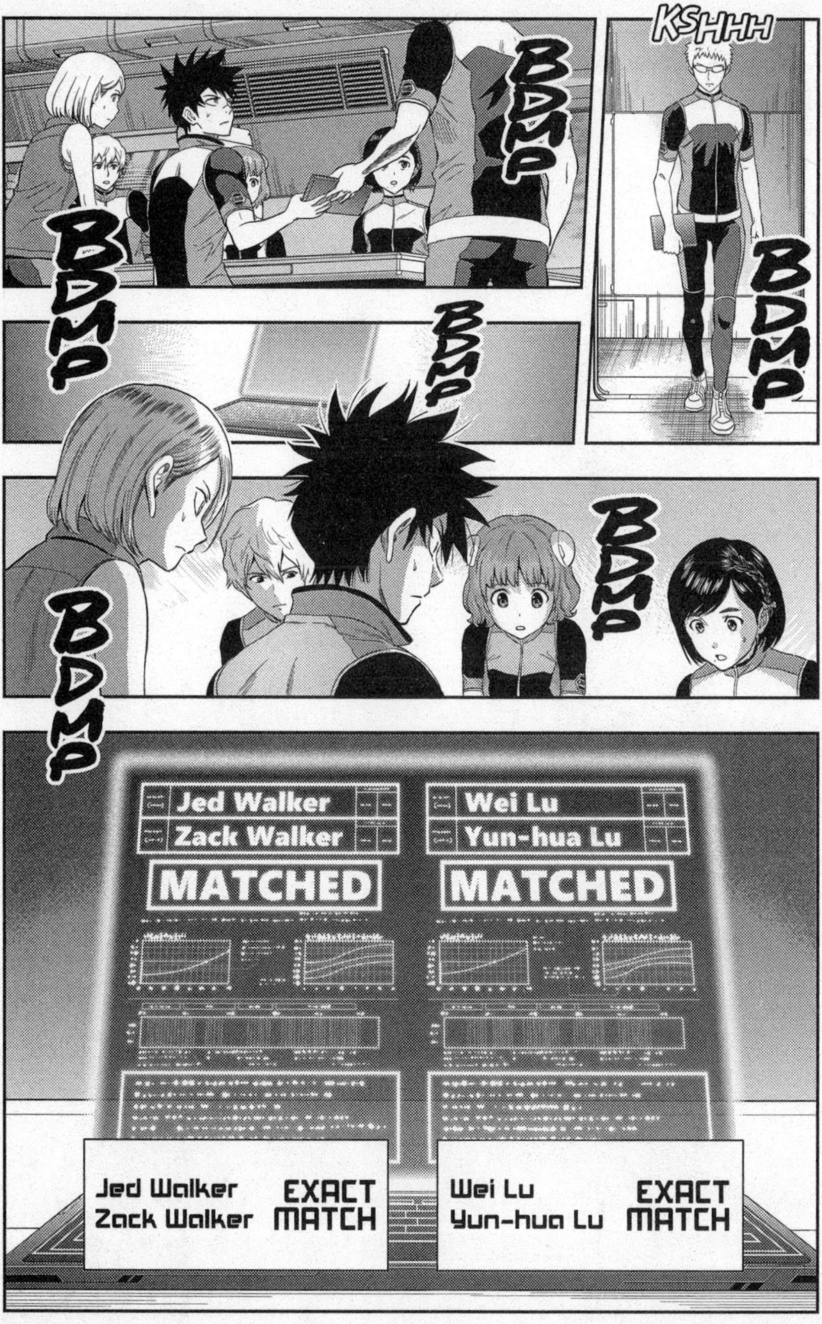
KSHHH
BDMP
BDMP
BDMP
BDMP
BDMP
BDMP
Wei Lu
Yun-hua Lu
MATCHED
Jed Walker
Zack Walker
MATCHED
Wei Lu
Yun-hua Lu
EXACT MATCH
Jed Walker
Zack Walker
EXACT MATCH

Material Collection
Character Profile **28**

POLINA LIVINSKAYA

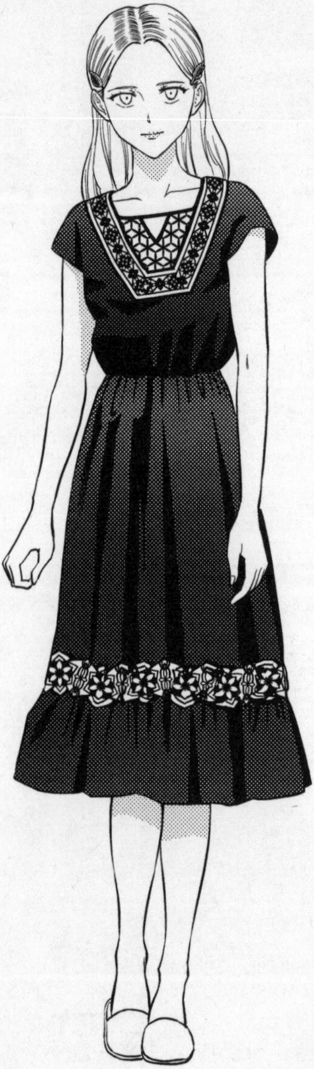

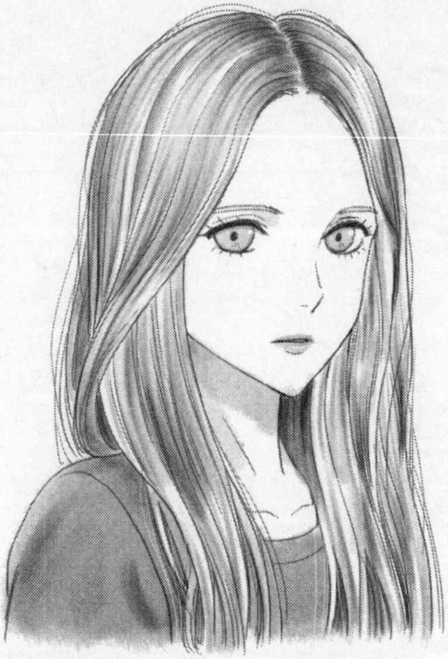

DATA

Name: **Polina Livinskaya**

Age: **28**

Birthday: **December 13**

Height: **5'5"**

Weight: **101 lbs.**

Blood Type: **A**

Eye Color: **Gray**

Hometown: **Russia**

A crew member on the *Ark VI* that crash-landed on the planet Icriss. After the rest of her crew died, she went into cryosleep until she was found by the crew of the *Astra*.

Her clothing is all borrowed from the Group B-5 crew.

ASTRA
LOST IN
SPACE

#34

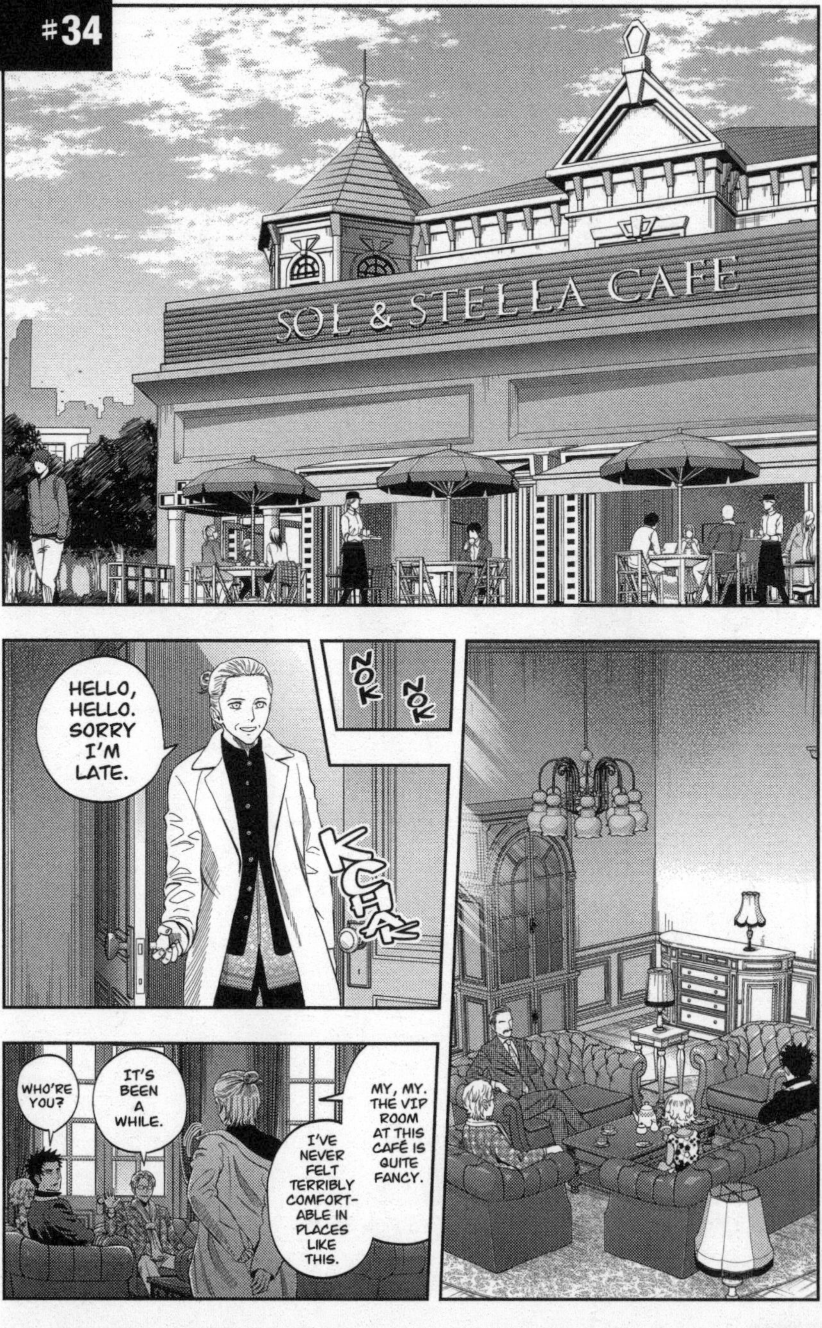
SOL & STELLA CAFE
NOK NOK
HELLO, HELLO. SORRY I'M LATE.
KCHAK
MY, MY. THE VIP ROOM AT THIS CAFÉ IS QUITE FANCY.
I'VE NEVER FELT TERRIBLY COMFORTABLE IN PLACES LIKE THIS.
IT'S BEEN A WHILE.
WHO'RE YOU?

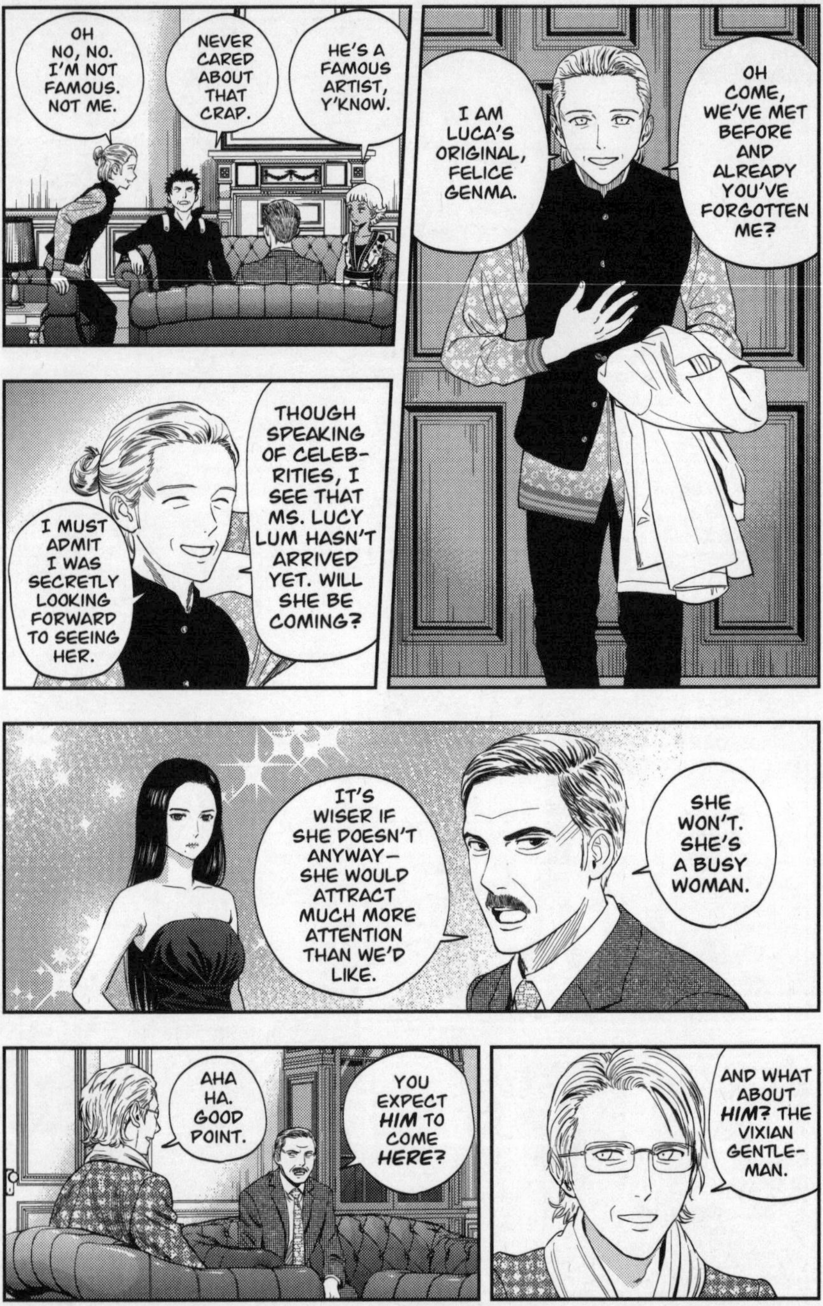
OH COME, WE'VE MET BEFORE AND ALREADY YOU'VE FORGOTTEN ME?
I AM LUCA'S ORIGINAL, FELICE GENMA.
HE'S A FAMOUS ARTIST, Y'KNOW.
NEVER CARED ABOUT THAT CRAP.
OH NO, NO. I'M NOT FAMOUS. NOT ME.
THOUGH SPEAKING OF CELEBRITIES, I SEE THAT MS. LUCY LUM HASN'T ARRIVED YET. WILL SHE BE COMING?
I MUST ADMIT I WAS SECRETLY LOOKING FORWARD TO SEEING HER.
SHE WON'T. SHE'S A BUSY WOMAN.
IT'S WISER IF SHE DOESN'T ANYWAY— SHE WOULD ATTRACT MUCH MORE ATTENTION THAN WE'D LIKE.
AND WHAT ABOUT *HIM*? THE VIXIAN GENTLEMAN.
YOU EXPECT *HIM* TO COME *HERE*?
AHA HA. GOOD POINT.

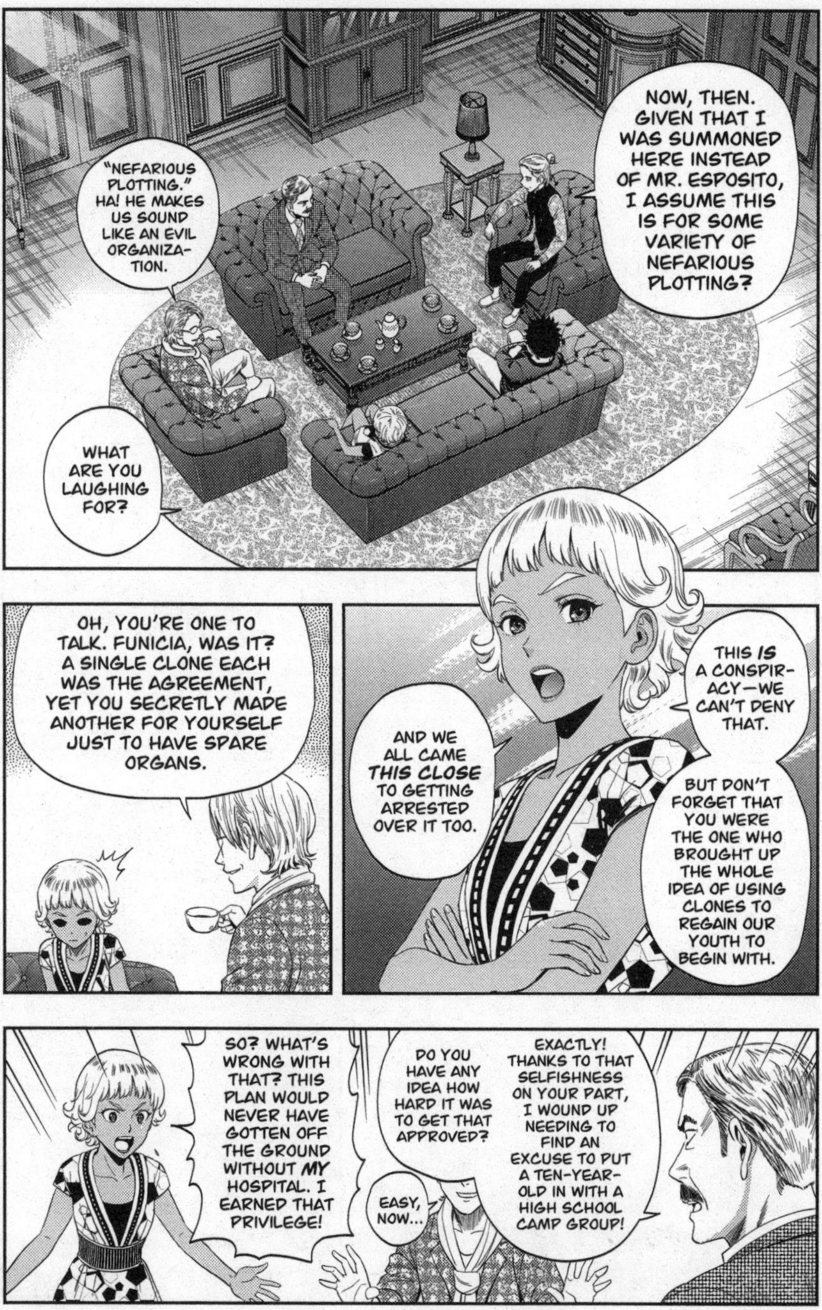
NOW, THEN. GIVEN THAT I WAS SUMMONED HERE INSTEAD OF MR. ESPOSITO, I ASSUME THIS IS FOR SOME VARIETY OF NEFARIOUS PLOTTING?
"NEFARIOUS PLOTTING." HA! HE MAKES US SOUND LIKE AN EVIL ORGANIZATION.
WHAT ARE YOU LAUGHING FOR?
THIS *IS* A CONSPIRACY—WE CAN'T DENY THAT.
BUT DON'T FORGET THAT YOU WERE THE ONE WHO BROUGHT UP THE WHOLE IDEA OF USING CLONES TO REGAIN OUR YOUTH TO BEGIN WITH.
AND WE ALL CAME ***THIS CLOSE*** TO GETTING ARRESTED OVER IT TOO.
OH, YOU'RE ONE TO TALK. FUNICIA, WAS IT? A SINGLE CLONE EACH WAS THE AGREEMENT, YET YOU SECRETLY MADE ANOTHER FOR YOURSELF JUST TO HAVE SPARE ORGANS.
EXACTLY! THANKS TO THAT SELFISHNESS ON YOUR PART, I WOUND UP NEEDING TO FIND AN EXCUSE TO PUT A TEN-YEAR-OLD IN WITH A HIGH SCHOOL CAMP GROUP!
DO YOU HAVE ANY IDEA HOW HARD IT WAS TO GET THAT APPROVED?
EASY, NOW...
SO? WHAT'S WRONG WITH THAT? THIS PLAN WOULD NEVER HAVE GOTTEN OFF THE GROUND WITHOUT *MY* HOSPITAL. I EARNED THAT PRIVILEGE!

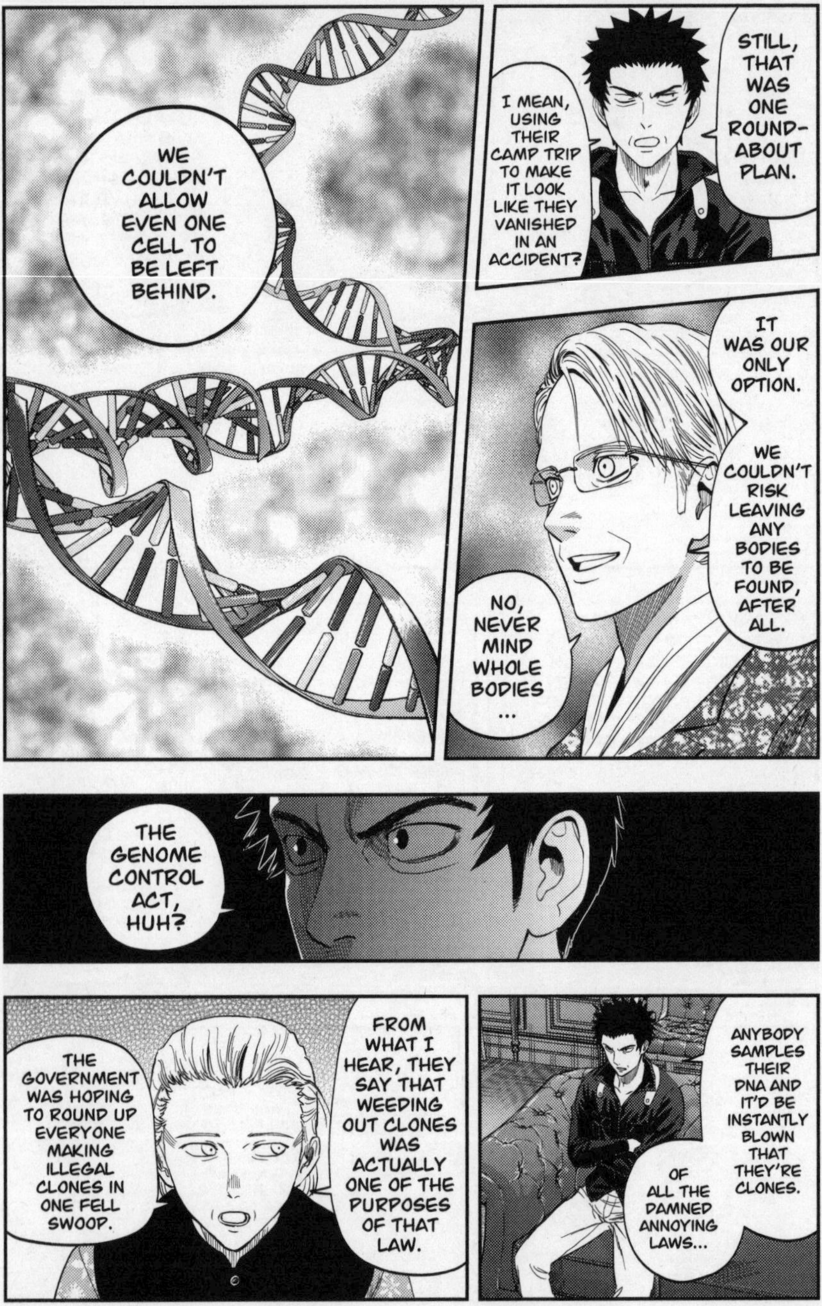
STILL, THAT WAS ONE ROUND-ABOUT PLAN.
I MEAN, USING THEIR CAMP TRIP TO MAKE IT LOOK LIKE THEY VANISHED IN AN ACCIDENT?
IT WAS OUR ONLY OPTION.
WE COULDN'T RISK LEAVING ANY BODIES TO BE FOUND, AFTER ALL.
NO, NEVER MIND WHOLE BODIES...
WE COULDN'T ALLOW EVEN ONE CELL TO BE LEFT BEHIND.
THE GENOME CONTROL ACT, HUH?
ANYBODY SAMPLES THEIR DNA AND IT'D BE INSTANTLY BLOWN THAT THEY'RE CLONES.
OF ALL THE DAMNED ANNOYING LAWS...
FROM WHAT I HEAR, THEY SAY THAT WEEDING OUT CLONES WAS ACTUALLY ONE OF THE PURPOSES OF THAT LAW.
THE GOVERNMENT WAS HOPING TO ROUND UP EVERYONE MAKING ILLEGAL CLONES IN ONE FELL SWOOP.

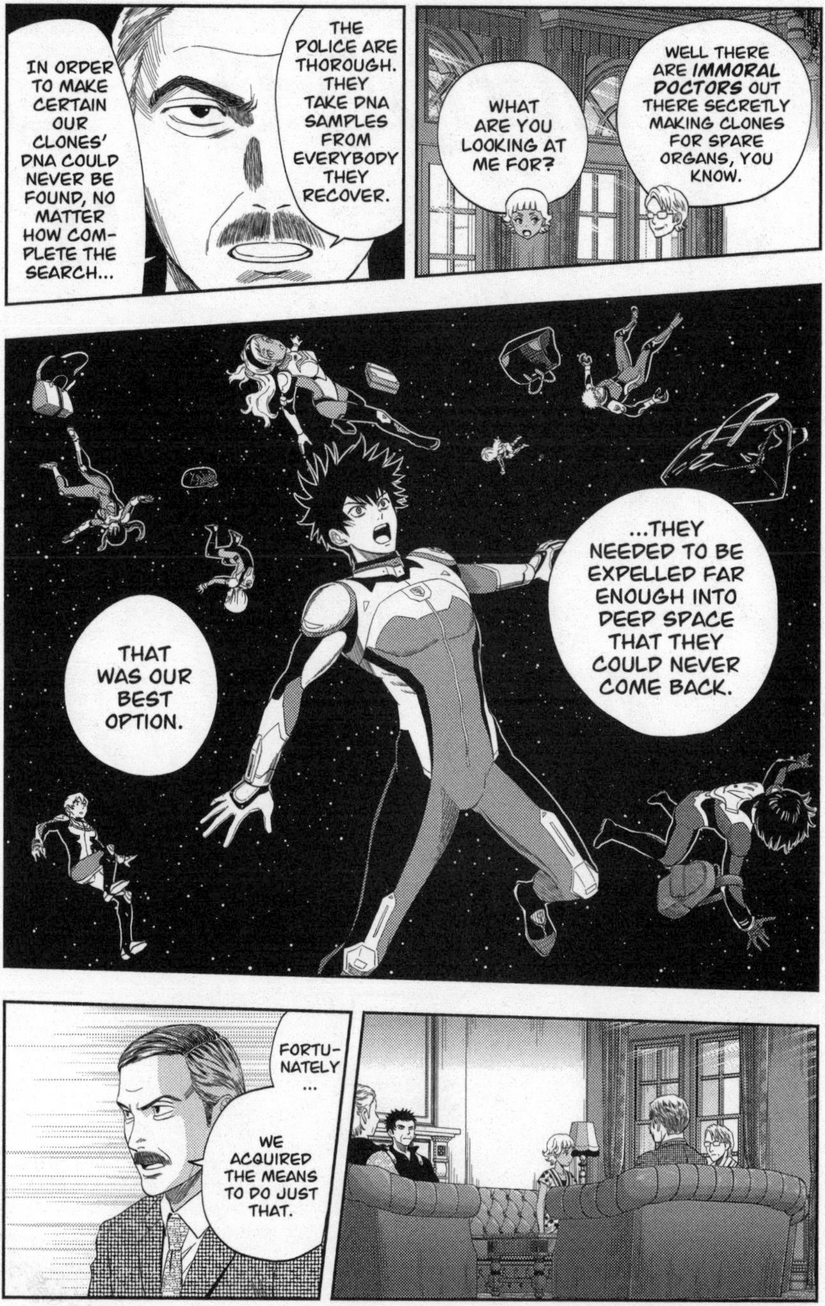
WELL THERE ARE IMMORAL DOCTORS OUT THERE SECRETLY MAKING CLONES FOR SPARE ORGANS, YOU KNOW.
WHAT ARE YOU LOOKING AT ME FOR?
THE POLICE ARE THOROUGH. THEY TAKE DNA SAMPLES FROM EVERYBODY THEY RECOVER.
IN ORDER TO MAKE CERTAIN OUR CLONES' DNA COULD NEVER BE FOUND, NO MATTER HOW COMPLETE THE SEARCH...
...THEY NEEDED TO BE EXPELLED FAR ENOUGH INTO DEEP SPACE THAT THEY COULD NEVER COME BACK.
THAT WAS OUR BEST OPTION.
FORTUNATELY...
WE ACQUIRED THE MEANS TO DO JUST THAT.

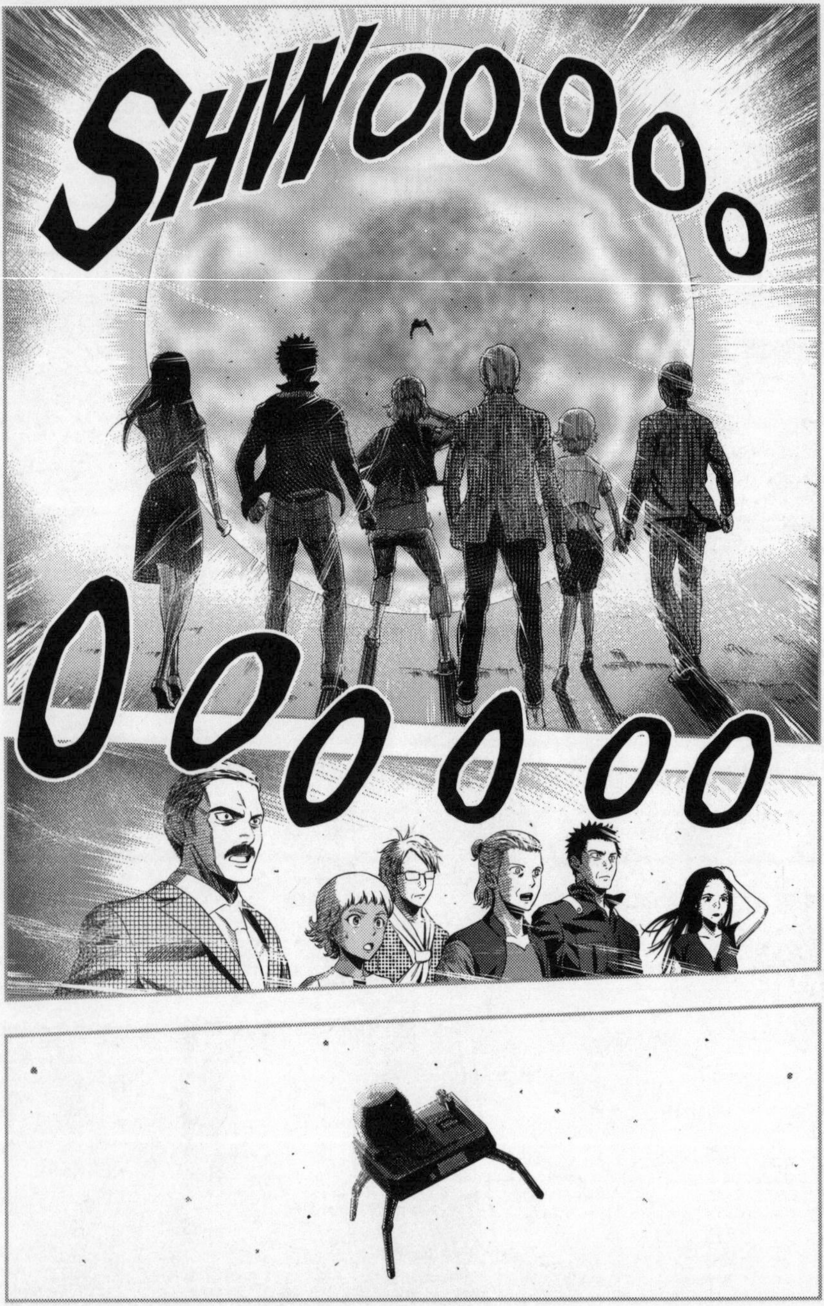

SHWOOOOOO
OOOOOOO

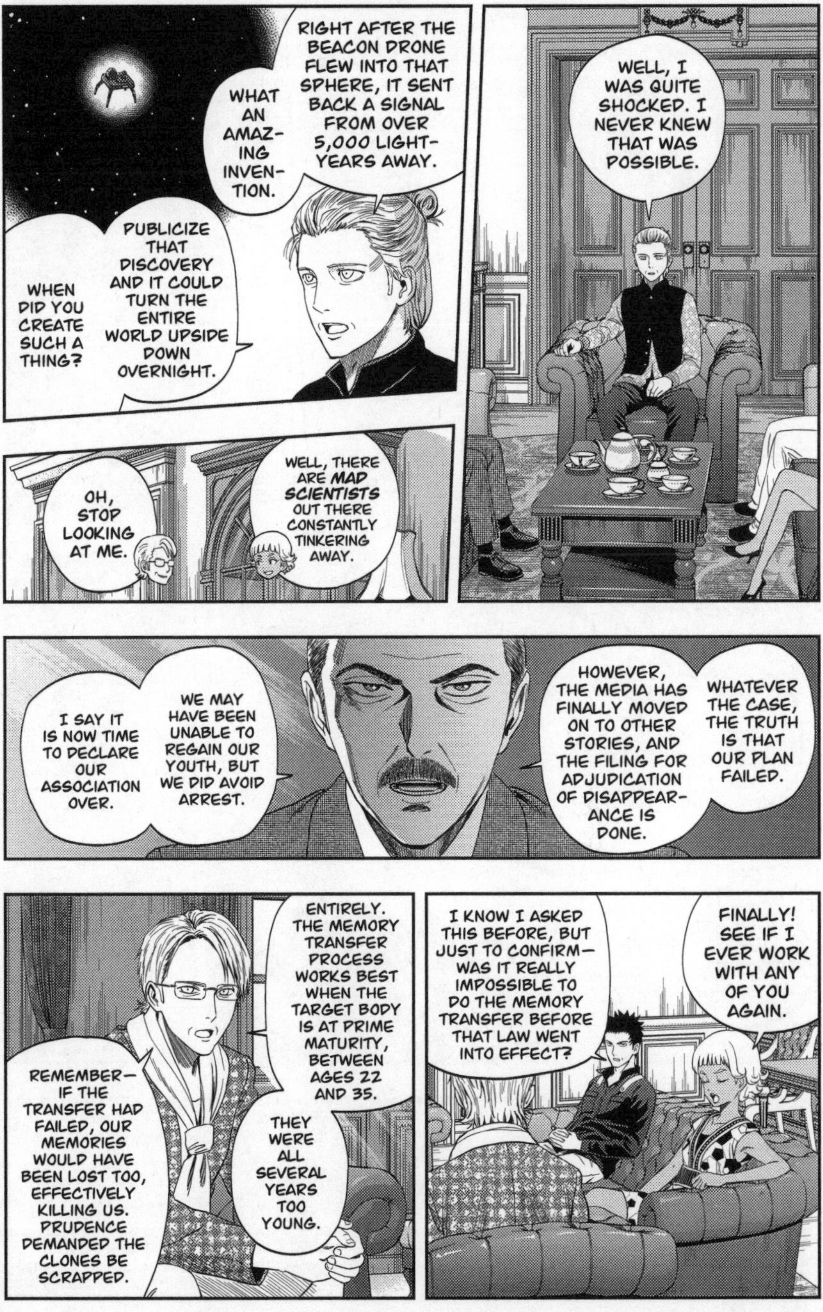
WELL, I WAS QUITE SHOCKED. I NEVER KNEW THAT WAS POSSIBLE.
RIGHT AFTER THE BEACON DRONE FLEW INTO THAT SPHERE, IT SENT BACK A SIGNAL FROM OVER 5,000 LIGHT-YEARS AWAY.
WHAT AN AMAZ-ING INVEN-TION.
PUBLICIZE THAT DISCOVERY AND IT COULD TURN THE ENTIRE WORLD UPSIDE DOWN OVERNIGHT.
WHEN DID YOU CREATE SUCH A THING?
WELL, THERE ARE ***MAD SCIENTISTS*** OUT THERE CONSTANTLY TINKERING AWAY.
OH, STOP LOOKING AT ME.
WHATEVER THE CASE, THE TRUTH IS THAT OUR PLAN FAILED.
HOWEVER, THE MEDIA HAS FINALLY MOVED ON TO OTHER STORIES, AND THE FILING FOR ADJUDICATION OF DISAPPEAR-ANCE IS DONE.
WE MAY HAVE BEEN UNABLE TO REGAIN OUR YOUTH, BUT WE DID AVOID ARREST.
I SAY IT IS NOW TIME TO DECLARE OUR ASSOCIATION OVER.
FINALLY! SEE IF I EVER WORK WITH ANY OF YOU AGAIN.
I KNOW I ASKED THIS BEFORE, BUT JUST TO CONFIRM—WAS IT REALLY IMPOSSIBLE TO DO THE MEMORY TRANSFER BEFORE THAT LAW WENT INTO EFFECT?
ENTIRELY. THE MEMORY TRANSFER PROCESS WORKS BEST WHEN THE TARGET BODY IS AT PRIME MATURITY, BETWEEN AGES 22 AND 35.
THEY WERE ALL SEVERAL YEARS TOO YOUNG.
REMEMBER—IF THE TRANSFER HAD FAILED, OUR MEMORIES WOULD HAVE BEEN LOST TOO, EFFECTIVELY KILLING US. PRUDENCE DEMANDED THE CLONES BE SCRAPPED.

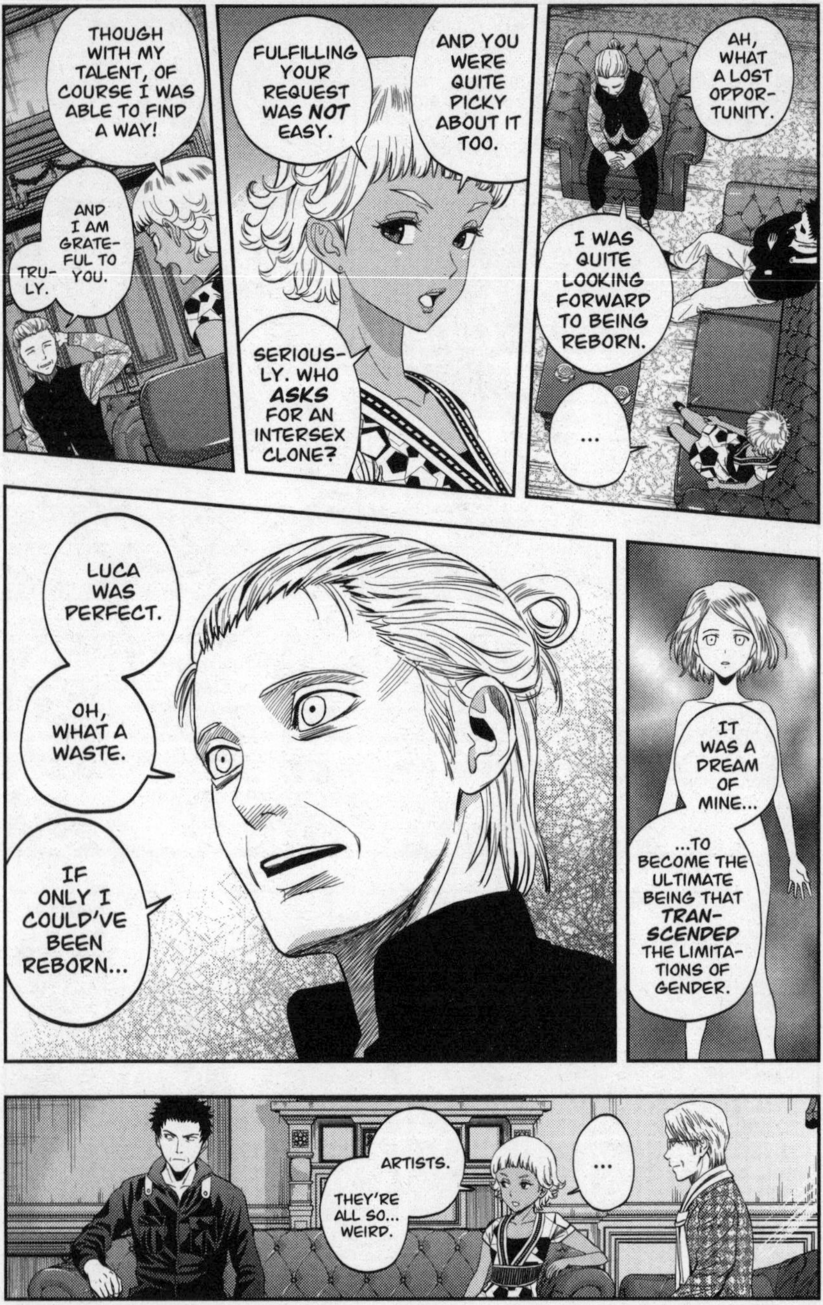
AH, WHAT A LOST OPPOR-TUNITY.
I WAS QUITE LOOKING FORWARD TO BEING REBORN.
...
AND YOU WERE QUITE PICKY ABOUT IT TOO.
FULFILLING YOUR REQUEST WAS **NOT** EASY.
SERIOUS-LY. WHO **ASKS** FOR AN INTERSEX CLONE?
THOUGH WITH MY TALENT, OF COURSE I WAS ABLE TO FIND A WAY!
AND I AM GRATE-FUL TO YOU.
TRU-LY.
IT WAS A DREAM OF MINE...
...TO BECOME THE ULTIMATE BEING THAT ***TRAN-SCENDED*** THE LIMITA-TIONS OF GENDER.
LUCA WAS PERFECT.
OH, WHAT A WASTE.
IF ONLY I COULD'VE BEEN REBORN...
...
ARTISTS.
THEY'RE ALL SO... WEIRD.

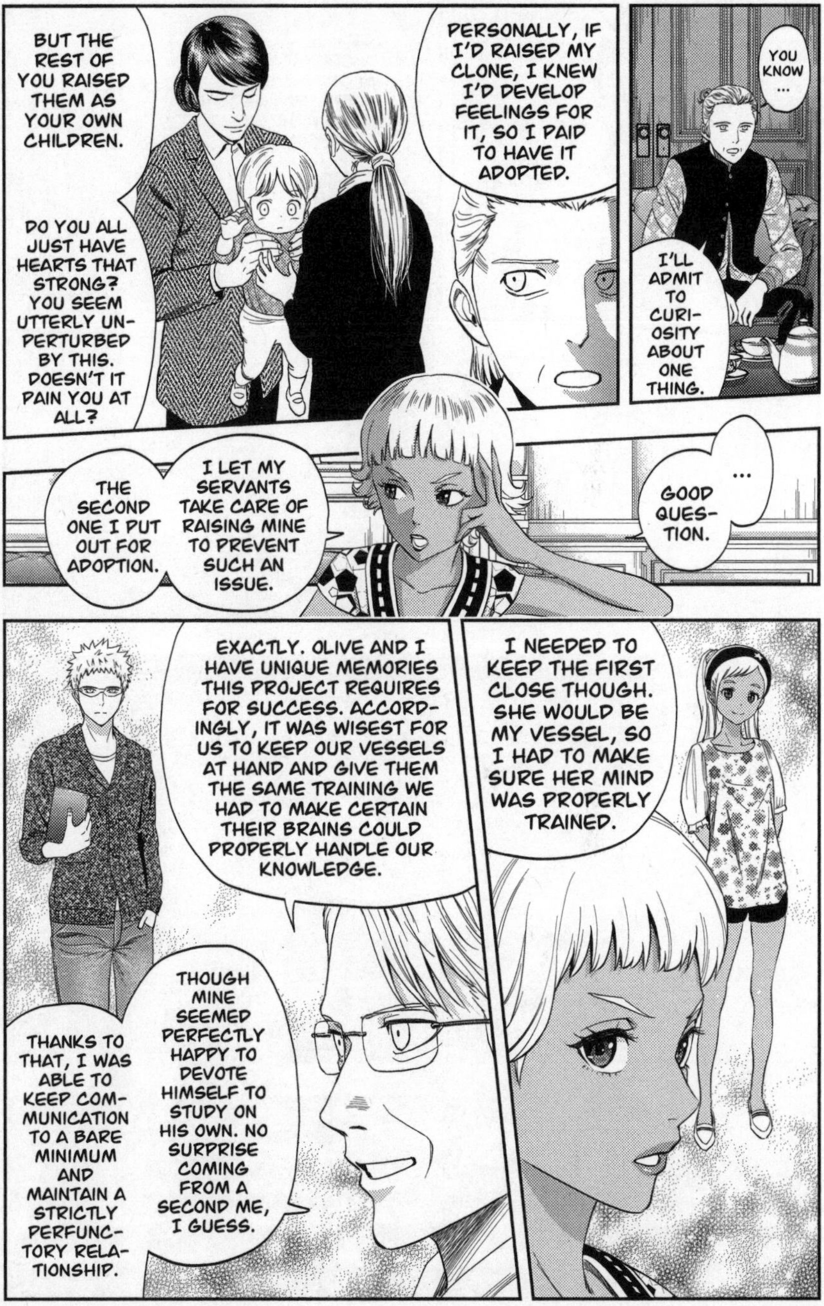
YOU KNOW ...
I'LL ADMIT TO CURIOSITY ABOUT ONE THING.
PERSONALLY, IF I'D RAISED MY CLONE, I KNEW I'D DEVELOP FEELINGS FOR IT, SO I PAID TO HAVE IT ADOPTED.
BUT THE REST OF YOU RAISED THEM AS YOUR OWN CHILDREN.
DO YOU ALL JUST HAVE HEARTS THAT STRONG? YOU SEEM UTTERLY UNPERTURBED BY THIS. DOESN'T IT PAIN YOU AT ALL?
... GOOD QUESTION.
I LET MY SERVANTS TAKE CARE OF RAISING MINE TO PREVENT SUCH AN ISSUE.
THE SECOND ONE I PUT OUT FOR ADOPTION.
I NEEDED TO KEEP THE FIRST CLOSE THOUGH. SHE WOULD BE MY VESSEL, SO I HAD TO MAKE SURE HER MIND WAS PROPERLY TRAINED.
EXACTLY. OLIVE AND I HAVE UNIQUE MEMORIES THIS PROJECT REQUIRES FOR SUCCESS. ACCORDINGLY, IT WAS WISEST FOR US TO KEEP OUR VESSELS AT HAND AND GIVE THEM THE SAME TRAINING WE HAD TO MAKE CERTAIN THEIR BRAINS COULD PROPERLY HANDLE OUR KNOWLEDGE.
THOUGH MINE SEEMED PERFECTLY HAPPY TO DEVOTE HIMSELF TO STUDY ON HIS OWN. NO SURPRISE COMING FROM A SECOND ME, I GUESS.
THANKS TO THAT, I WAS ABLE TO KEEP COMMUNICATION TO A BARE MINIMUM AND MAINTAIN A STRICTLY PERFUNCTORY RELATIONSHIP.

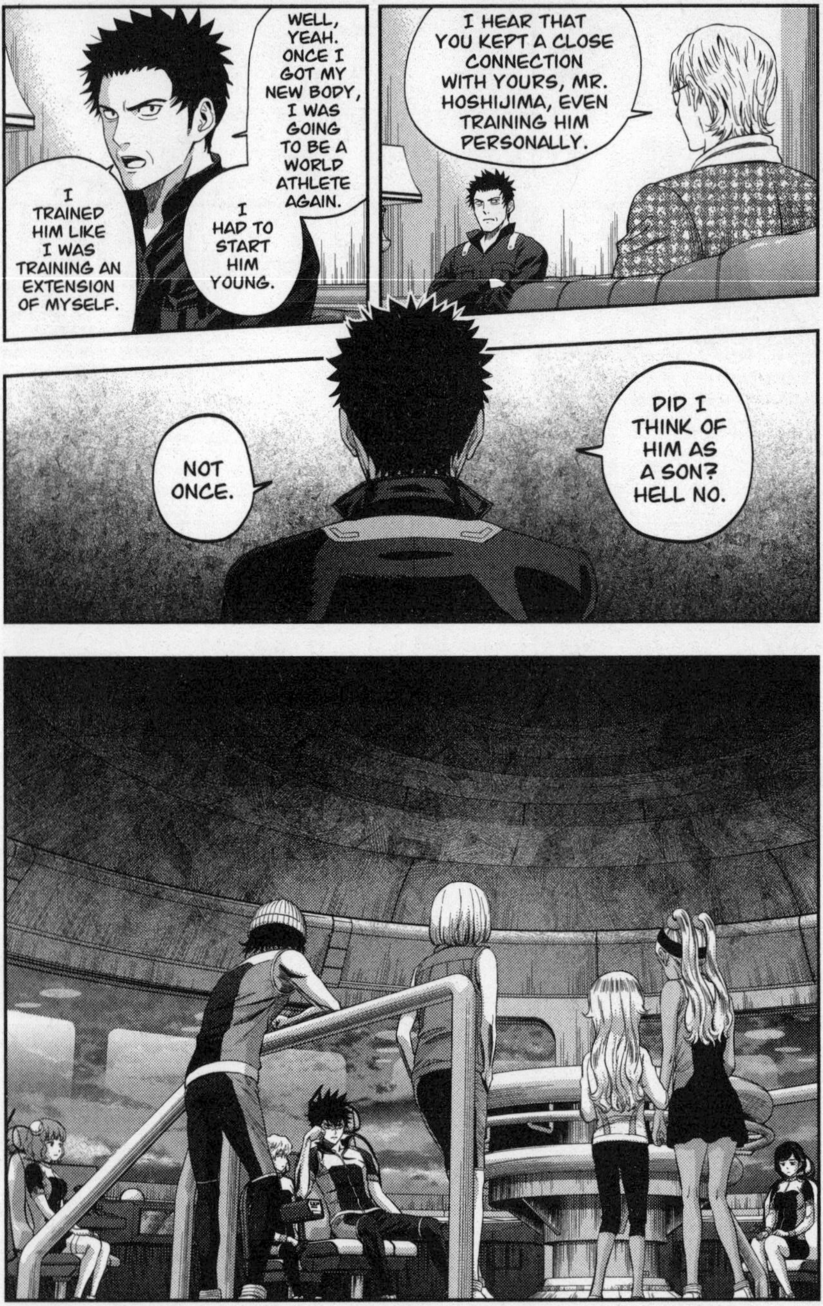
I HEAR THAT YOU KEPT A CLOSE CONNECTION WITH YOURS, MR. HOSHIJIMA, EVEN TRAINING HIM PERSONALLY.
WELL, YEAH. ONCE I GOT MY NEW BODY, I WAS GOING TO BE A WORLD ATHLETE AGAIN.
I HAD TO START HIM YOUNG.
I TRAINED HIM LIKE I WAS TRAINING AN EXTENSION OF MYSELF.
DID I THINK OF HIM AS A SON? HELL NO.
NOT ONCE.

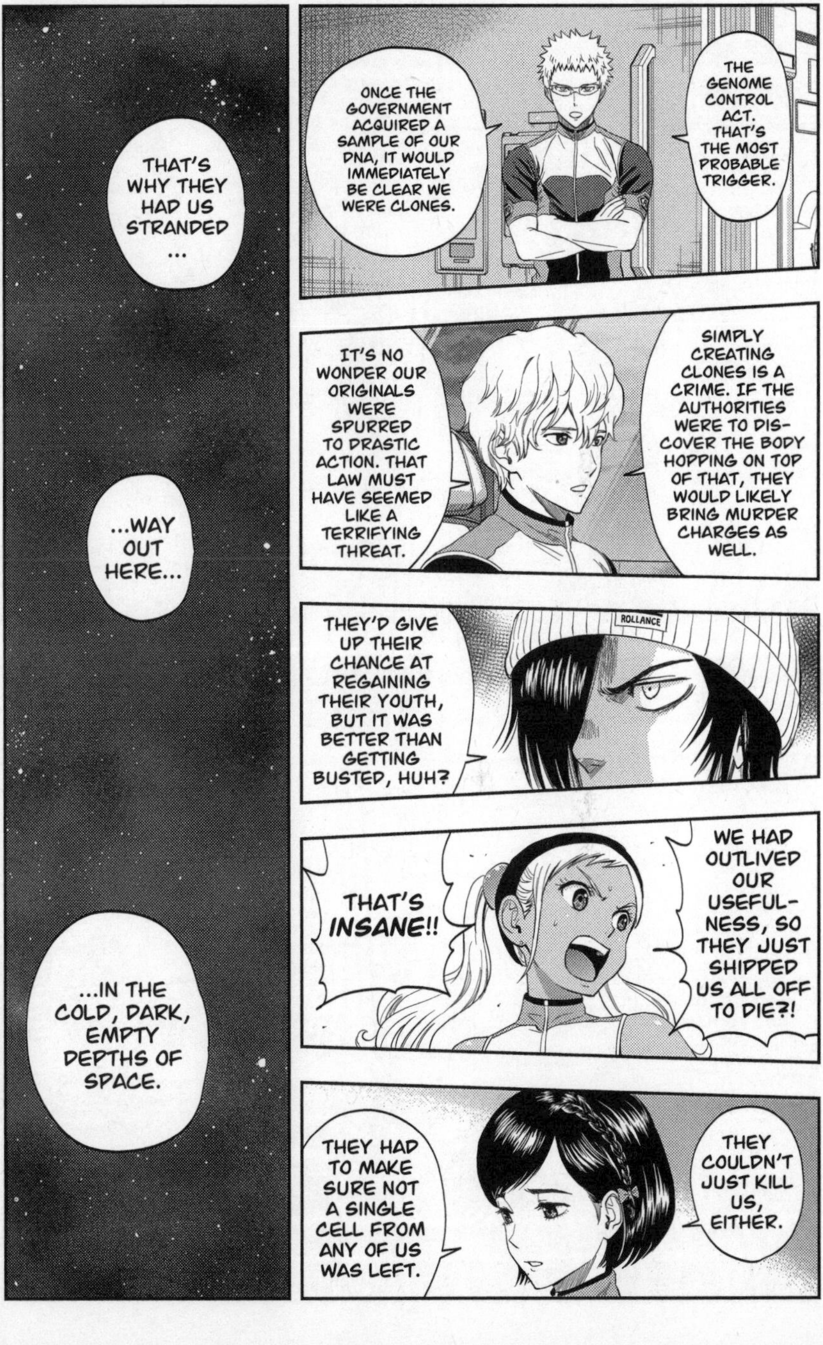
THE GENOME CONTROL ACT. THAT'S THE MOST PROBABLE TRIGGER.
ONCE THE GOVERNMENT ACQUIRED A SAMPLE OF OUR DNA, IT WOULD IMMEDIATELY BE CLEAR WE WERE CLONES.
SIMPLY CREATING CLONES IS A CRIME. IF THE AUTHORITIES WERE TO DIS-COVER THE BODY HOPPING ON TOP OF THAT, THEY WOULD LIKELY BRING MURDER CHARGES AS WELL.
IT'S NO WONDER OUR ORIGINALS WERE SPURRED TO DRASTIC ACTION. THAT LAW MUST HAVE SEEMED LIKE A TERRIFYING THREAT.
ROLLANCE
THEY'D GIVE UP THEIR CHANCE AT REGAINING THEIR YOUTH, BUT IT WAS BETTER THAN GETTING BUSTED, HUH?
WE HAD OUTLIVED OUR USEFUL-NESS, SO THEY JUST SHIPPED US ALL OFF TO DIE?!
THAT'S ***INSANE***!!
THEY COULDN'T JUST KILL US, EITHER.
THEY HAD TO MAKE SURE NOT A SINGLE CELL FROM ANY OF US WAS LEFT.
THAT'S WHY THEY HAD US STRANDED...
...WAY OUT HERE...
...IN THE COLD, DARK, EMPTY DEPTHS OF SPACE.

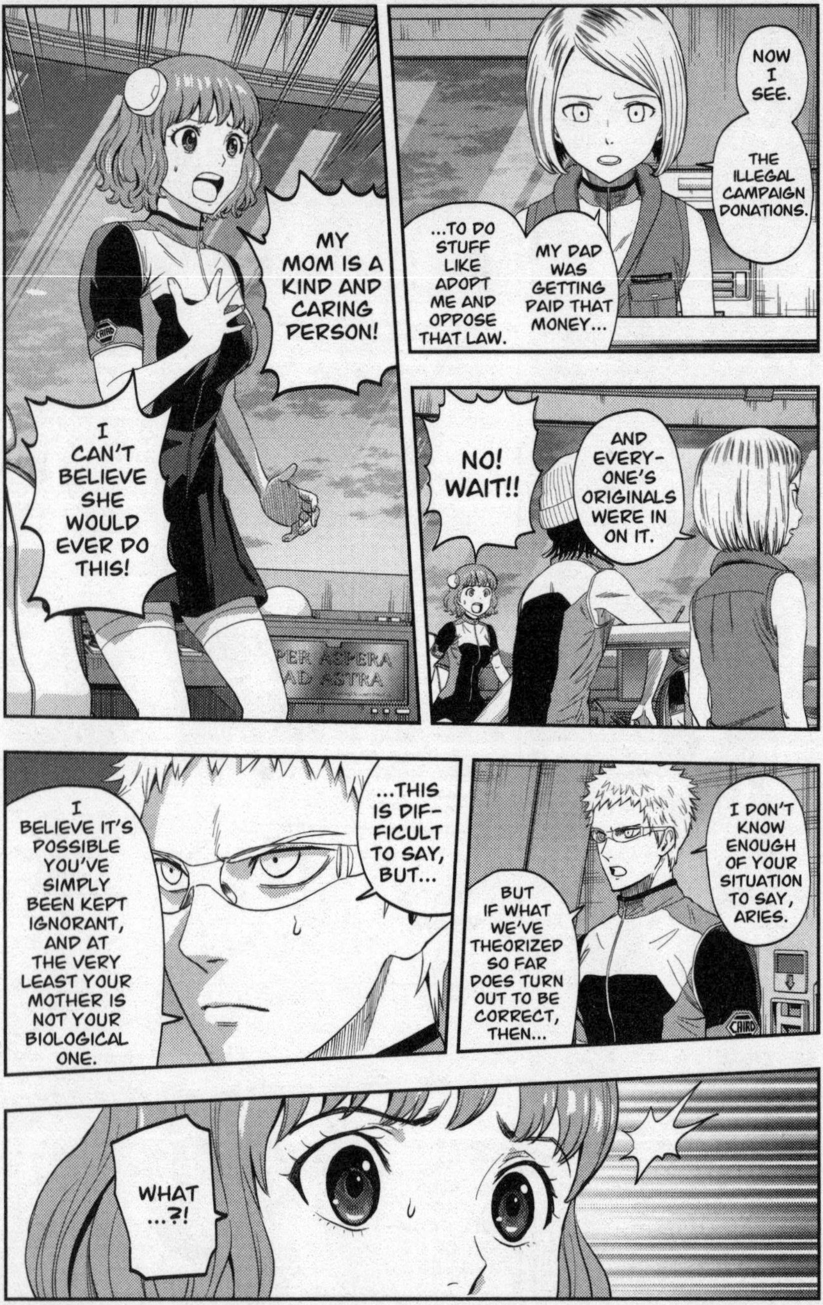
NOW I SEE.
THE ILLEGAL CAMPAIGN DONATIONS.
MY DAD WAS GETTING PAID THAT MONEY...
...TO DO STUFF LIKE ADOPT ME AND OPPOSE THAT LAW.
AND EVERY-ONE'S ORIGINALS WERE IN ON IT.
NO! WAIT!!
MY MOM IS A KIND AND CARING PERSON!
I CAN'T BELIEVE SHE WOULD EVER DO THIS!
PER ASPERA AD ASTRA
I DON'T KNOW ENOUGH OF YOUR SITUATION TO SAY, ARIES.
BUT IF WHAT WE'VE THEORIZED SO FAR DOES TURN OUT TO BE CORRECT, THEN...
...THIS IS DIF-FICULT TO SAY, BUT...
I BELIEVE IT'S POSSIBLE YOU'VE SIMPLY BEEN KEPT IGNORANT, AND AT THE VERY LEAST YOUR MOTHER IS NOT YOUR BIOLOGICAL ONE.
WHAT ...?!

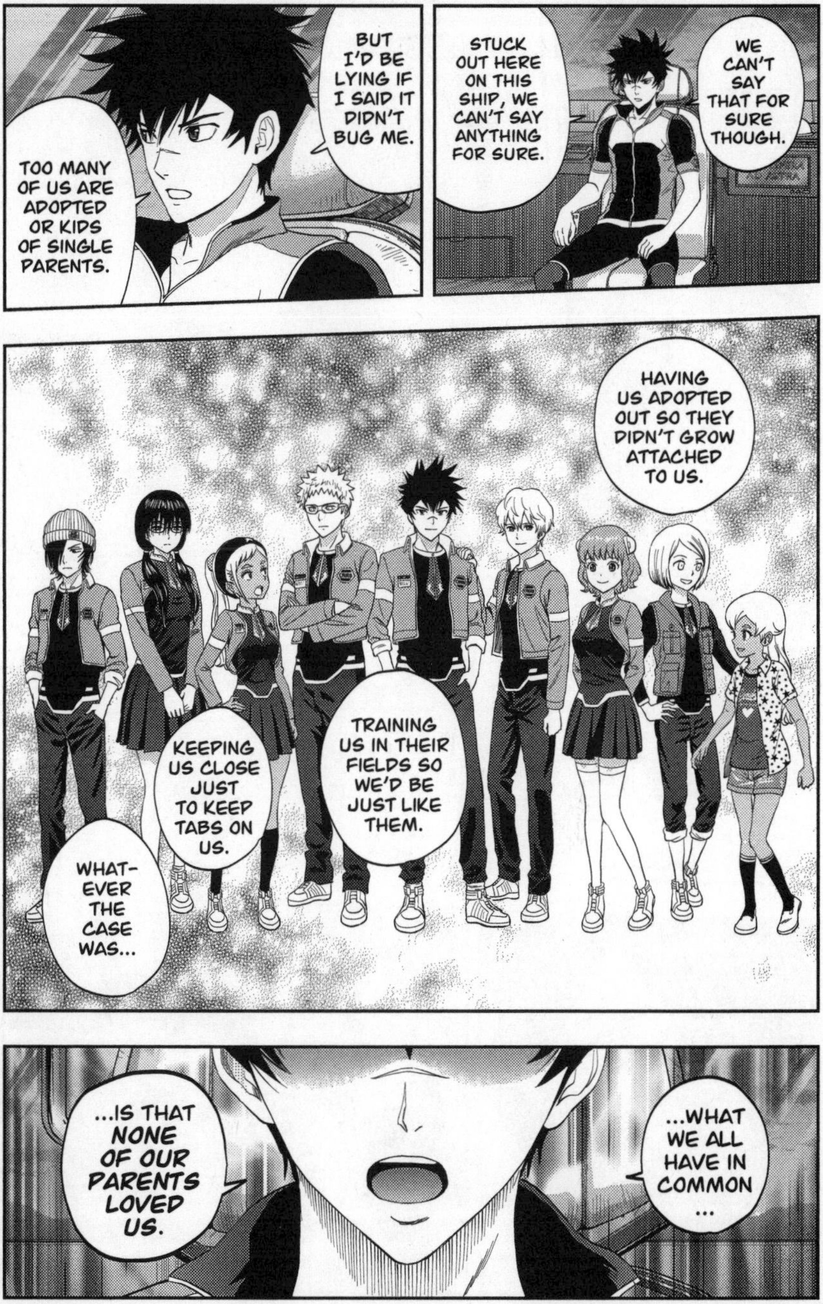
WE CAN'T SAY THAT FOR SURE THOUGH.
STUCK OUT HERE ON THIS SHIP, WE CAN'T SAY ANYTHING FOR SURE.
BUT I'D BE LYING IF I SAID IT DIDN'T BUG ME.
TOO MANY OF US ARE ADOPTED OR KIDS OF SINGLE PARENTS.
HAVING US ADOPTED OUT SO THEY DIDN'T GROW ATTACHED TO US.
TRAINING US IN THEIR FIELDS SO WE'D BE JUST LIKE THEM.
KEEPING US CLOSE JUST TO KEEP TABS ON US.
WHAT-EVER THE CASE WAS...
...WHAT WE ALL HAVE IN COMMON ...
...IS THAT NONE OF OUR PARENTS LOVED US.

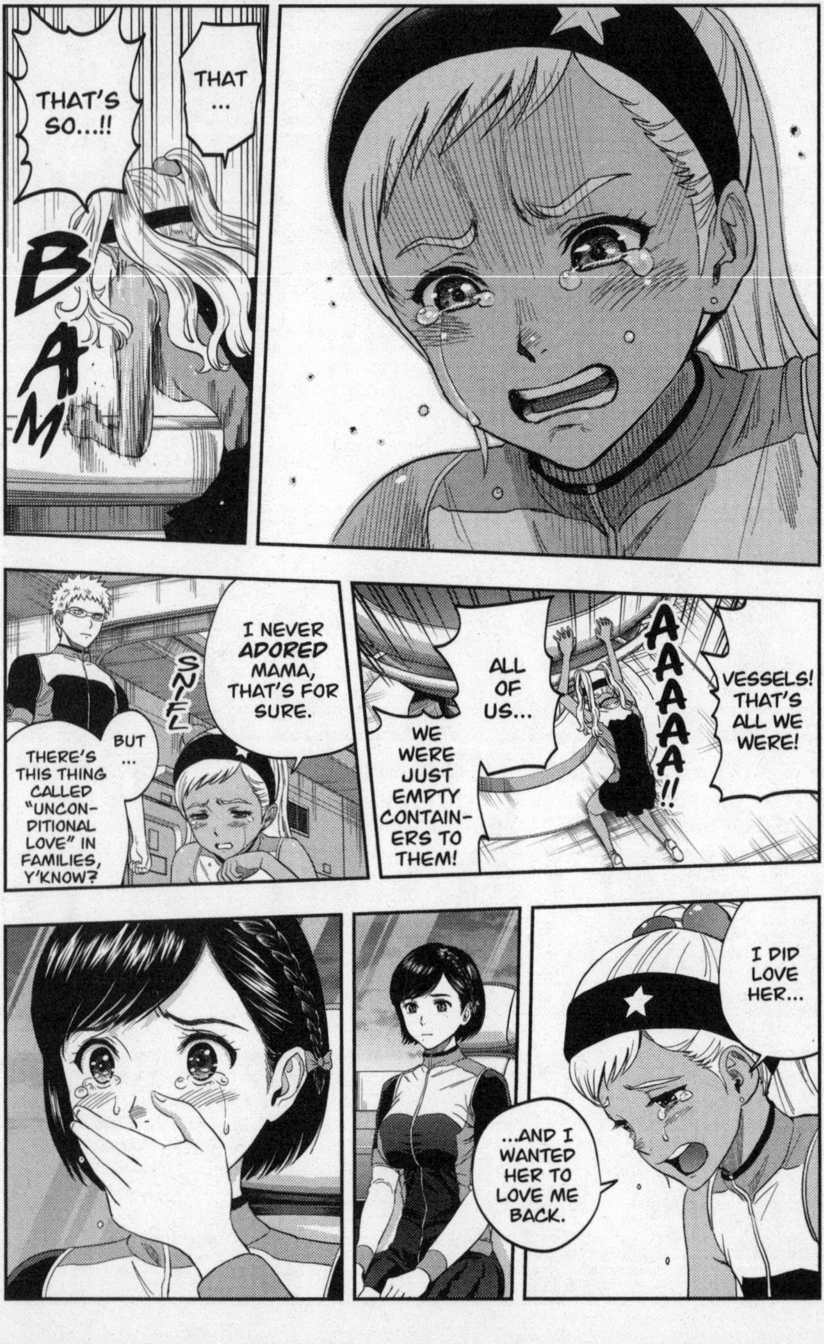
THAT ...
THAT'S SO...!!
BAM
VESSELS! THAT'S ALL WE WERE!
AAAAA!!
ALL OF US...
WE WERE JUST EMPTY CONTAINERS TO THEM!
I NEVER ADORED MAMA, THAT'S FOR SURE.
SNIFL
BUT ...
THERE'S THIS THING CALLED "UNCONDITIONAL LOVE" IN FAMILIES, Y'KNOW?
I DID LOVE HER...
...AND I WANTED HER TO LOVE ME BACK.

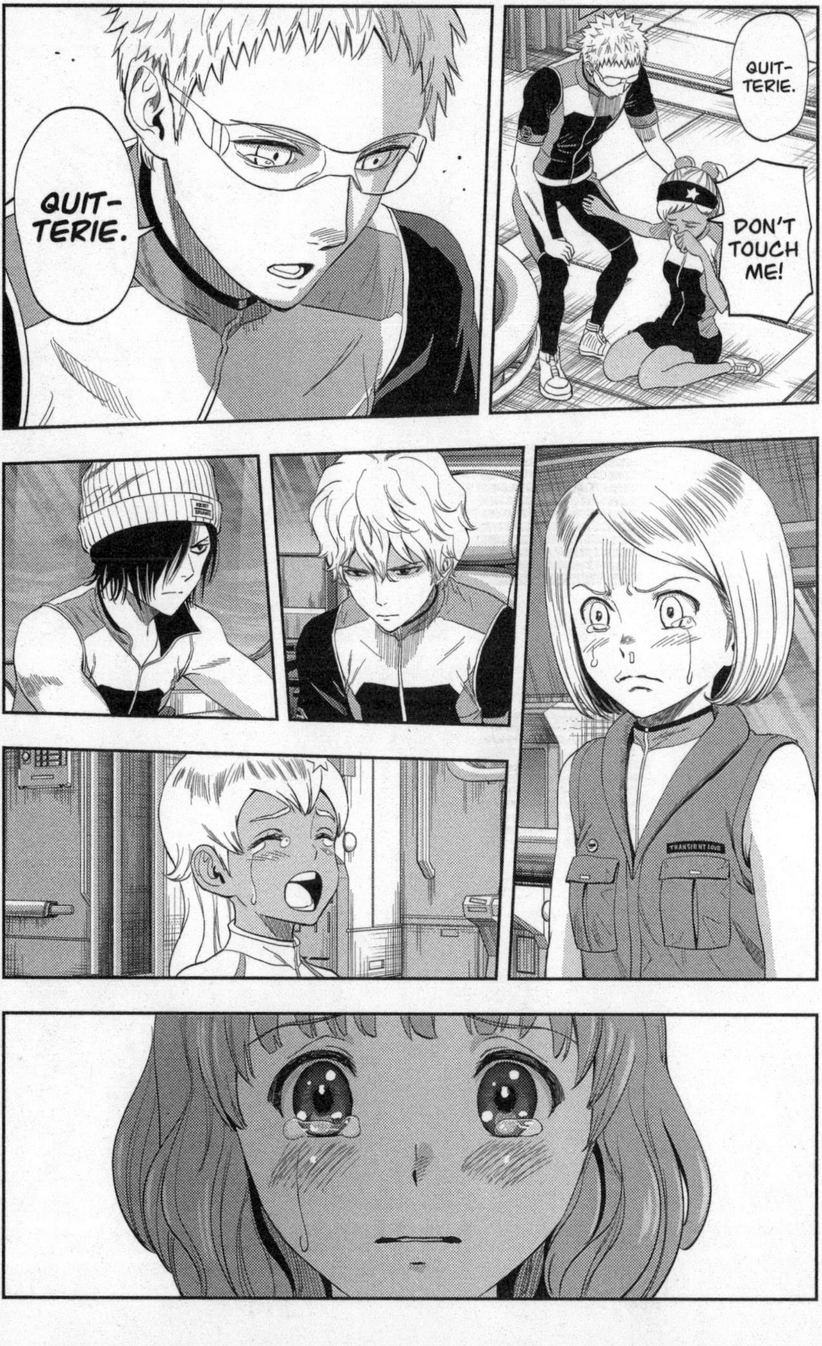
QUIT-TERIE.
DON'T TOUCH ME!
QUIT-TERIE.

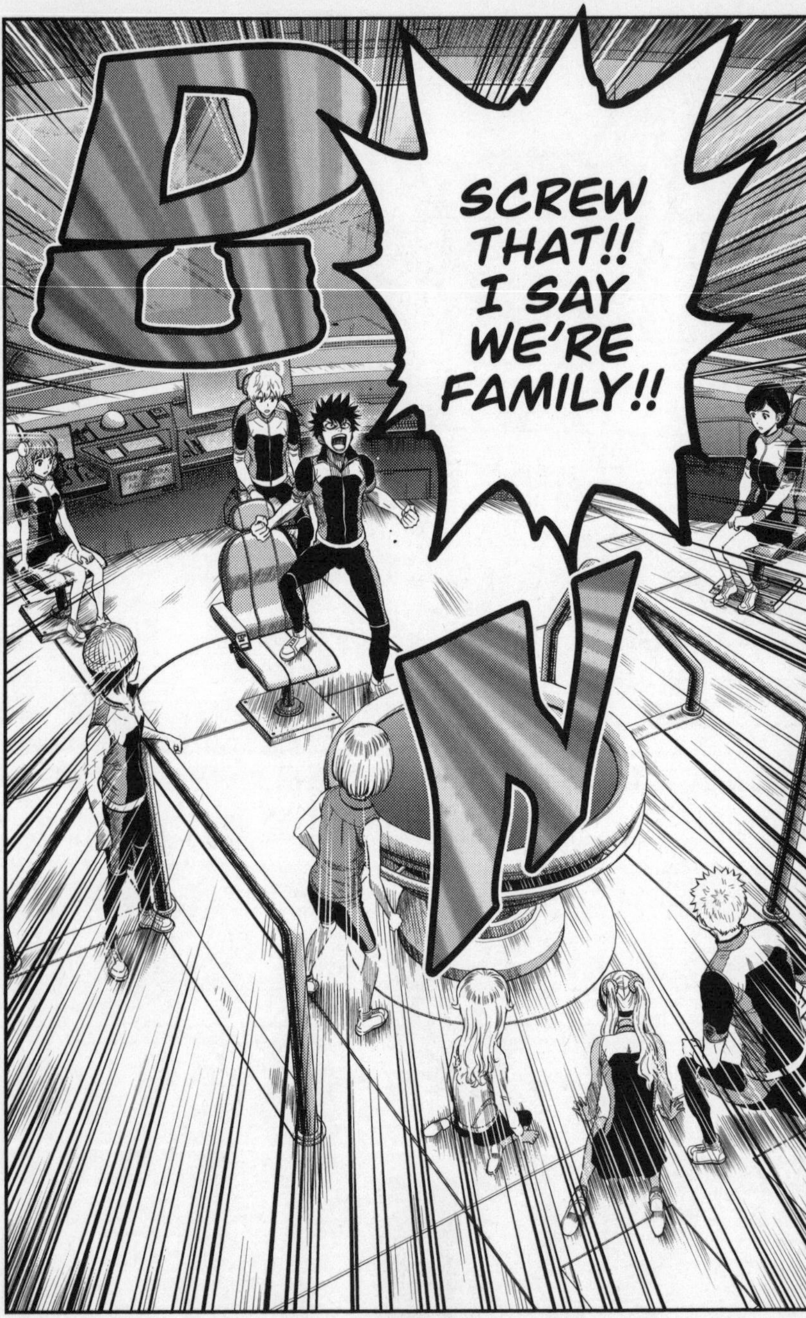
SCREW THAT!! I SAY WE'RE FAMILY!!

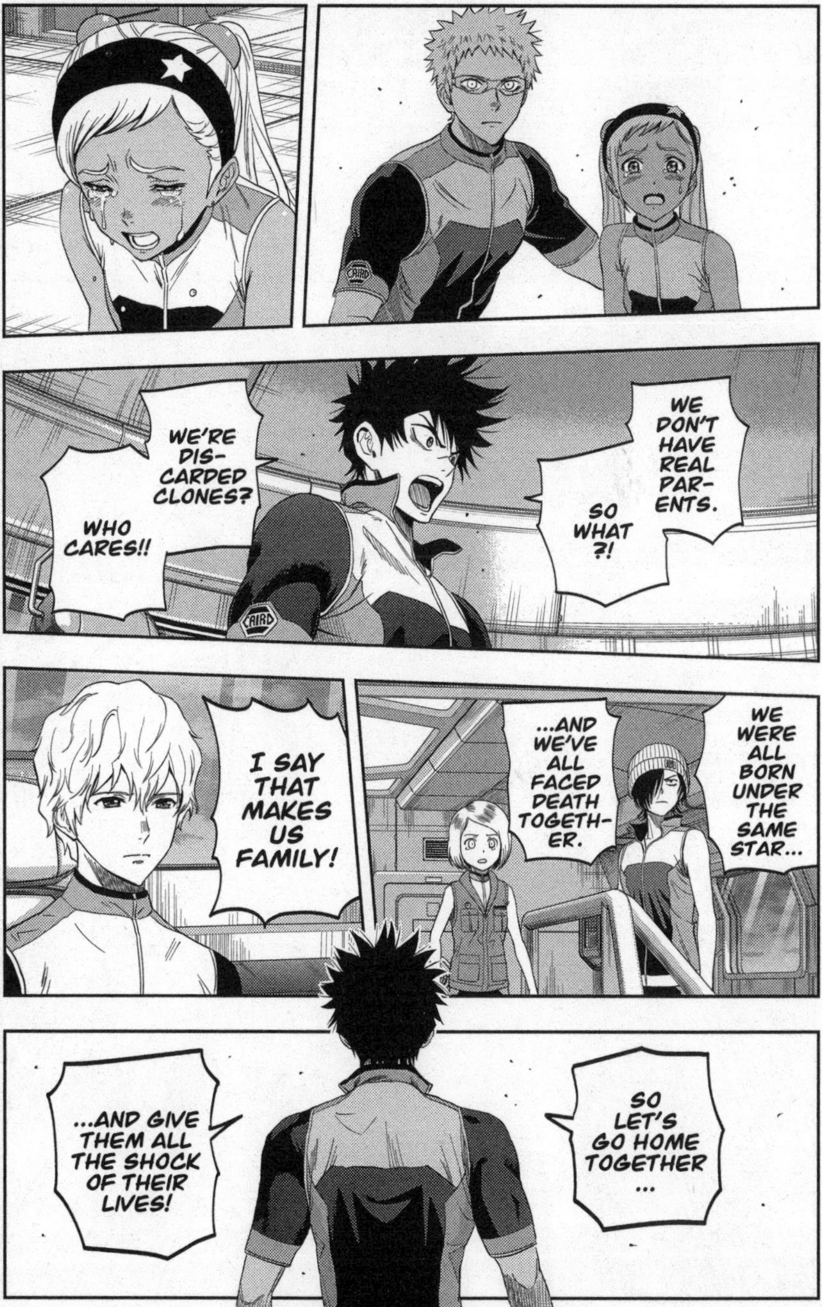
WE DON'T HAVE REAL PAR-ENTS.
SO WHAT ?!
WE'RE DIS-CARDED CLONES?
WHO CARES!!
WE WERE ALL BORN UNDER THE SAME STAR...
...AND WE'VE ALL FACED DEATH TOGETH-ER.
I SAY THAT MAKES US FAMILY!
SO LET'S GO HOME TOGETHER ...
...AND GIVE THEM ALL THE SHOCK OF THEIR LIVES!

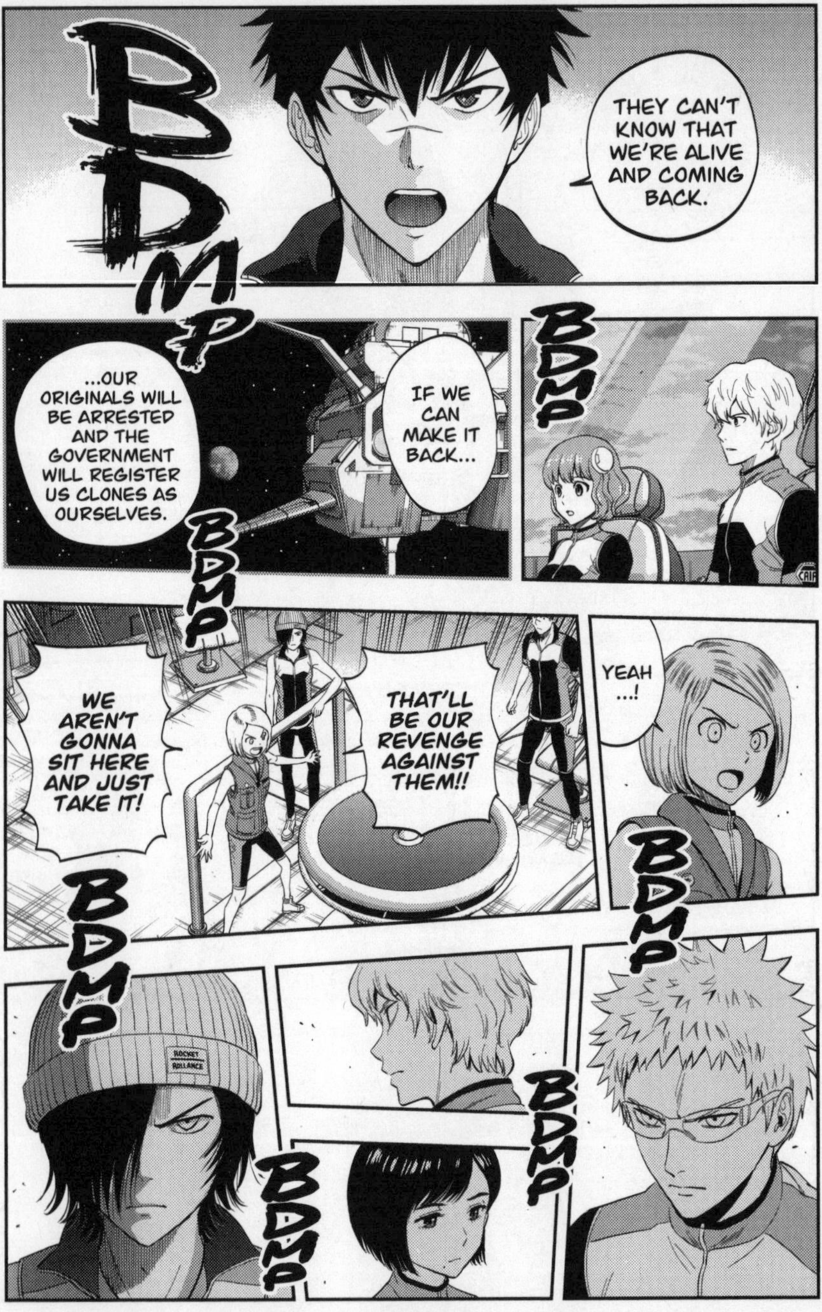
THEY CAN'T KNOW THAT WE'RE ALIVE AND COMING BACK.
BDMP
BDMP
IF WE CAN MAKE IT BACK...
...OUR ORIGINALS WILL BE ARRESTED AND THE GOVERNMENT WILL REGISTER US CLONES AS OURSELVES.
BDMP
YEAH ...!
BDMP
THAT'LL BE OUR REVENGE AGAINST THEM!!
WE AREN'T GONNA SIT HERE AND JUST TAKE IT!
BDMP
BDMP
BDMP

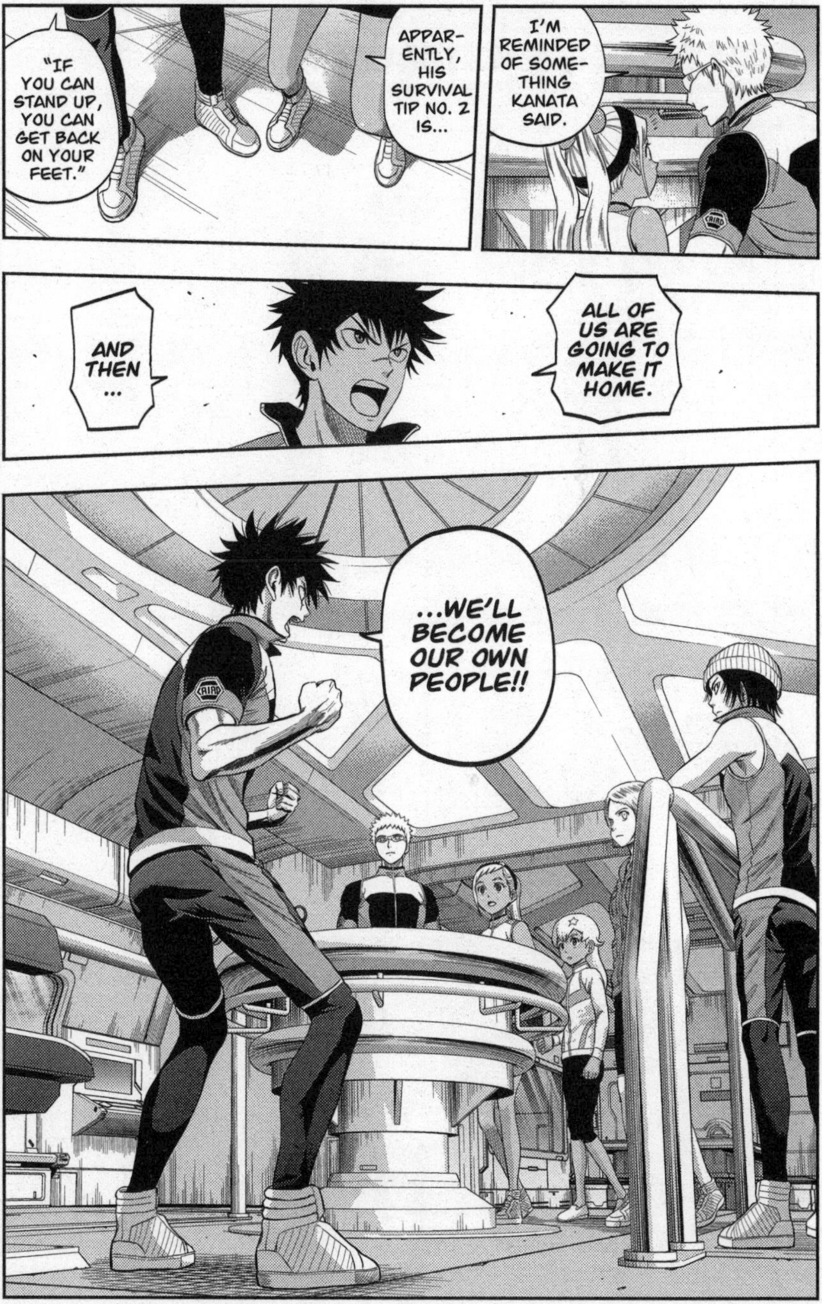
I'M REMINDED OF SOMETHING KANATA SAID.
APPARENTLY, HIS SURVIVAL TIP NO. 2 IS...
"IF YOU CAN STAND UP, YOU CAN GET BACK ON YOUR FEET."
ALL OF US ARE GOING TO MAKE IT HOME.
AND THEN...
...WE'LL BECOME OUR OWN PEOPLE!!

Material Collection

CRYOSTASIS POD

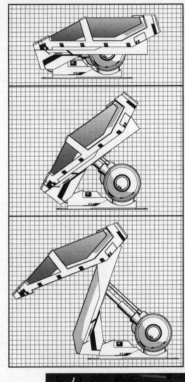

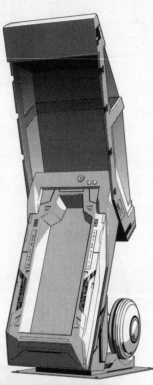

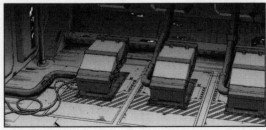

ASTRA
LOST IN SPACE
#35

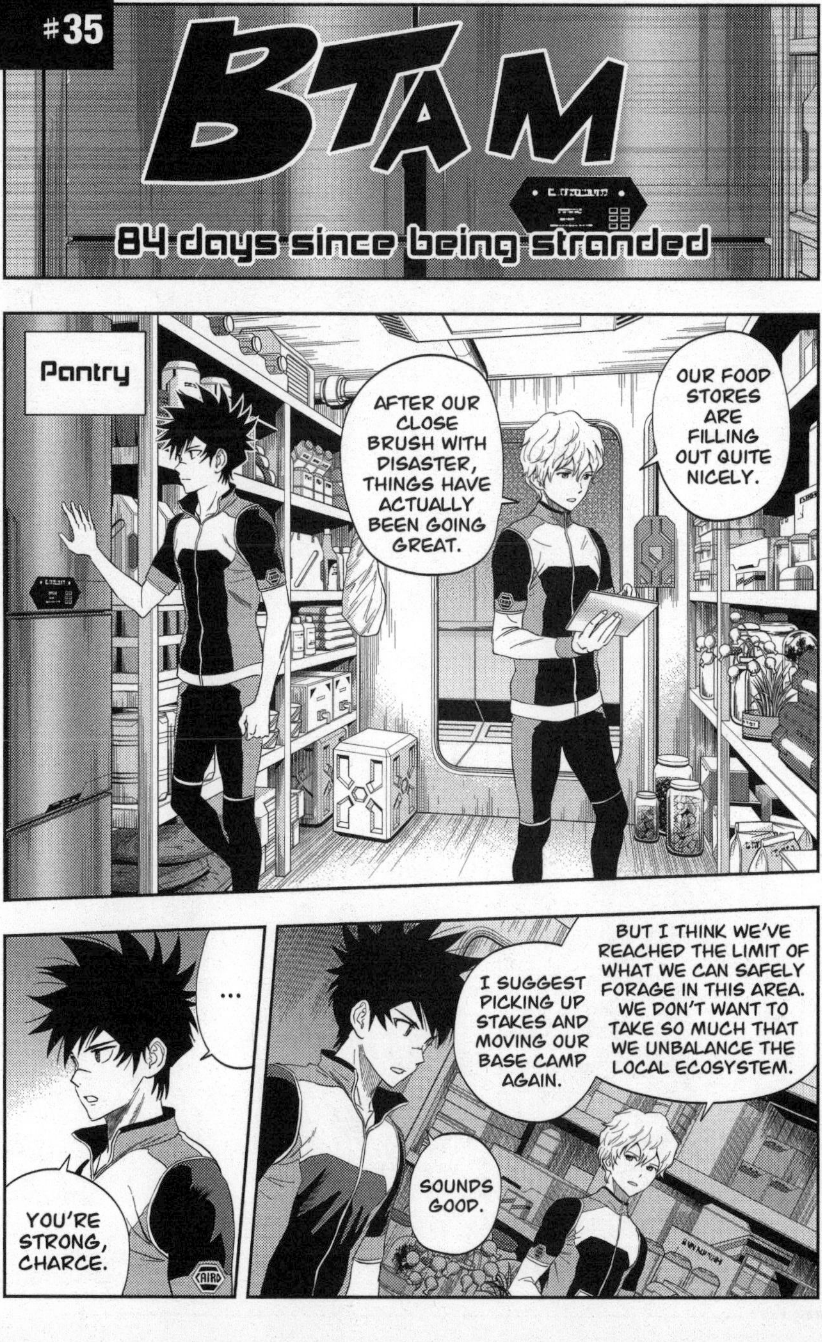
BTAM
84 days since being stranded
OUR FOOD STORES ARE FILLING OUT QUITE NICELY.
AFTER OUR CLOSE BRUSH WITH DISASTER, THINGS HAVE ACTUALLY BEEN GOING GREAT.
Pantry
BUT I THINK WE'VE REACHED THE LIMIT OF WHAT WE CAN SAFELY FORAGE IN THIS AREA. WE DON'T WANT TO TAKE SO MUCH THAT WE UNBALANCE THE LOCAL ECOSYSTEM.
I SUGGEST PICKING UP STAKES AND MOVING OUR BASE CAMP AGAIN.
SOUNDS GOOD.
...
YOU'RE STRONG, CHARCE.

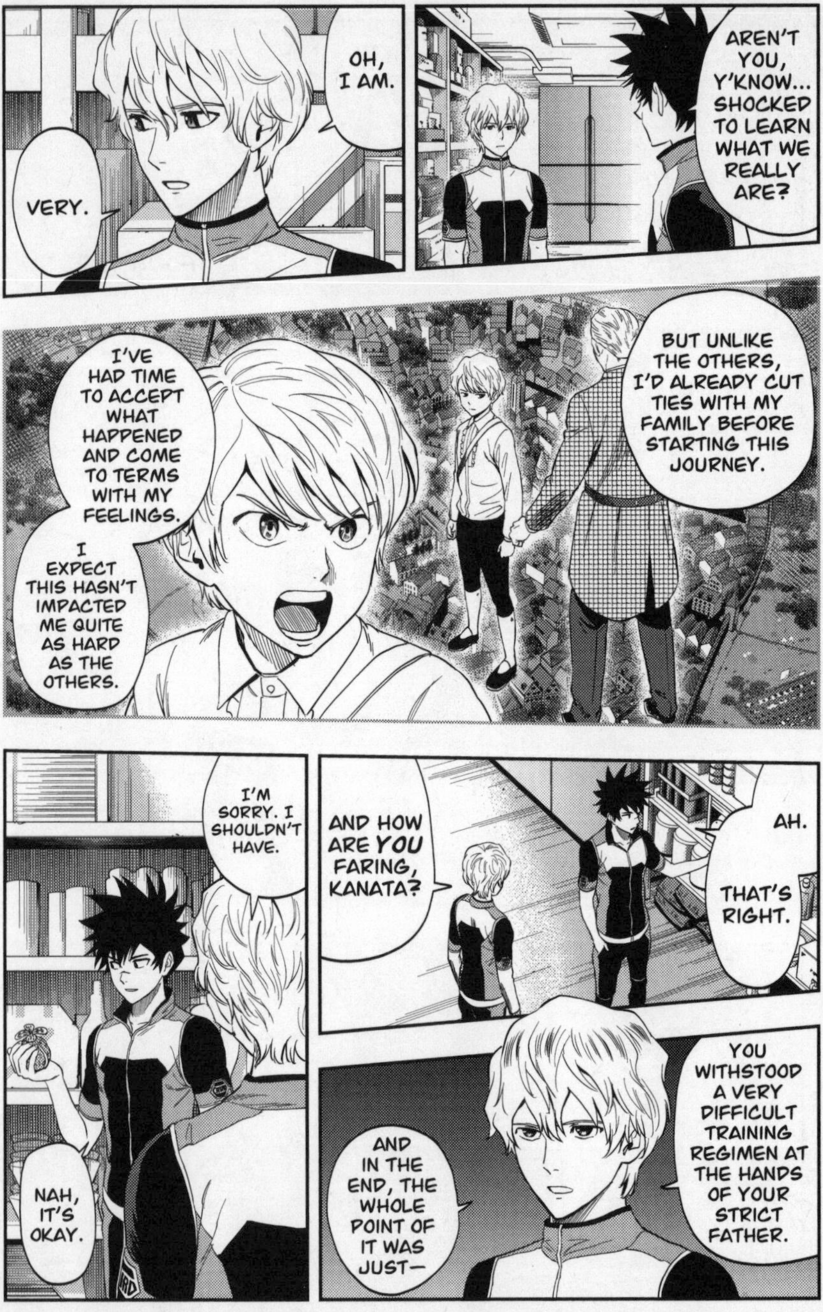
AREN'T YOU, Y'KNOW... SHOCKED TO LEARN WHAT WE REALLY ARE?
OH, I AM.
VERY.
BUT UNLIKE THE OTHERS, I'D ALREADY CUT TIES WITH MY FAMILY BEFORE STARTING THIS JOURNEY.
I'VE HAD TIME TO ACCEPT WHAT HAPPENED AND COME TO TERMS WITH MY FEELINGS.
I EXPECT THIS HASN'T IMPACTED ME QUITE AS HARD AS THE OTHERS.
AH.
THAT'S RIGHT.
AND HOW ARE *YOU* FARING, KANATA?
YOU WITHSTOOD A VERY DIFFICULT TRAINING REGIMEN AT THE HANDS OF YOUR STRICT FATHER.
AND IN THE END, THE WHOLE POINT OF IT WAS JUST—
I'M SORRY. I SHOULDN'T HAVE.
NAH, IT'S OKAY.

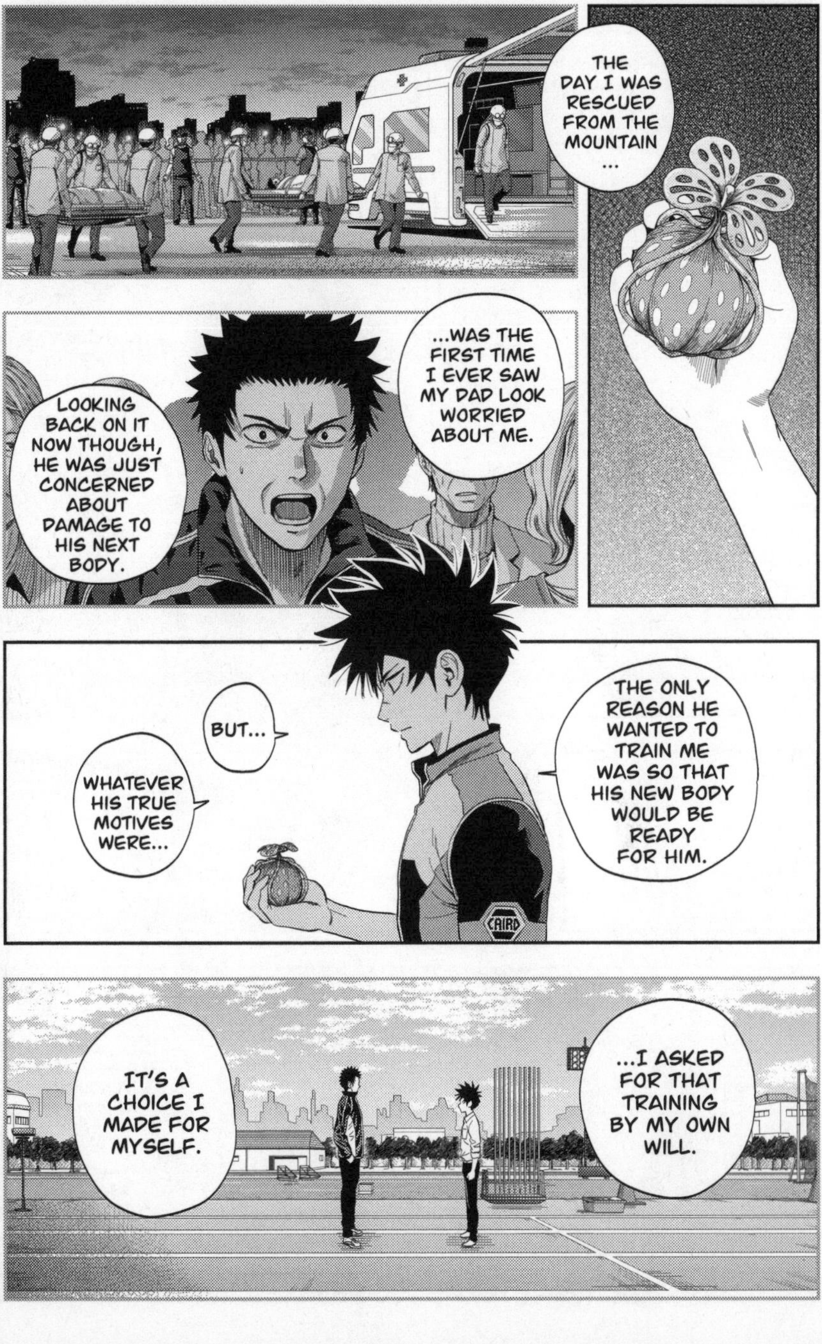
THE DAY I WAS RESCUED FROM THE MOUNTAIN ...
...WAS THE FIRST TIME I EVER SAW MY DAD LOOK WORRIED ABOUT ME.
LOOKING BACK ON IT NOW THOUGH, HE WAS JUST CONCERNED ABOUT DAMAGE TO HIS NEXT BODY.
THE ONLY REASON HE WANTED TO TRAIN ME WAS SO THAT HIS NEW BODY WOULD BE READY FOR HIM.
BUT...
WHATEVER HIS TRUE MOTIVES WERE...
CAIRD
...I ASKED FOR THAT TRAINING BY MY OWN WILL.
IT'S A CHOICE I MADE FOR MYSELF.

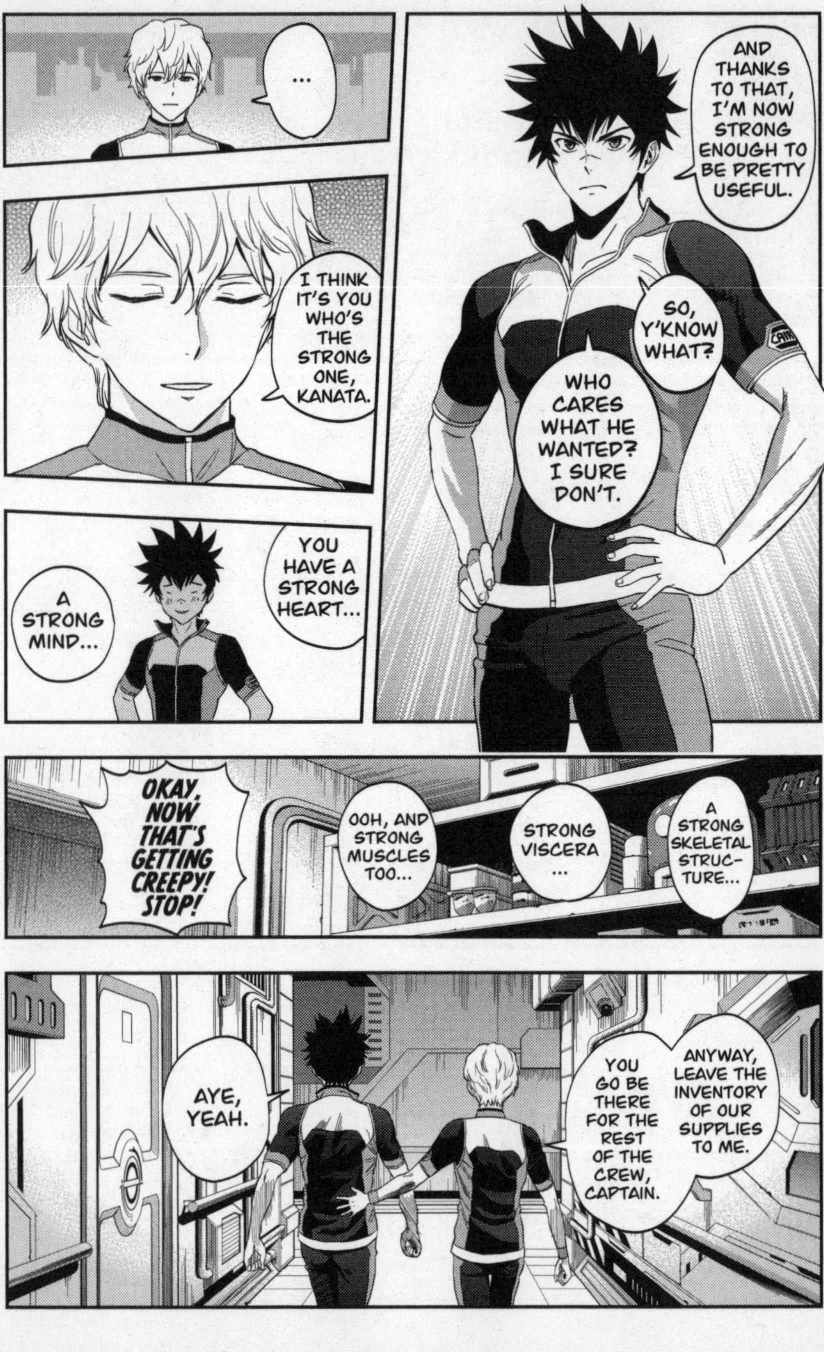
AND THANKS TO THAT, I'M NOW STRONG ENOUGH TO BE PRETTY USEFUL.
SO, Y'KNOW WHAT?
WHO CARES WHAT HE WANTED? I SURE DON'T.
...
I THINK IT'S YOU WHO'S THE STRONG ONE, KANATA.
YOU HAVE A STRONG HEART...
A STRONG MIND...
A STRONG SKELETAL STRUC-TURE...
STRONG VISCERA ...
OOH, AND STRONG MUSCLES TOO...
OKAY, NOW THAT'S GETTING CREEPY! STOP!
ANYWAY, LEAVE THE INVENTORY OF OUR SUPPLIES TO ME.
YOU GO BE THERE FOR THE REST OF THE CREW, CAPTAIN.
AYE, YEAH.

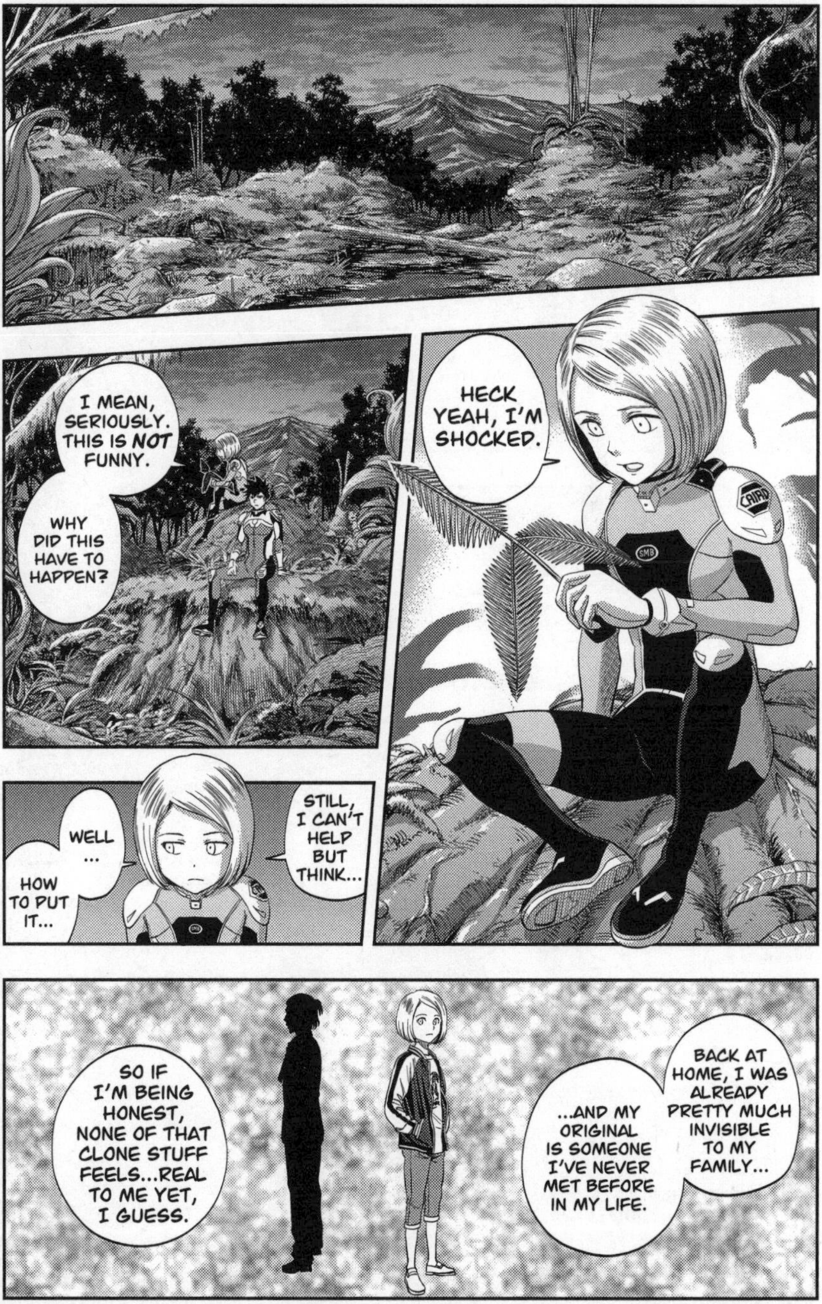
HECK YEAH, I'M SHOCKED.
I MEAN, SERIOUSLY. THIS IS *NOT* FUNNY.
WHY DID THIS HAVE TO HAPPEN?
STILL, I CAN'T HELP BUT THINK...
WELL ...
HOW TO PUT IT...
BACK AT HOME, I WAS ALREADY PRETTY MUCH INVISIBLE TO MY FAMILY...
...AND MY ORIGINAL IS SOMEONE I'VE NEVER MET BEFORE IN MY LIFE.
SO IF I'M BEING HONEST, NONE OF THAT CLONE STUFF FEELS...REAL TO ME YET, I GUESS.

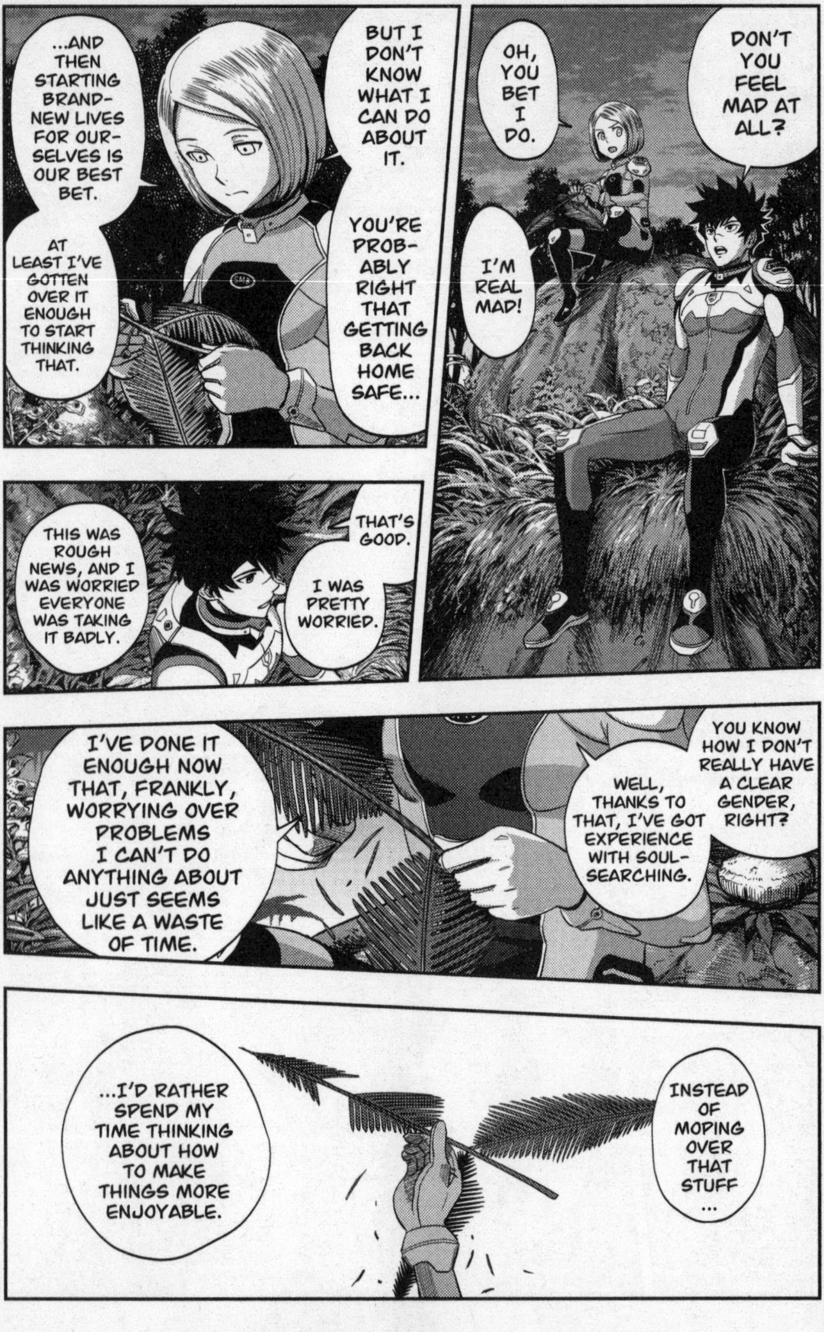
DON'T YOU FEEL MAD AT ALL?
OH, YOU BET I DO.
I'M REAL MAD!
BUT I DON'T KNOW WHAT I CAN DO ABOUT IT.
YOU'RE PROBABLY RIGHT THAT GETTING BACK HOME SAFE...
...AND THEN STARTING BRAND-NEW LIVES FOR OURSELVES IS OUR BEST BET.
AT LEAST I'VE GOTTEN OVER IT ENOUGH TO START THINKING THAT.
THAT'S GOOD.
I WAS PRETTY WORRIED.
THIS WAS ROUGH NEWS, AND I WAS WORRIED EVERYONE WAS TAKING IT BADLY.
YOU KNOW HOW I DON'T REALLY HAVE A CLEAR GENDER, RIGHT?
WELL, THANKS TO THAT, I'VE GOT EXPERIENCE WITH SOUL-SEARCHING.
I'VE DONE IT ENOUGH NOW THAT, FRANKLY, WORRYING OVER PROBLEMS I CAN'T DO ANYTHING ABOUT JUST SEEMS LIKE A WASTE OF TIME.
INSTEAD OF MOPING OVER THAT STUFF...
...I'D RATHER SPEND MY TIME THINKING ABOUT HOW TO MAKE THINGS MORE ENJOYABLE.

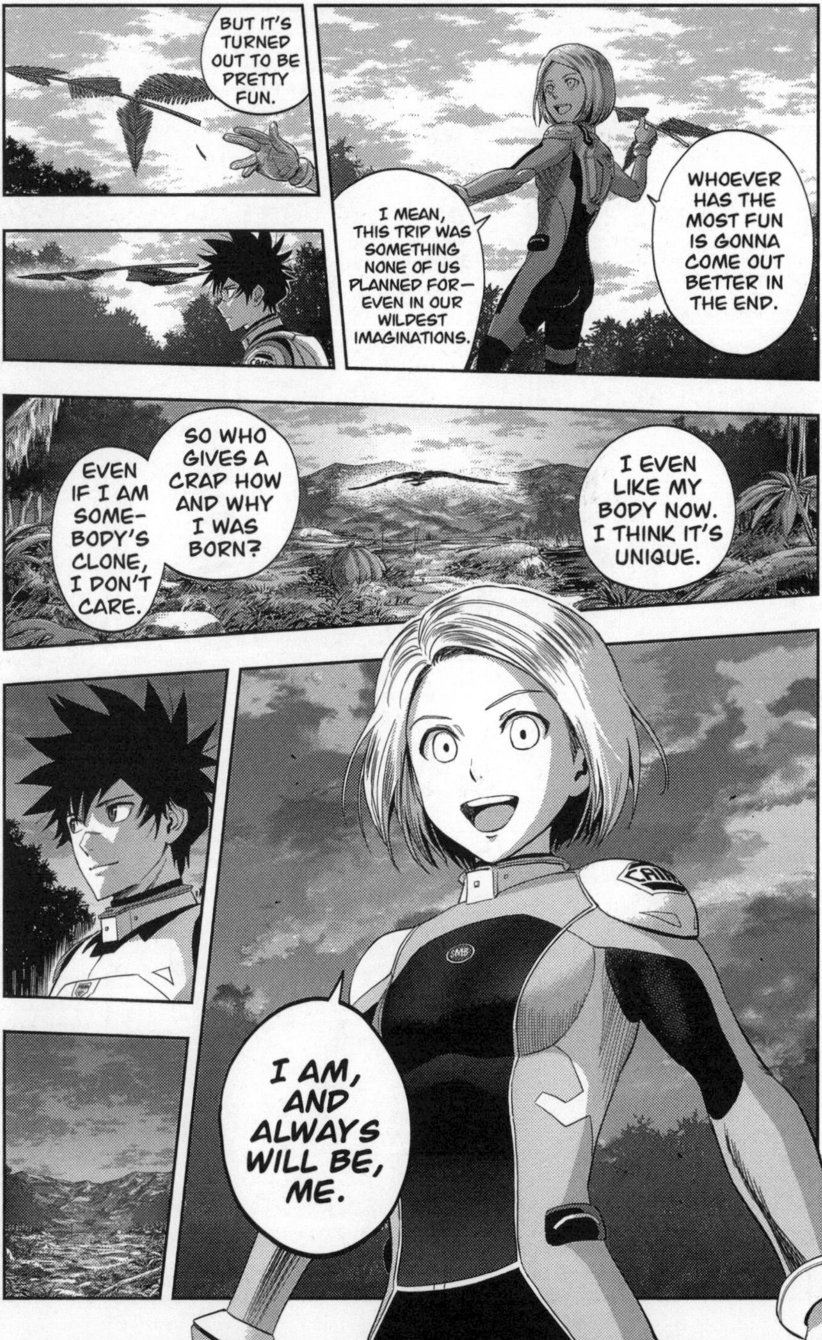
WHOEVER HAS THE MOST FUN IS GONNA COME OUT BETTER IN THE END.
I MEAN, THIS TRIP WAS SOMETHING NONE OF US PLANNED FOR—EVEN IN OUR WILDEST IMAGINATIONS.
BUT IT'S TURNED OUT TO BE PRETTY FUN.
I EVEN LIKE MY BODY NOW. I THINK IT'S UNIQUE.
SO WHO GIVES A CRAP HOW AND WHY I WAS BORN?
EVEN IF I AM SOMEBODY'S CLONE, I DON'T CARE.
I AM, AND ALWAYS WILL BE, ME.

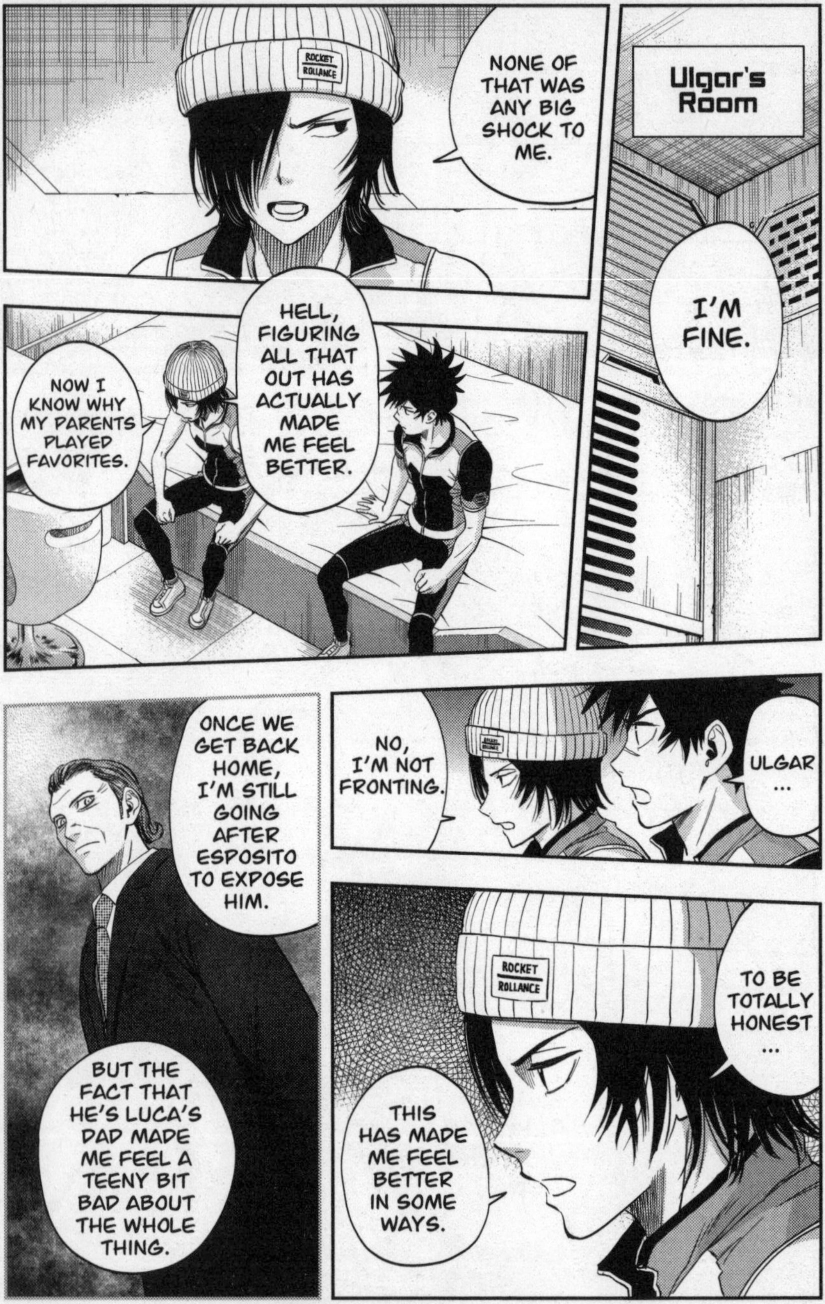
Ulgar's Room
I'M FINE.
NONE OF THAT WAS ANY BIG SHOCK TO ME.
HELL, FIGURING ALL THAT OUT HAS ACTUALLY MADE ME FEEL BETTER.
NOW I KNOW WHY MY PARENTS PLAYED FAVORITES.
ULGAR ...
NO, I'M NOT FRONTING.
TO BE TOTALLY HONEST ...
THIS HAS MADE ME FEEL BETTER IN SOME WAYS.
ONCE WE GET BACK HOME, I'M STILL GOING AFTER ESPOSITO TO EXPOSE HIM.
BUT THE FACT THAT HE'S LUCA'S DAD MADE ME FEEL A TEENY BIT BAD ABOUT THE WHOLE THING.

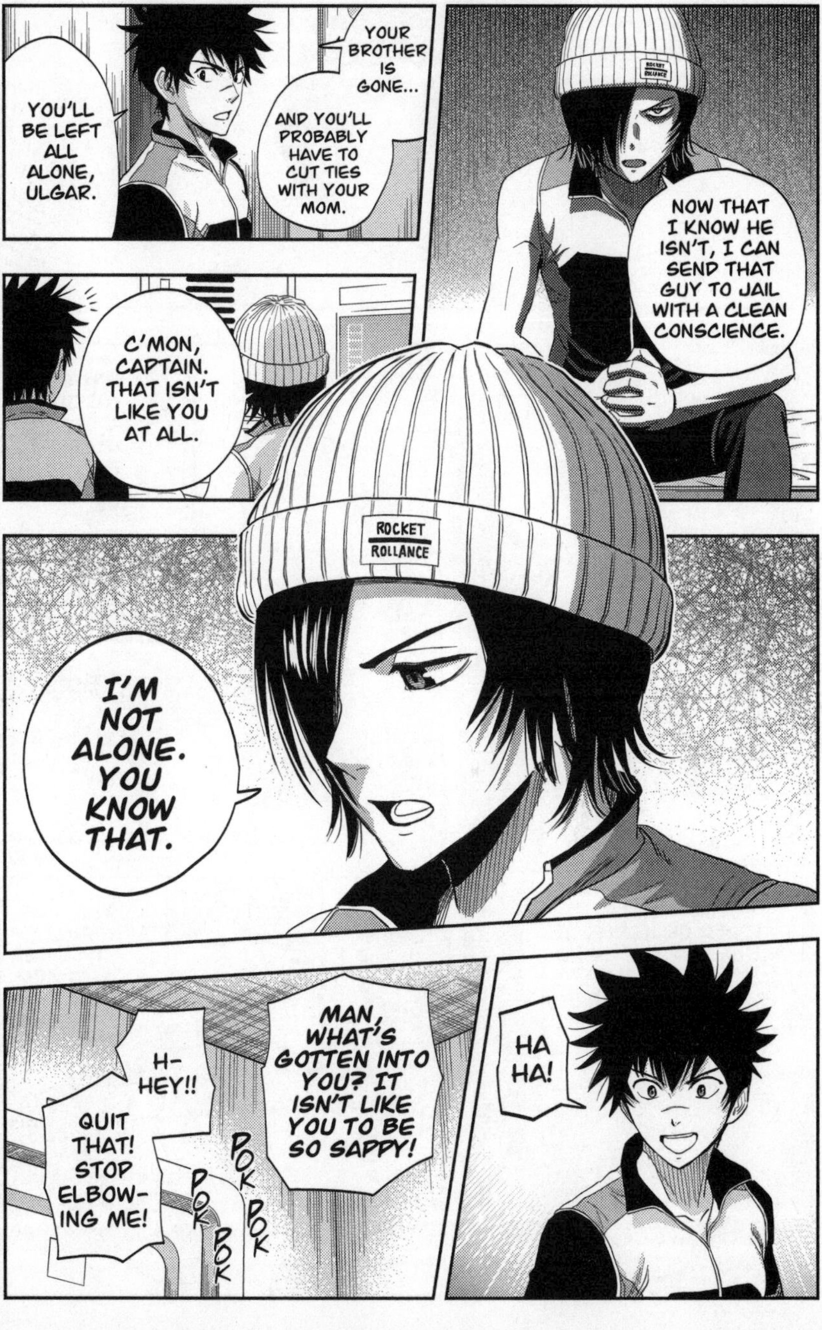
ROCKET ROLLANCE
NOW THAT I KNOW HE ISN'T, I CAN SEND THAT GUY TO JAIL WITH A CLEAN CONSCIENCE.
YOUR BROTHER IS GONE...
AND YOU'LL PROBABLY HAVE TO CUT TIES WITH YOUR MOM.
YOU'LL BE LEFT ALL ALONE, ULGAR.
C'MON, CAPTAIN. THAT ISN'T LIKE YOU AT ALL.
ROCKET ROLLANCE
I'M NOT ALONE. YOU KNOW THAT.
HA HA!
MAN, WHAT'S GOTTEN INTO YOU? IT ISN'T LIKE YOU TO BE SO SAPPY!
POK POK POK POK
H-HEY!!
QUIT THAT! STOP ELBOWING ME!

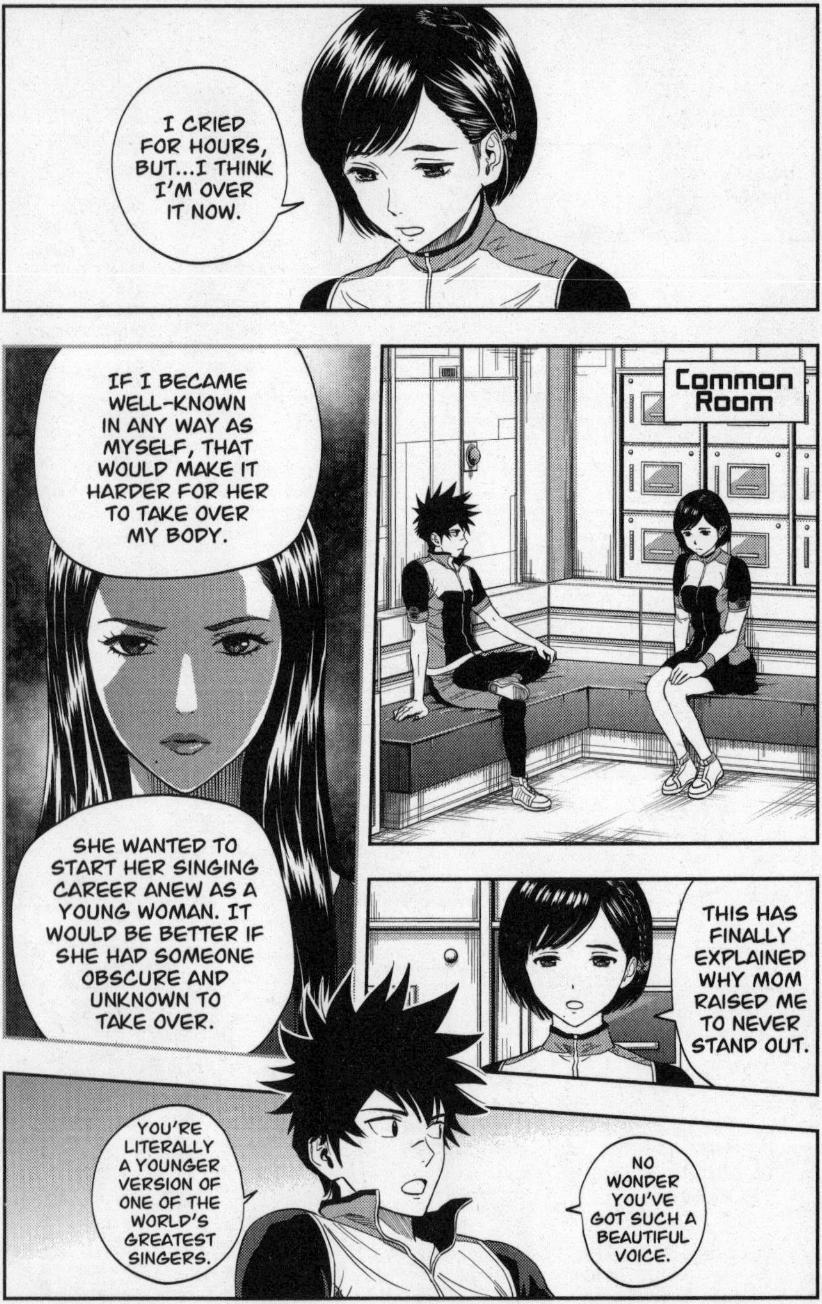
I CRIED FOR HOURS, BUT...I THINK I'M OVER IT NOW.
Common Room
THIS HAS FINALLY EXPLAINED WHY MOM RAISED ME TO NEVER STAND OUT.
IF I BECAME WELL-KNOWN IN ANY WAY AS MYSELF, THAT WOULD MAKE IT HARDER FOR HER TO TAKE OVER MY BODY.
SHE WANTED TO START HER SINGING CAREER ANEW AS A YOUNG WOMAN. IT WOULD BE BETTER IF SHE HAD SOMEONE OBSCURE AND UNKNOWN TO TAKE OVER.
NO WONDER YOU'VE GOT SUCH A BEAUTIFUL VOICE.
YOU'RE LITERALLY A YOUNGER VERSION OF ONE OF THE WORLD'S GREATEST SINGERS.

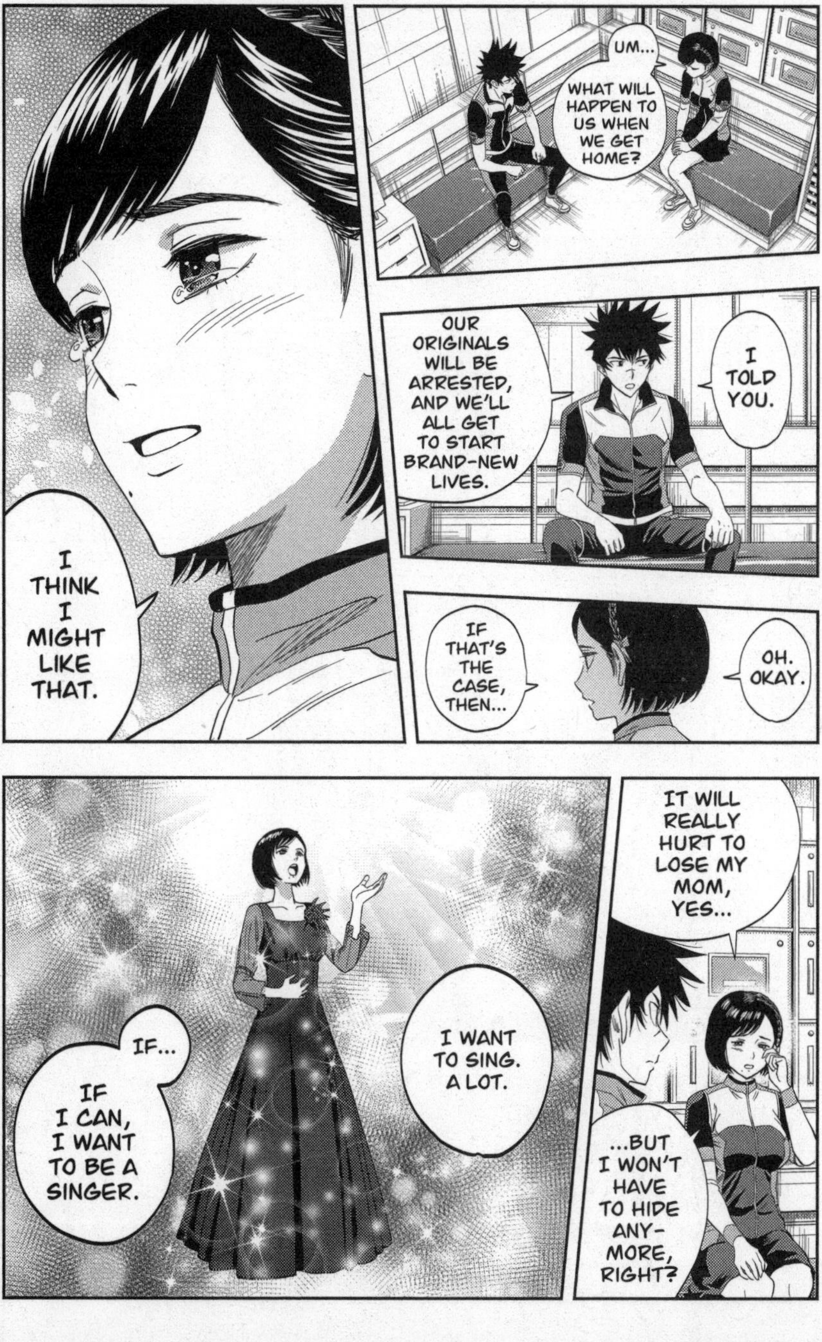
UM...
WHAT WILL HAPPEN TO US WHEN WE GET HOME?
I TOLD YOU.
OUR ORIGINALS WILL BE ARRESTED, AND WE'LL ALL GET TO START BRAND-NEW LIVES.
OH. OKAY.
IF THAT'S THE CASE, THEN...
I THINK I MIGHT LIKE THAT.
IT WILL REALLY HURT TO LOSE MY MOM, YES...
...BUT I WON'T HAVE TO HIDE ANY-MORE, RIGHT?
I WANT TO SING. A LOT.
IF...
IF I CAN, I WANT TO BE A SINGER.

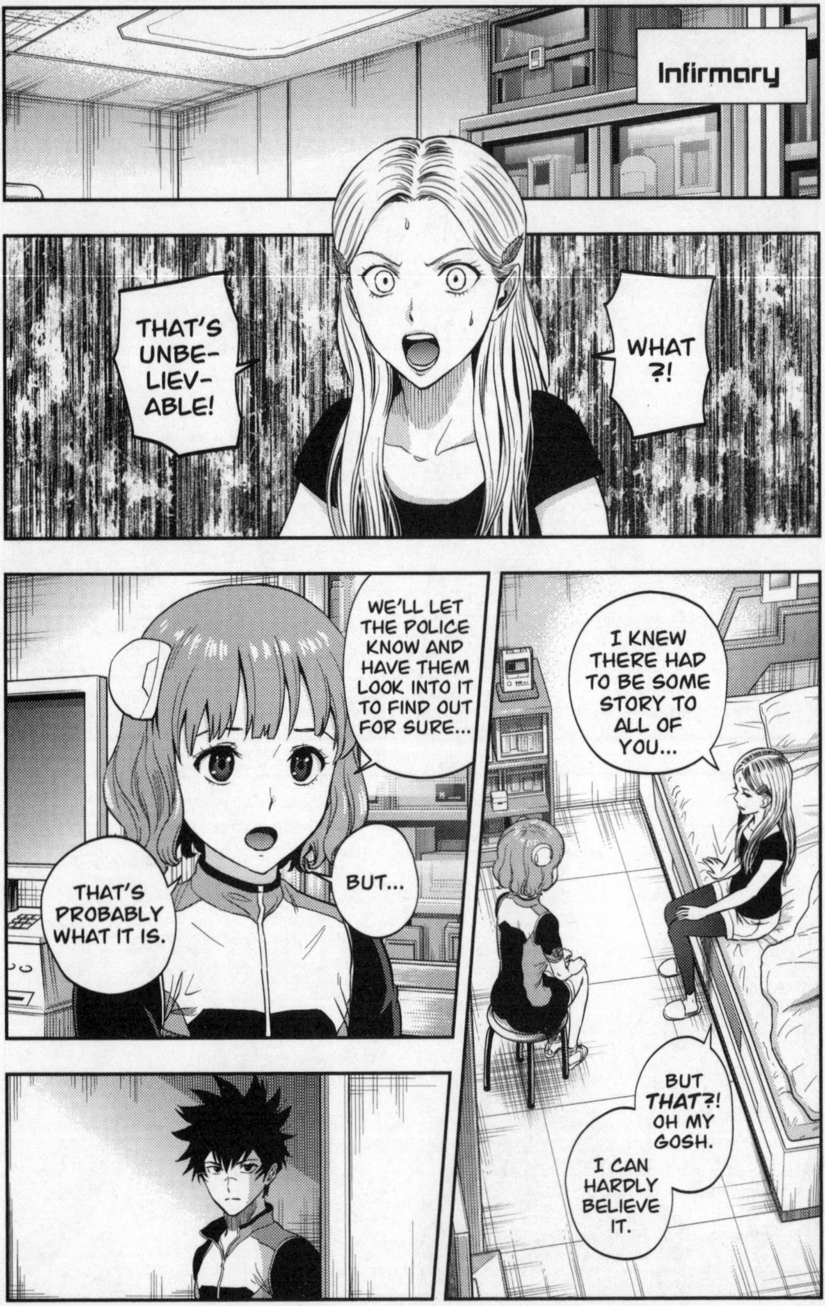
Infirmary
WHAT?!
THAT'S UNBE-LIEV-ABLE!
I KNEW THERE HAD TO BE SOME STORY TO ALL OF YOU...
BUT THAT?! OH MY GOSH.
I CAN HARDLY BELIEVE IT.
WE'LL LET THE POLICE KNOW AND HAVE THEM LOOK INTO IT TO FIND OUT FOR SURE...
BUT...
THAT'S PROBABLY WHAT IT IS.

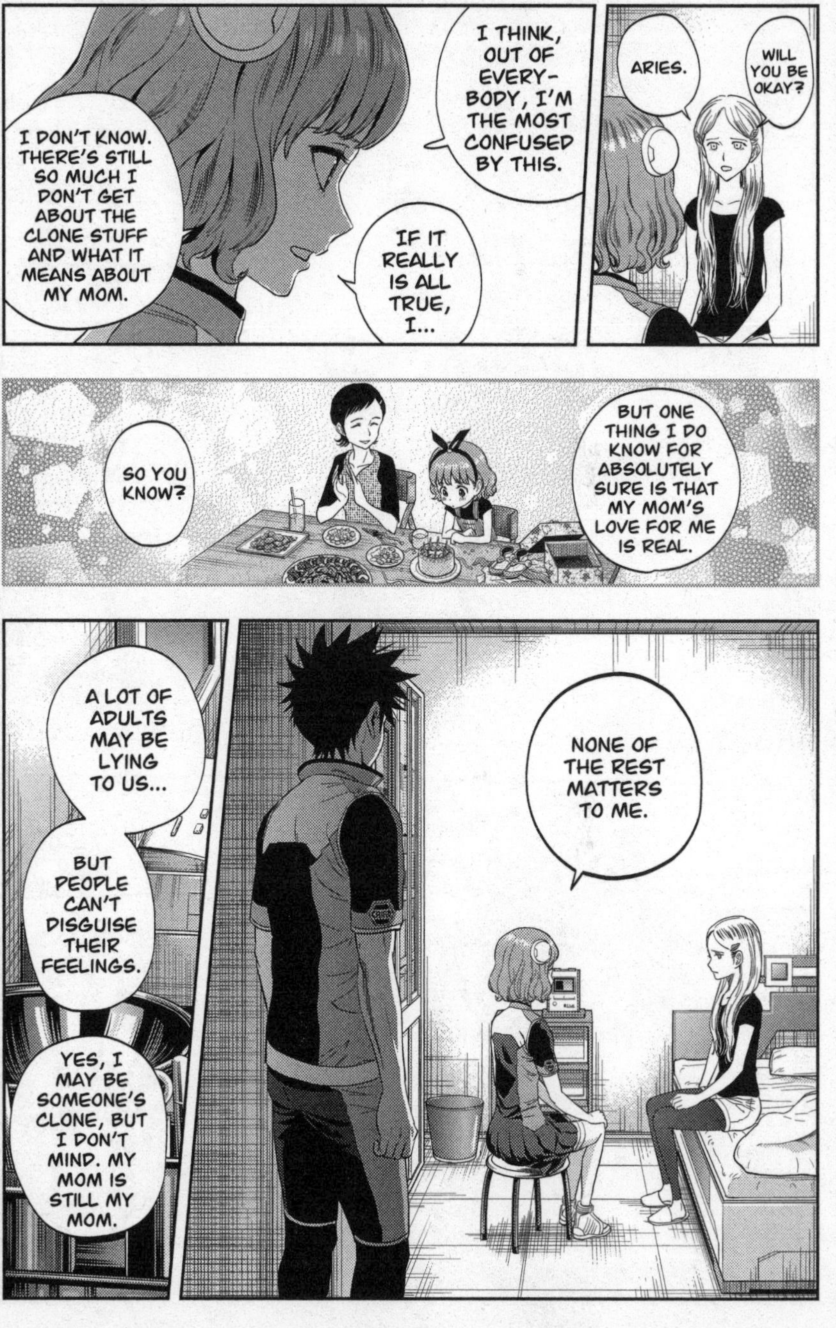

WILL YOU BE OKAY?
ARIES.
I DON'T KNOW. THERE'S STILL SO MUCH I DON'T GET ABOUT THE CLONE STUFF AND WHAT IT MEANS ABOUT MY MOM.
I THINK, OUT OF EVERY-BODY, I'M THE MOST CONFUSED BY THIS.
IF IT REALLY IS ALL TRUE, I...
BUT ONE THING I DO KNOW FOR ABSOLUTELY SURE IS THAT MY MOM'S LOVE FOR ME IS REAL.
SO YOU KNOW?
NONE OF THE REST MATTERS TO ME.
A LOT OF ADULTS MAY BE LYING TO US...
BUT PEOPLE CAN'T DISGUISE THEIR FEELINGS.
YES, I MAY BE SOMEONE'S CLONE, BUT I DON'T MIND. MY MOM IS STILL MY MOM.

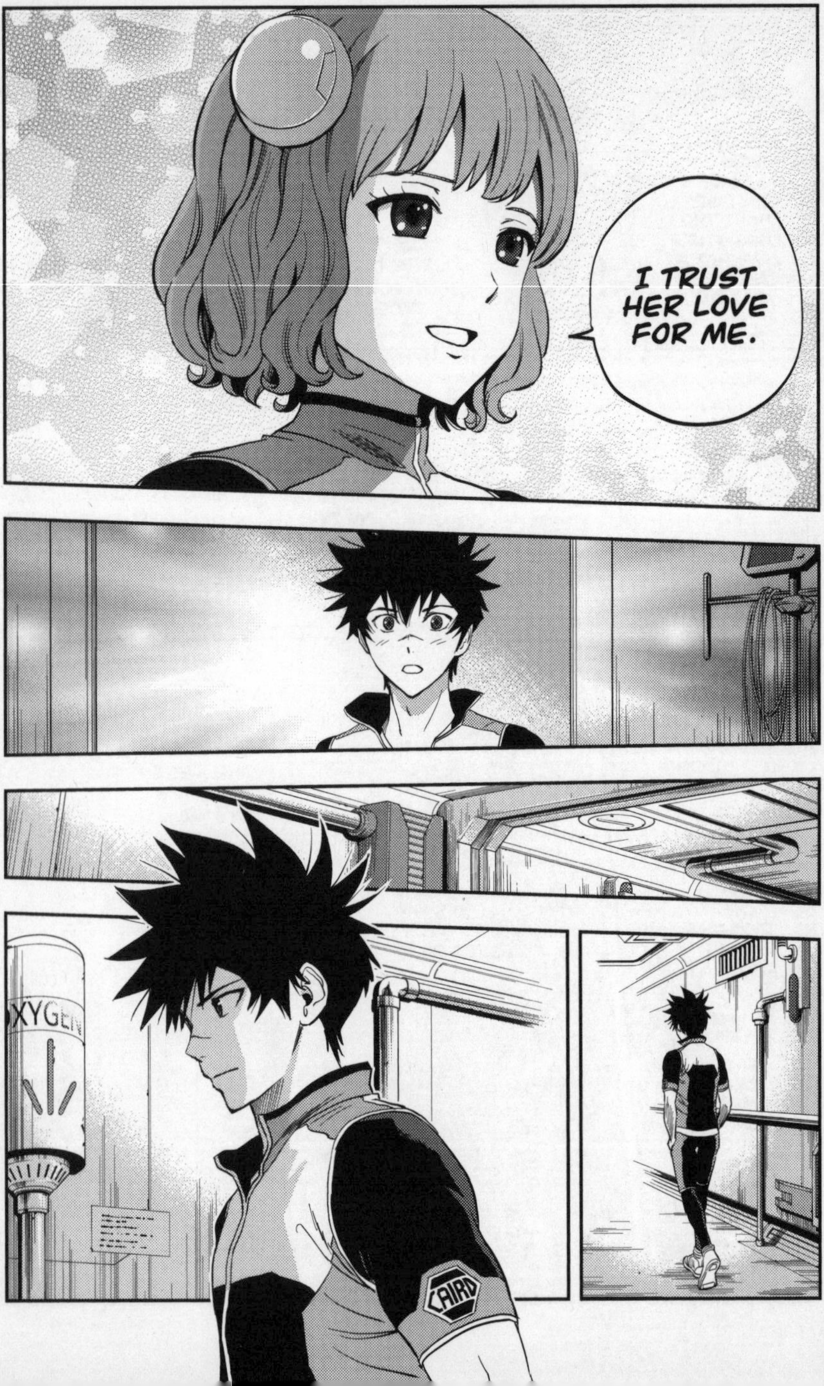
I TRUST HER LOVE FOR ME.
OXYGEN
CAIRD

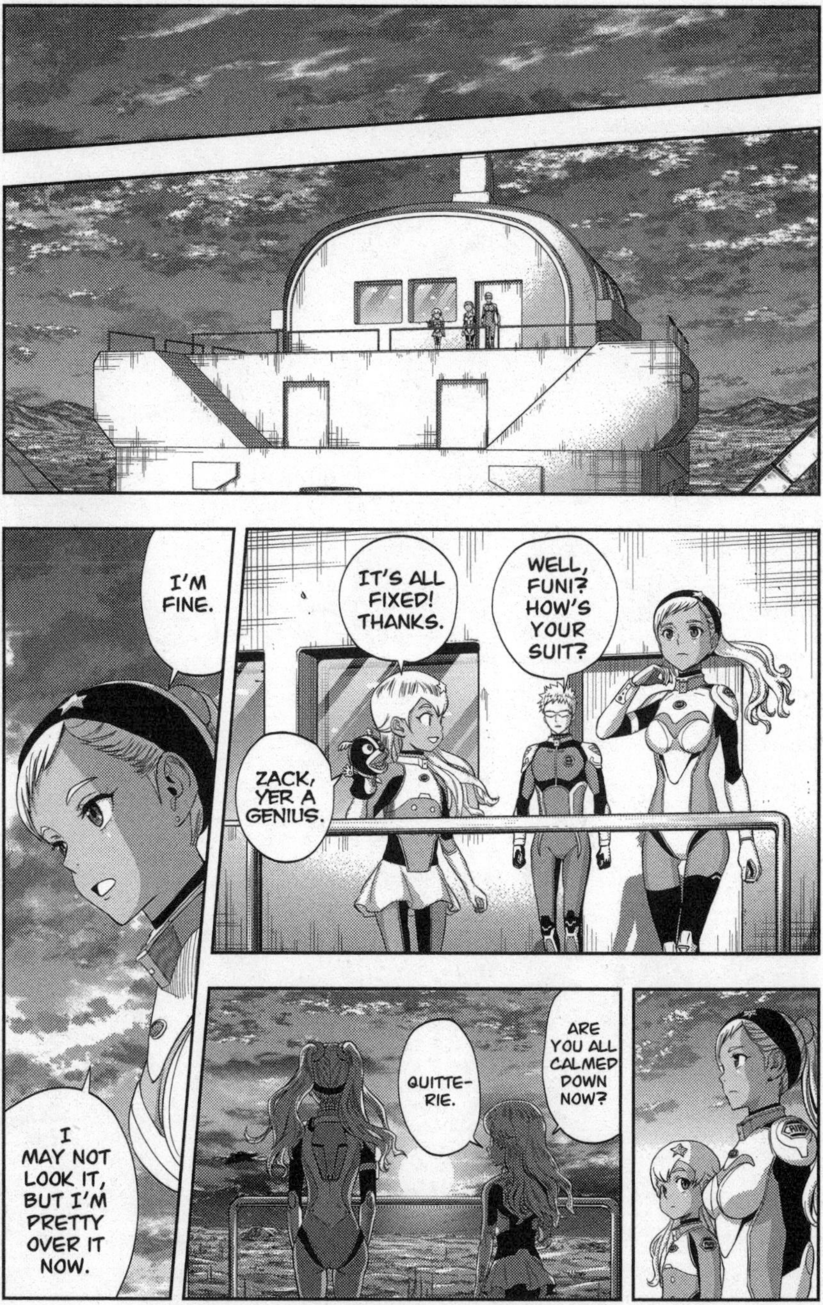
WELL, FUNI? HOW'S YOUR SUIT?
IT'S ALL FIXED! THANKS.
ZACK, YER A GENIUS.
ARE YOU ALL CALMED DOWN NOW?
QUITTE-RIE.
I'M FINE.
I MAY NOT LOOK IT, BUT I'M PRETTY OVER IT NOW.

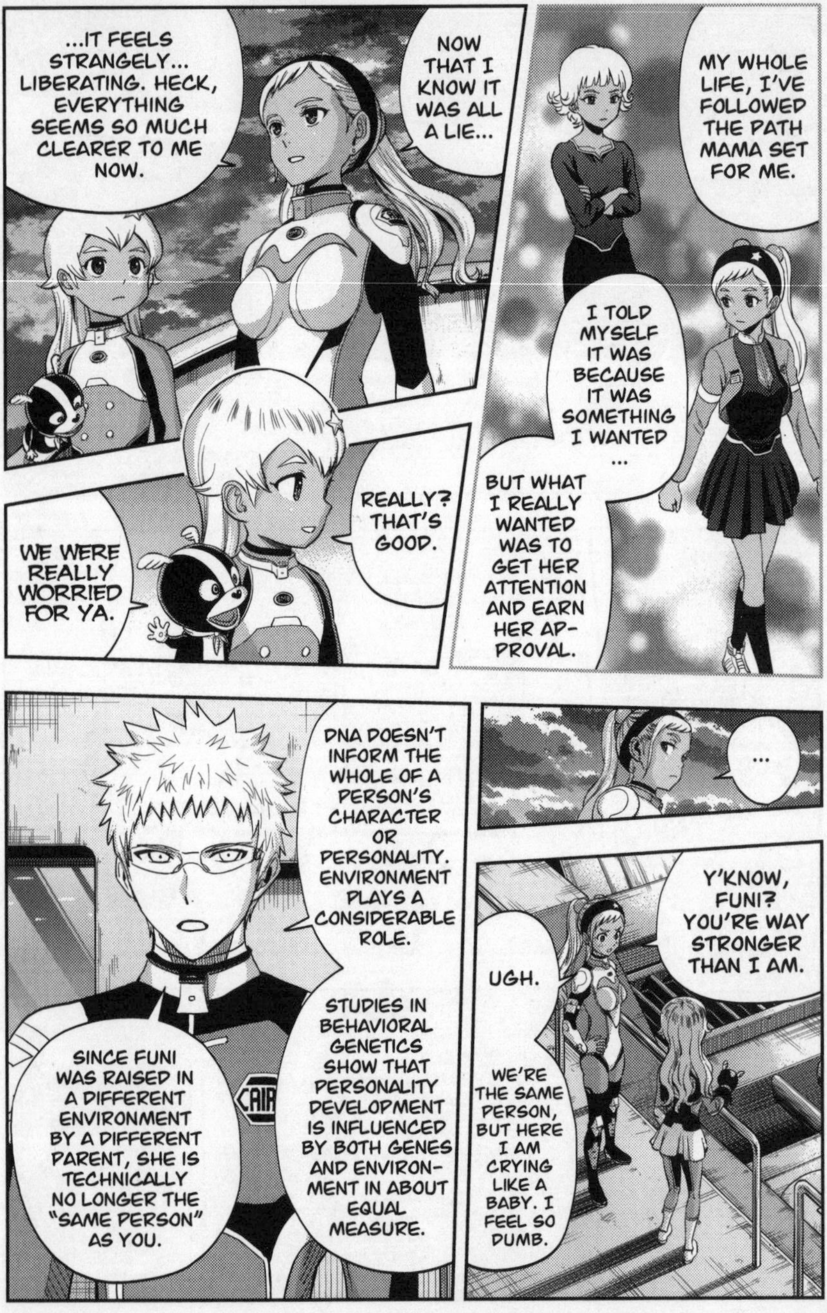
MY WHOLE LIFE, I'VE FOLLOWED THE PATH MAMA SET FOR ME.
I TOLD MYSELF IT WAS BECAUSE IT WAS SOMETHING I WANTED ...
BUT WHAT I REALLY WANTED WAS TO GET HER ATTENTION AND EARN HER AP-PROVAL.
NOW THAT I KNOW IT WAS ALL A LIE...
...IT FEELS STRANGELY... LIBERATING. HECK, EVERYTHING SEEMS SO MUCH CLEARER TO ME NOW.
REALLY? THAT'S GOOD.
WE WERE REALLY WORRIED FOR YA.
...
Y'KNOW, FUNI? YOU'RE WAY STRONGER THAN I AM.
UGH.
WE'RE THE SAME PERSON, BUT HERE I AM CRYING LIKE A BABY. I FEEL SO DUMB.
DNA DOESN'T INFORM THE WHOLE OF A PERSON'S CHARACTER OR PERSONALITY. ENVIRONMENT PLAYS A CONSIDERABLE ROLE.
STUDIES IN BEHAVIORAL GENETICS SHOW THAT PERSONALITY DEVELOPMENT IS INFLUENCED BY BOTH GENES AND ENVIRON-MENT IN ABOUT EQUAL MEASURE.
SINCE FUNI WAS RAISED IN A DIFFERENT ENVIRONMENT BY A DIFFERENT PARENT, SHE IS TECHNICALLY NO LONGER THE "SAME PERSON" AS YOU.

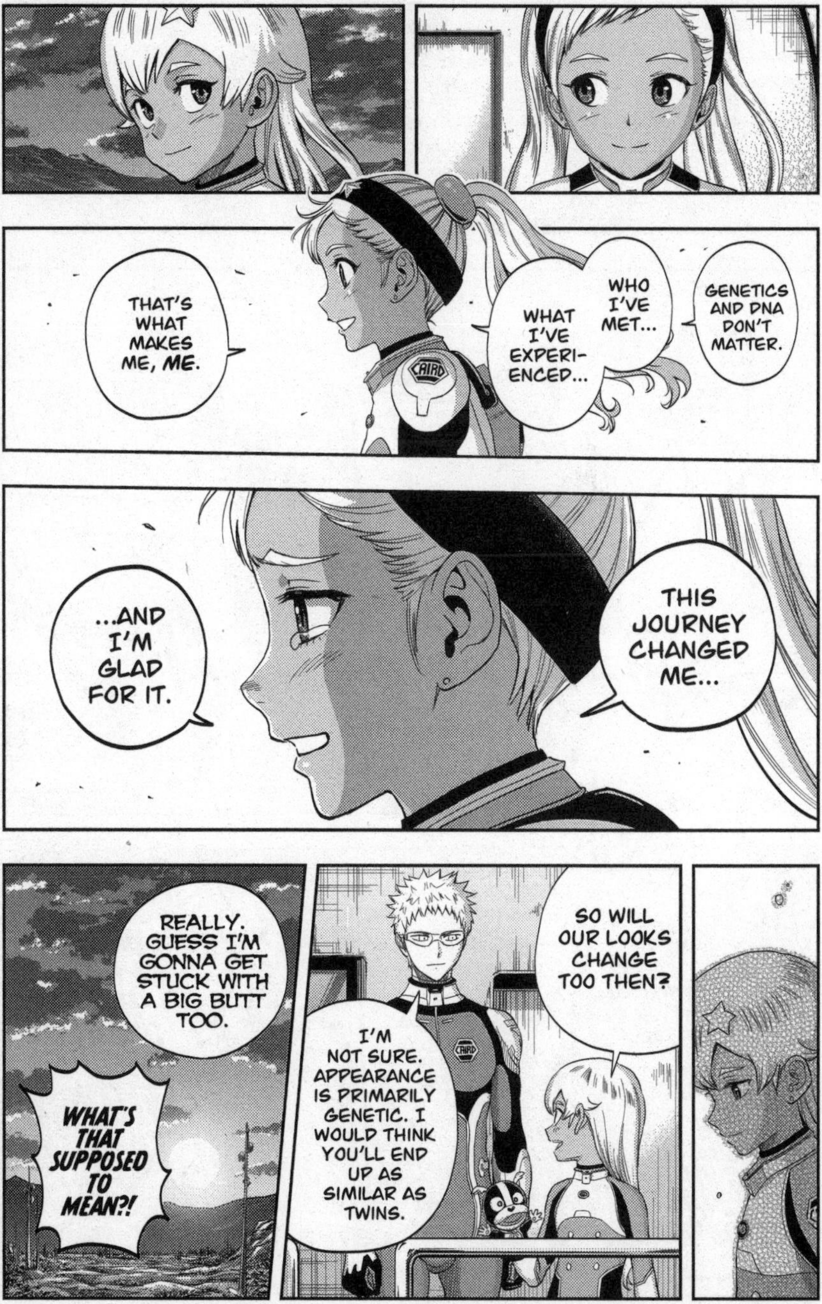
GENETICS AND DNA DON'T MATTER.
WHO I'VE MET...
WHAT I'VE EXPERIENCED...
THAT'S WHAT MAKES ME, ME.
THIS JOURNEY CHANGED ME...
...AND I'M GLAD FOR IT.
SO WILL OUR LOOKS CHANGE TOO THEN?
I'M NOT SURE. APPEARANCE IS PRIMARILY GENETIC. I WOULD THINK YOU'LL END UP AS SIMILAR AS TWINS.
REALLY. GUESS I'M GONNA GET STUCK WITH A BIG BUTT TOO.
WHAT'S THAT SUPPOSED TO MEAN?!

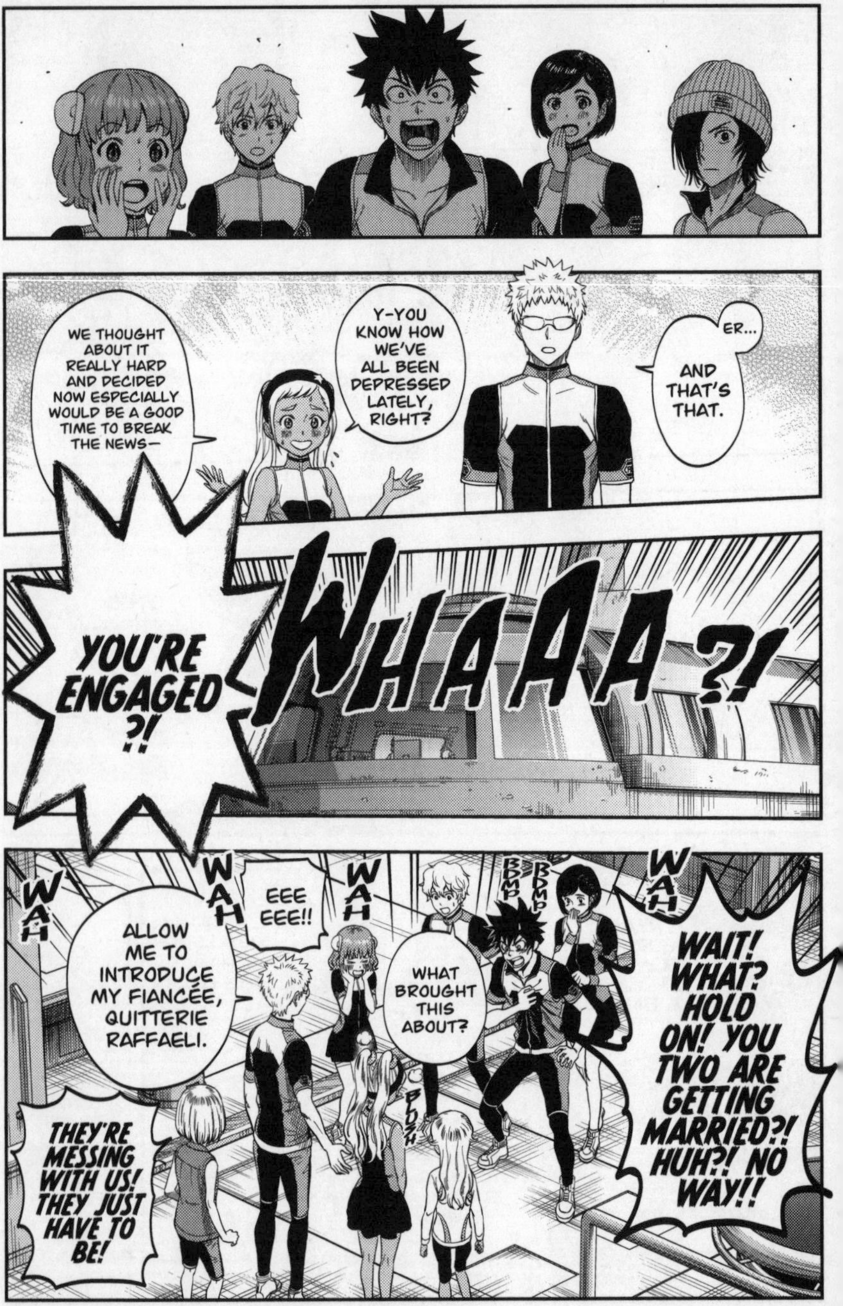
ER...
AND THAT'S THAT.
Y-YOU KNOW HOW WE'VE ALL BEEN DEPRESSED LATELY, RIGHT?
WE THOUGHT ABOUT IT REALLY HARD AND DECIDED NOW ESPECIALLY WOULD BE A GOOD TIME TO BREAK THE NEWS—
WHAAAA ?!
YOU'RE ENGAGED ?!
WAH
WAIT! WHAT? HOLD ON! YOU TWO ARE GETTING MARRIED?! HUH?! NO WAY!!
BDMP BDMP
WHAT BROUGHT THIS ABOUT?
WAH
EEE EEE!!
WAH
ALLOW ME TO INTRODUCE MY FIANCÉE, QUITTERIE RAFFAELI.
WAH
BLUSH
THEY'RE MESSING WITH US! THEY JUST HAVE TO BE!

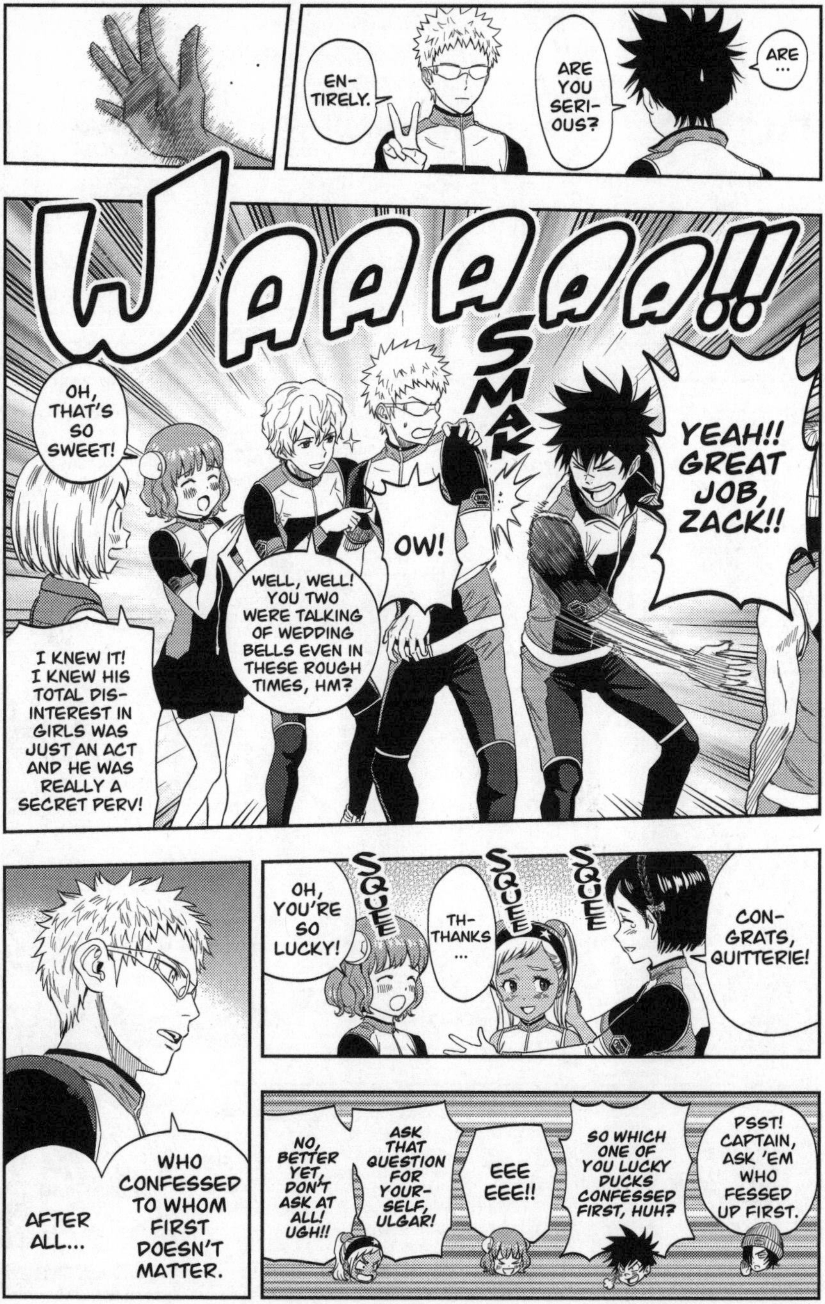
ARE ...
ARE YOU SERI-OUS?
EN-TIRELY.
WAAAAA!!
YEAH!! GREAT JOB, ZACK!!
SMAK
OW!
OH, THAT'S SO SWEET!
WELL, WELL! YOU TWO WERE TALKING OF WEDDING BELLS EVEN IN THESE ROUGH TIMES, HM?
I KNEW IT! I KNEW HIS TOTAL DIS-INTEREST IN GIRLS WAS JUST AN ACT AND HE WAS REALLY A SECRET PERV!
CON-GRATS, QUITTERIE!
SQUEE
SQUEE
TH-THANKS ...
SQUEE
OH, YOU'RE SO LUCKY!
PSST! CAPTAIN, ASK 'EM WHO FESSED UP FIRST.
SO WHICH ONE OF YOU LUCKY DUCKS CONFESSED FIRST, HUH?
EEE EEE!!
ASK THAT QUESTION FOR YOUR-SELF, ULGAR!
NO, BETTER YET, DON'T ASK AT ALL! UGH!!
WHO CONFESSED TO WHOM FIRST DOESN'T MATTER.
AFTER ALL...

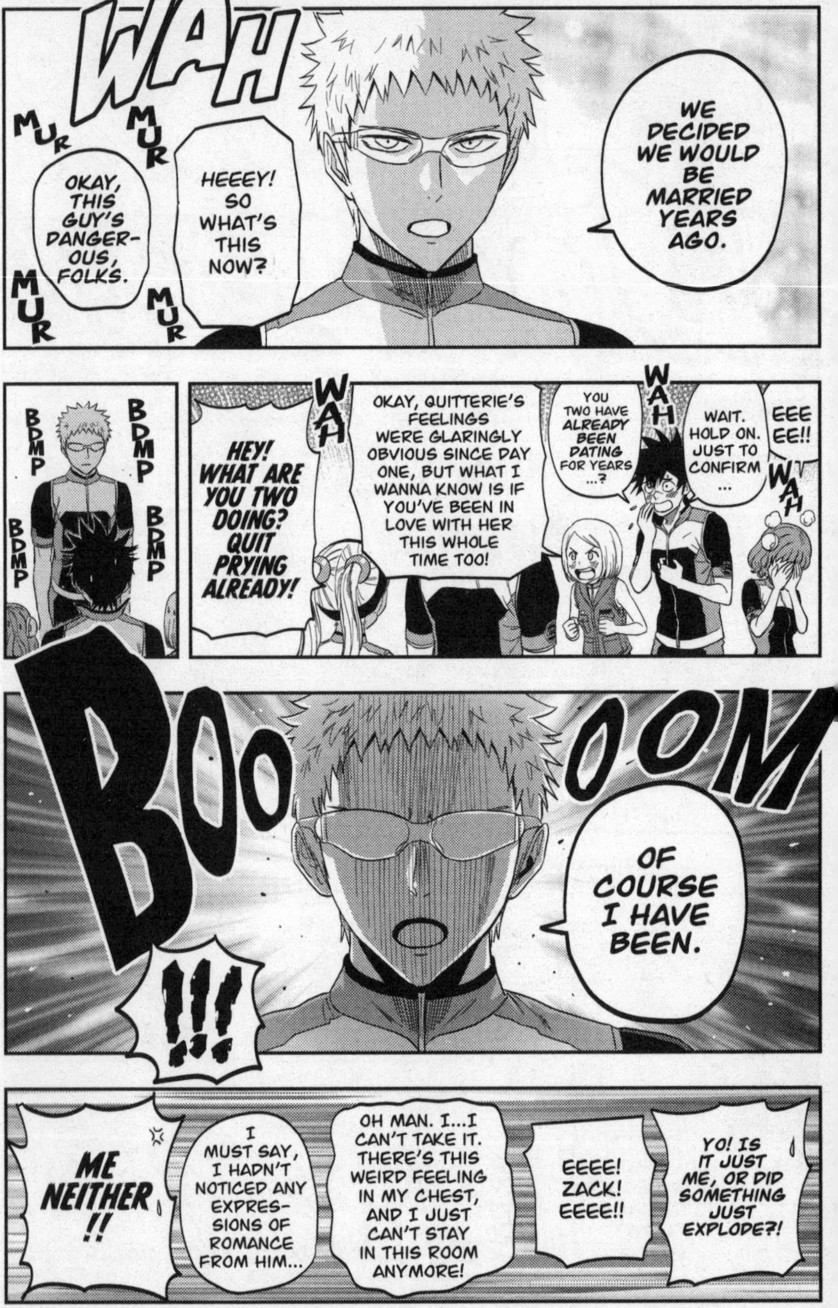
WE DECIDED WE WOULD BE MARRIED YEARS AGO.
WAH
HEEEY! SO WHAT'S THIS NOW?
MUR MUR
MUR MUR
OKAY, THIS GUY'S DANGEROUS, FOLKS.
EEEEE!!
WAH
WAIT. HOLD ON. JUST TO CONFIRM...
WAH
YOU TWO HAVE ALREADY BEEN DATING FOR YEARS...?
OKAY, QUITTERIE'S FEELINGS WERE GLARINGLY OBVIOUS SINCE DAY ONE, BUT WHAT I WANNA KNOW IS IF YOU'VE BEEN IN LOVE WITH HER THIS WHOLE TIME TOO!
WAH
HEY! WHAT ARE YOU TWO DOING? QUIT PRYING ALREADY!
BDMP BDMP
BDMP BDMP
OF COURSE I HAVE BEEN.
BOOOOM!!!
YO! IS IT JUST ME, OR DID SOMETHING JUST EXPLODE?!
EEEE! ZACK! EEEE!!
OH MAN. I...I CAN'T TAKE IT. THERE'S THIS WEIRD FEELING IN MY CHEST, AND I JUST CAN'T STAY IN THIS ROOM ANYMORE!
I MUST SAY, I HADN'T NOTICED ANY EXPRESSIONS OF ROMANCE FROM HIM...
ME NEITHER!!

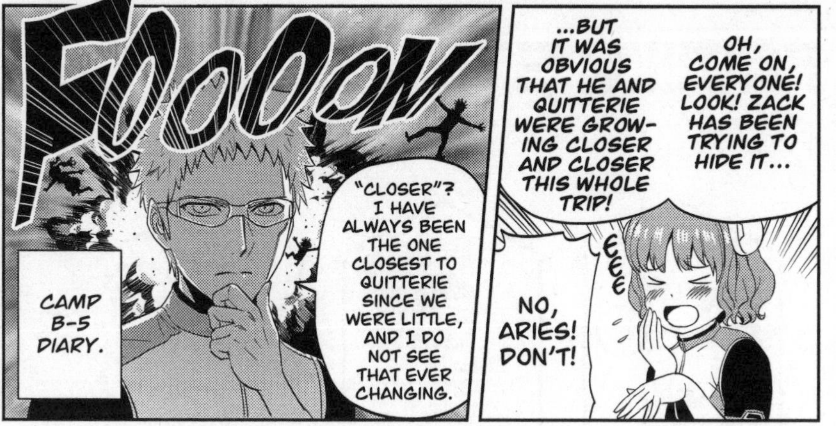
OH, COME ON, EVERYONE! LOOK! ZACK HAS BEEN TRYING TO HIDE IT...
...BUT IT WAS OBVIOUS THAT HE AND QUITTERIE WERE GROWING CLOSER AND CLOSER THIS WHOLE TRIP!
EEE
NO, ARIES! DON'T!
FOOOOM
"CLOSER"? I HAVE ALWAYS BEEN THE ONE CLOSEST TO QUITTERIE SINCE WE WERE LITTLE, AND I DO NOT SEE THAT EVER CHANGING.
CAMP B-5 DIARY.

NO MATTER WHAT HAPPENS, THIS CREW ALWAYS STAYS UPBEAT.

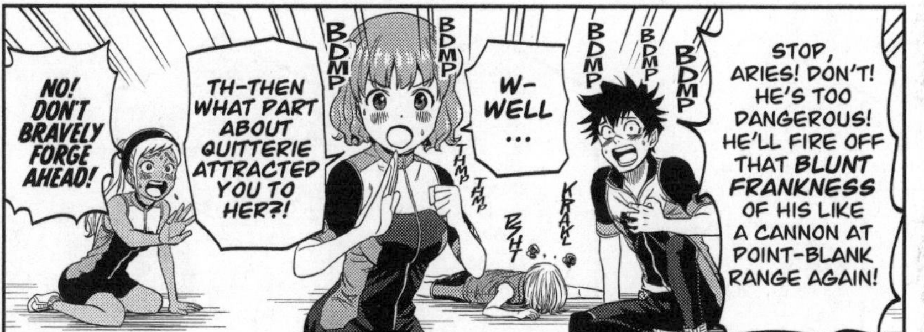
STOP, ARIES! DON'T! HE'S TOO DANGEROUS! HE'LL FIRE OFF THAT **BLUNT FRANKNESS** OF HIS LIKE A CANNON AT POINT-BLANK RANGE AGAIN!
BDMP BDMP BDMP
BDMP BDMP
W-WELL...
THMP THMP
TH-THEN WHAT PART ABOUT QUITTERIE ATTRACTED YOU TO HER?!
NO! DON'T BRAVELY FORGE AHEAD!

THEY'RE ALL SO VERY STRONG... NO.

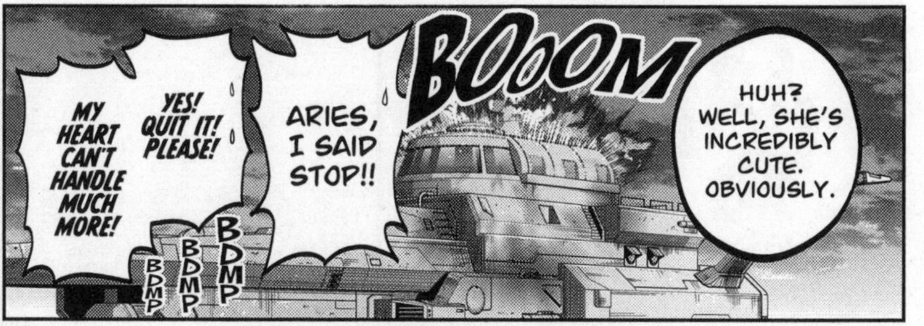
HUH? WELL, SHE'S INCREDIBLY CUTE. OBVIOUSLY.
BOOOM
ARIES, I SAID STOP!!
YES! QUIT IT! PLEASE!
MY HEART CAN'T HANDLE MUCH MORE!
BDMP BDMP BDMP

THEY'RE **INVINCIBLE**.

Material Collection
FAMILY STRUCTURE

HOSHIJIMA

Biological Dad — Mom

Rei

Kanata

SPRING

Adoptive Mom

Emma

Aries

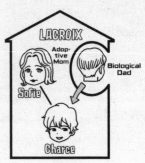

LACROIX

Adoptive Mom — Biological Dad

Sofie

Charce

RAFFAELI

Q. Biological Mom
F. Adoptive Mom

Olive

Adoptive Sisters — Adopted

Quitterie — Funicia

WALKER

Biological Dad

Jed

Zack

ESPOSITO

Adoptive Dad

Felice — Marco — Mom

Adoptive Brothers

Luca — Ricardo

LU

Biological Mom

Wei

Yun-hua

ZWEIG

Biological Dad — Mom

Gert

Brother

Ulgar — Finn

*This is a diagram of the familial structures of each character, as revealed in the story.

⇨ This arrow denotes the original-to-clone relationship.

ASTRA
LOST IN SPACE

#36

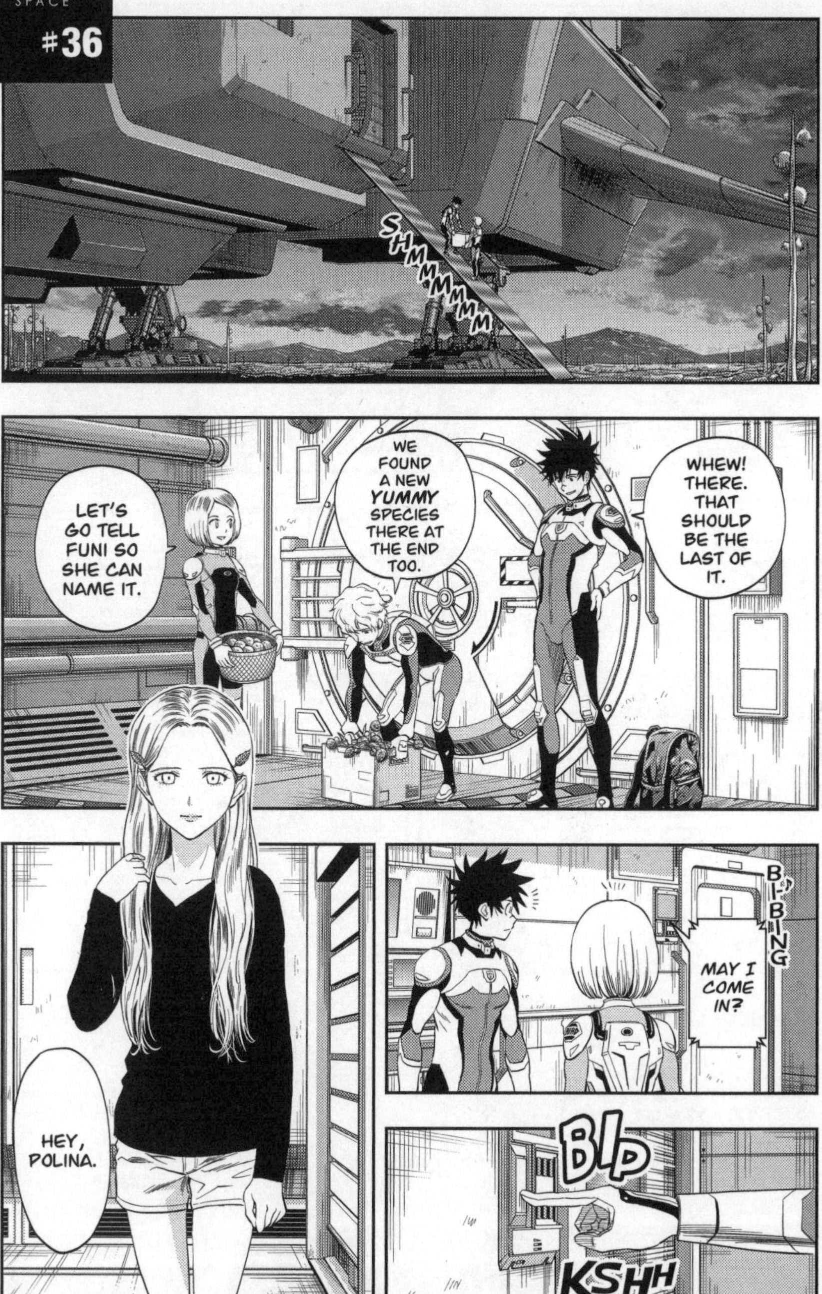
SHMMMMMM
WHEW! THERE. THAT SHOULD BE THE LAST OF IT.
WE FOUND A NEW *YUMMY* SPECIES THERE AT THE END TOO.
LET'S GO TELL FUNI SO SHE CAN NAME IT.
BI-BING
MAY I COME IN?
BIP
KSHH
HEY, POLINA.

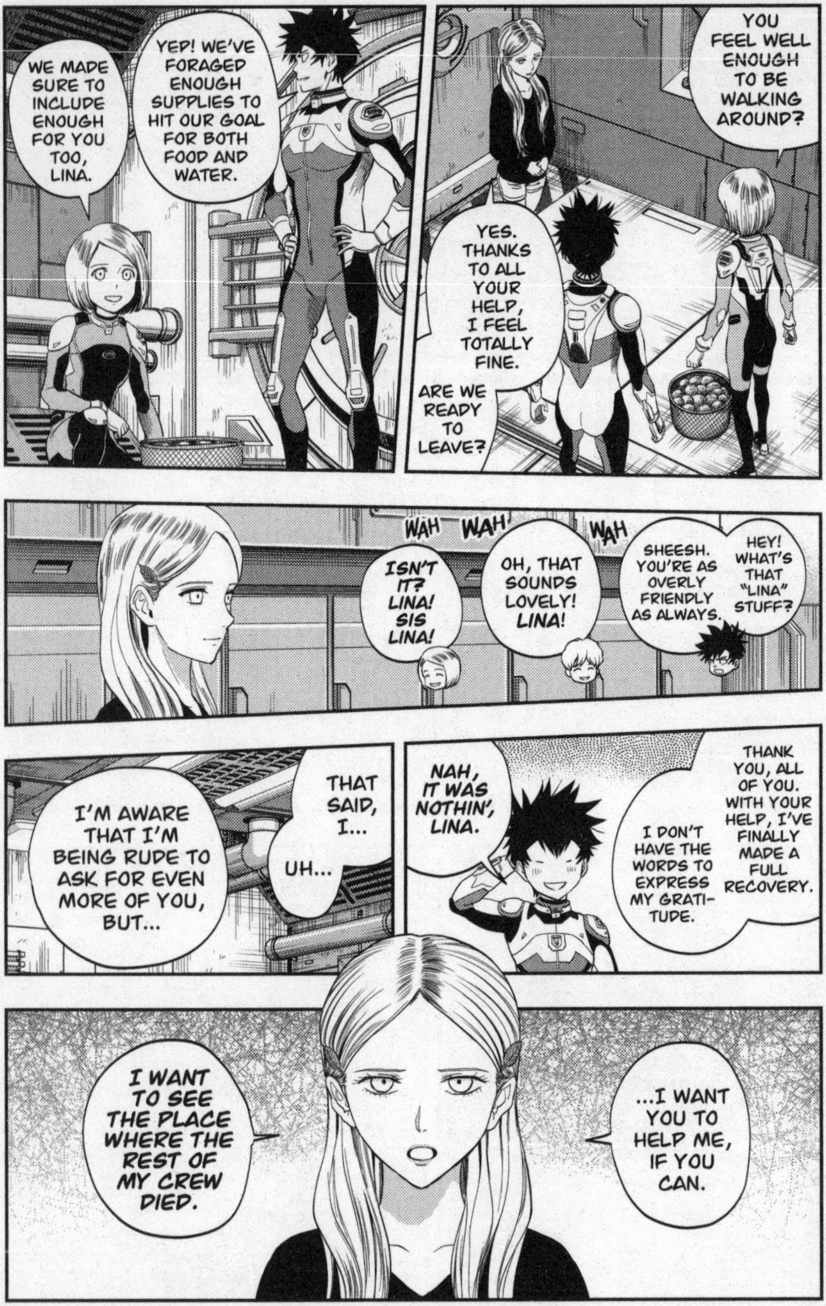
YOU FEEL WELL ENOUGH TO BE WALKING AROUND?
YES. THANKS TO ALL YOUR HELP, I FEEL TOTALLY FINE.
ARE WE READY TO LEAVE?
YEP! WE'VE FORAGED ENOUGH SUPPLIES TO HIT OUR GOAL FOR BOTH FOOD AND WATER.
WE MADE SURE TO INCLUDE ENOUGH FOR YOU TOO, LINA.
HEY! WHAT'S THAT "LINA" STUFF?
SHEESH. YOU'RE AS OVERLY FRIENDLY AS ALWAYS.
WAH
WAH
WAH
OH, THAT SOUNDS LOVELY! LINA!
ISN'T IT? LINA! SIS LINA!
THANK YOU, ALL OF YOU. WITH YOUR HELP, I'VE FINALLY MADE A FULL RECOVERY.
I DON'T HAVE THE WORDS TO EXPRESS MY GRATITUDE.
NAH, IT WAS NOTHIN', LINA.
THAT SAID, I...
UH...
I'M AWARE THAT I'M BEING RUDE TO ASK FOR EVEN MORE OF YOU, BUT...
...I WANT YOU TO HELP ME, IF YOU CAN.
I WANT TO SEE THE PLACE WHERE THE REST OF MY CREW DIED.

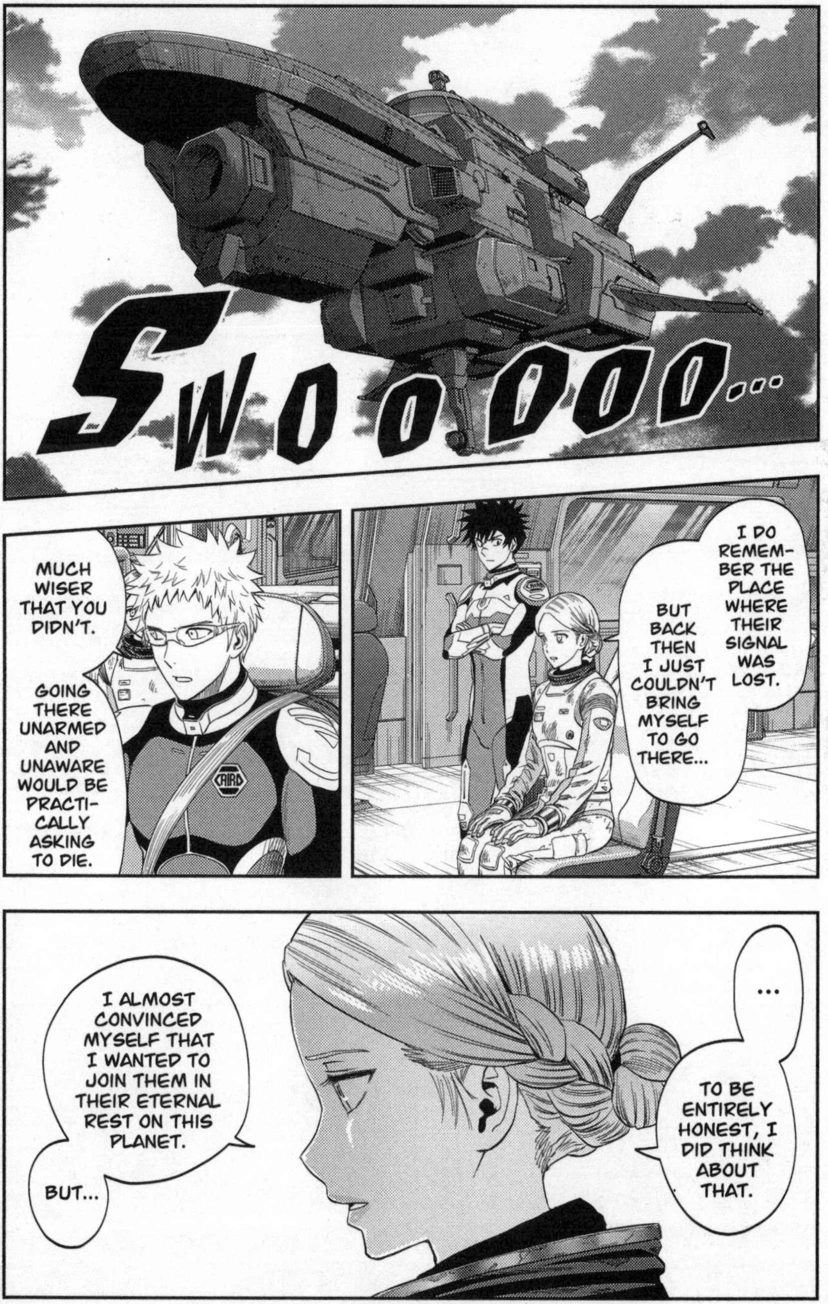
SWOOOOO...
I DO REMEMBER THE PLACE WHERE THEIR SIGNAL WAS LOST.
BUT BACK THEN I JUST COULDN'T BRING MYSELF TO GO THERE...
MUCH WISER THAT YOU DIDN'T.
GOING THERE UNARMED AND UNAWARE WOULD BE PRACTICALLY ASKING TO DIE.
...
TO BE ENTIRELY HONEST, I DID THINK ABOUT THAT.
I ALMOST CONVINCED MYSELF THAT I WANTED TO JOIN THEM IN THEIR ETERNAL REST ON THIS PLANET.
BUT...

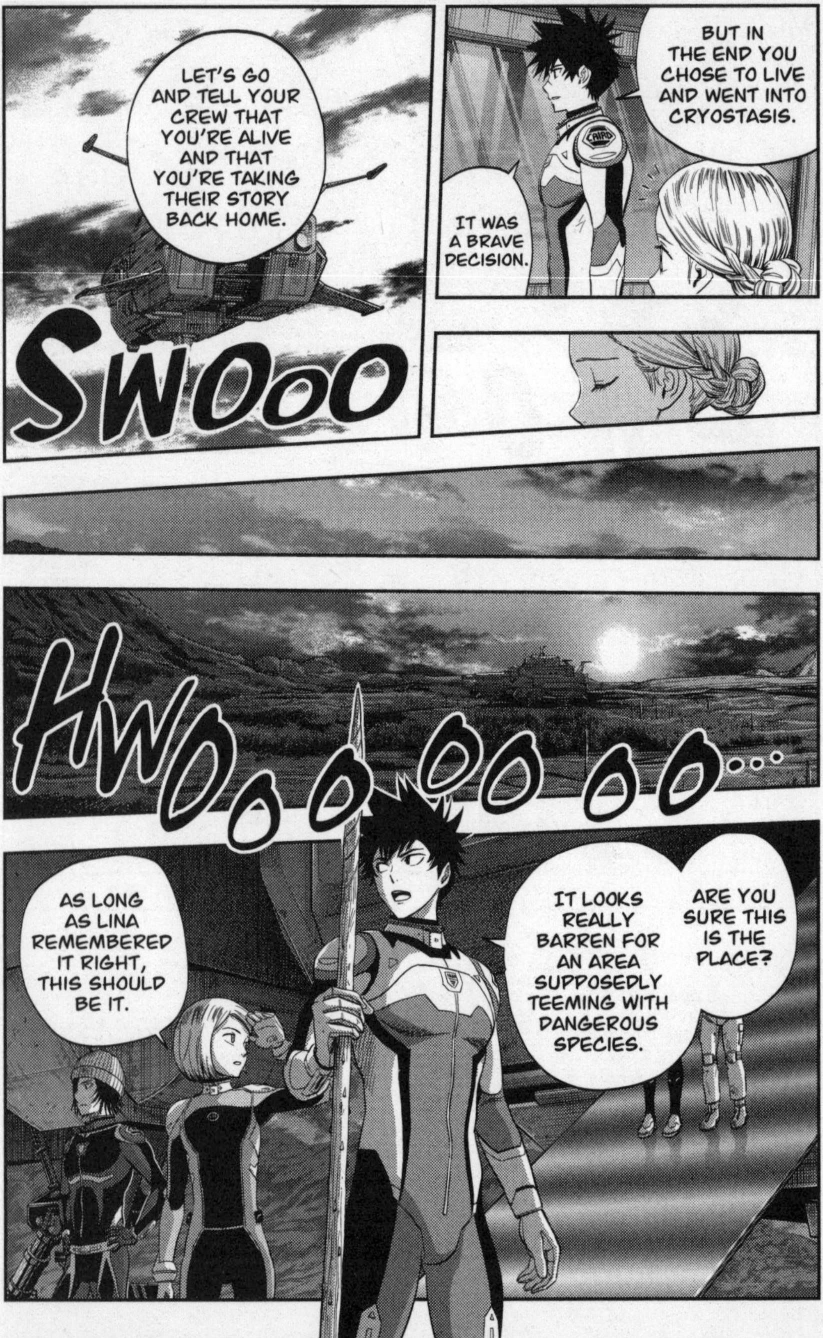
BUT IN THE END YOU CHOSE TO LIVE AND WENT INTO CRYOSTASIS.
IT WAS A BRAVE DECISION.
LET'S GO AND TELL YOUR CREW THAT YOU'RE ALIVE AND THAT YOU'RE TAKING THEIR STORY BACK HOME.
SWOOO
HWOOO OO OO...
ARE YOU SURE THIS IS THE PLACE?
IT LOOKS REALLY BARREN FOR AN AREA SUPPOSEDLY TEEMING WITH DANGEROUS SPECIES.
AS LONG AS LINA REMEMBERED IT RIGHT, THIS SHOULD BE IT.

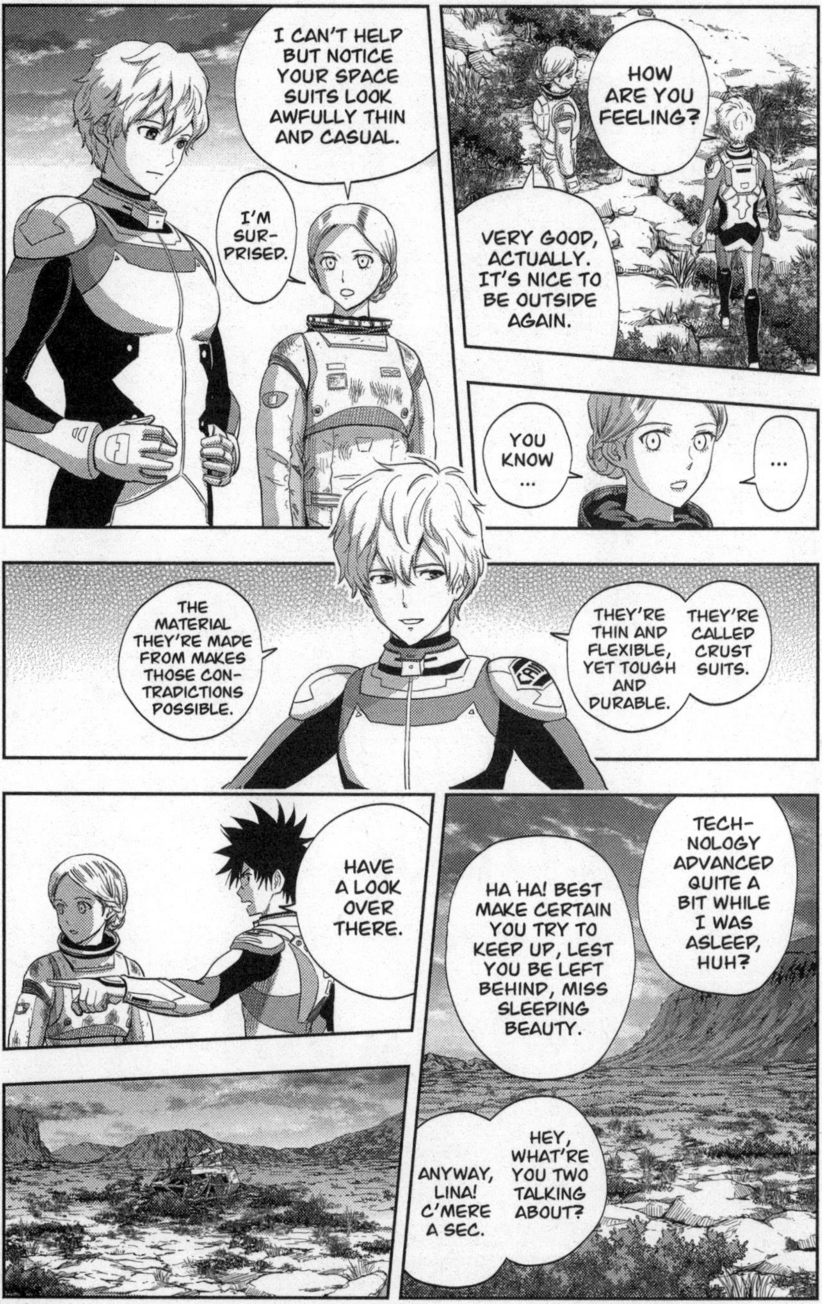

HOW ARE YOU FEELING?
VERY GOOD, ACTUALLY. IT'S NICE TO BE OUTSIDE AGAIN.
...
YOU KNOW ...
I CAN'T HELP BUT NOTICE YOUR SPACE SUITS LOOK AWFULLY THIN AND CASUAL.
I'M SUR-PRISED.
THEY'RE CALLED CRUST SUITS.
THEY'RE THIN AND FLEXIBLE, YET TOUGH AND DURABLE.
THE MATERIAL THEY'RE MADE FROM MAKES THOSE CON-TRADICTIONS POSSIBLE.
TECH-NOLOGY ADVANCED QUITE A BIT WHILE I WAS ASLEEP, HUH?
HA HA! BEST MAKE CERTAIN YOU TRY TO KEEP UP, LEST YOU BE LEFT BEHIND, MISS SLEEPING BEAUTY.
HEY, WHAT'RE YOU TWO TALKING ABOUT?
ANYWAY, LINA! C'MERE A SEC.
HAVE A LOOK OVER THERE.

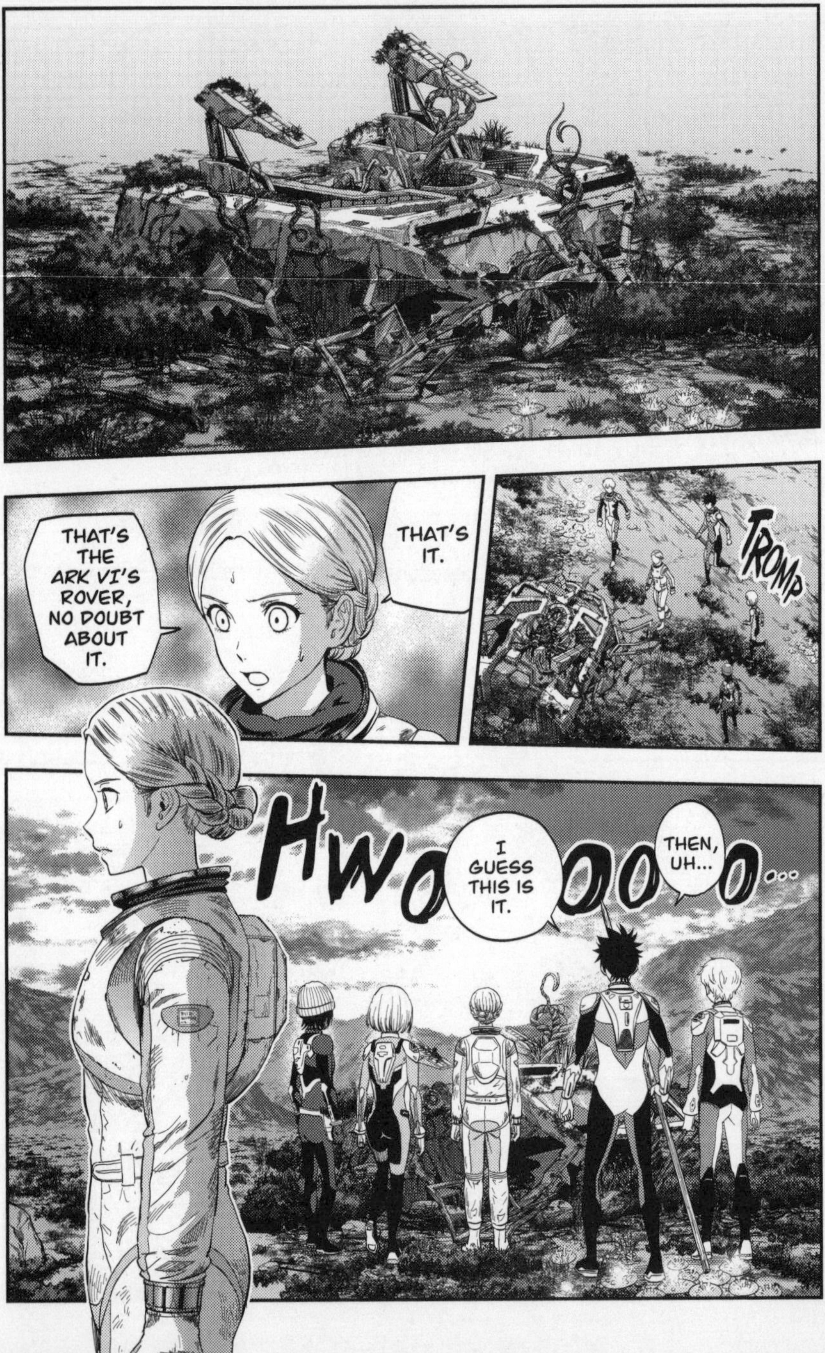
TROMP
THAT'S IT.
THAT'S THE ARK VI'S ROVER, NO DOUBT ABOUT IT.
HWOOOOOO...
THEN, UH...
I GUESS THIS IS IT.

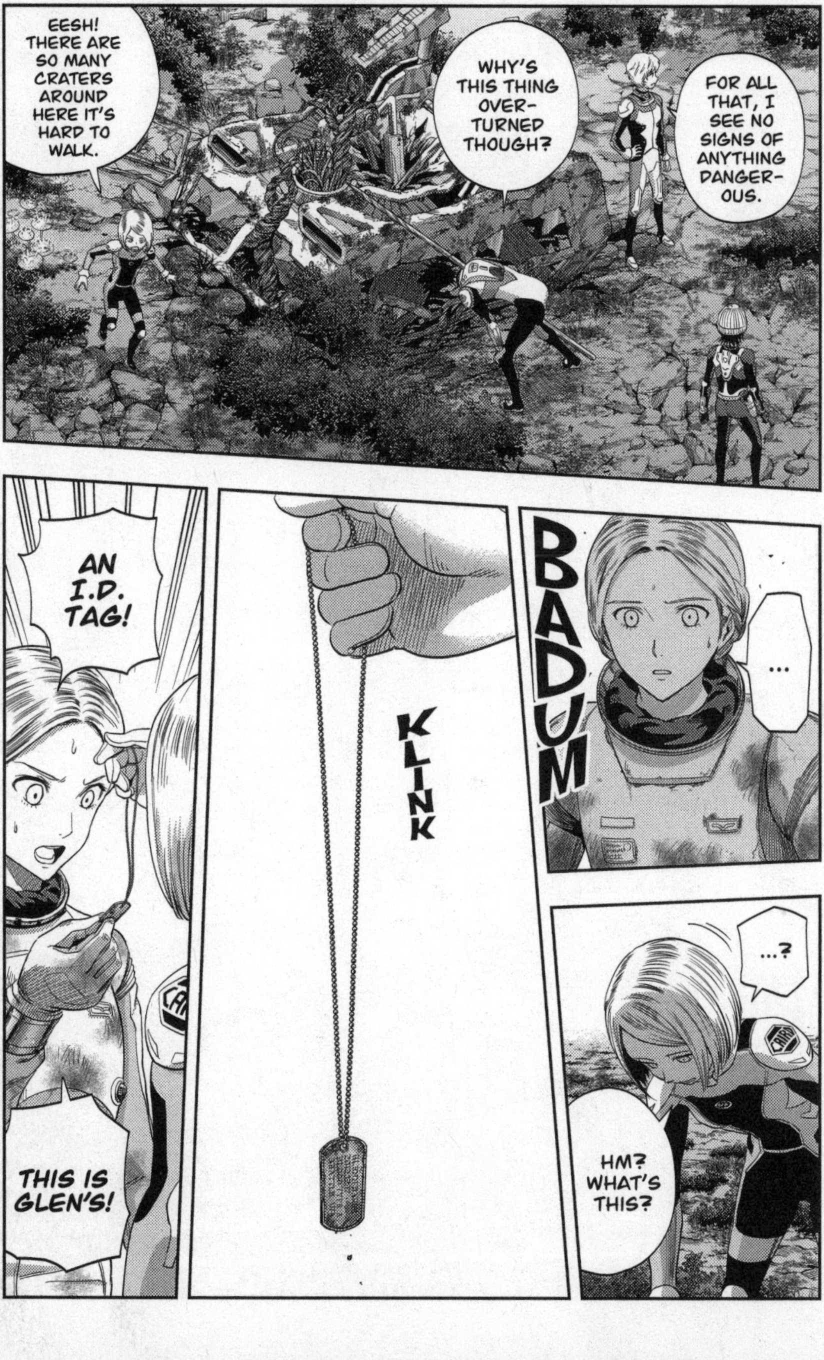
FOR ALL THAT, I SEE NO SIGNS OF ANYTHING DANGER-OUS.
WHY'S THIS THING OVER-TURNED THOUGH?
EESH! THERE ARE SO MANY CRATERS AROUND HERE IT'S HARD TO WALK.
BADUM
...
...?
HM? WHAT'S THIS?
KLINK
AN I.D. TAG!
THIS IS GLEN'S!

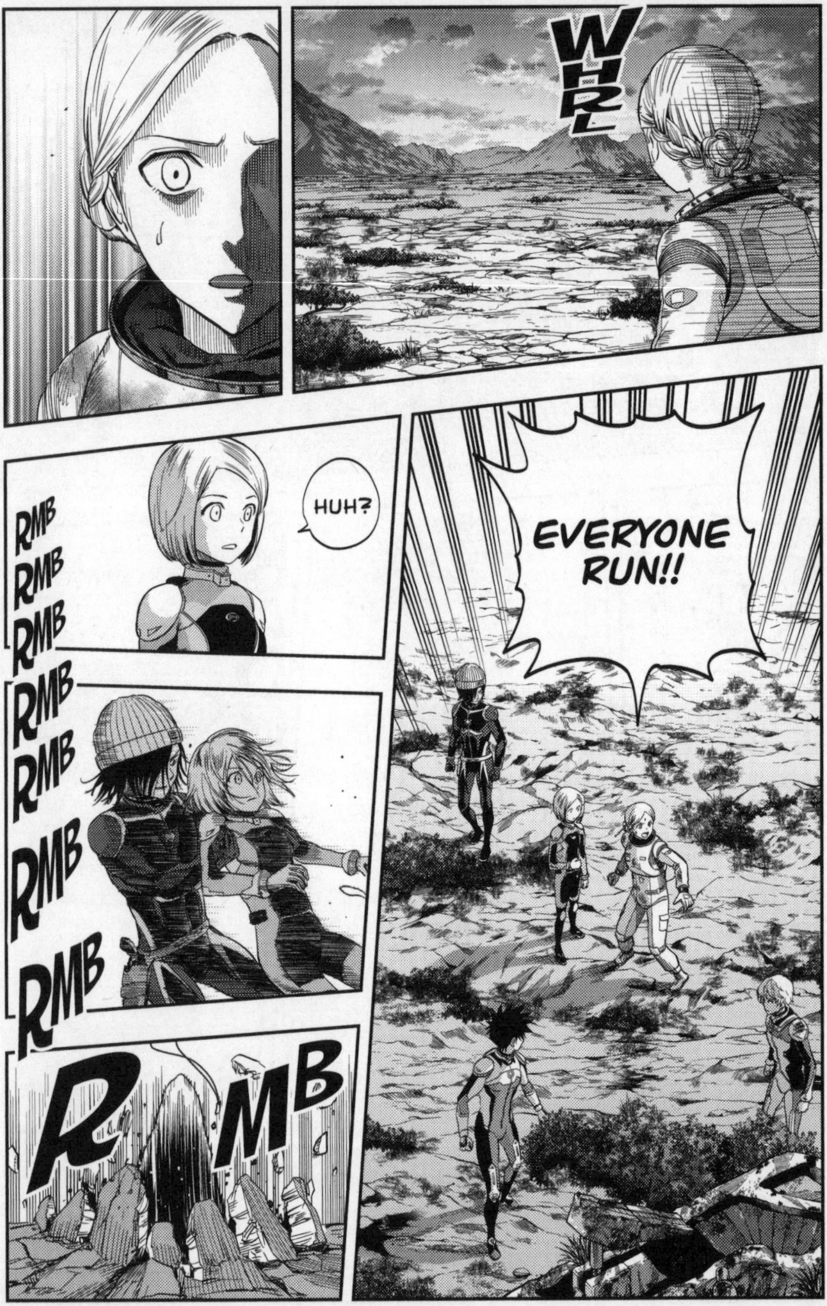
WHRL
EVERYONE RUN!!
HUH?
RMB
RMB
RMB
RMB
RMB
RMB
RMB
RMB

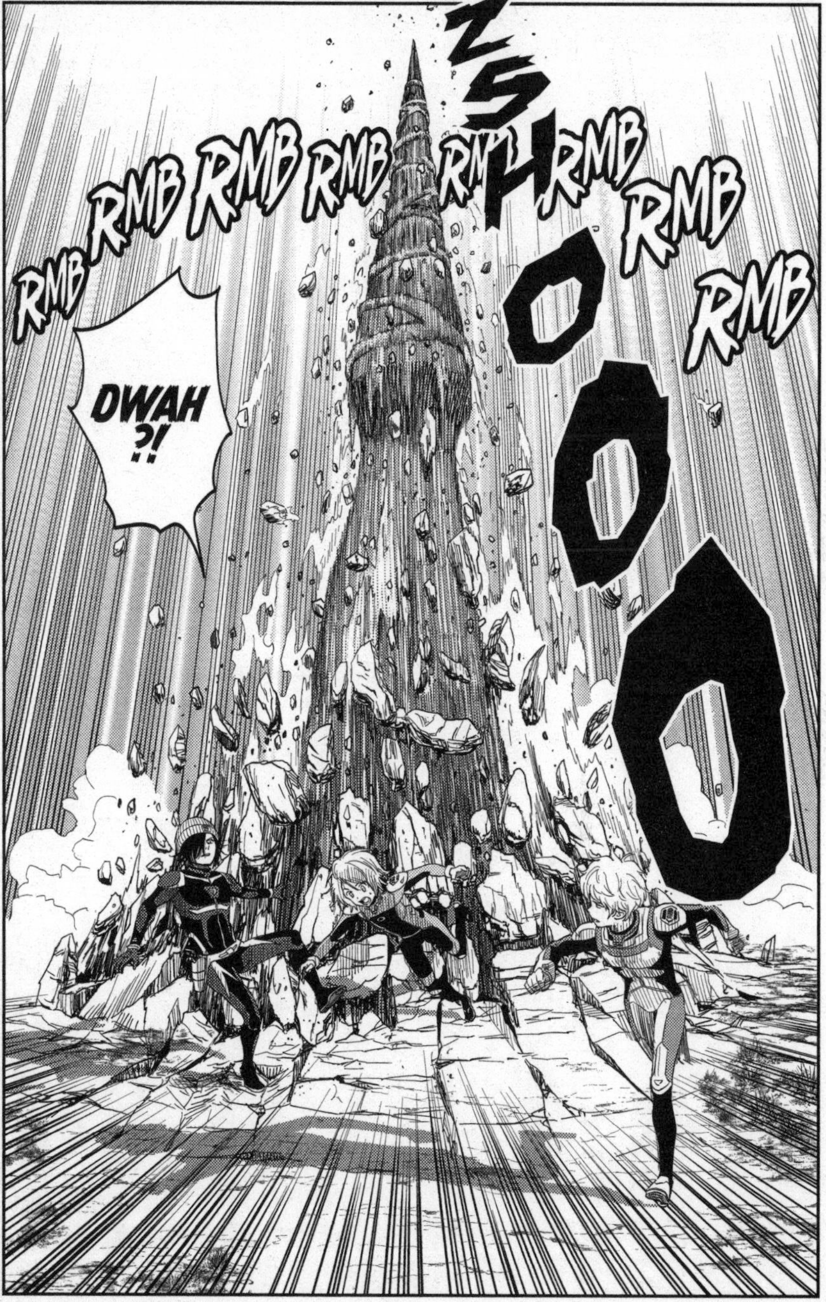

ZSHOOOO
RMB RMB RMB RMB RMB RMB RMB RMB RMB
DWAH ?!

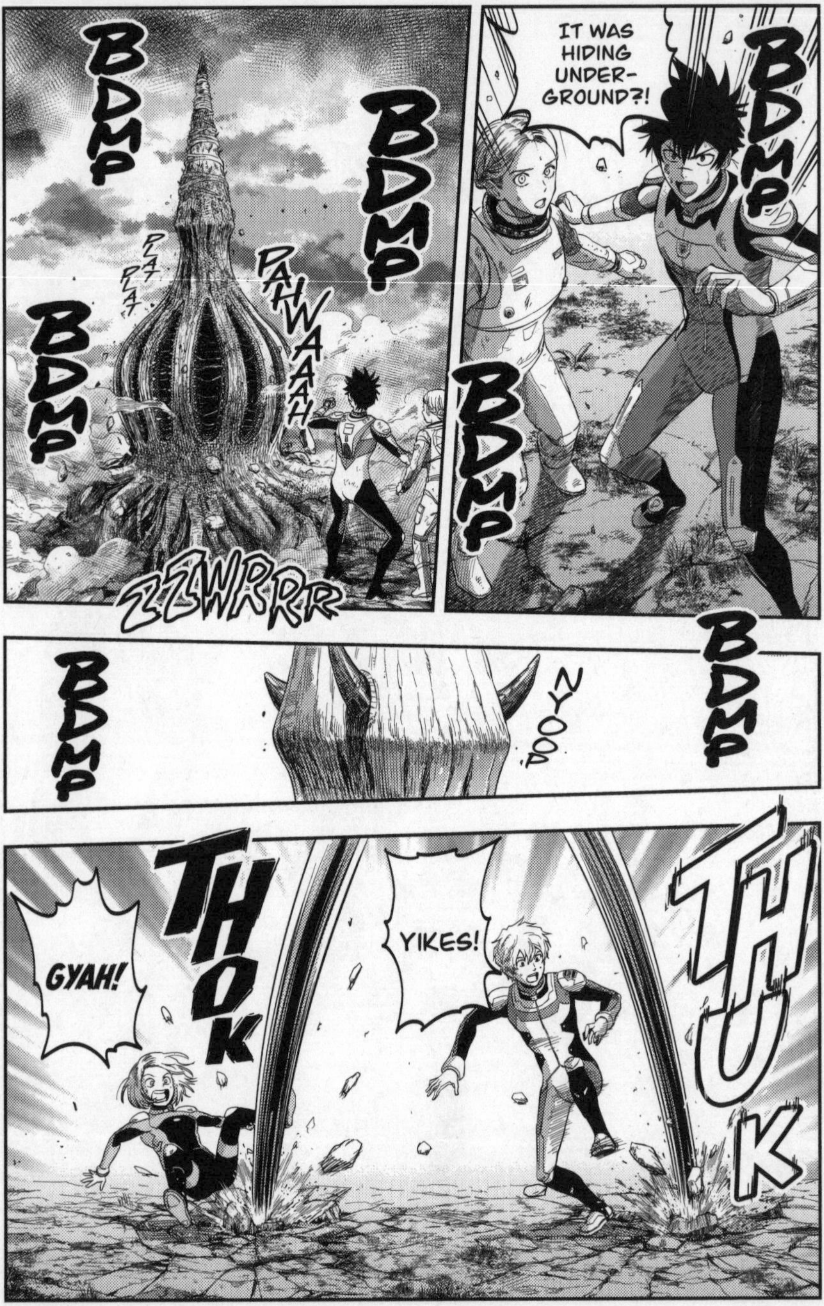

BDMP
IT WAS HIDING UNDER-GROUND?!
BDMP
BDMP
BDMP
PLAT PLAT
PAHWAAAH
BDMP
ZZWRRRR
BDMP
NYOOOP
BDMP
THUK
YIKES!
THOK
GYAH!

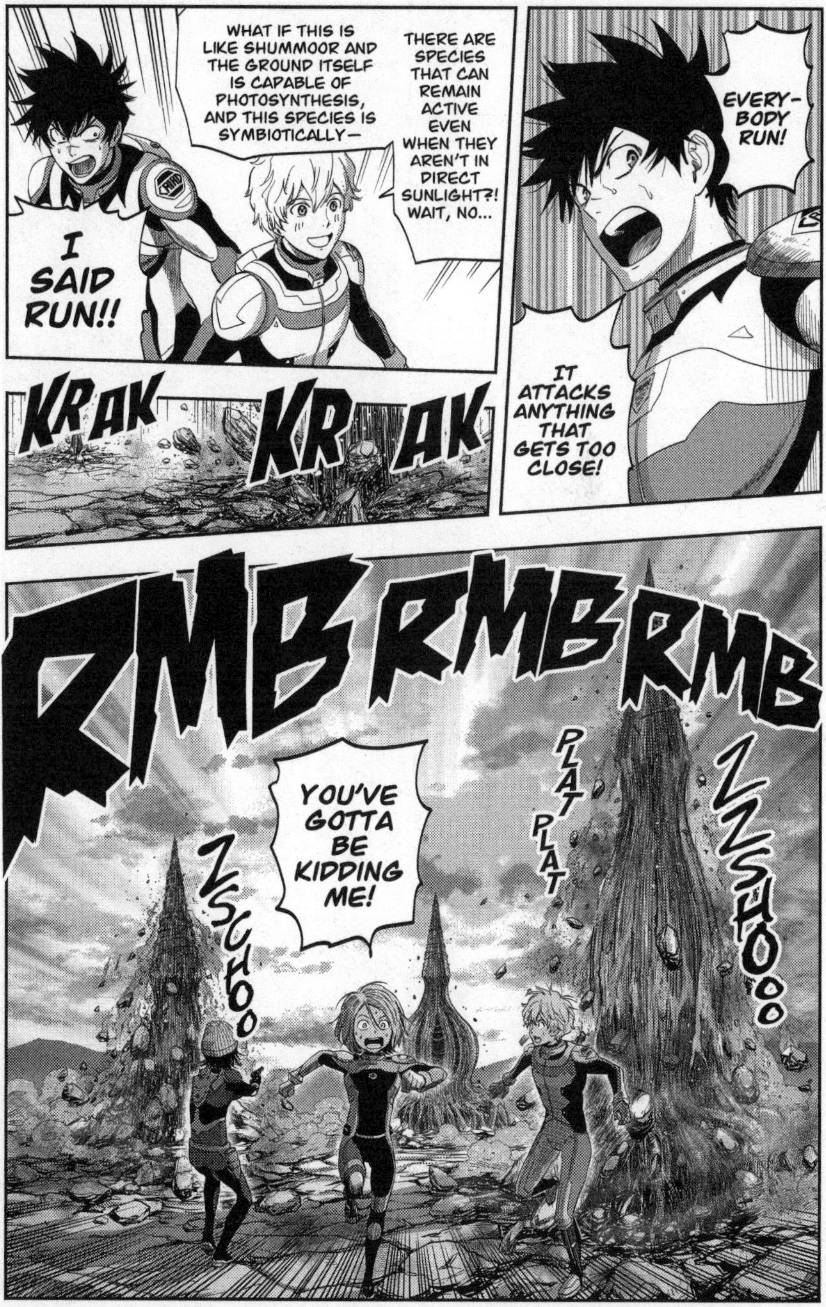
EVERY-BODY RUN!
IT ATTACKS ANYTHING THAT GETS TOO CLOSE!
THERE ARE SPECIES THAT CAN REMAIN ACTIVE EVEN WHEN THEY AREN'T IN DIRECT SUNLIGHT?! WAIT, NO...
WHAT IF THIS IS LIKE SHUMMOOR AND THE GROUND ITSELF IS CAPABLE OF PHOTOSYNTHESIS, AND THIS SPECIES IS SYMBIOTICALLY—
I SAID RUN!!
KRAK
KRAK
RMB RMB RMB
ZZSHOOO
PLAT
PLAT PLAT
YOU'VE GOTTA BE KIDDING ME!
ZSSHOO

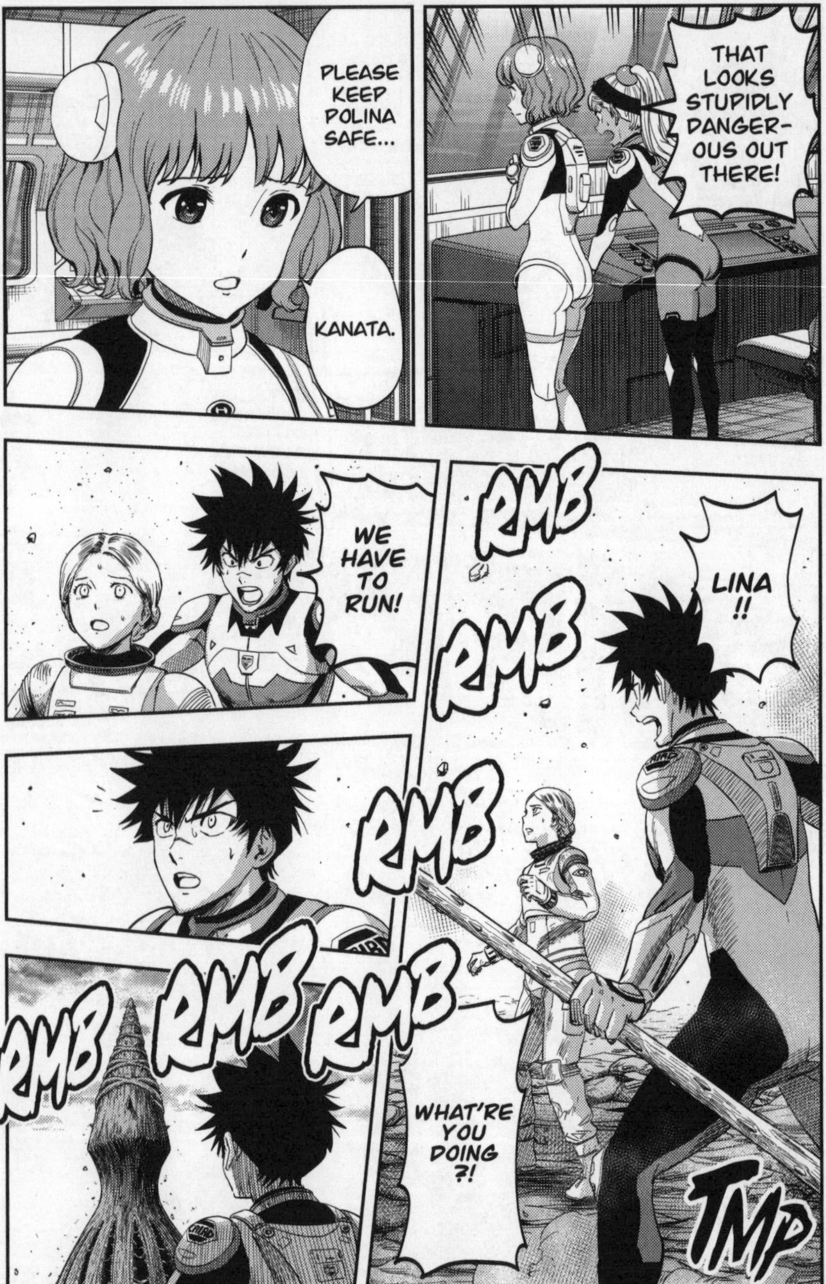
THAT LOOKS STUPIDLY DANGER-OUS OUT THERE!
PLEASE KEEP POLINA SAFE...
KANATA.
RMB
RMB
LINA !!
RMB
WHAT'RE YOU DOING ?!
TMP
WE HAVE TO RUN!
RMB
RMB
RMB

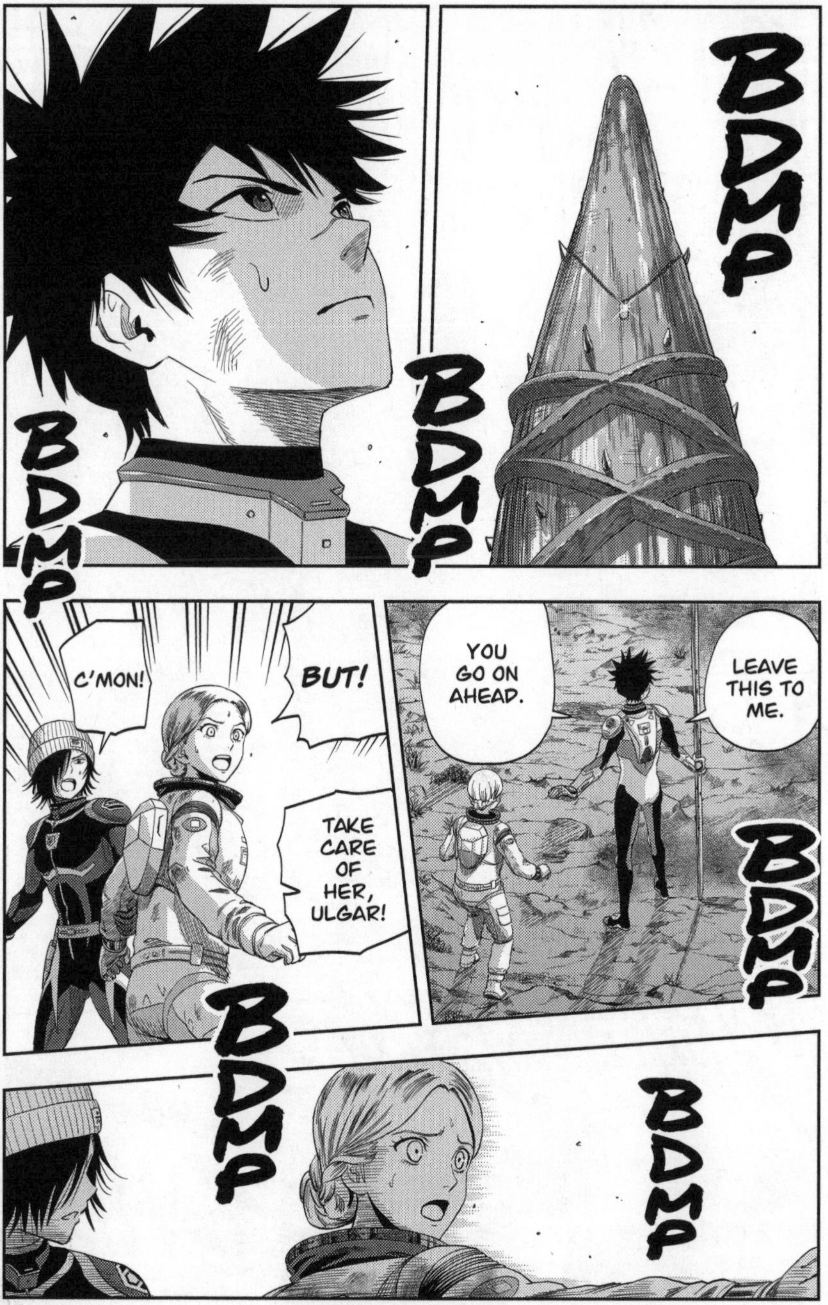
BDMP
BDMP
BDMP
LEAVE THIS TO ME.
YOU GO ON AHEAD.
BDMP
BUT!
C'MON!
TAKE CARE OF HER, ULGAR!
BDMP
BDMP
BDMP

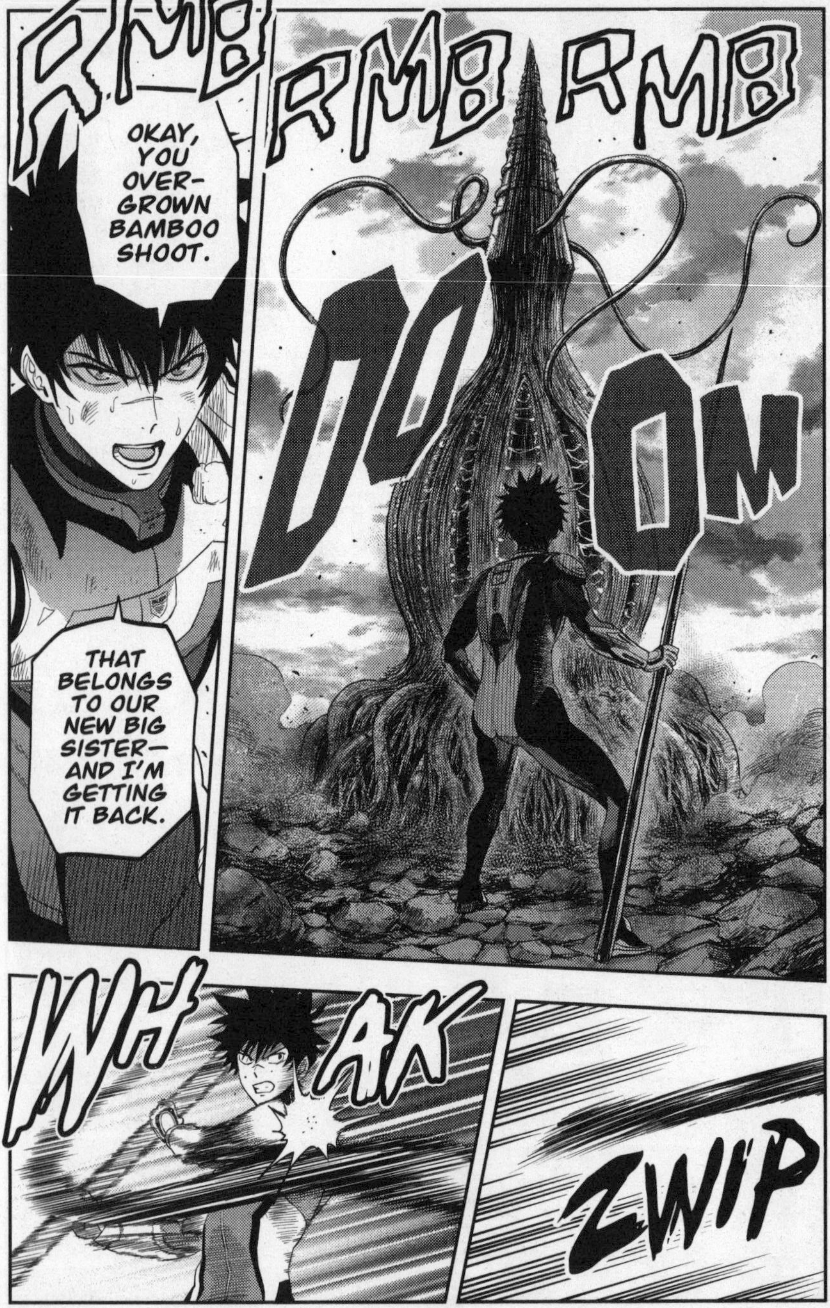
RMB RMB
DOOM
RMB
OKAY, YOU OVER-GROWN BAMBOO SHOOT.
THAT BELONGS TO OUR NEW BIG SISTER—AND I'M GETTING IT BACK.
ZWIP
WHAK

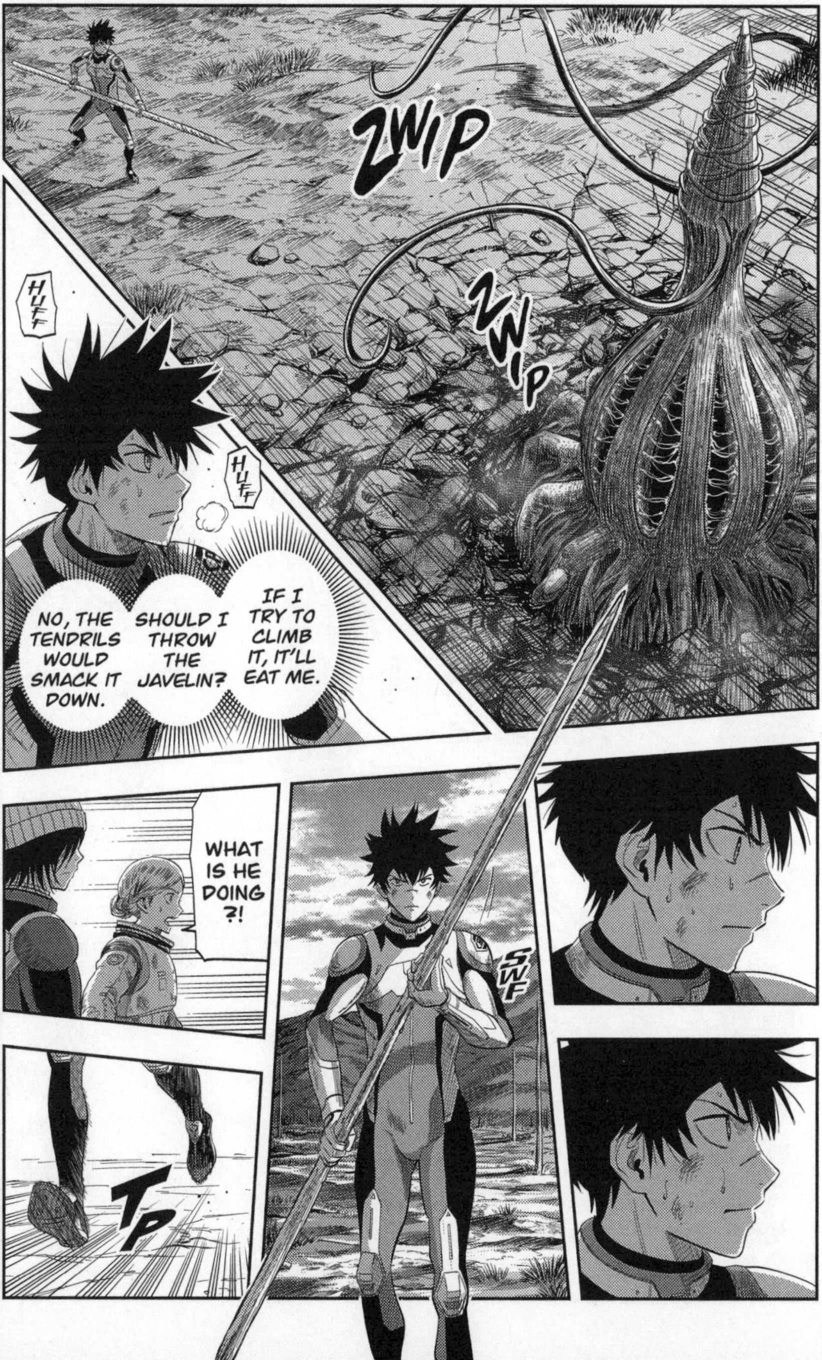
ZWIP
ZWIP
HUFF
HUFF
IF I TRY TO CLIMB IT, IT'LL EAT ME.
SHOULD I THROW THE JAVELIN?
NO, THE TENDRILS WOULD SMACK IT DOWN.
SWF
WHAT IS HE DOING?!
TP

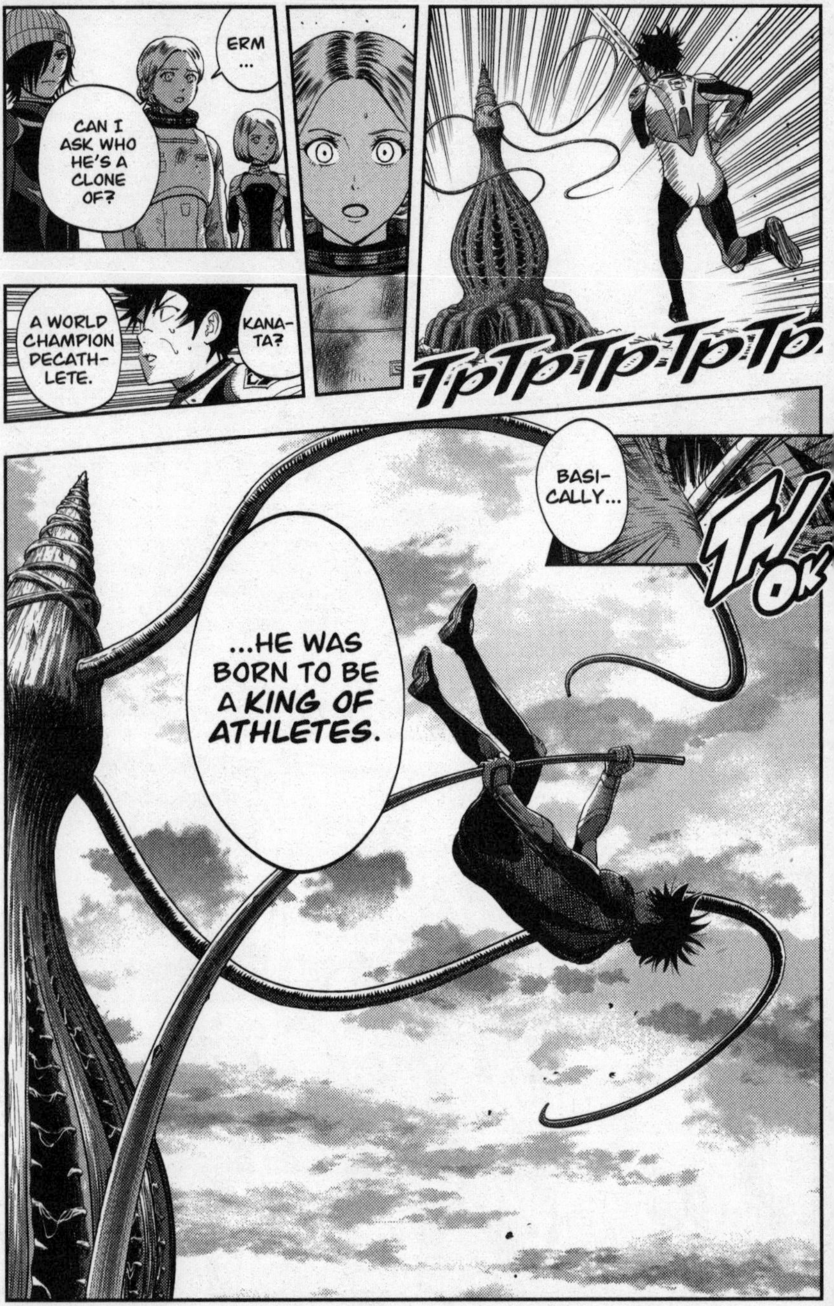

TpTpTpTpTp
ERM ...
CAN I ASK WHO HE'S A CLONE OF?
KANA-TA?
A WORLD CHAMPION DECATHLETE.
BASICALLY...
THOK
...HE WAS BORN TO BE A KING OF ATHLETES.

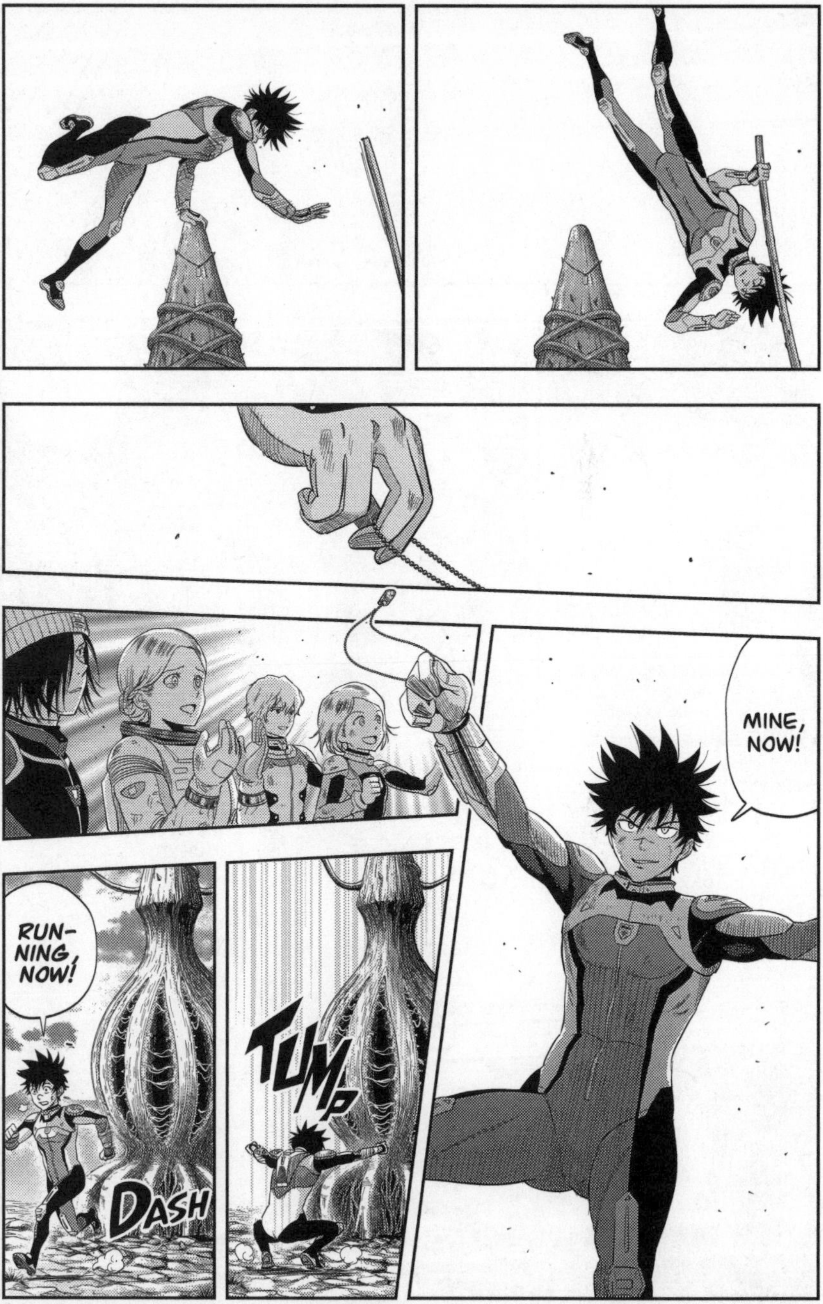
MINE, NOW!
TUMP
RUN-NING, NOW!
DASH

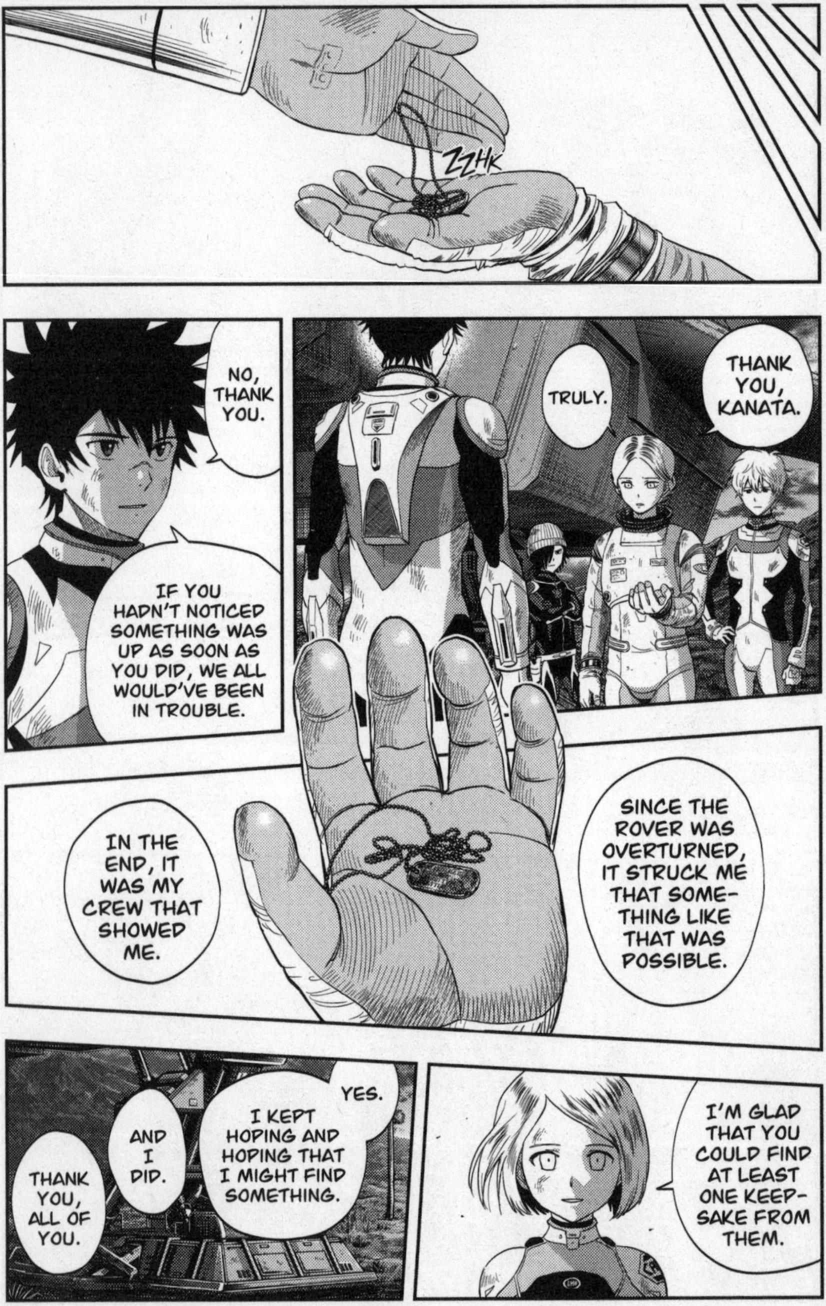
ZZHK
THANK YOU, KANATA.
TRULY.
NO, THANK YOU.
IF YOU HADN'T NOTICED SOMETHING WAS UP AS SOON AS YOU DID, WE ALL WOULD'VE BEEN IN TROUBLE.
SINCE THE ROVER WAS OVERTURNED, IT STRUCK ME THAT SOME-THING LIKE THAT WAS POSSIBLE.
IN THE END, IT WAS MY CREW THAT SHOWED ME.
I'M GLAD THAT YOU COULD FIND AT LEAST ONE KEEP-SAKE FROM THEM.
YES.
I KEPT HOPING AND HOPING THAT I MIGHT FIND SOMETHING.
AND I DID.
THANK YOU, ALL OF YOU.

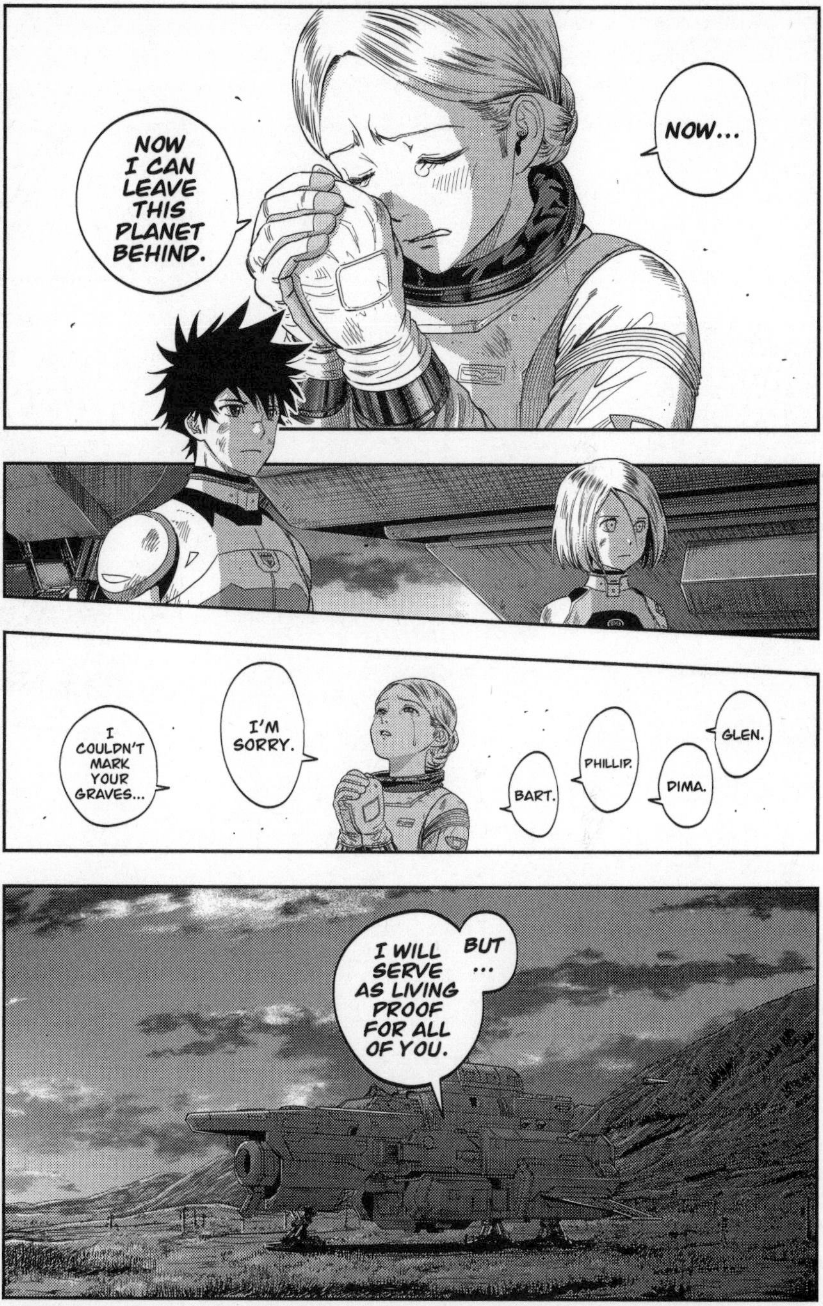
NOW...
NOW I CAN LEAVE THIS PLANET BEHIND.
GLEN.
DIMA.
PHILLIP.
BART.
I'M SORRY.
I COULDN'T MARK YOUR GRAVES...
BUT...
I WILL SERVE AS LIVING PROOF FOR ALL OF YOU.

ASTRA

LOST IN SPACE

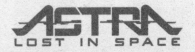

ASTRA
LOST IN SPACE
#37

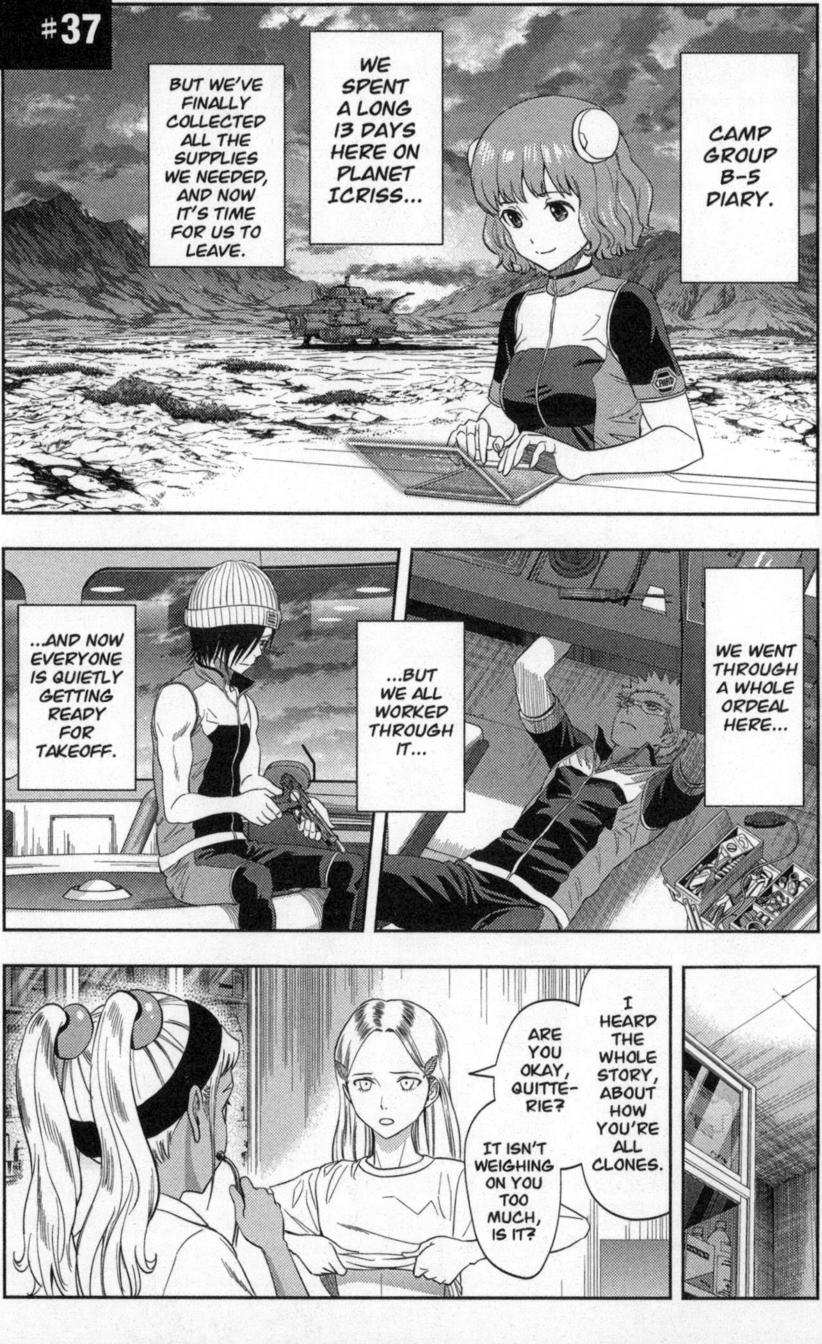
CAMP GROUP B-5 DIARY.
WE SPENT A LONG 13 DAYS HERE ON PLANET ICRISS...
BUT WE'VE FINALLY COLLECTED ALL THE SUPPLIES WE NEEDED, AND NOW IT'S TIME FOR US TO LEAVE.
WE WENT THROUGH A WHOLE ORDEAL HERE...
...BUT WE ALL WORKED THROUGH IT...
...AND NOW EVERYONE IS QUIETLY GETTING READY FOR TAKEOFF.
I HEARD THE WHOLE STORY, ABOUT HOW YOU'RE ALL CLONES.
ARE YOU OKAY, QUITTE-RIE?
IT ISN'T WEIGHING ON YOU TOO MUCH, IS IT?

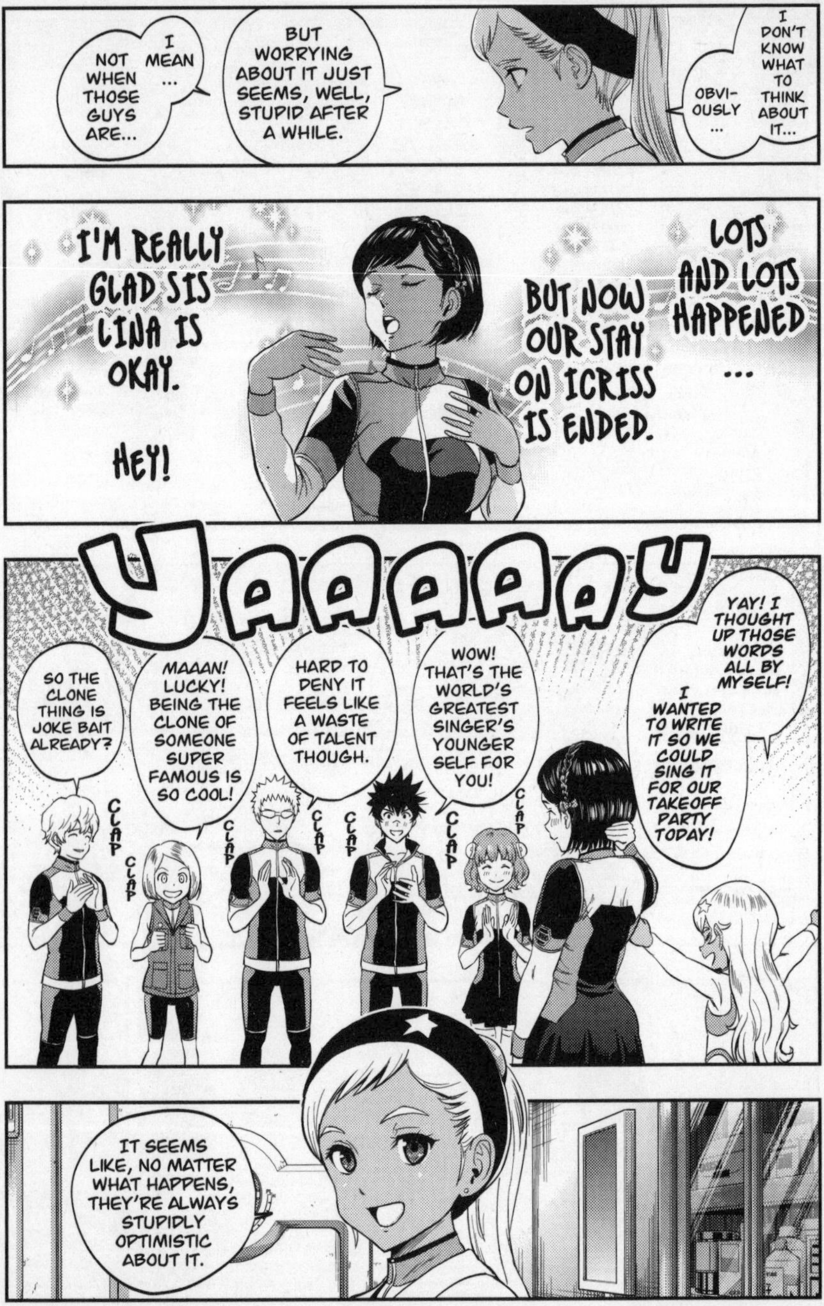
I DON'T KNOW WHAT TO THINK ABOUT IT... OBVIOUSLY...
BUT WORRYING ABOUT IT JUST SEEMS, WELL, STUPID AFTER A WHILE.
I MEAN... NOT WHEN THOSE GUYS ARE...
LOTS AND LOTS HAPPENED...
BUT NOW OUR STAY ON ICRISS IS ENDED.
I'M REALLY GLAD SIS LINA IS OKAY.
HEY!
YAAAAAY
YAY! I THOUGHT UP THOSE WORDS ALL BY MYSELF!
I WANTED TO WRITE IT SO WE COULD SING IT FOR OUR TAKEOFF PARTY TODAY!
CLAP
WOW! THAT'S THE WORLD'S GREATEST SINGER'S YOUNGER SELF FOR YOU!
CLAP
CLAP
HARD TO DENY IT FEELS LIKE A WASTE OF TALENT THOUGH.
CLAP
CLAP
MAAAN! LUCKY! BEING THE CLONE OF SOMEONE SUPER FAMOUS IS SO COOL!
CLAP
SO THE CLONE THING IS JOKE BAIT ALREADY?
CLAP
IT SEEMS LIKE, NO MATTER WHAT HAPPENS, THEY'RE ALWAYS STUPIDLY OPTIMISTIC ABOUT IT.

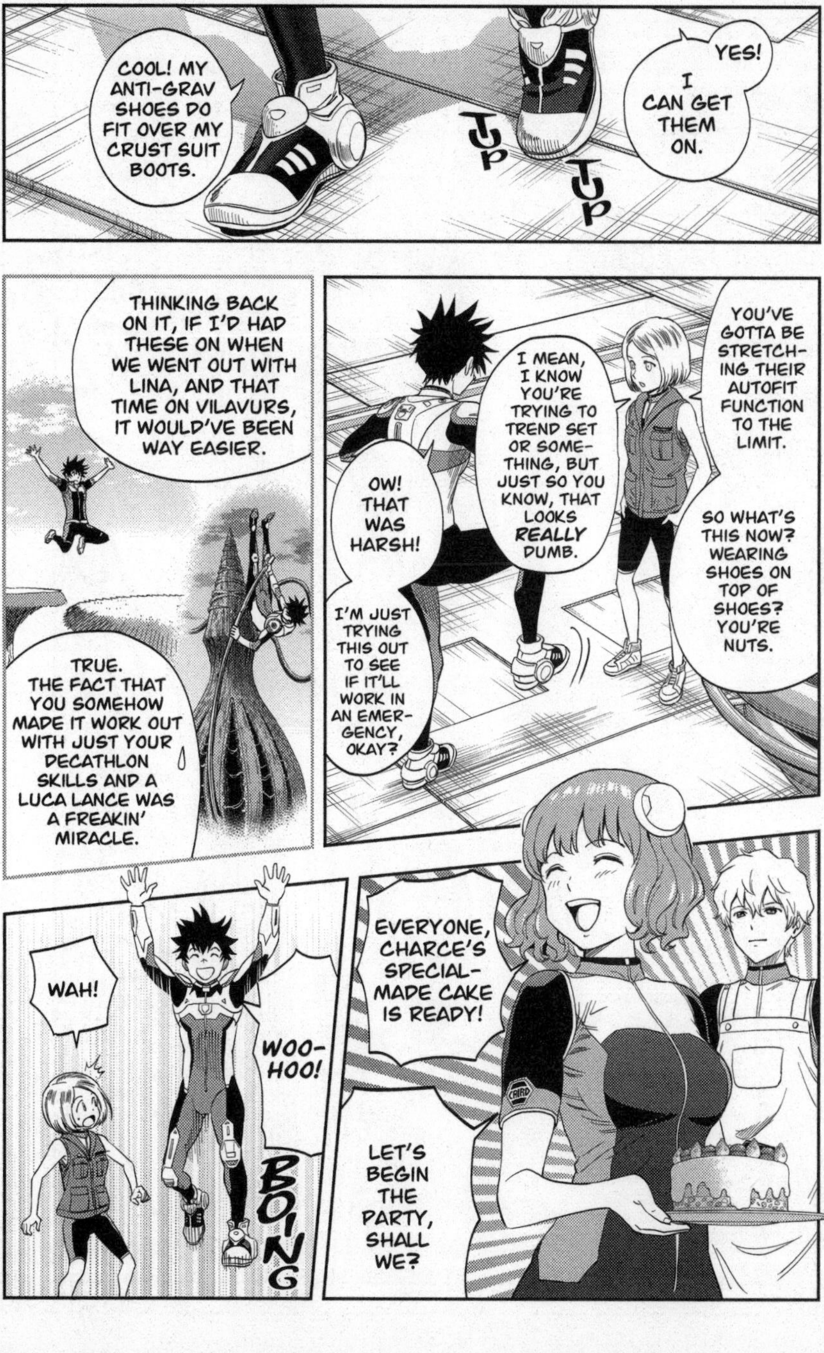
YES! I CAN GET THEM ON.
TUP
TUP
COOL! MY ANTI-GRAV SHOES DO FIT OVER MY CRUST SUIT BOOTS.
YOU'VE GOTTA BE STRETCHING THEIR AUTOFIT FUNCTION TO THE LIMIT.
SO WHAT'S THIS NOW? WEARING SHOES ON TOP OF SHOES? YOU'RE NUTS.
I MEAN, I KNOW YOU'RE TRYING TO TREND SET OR SOMETHING, BUT JUST SO YOU KNOW, THAT LOOKS REALLY DUMB.
OW! THAT WAS HARSH!
I'M JUST TRYING THIS OUT TO SEE IF IT'LL WORK IN AN EMERGENCY, OKAY?
THINKING BACK ON IT, IF I'D HAD THESE ON WHEN WE WENT OUT WITH LINA, AND THAT TIME ON VILAVURS, IT WOULD'VE BEEN WAY EASIER.
TRUE. THE FACT THAT YOU SOMEHOW MADE IT WORK OUT WITH JUST YOUR DECATHLON SKILLS AND A LUCA LANCE WAS A FREAKIN' MIRACLE.
EVERYONE, CHARCE'S SPECIAL-MADE CAKE IS READY!
LET'S BEGIN THE PARTY, SHALL WE?
WOO-HOO!
WAH!
BOING

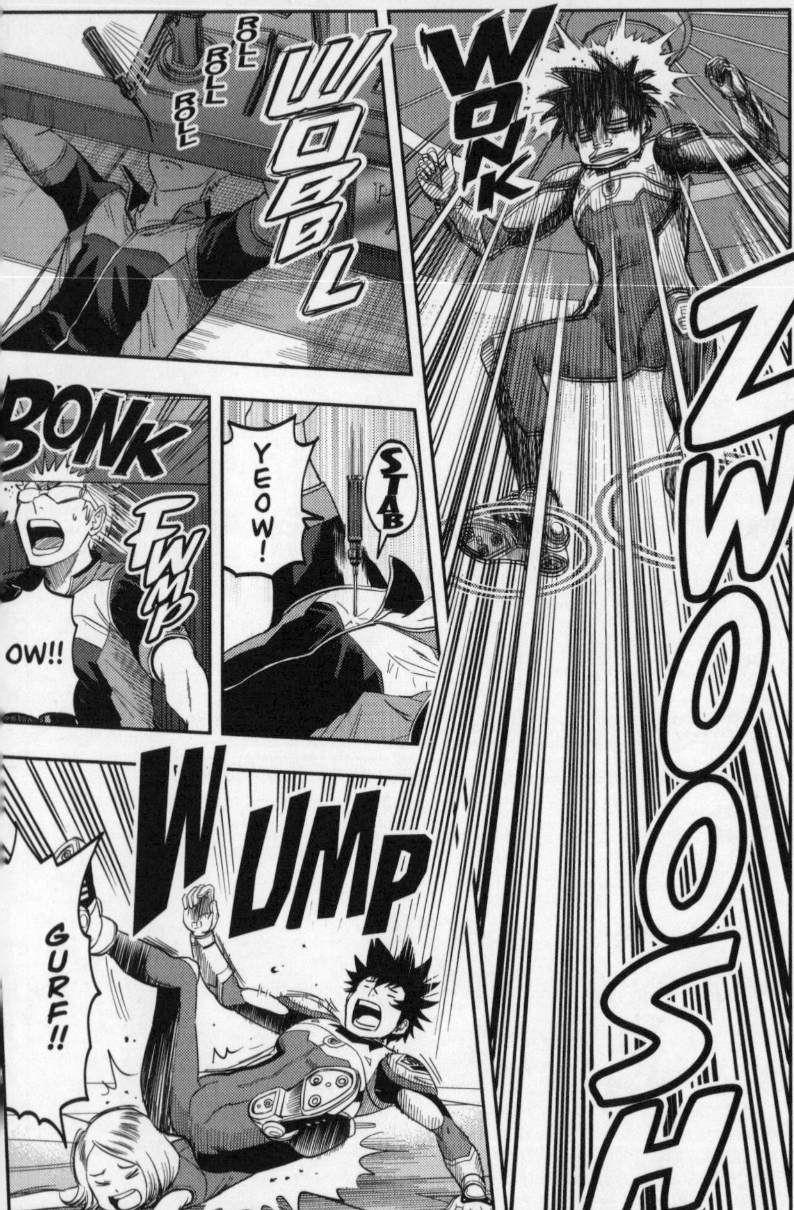
WONK
ZWOOSH
WOBBL
ROLL
ROLL
ROLL
STAB
YEOW!
BONK
FWMP
OW!!
WUMP
GURF!!

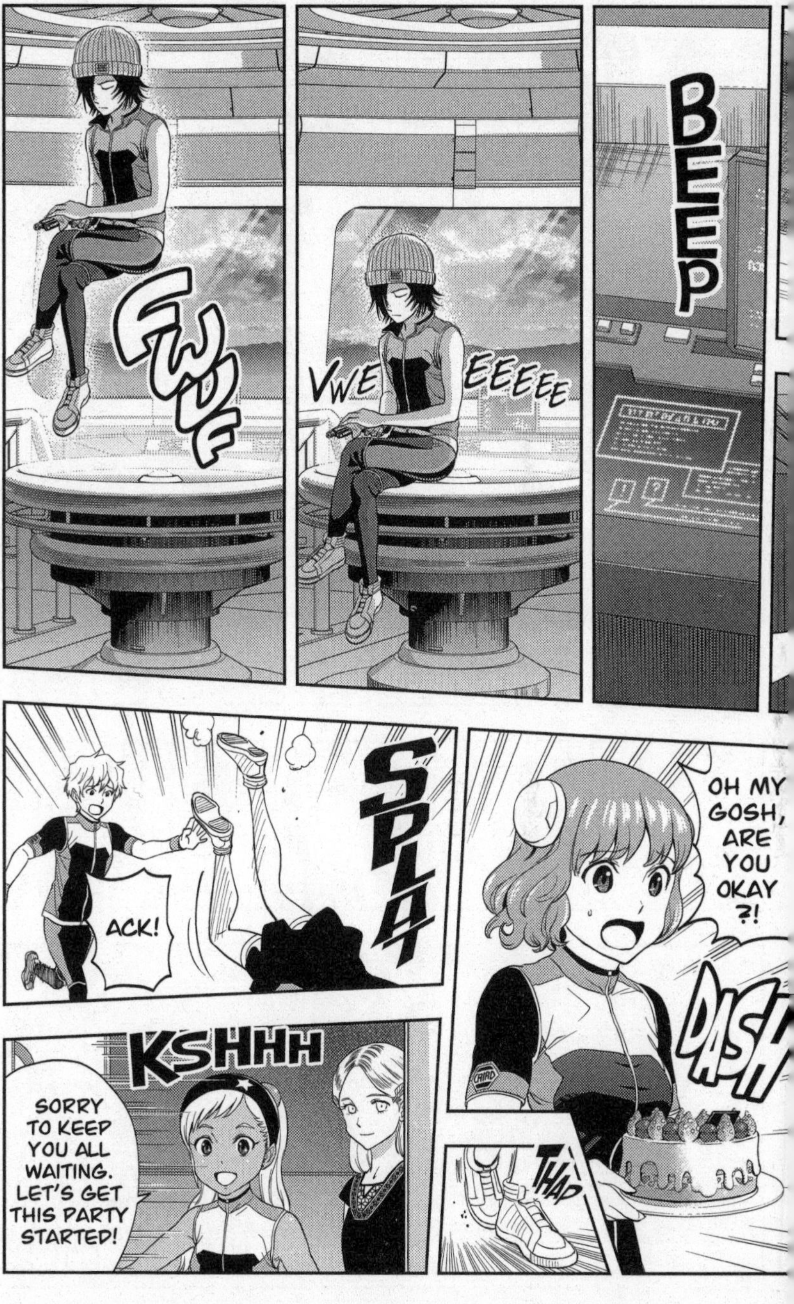
BEEP
VWEEEEEE
FWUF
OH MY GOSH, ARE YOU OKAY ?!
DASH
THAP
SPLAT
ACK!
KSHHH
SORRY TO KEEP YOU ALL WAITING. LET'S GET THIS PARTY STARTED!

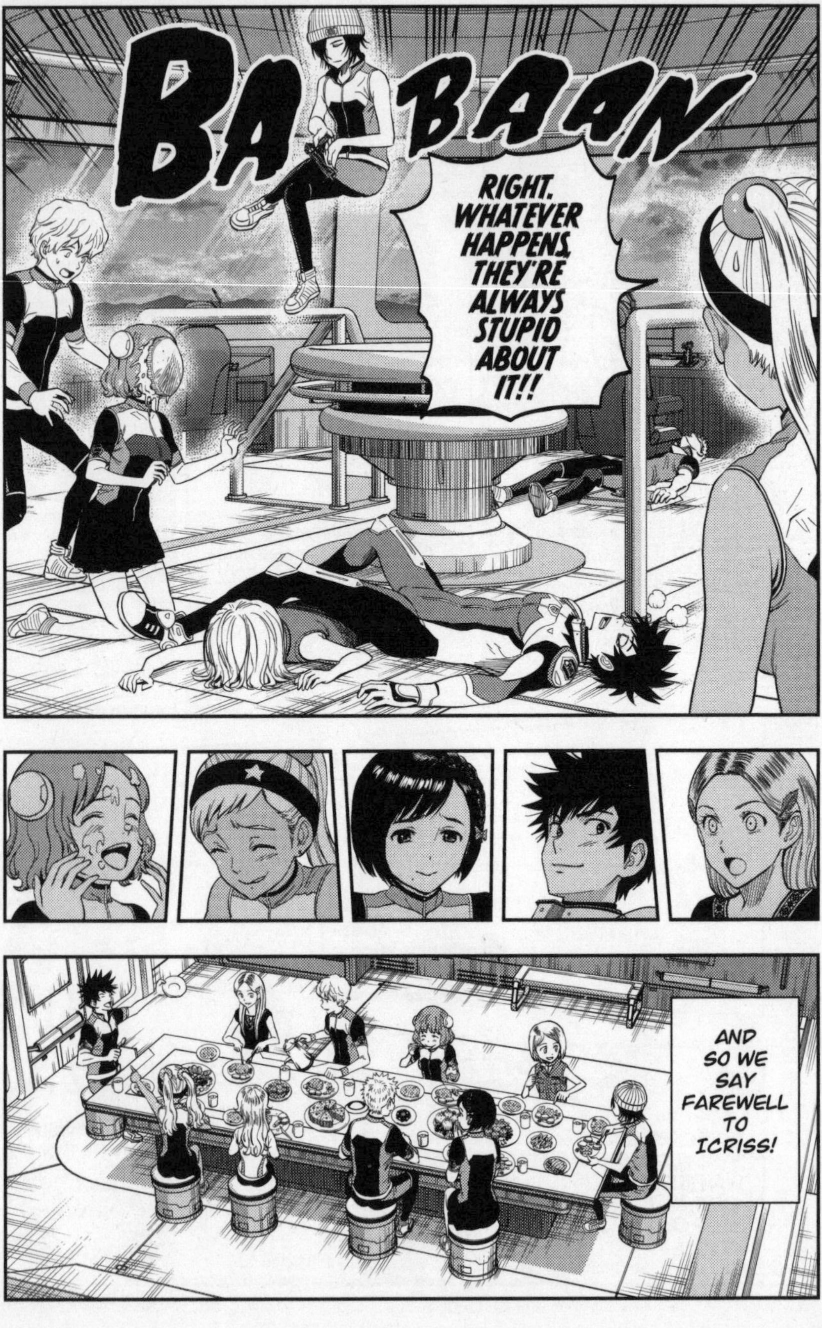
BA BAAN
RIGHT. WHATEVER HAPPENS, THEY'RE ALWAYS STUPID ABOUT IT!!
AND SO WE SAY FAREWELL TO ICRISS!

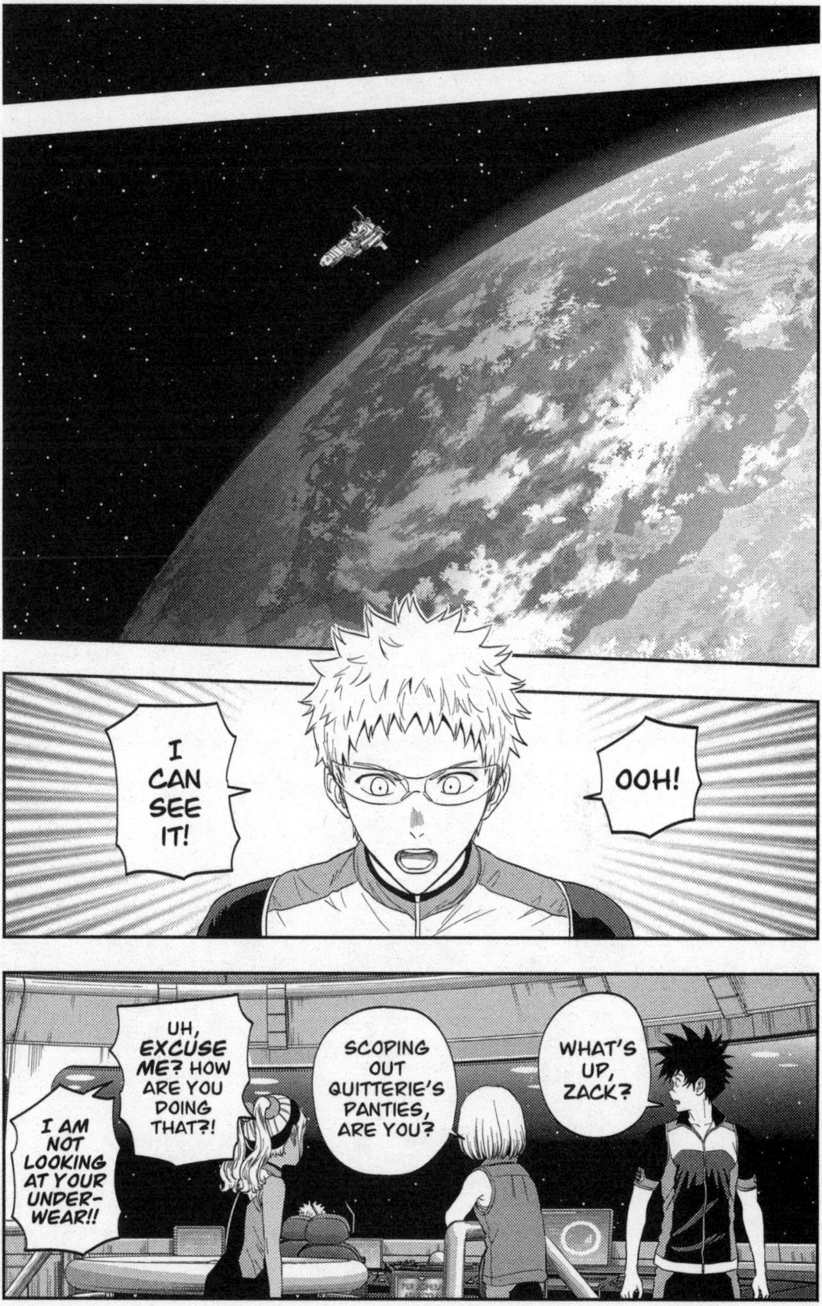
OOH!
I CAN SEE IT!
WHAT'S UP, ZACK?
SCOPING OUT QUITTERIE'S PANTIES, ARE YOU?
UH, EXCUSE ME? HOW ARE YOU DOING THAT?!
I AM NOT LOOKING AT YOUR UNDER-WEAR!!

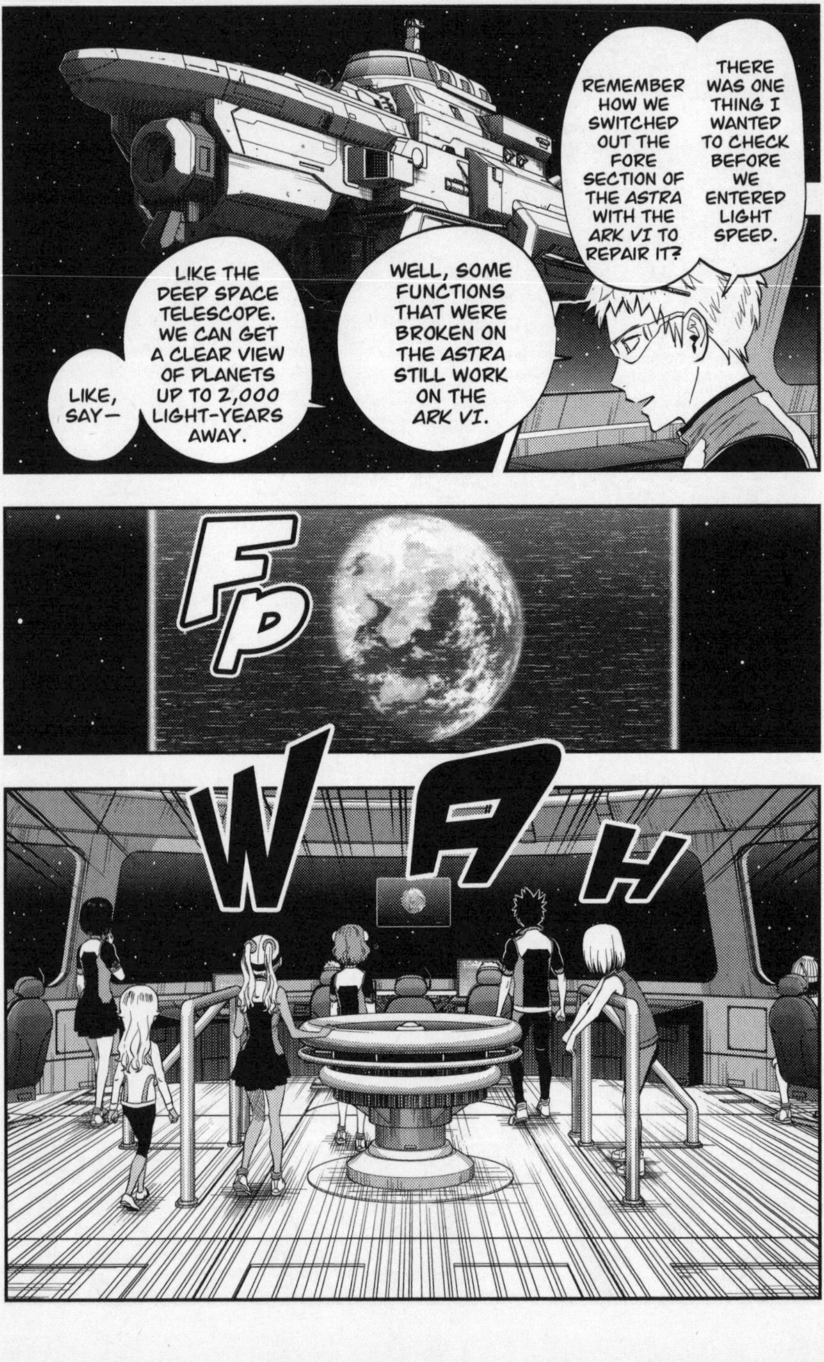
THERE WAS ONE THING I WANTED TO CHECK BEFORE WE ENTERED LIGHT SPEED.
REMEMBER HOW WE SWITCHED OUT THE FORE SECTION OF THE ASTRA WITH THE ARK VI TO REPAIR IT?
WELL, SOME FUNCTIONS THAT WERE BROKEN ON THE ASTRA STILL WORK ON THE ARK VI.
LIKE THE DEEP SPACE TELESCOPE. WE CAN GET A CLEAR VIEW OF PLANETS UP TO 2,000 LIGHT-YEARS AWAY.
LIKE, SAY—
FP
WAAH

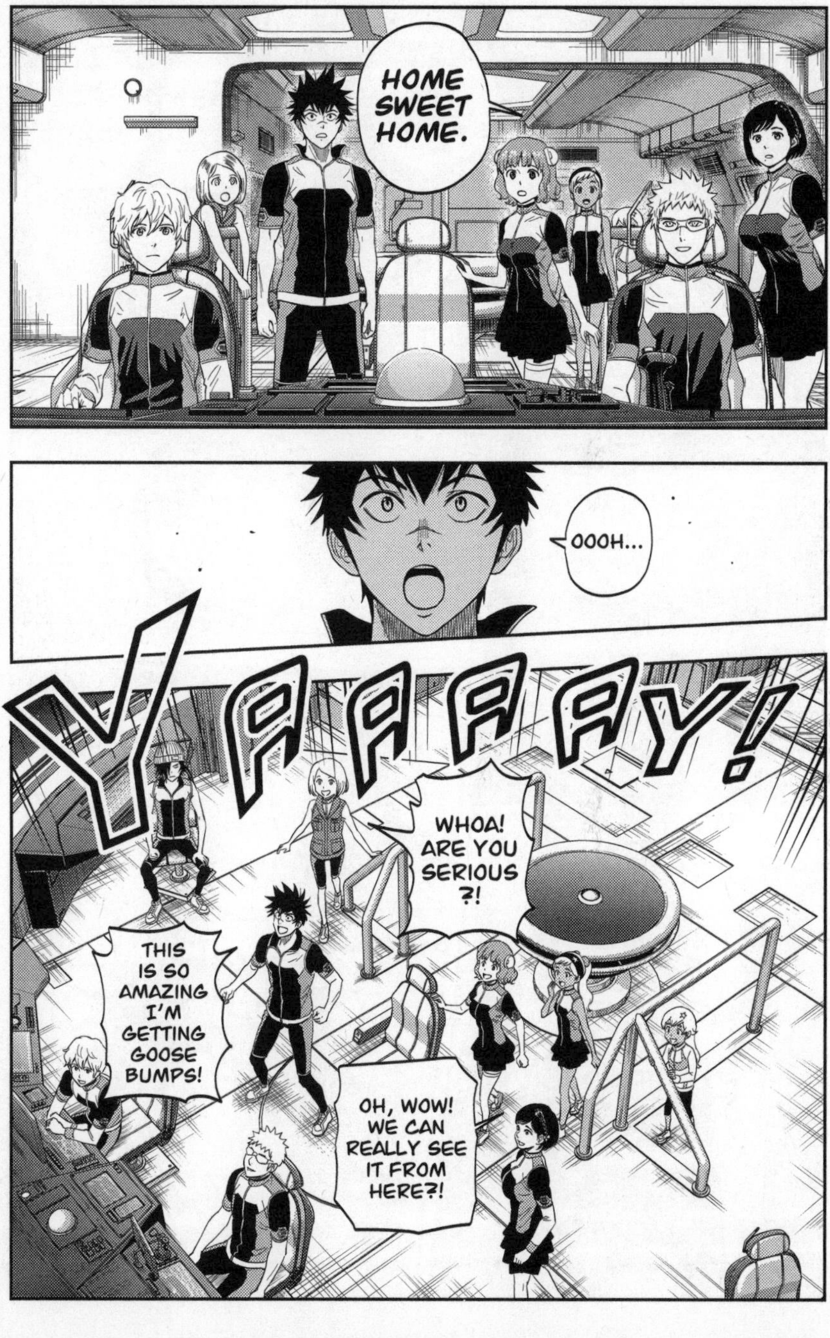
HOME SWEET HOME.
OOOH...
YAAAAY!
WHOA! ARE YOU SERIOUS?!
OH, WOW! WE CAN REALLY SEE IT FROM HERE?!
THIS IS SO AMAZING I'M GETTING GOOSE BUMPS!

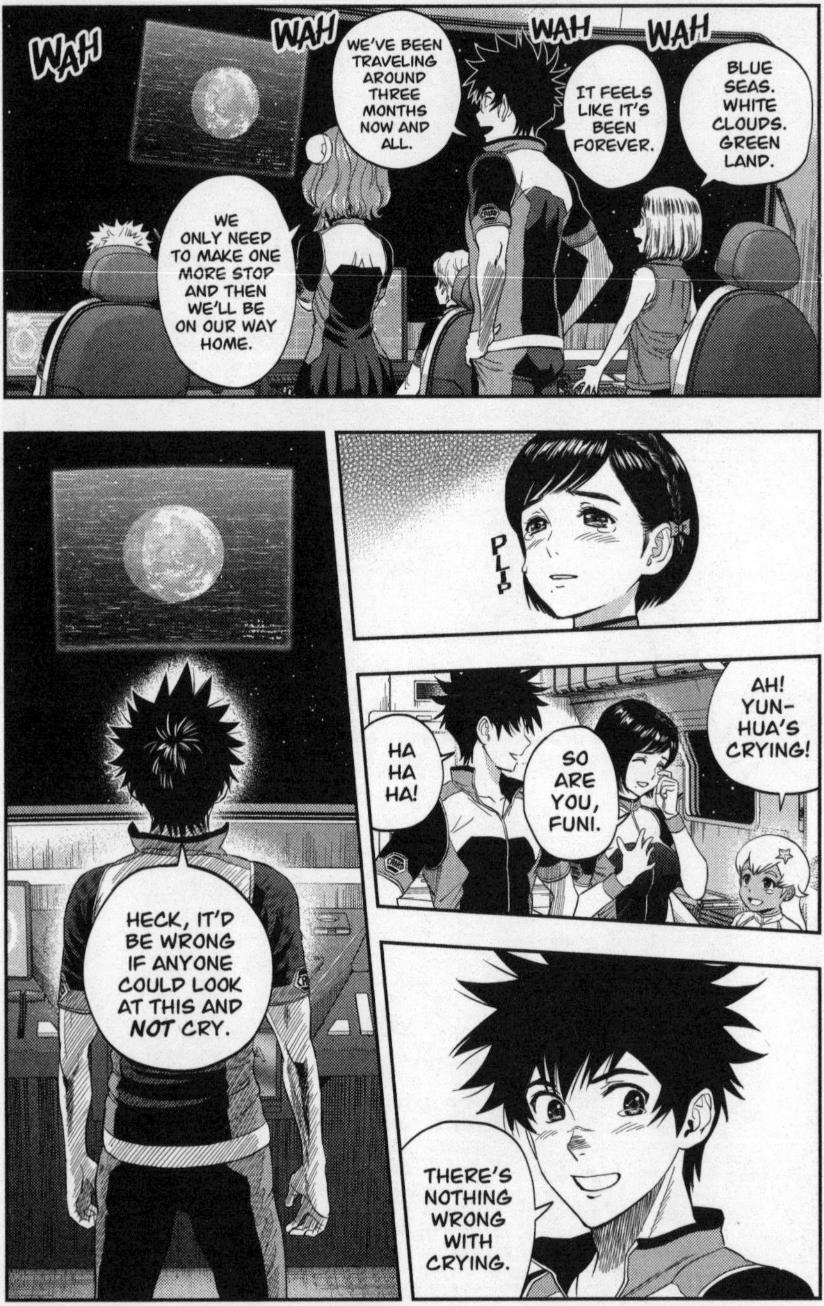
WAH
BLUE SEAS. WHITE CLOUDS. GREEN LAND.
WAH
IT FEELS LIKE IT'S BEEN FOREVER.
WAH
WE'VE BEEN TRAVELING AROUND THREE MONTHS NOW AND ALL.
WAH
WE ONLY NEED TO MAKE ONE MORE STOP AND THEN WE'LL BE ON OUR WAY HOME.
PLIP
AH! YUN-HUA'S CRYING!
SO ARE YOU, FUNI.
HA HA HA!
THERE'S NOTHING WRONG WITH CRYING.
HECK, IT'D BE WRONG IF ANYONE COULD LOOK AT THIS AND *NOT* CRY.

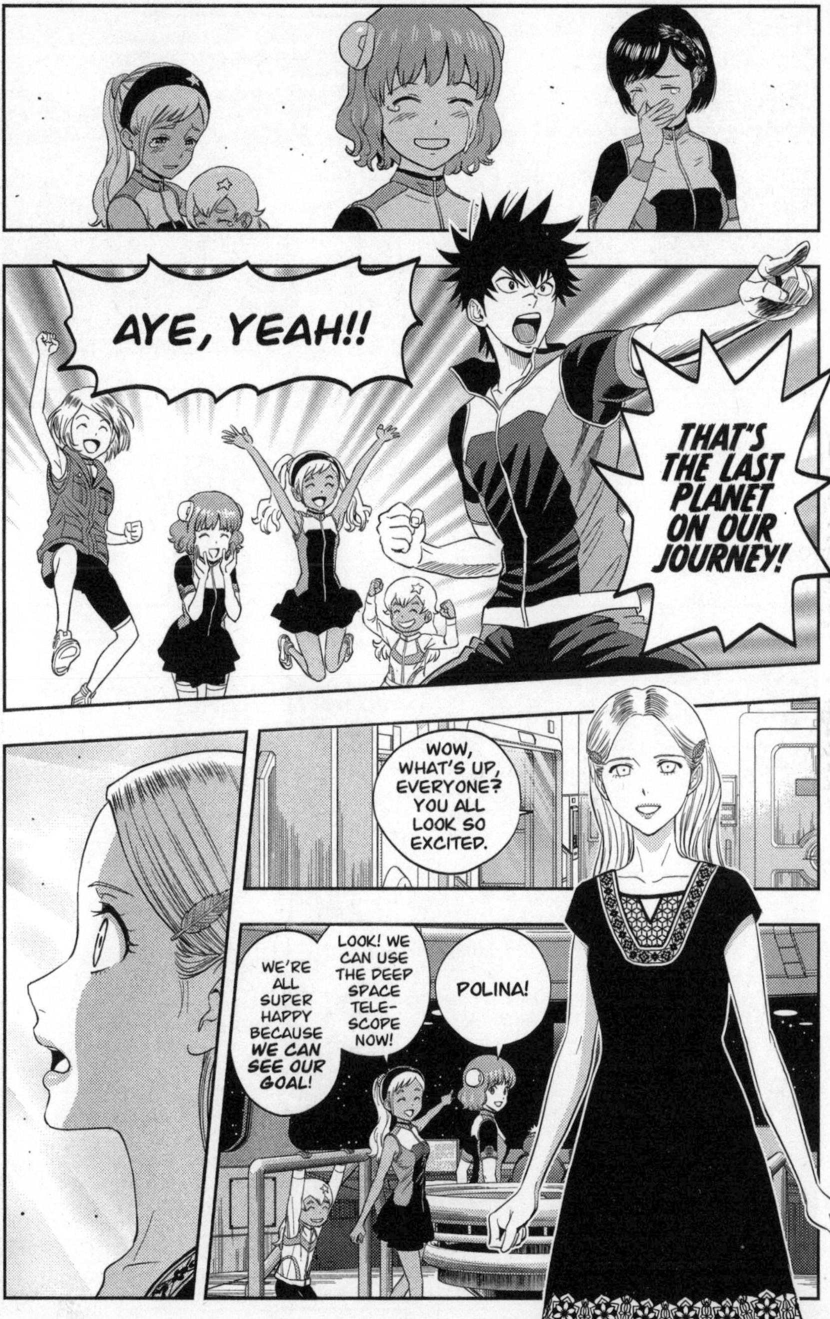
THAT'S THE LAST PLANET ON OUR JOURNEY!
AYE, YEAH!!
WOW, WHAT'S UP, EVERYONE? YOU ALL LOOK SO EXCITED.
POLINA!
LOOK! WE CAN USE THE DEEP SPACE TELE-SCOPE NOW!
WE'RE ALL SUPER HAPPY BECAUSE WE CAN SEE OUR GOAL!

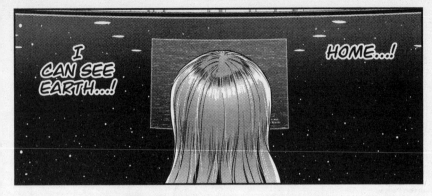

HOME...!
I CAN SEE EARTH...!
PLIP
THIS TIME... IT ISN'T A DREAM, IS IT?
I REALLY CAN GO HOME.
POLINA ...
I DREAMED OF THIS SO MANY TIMES... SO MANY TIMES.
THOSE OCEANS ...
THOSE CONTI-NENTS...

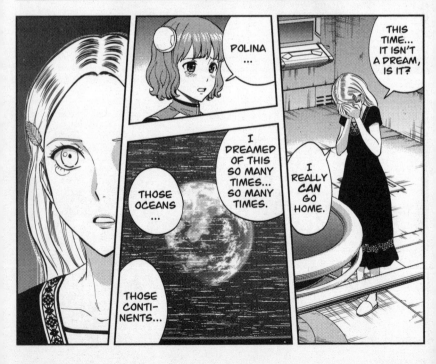

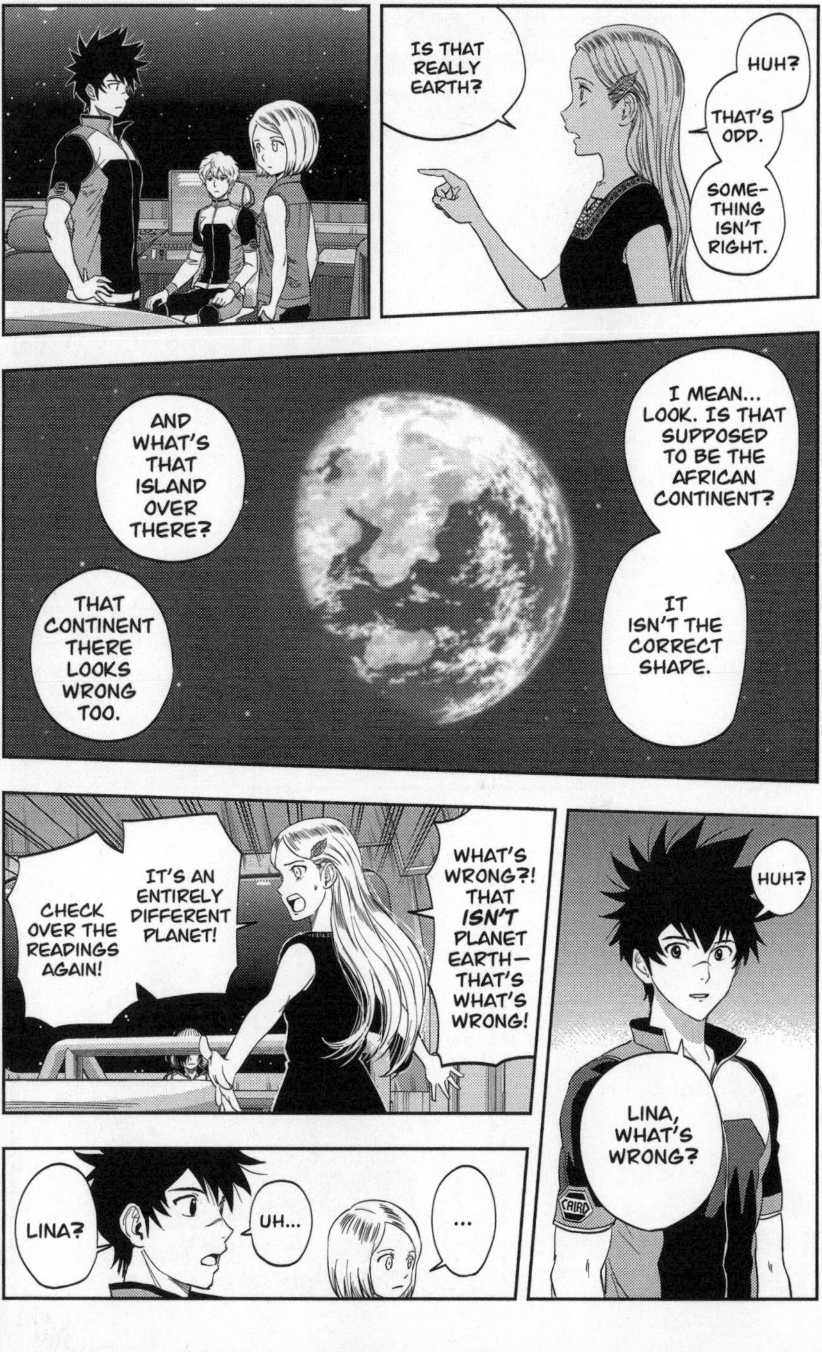
HUH?
THAT'S ODD.
SOME-THING ISN'T RIGHT.
IS THAT REALLY EARTH?
I MEAN... LOOK. IS THAT SUPPOSED TO BE THE AFRICAN CONTINENT?
IT ISN'T THE CORRECT SHAPE.
AND WHAT'S THAT ISLAND OVER THERE?
THAT CONTINENT THERE LOOKS WRONG TOO.
HUH?
LINA, WHAT'S WRONG?
WHAT'S WRONG?! THAT *ISN'T* PLANET EARTH—THAT'S WHAT'S WRONG!
IT'S AN ENTIRELY DIFFERENT PLANET!
CHECK OVER THE READINGS AGAIN!
...
UH...
LINA?

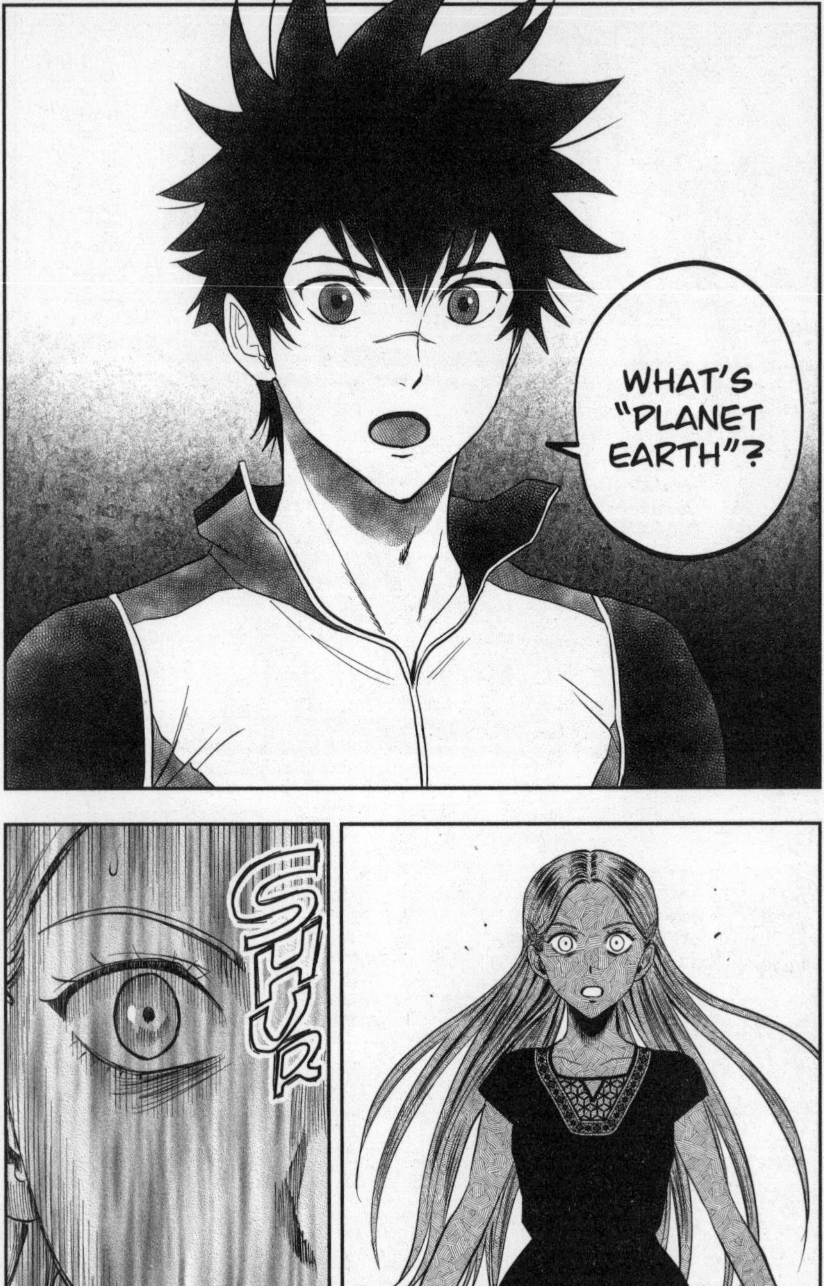
WHAT'S "PLANET EARTH"?
SHUR

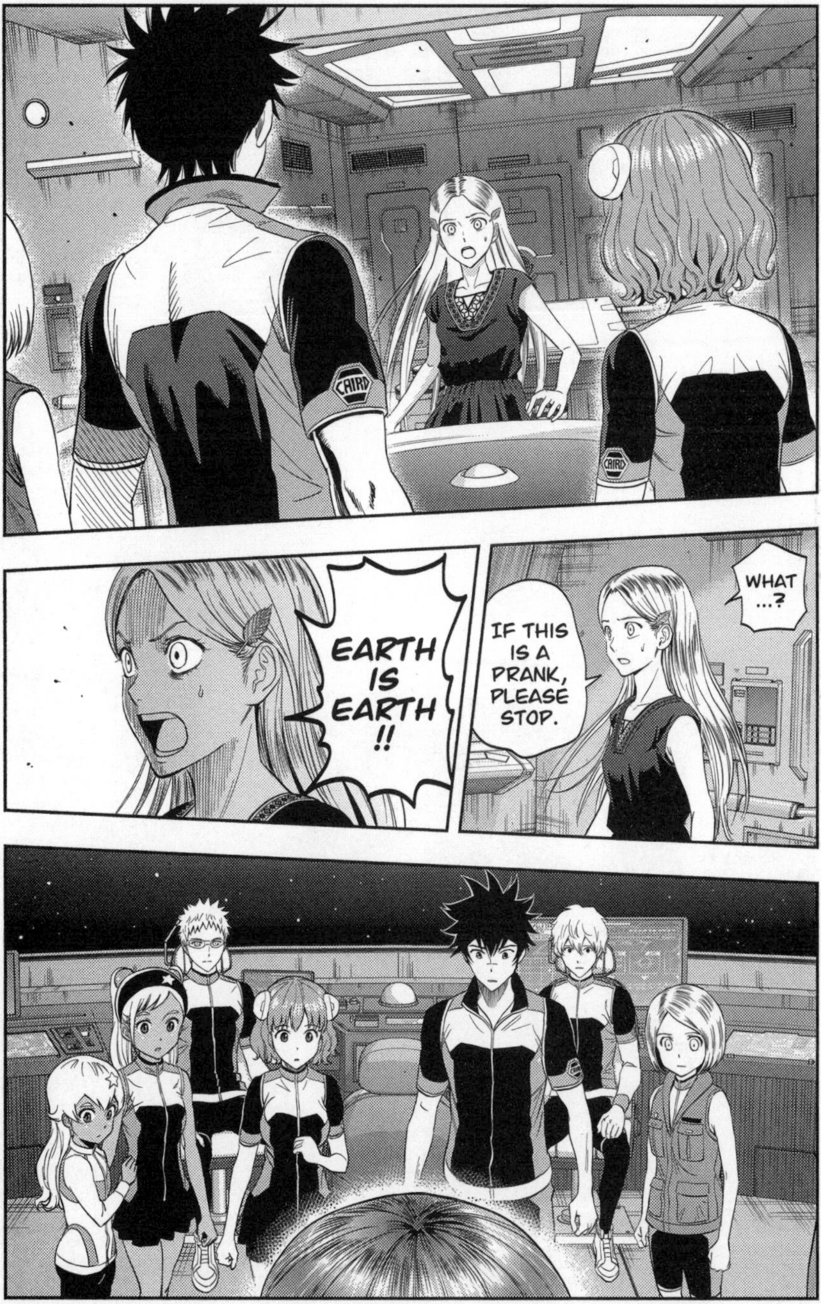
WHAT ...?
IF THIS IS A PRANK, PLEASE STOP.
EARTH IS EARTH !!

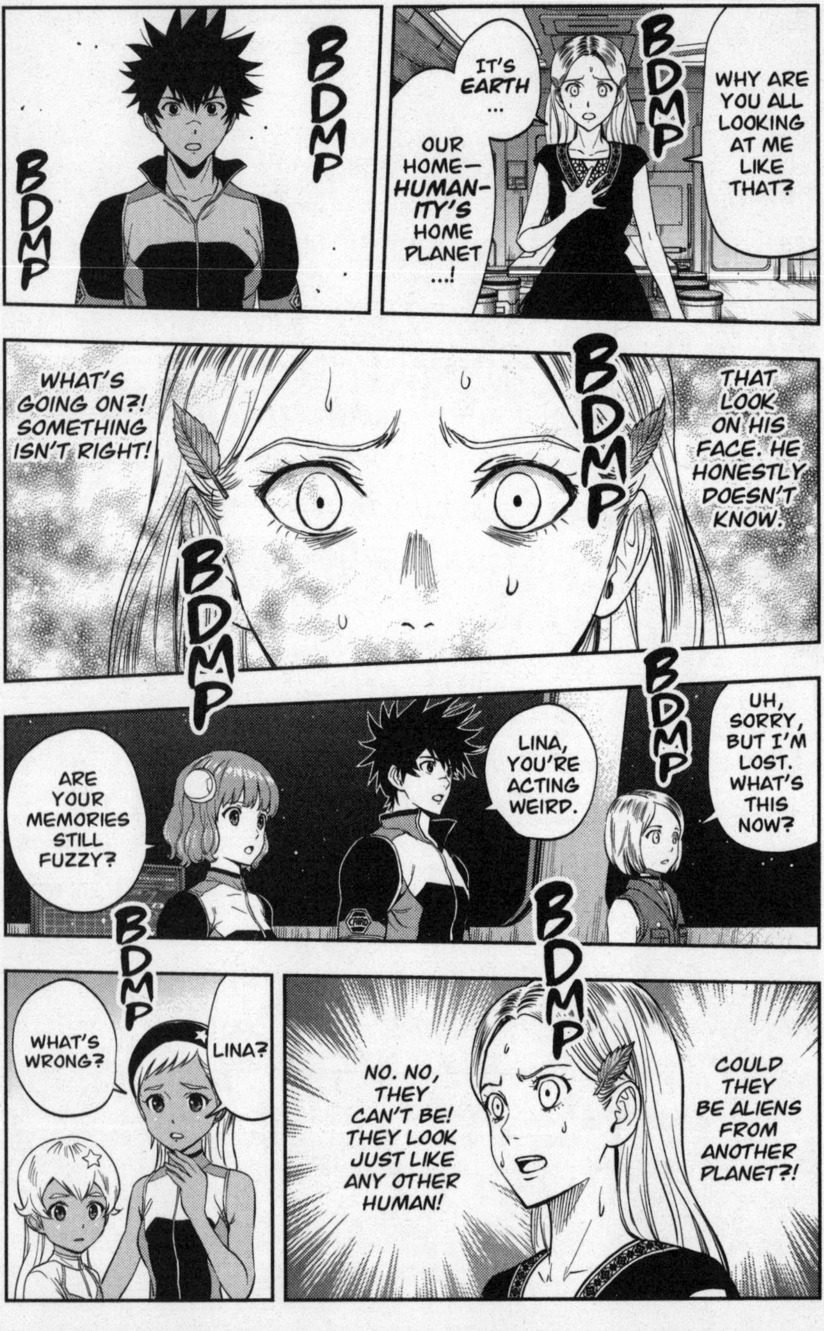
BDMP
WHY ARE YOU ALL LOOKING AT ME LIKE THAT?
IT'S EARTH ...
OUR HOME— HUMAN-ITY'S HOME PLANET ...!
BDMP
BDMP
THAT LOOK ON HIS FACE. HE HONESTLY DOESN'T KNOW.
BDMP
WHAT'S GOING ON?! SOMETHING ISN'T RIGHT!
BDMP
BDMP
UH, SORRY, BUT I'M LOST. WHAT'S THIS NOW?
LINA, YOU'RE ACTING WEIRD.
ARE YOUR MEMORIES STILL FUZZY?
BDMP
COULD THEY BE ALIENS FROM ANOTHER PLANET?!
NO. NO, THEY CAN'T BE! THEY LOOK JUST LIKE ANY OTHER HUMAN!
BDMP
LINA?
WHAT'S WRONG?
BDMP

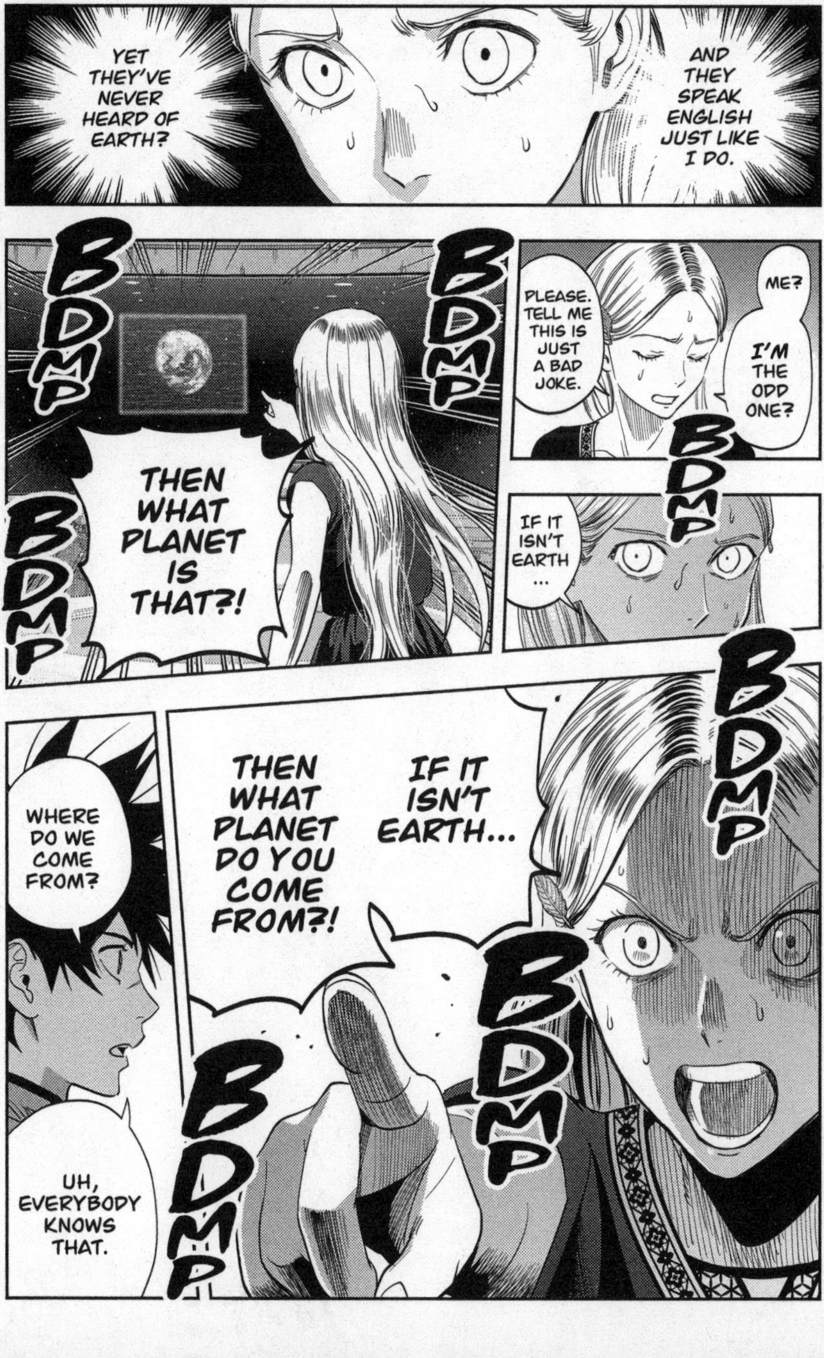
AND THEY SPEAK ENGLISH JUST LIKE I DO.
YET THEY'VE NEVER HEARD OF EARTH?
BDMP
ME?
I'M THE ODD ONE?
PLEASE. TELL ME THIS IS JUST A BAD JOKE.
BDMP
IF IT ISN'T EARTH ...
BDMP
THEN WHAT PLANET IS THAT?!
BDMP
BDMP
IF IT ISN'T EARTH...
THEN WHAT PLANET DO YOU COME FROM?!
BDMP
BDMP
WHERE DO WE COME FROM?
UH, EVERYBODY KNOWS THAT.

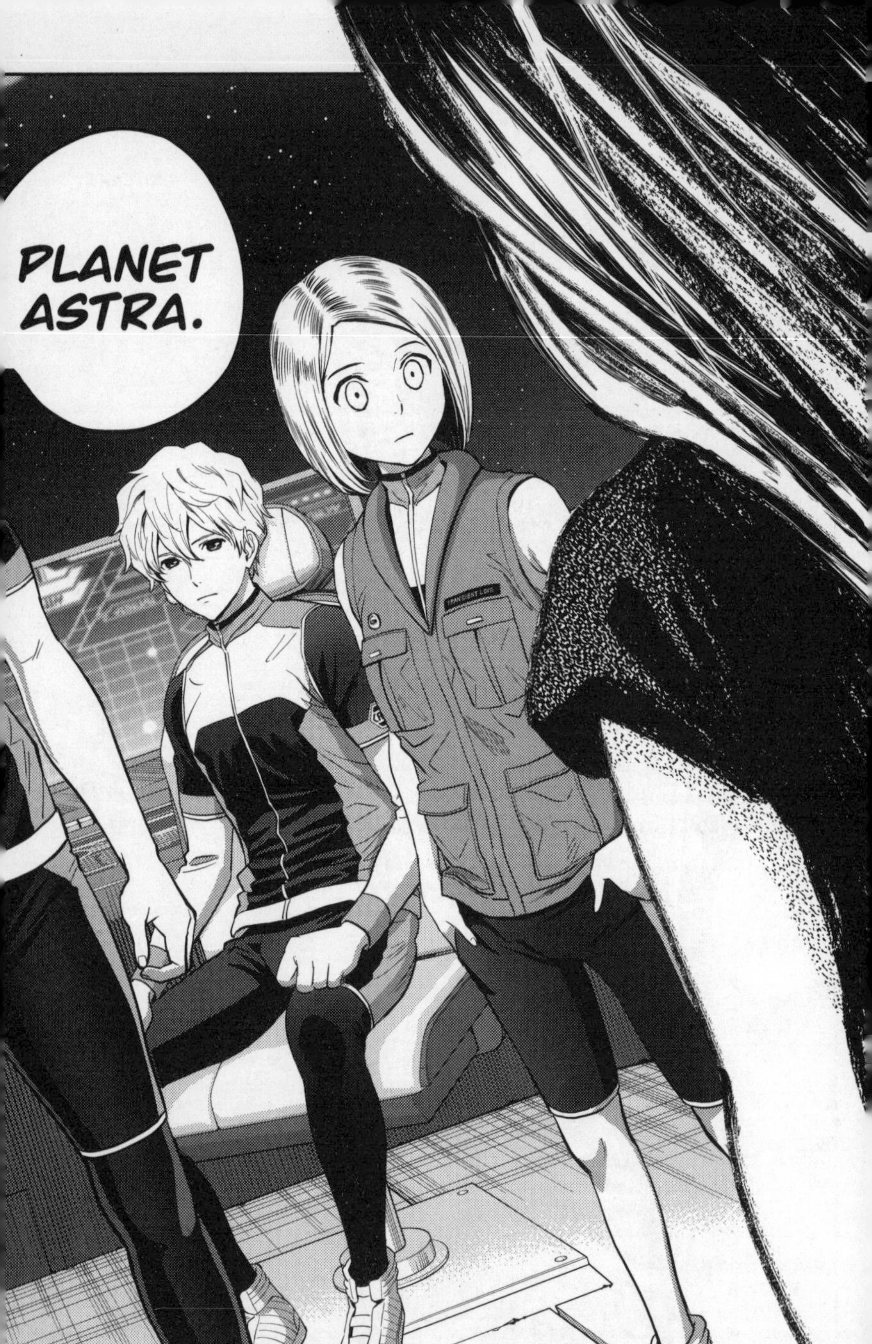
PLANET ASTRA.

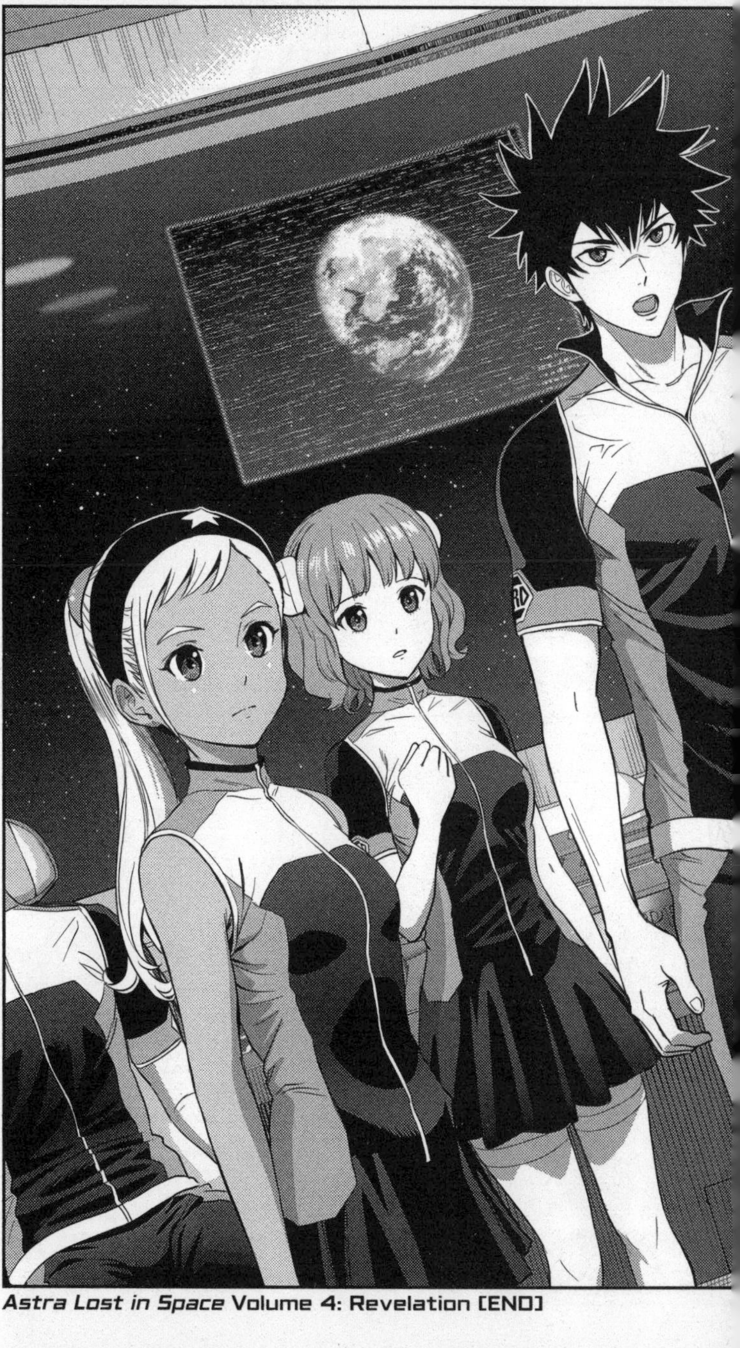

Astra Lost in Space Volume 4: Revelation [END]

Luca's Having Fun

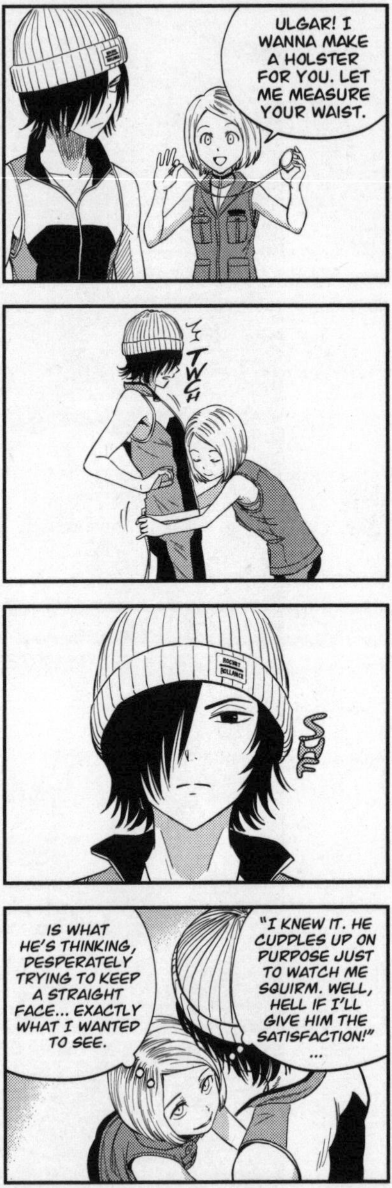
ULGAR! I WANNA MAKE A HOLSTER FOR YOU. LET ME MEASURE YOUR WAIST.
TWCH
"I KNEW IT. HE CUDDLES UP ON PURPOSE JUST TO WATCH ME SQUIRM. WELL, HELL IF I'LL GIVE HIM THE SATISFACTION!" ...
IS WHAT HE'S THINKING, DESPERATELY TRYING TO KEEP A STRAIGHT FACE... EXACTLY WHAT I WANTED TO SEE.

Luca's Having Fun 2

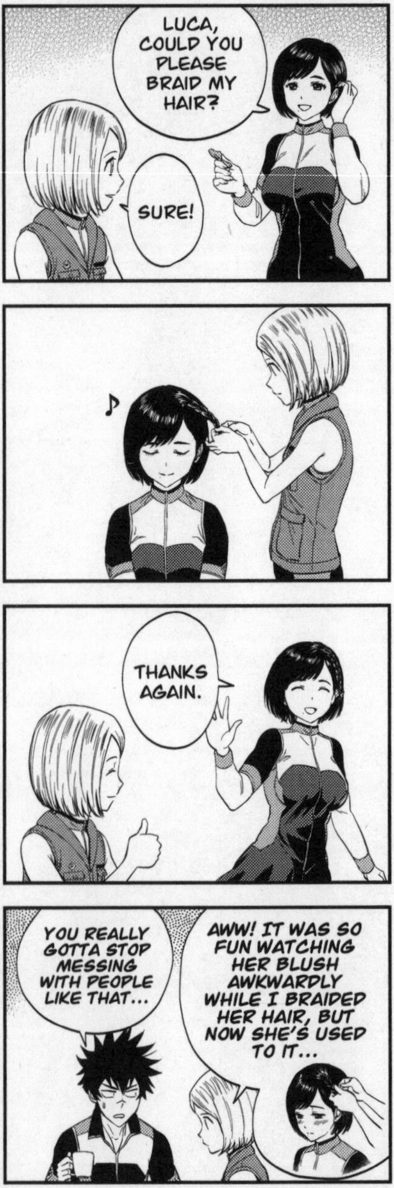
LUCA, COULD YOU PLEASE BRAID MY HAIR?
SURE!
♪
THANKS AGAIN.
AWW! IT WAS SO FUN WATCHING HER BLUSH AWKWARDLY WHILE I BRAIDED HER HAIR, BUT NOW SHE'S USED TO IT...
YOU REALLY GOTTA STOP MESSING WITH PEOPLE LIKE THAT...

Drawing Manga Characters from Memory Contest

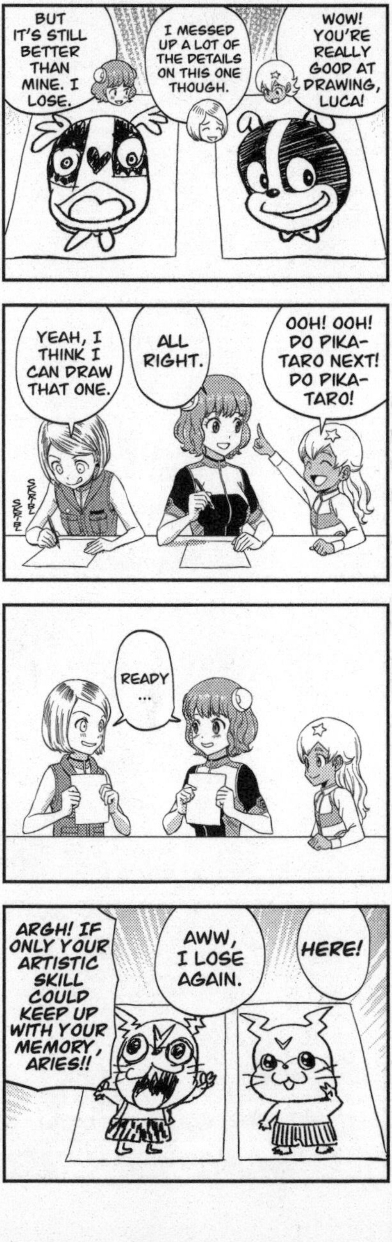
WOW! YOU'RE REALLY GOOD AT DRAWING, LUCA!
I MESSED UP A LOT OF THE DETAILS ON THIS ONE THOUGH.
BUT IT'S STILL BETTER THAN MINE. I LOSE.
OOH! OOH! DO PIKA-TARO NEXT! DO PIKA-TARO!
ALL RIGHT.
YEAH, I THINK I CAN DRAW THAT ONE.
SKRIBL SKRIBL
READY...
HERE!
AWW, I LOSE AGAIN.
ARGH! IF ONLY YOUR ARTISTIC SKILL COULD KEEP UP WITH YOUR MEMORY, ARIES!!

Peeping Tom...?

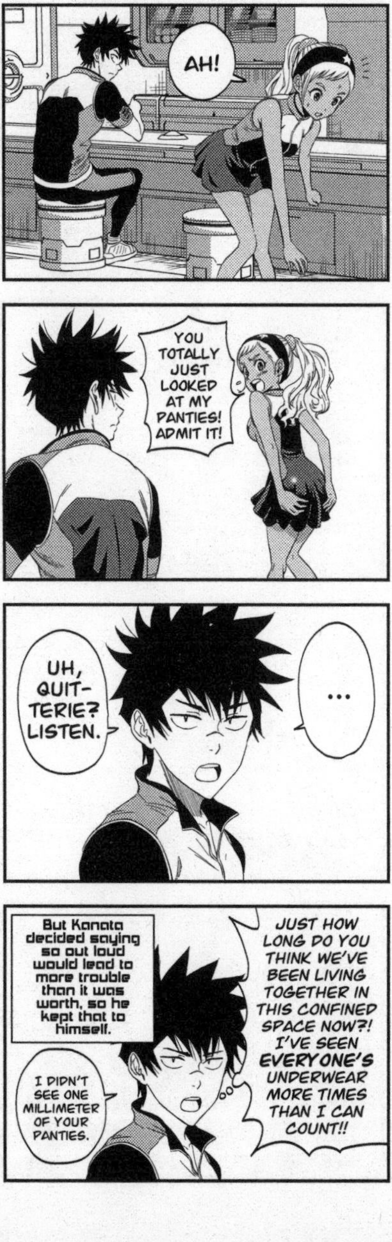
AH!
YOU TOTALLY JUST LOOKED AT MY PANTIES! ADMIT IT!
...
UH, QUIT-TERIE? LISTEN.
JUST HOW LONG DO YOU THINK WE'VE BEEN LIVING TOGETHER IN THIS CONFINED SPACE NOW?! I'VE SEEN EVERYONE'S UNDERWEAR MORE TIMES THAN I CAN COUNT!!
But Kanata decided saying so out loud would lead to more trouble than it was worth, so he kept that to himself.
I DIDN'T SEE ONE MILLIMETER OF YOUR PANTIES.

Snack Wars

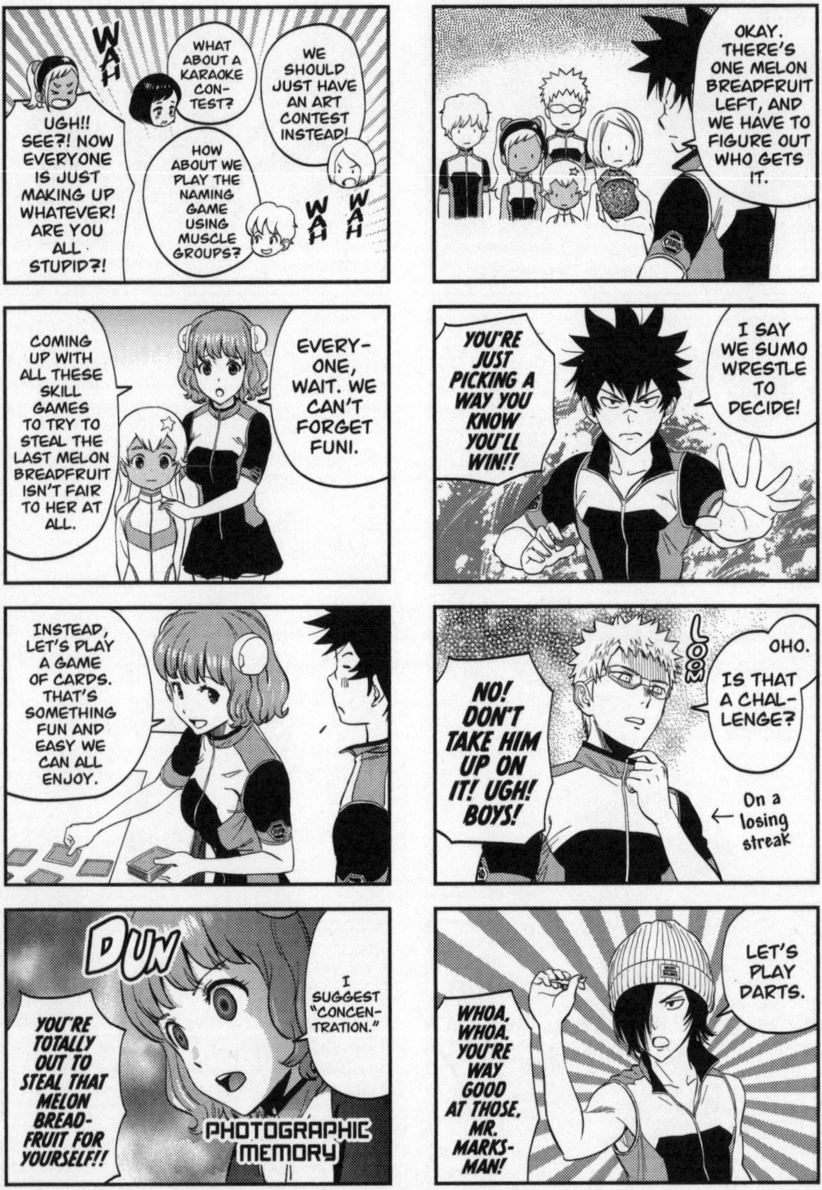
OKAY. THERE'S ONE MELON BREADFRUIT LEFT, AND WE HAVE TO FIGURE OUT WHO GETS IT.
I SAY WE SUMO WRESTLE TO DECIDE!
YOU'RE JUST PICKING A WAY YOU KNOW YOU'LL WIN!!
OHO.
IS THAT A CHALLENGE?
LOOM
NO! DON'T TAKE HIM UP ON IT! UGH! BOYS!
On a losing streak
LET'S PLAY DARTS.
WHOA, WHOA. YOU'RE WAY GOOD AT THOSE, MR. MARKSMAN!
WE SHOULD JUST HAVE AN ART CONTEST INSTEAD!
WAH
WAH
WHAT ABOUT A KARAOKE CONTEST?
HOW ABOUT WE PLAY THE NAMING GAME USING MUSCLE GROUPS?
WAH
UGH!! SEE?! NOW EVERYONE IS JUST MAKING UP WHATEVER! ARE YOU ALL STUPID?!
EVERYONE, WAIT. WE CAN'T FORGET FUNI.
COMING UP WITH ALL THESE SKILL GAMES TO TRY TO STEAL THE LAST MELON BREADFRUIT ISN'T FAIR TO HER AT ALL.
INSTEAD, LET'S PLAY A GAME OF CARDS. THAT'S SOMETHING FUN AND EASY WE CAN ALL ENJOY.
I SUGGEST "CONCENTRATION."
DUN
YOU'RE TOTALLY OUT TO STEAL THAT MELON BREADFRUIT FOR YOURSELF!!
PHOTOGRAPHIC MEMORY

Taking the Initiative 1

EVERYONE, LET ME INTRODUCE YOU TO OUR NEW CREW MEMBER, POLINA LIVINSKAYA.
YAAAAAY
WOO WOO
FWEE-WEE
CLAP CLAP CLAP CLAP
SHF SHF SHF SHF
WHERE ARE YOU FROM?
HOW OLD ARE YOU?
YOU HAVE SUCH PRETTY WHITE SKIN!
WHAT'S YOUR FAVORITE INTERNAL ORGAN?
WHOA, WHOA! SHE HASN'T FULLY RECOVERED YET!
QUIT BOMBARDING HER WITH QUESTIONS AND GIVE HER SPACE TO BREATHE, OKAY?!
WOULD YOU CARE TO JOIN ME FOR A BATH THIS EVENING?
AND QUIT TRYING TO CON HER BEFORE SHE KNOWS!!

Taking the Initiative 2

SO YOU WERE THE ARK VI'S ENGINEER? I SEE.
THEN I HAVE A FEW QUESTIONS FOR YOU.
AHA. I SEE.
SO THAT'S HOW THAT WORKS.
THANKS. THIS IS ENLIGHTENING. I'M GLAD YOU'RE HERE.
CHIT CHAT CHIT CHAT
JUST SO YOU KNOW, HE AND CHARCE ARE AN ITEM.
REALLY?

My Boyfriend's a Nitpicker

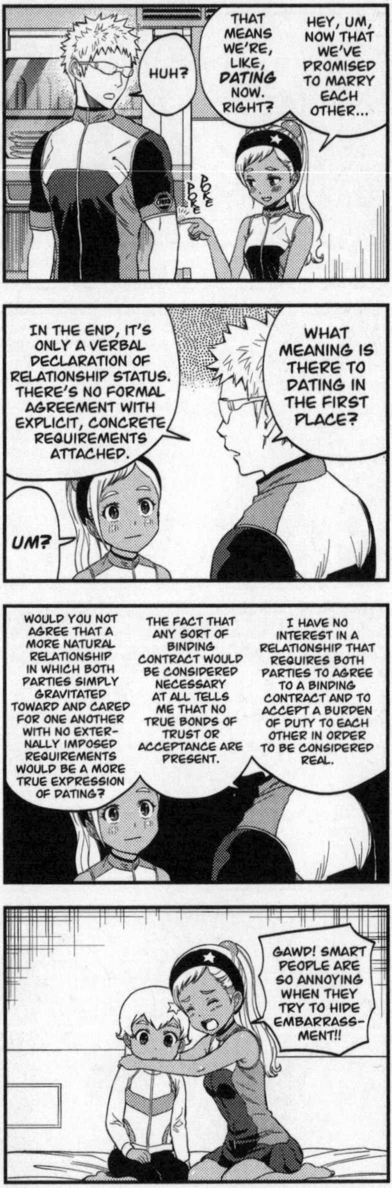
HEY, UM, NOW THAT WE'VE PROMISED TO MARRY EACH OTHER...
THAT MEANS WE'RE, LIKE, *DATING* NOW. RIGHT?
HUH?
POKE POKE
WHAT MEANING IS THERE TO DATING IN THE FIRST PLACE?
IN THE END, IT'S ONLY A VERBAL DECLARATION OF RELATIONSHIP STATUS. THERE'S NO FORMAL AGREEMENT WITH EXPLICIT, CONCRETE REQUIREMENTS ATTACHED.
UM?
I HAVE NO INTEREST IN A RELATIONSHIP THAT REQUIRES BOTH PARTIES TO AGREE TO A BINDING CONTRACT AND TO ACCEPT A BURDEN OF DUTY TO EACH OTHER IN ORDER TO BE CONSIDERED REAL.
THE FACT THAT ANY SORT OF BINDING CONTRACT WOULD BE CONSIDERED NECESSARY AT ALL TELLS ME THAT NO TRUE BONDS OF TRUST OR ACCEPTANCE ARE PRESENT.
WOULD YOU NOT AGREE THAT A MORE NATURAL RELATIONSHIP IN WHICH BOTH PARTIES SIMPLY GRAVITATED TOWARD AND CARED FOR ONE ANOTHER WITH NO EXTERNALLY IMPOSED REQUIREMENTS WOULD BE A MORE TRUE EXPRESSION OF DATING?
GAWD! SMART PEOPLE ARE SO ANNOYING WHEN THEY TRY TO HIDE EMBARRASSMENT!!

"How Old Are You, Polina?"

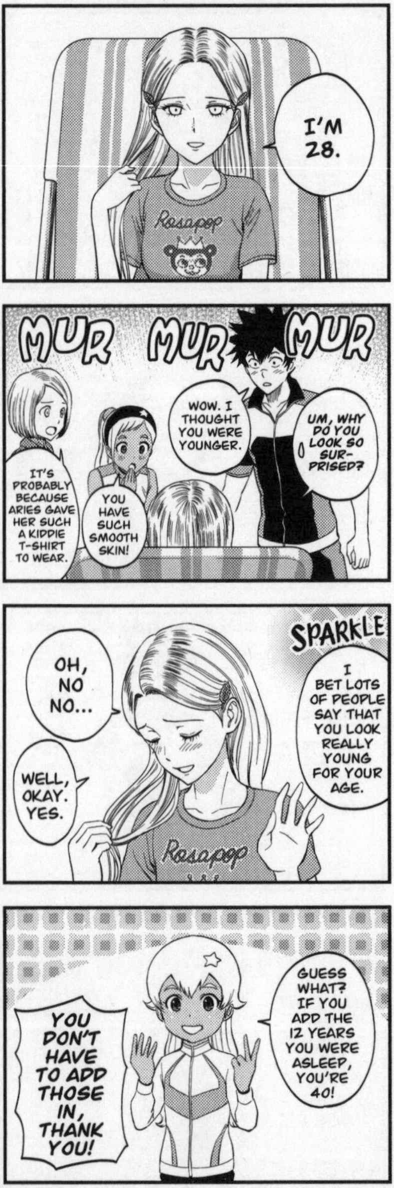
I'M 28.
Rosapop
MUR MUR MUR
UM, WHY DO YOU LOOK SO SURPRISED?
WOW. I THOUGHT YOU WERE YOUNGER.
YOU HAVE SUCH SMOOTH SKIN!
IT'S PROBABLY BECAUSE ARIES GAVE HER SUCH A KIDDIE T-SHIRT TO WEAR.
SPARKLE
I BET LOTS OF PEOPLE SAY THAT YOU LOOK REALLY YOUNG FOR YOUR AGE.
OH, NO NO...
WELL, OKAY. YES.
Rosapop
GUESS WHAT? IF YOU ADD THE 12 YEARS YOU WERE ASLEEP, YOU'RE 40!
YOU DON'T HAVE TO ADD THOSE IN, THANK YOU!

He's Used to It

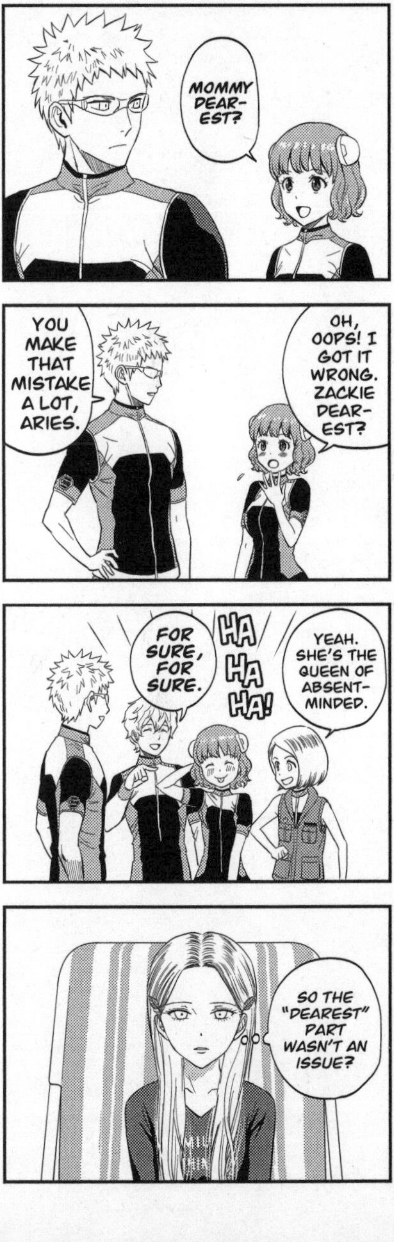
MOMMY DEAREST?
OH, OOPS! I GOT IT WRONG. ZACKIE DEAREST?
YOU MAKE THAT MISTAKE A LOT, ARIES.
YEAH. SHE'S THE QUEEN OF ABSENT-MINDED.
HA HA HA!
FOR SURE, FOR SURE.
SO THE "DEAREST" PART WASN'T AN ISSUE?

Midnight Visitor

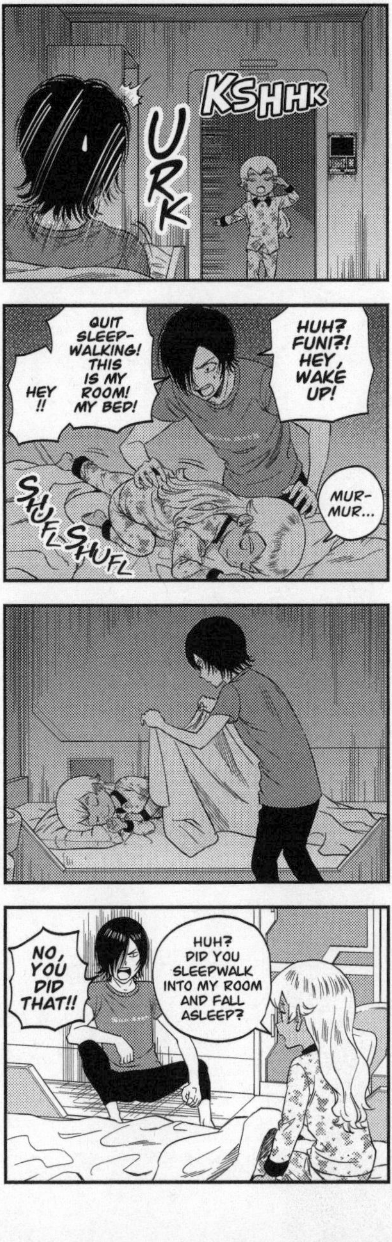
KSHHHK
URK
HUH? FUNI?! HEY, WAKE UP!
MUR-MUR...
QUIT SLEEP-WALKING! THIS IS MY ROOM! MY BED!
HEY!!
SHUFL SHUFL
HUH? DID YOU SLEEPWALK INTO MY ROOM AND FALL ASLEEP?
NO, YOU DID THAT!!

KENTA SHINOHARA started his manga career as an assistant to the legendary creator Hideaki Sorachi of **Gin Tama**. In 2006, he wrote and published a one-shot, **Sket Dance**, that began serialization in 2007 in **Weekly Shonen Jump** in Japan. **Sket Dance** went on to win the 55th Shogakukan Manga Award in the shonen manga category and inspired an anime in 2011. Shinohara began writing **Astra Lost in Space** in 2016 for **Jump+**.

ASTRA
LOST IN SPACE 4

SHONEN JUMP MANGA EDITION

STORY AND ART BY KENTA SHINOHARA

Translation/Adrienne Beck
Touch-Up Art & Lettering/Annaliese Christman
Design/Julian [JR] Robinson
Editor/Marlene First

NEXT PLANET

Printed in the U.S.A.

Published by VIZ Media, LLC
P.O. Box 77010
San Francisco, CA 94107

10 9 8 7 6 5 4 3 2 1
First printing, September 2018

viz.com

shonenjump.com

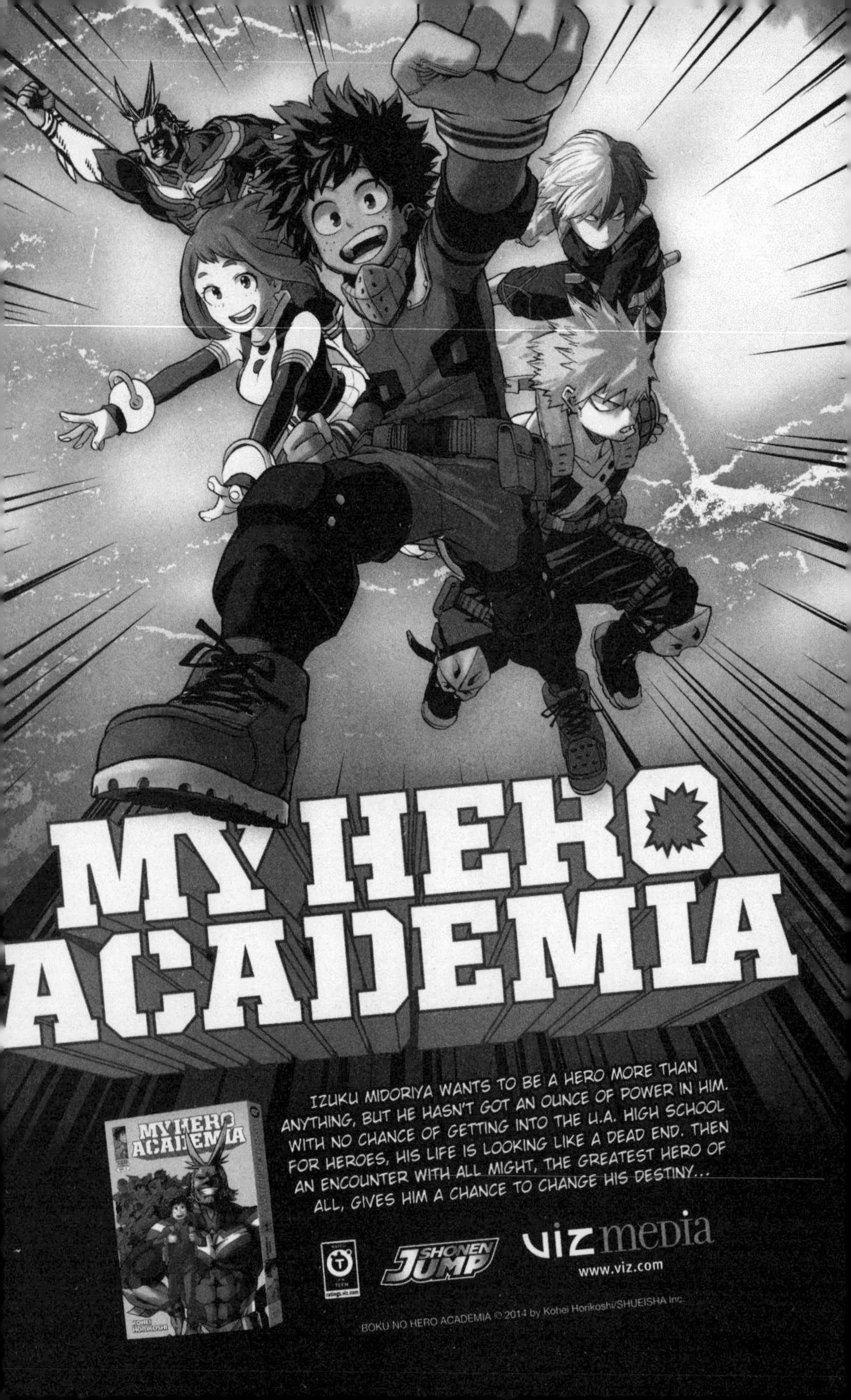
MY HERO ACADEMIA
IZUKU MIDORIYA WANTS TO BE A HERO MORE THAN ANYTHING, BUT HE HASN'T GOT AN OUNCE OF POWER IN HIM. WITH NO CHANCE OF GETTING INTO THE U.A. HIGH SCHOOL FOR HEROES, HIS LIFE IS LOOKING LIKE A DEAD END. THEN AN ENCOUNTER WITH ALL MIGHT, THE GREATEST HERO OF ALL, GIVES HIM A CHANCE TO CHANGE HIS DESTINY...
SHONEN JUMP
VIZ media
www.viz.com
BOKU NO HERO ACADEMIA © 2014 by Kohei Horikoshi/SHUEISHA Inc.

DRAGON BALL SUPER

STORY BY **Akira Toriyama**   ART BY **Toyotarou**

Goku's adventure from the best-selling classic manga *Dragon Ball* continues in this new series!

Ever since Goku became Earth's greatest hero and gathered the seven Dragon Balls to defeat the evil Boo, his life on Earth has grown a little dull. But new threats loom overhead, and Goku and his friends will have to defend the planet once again!

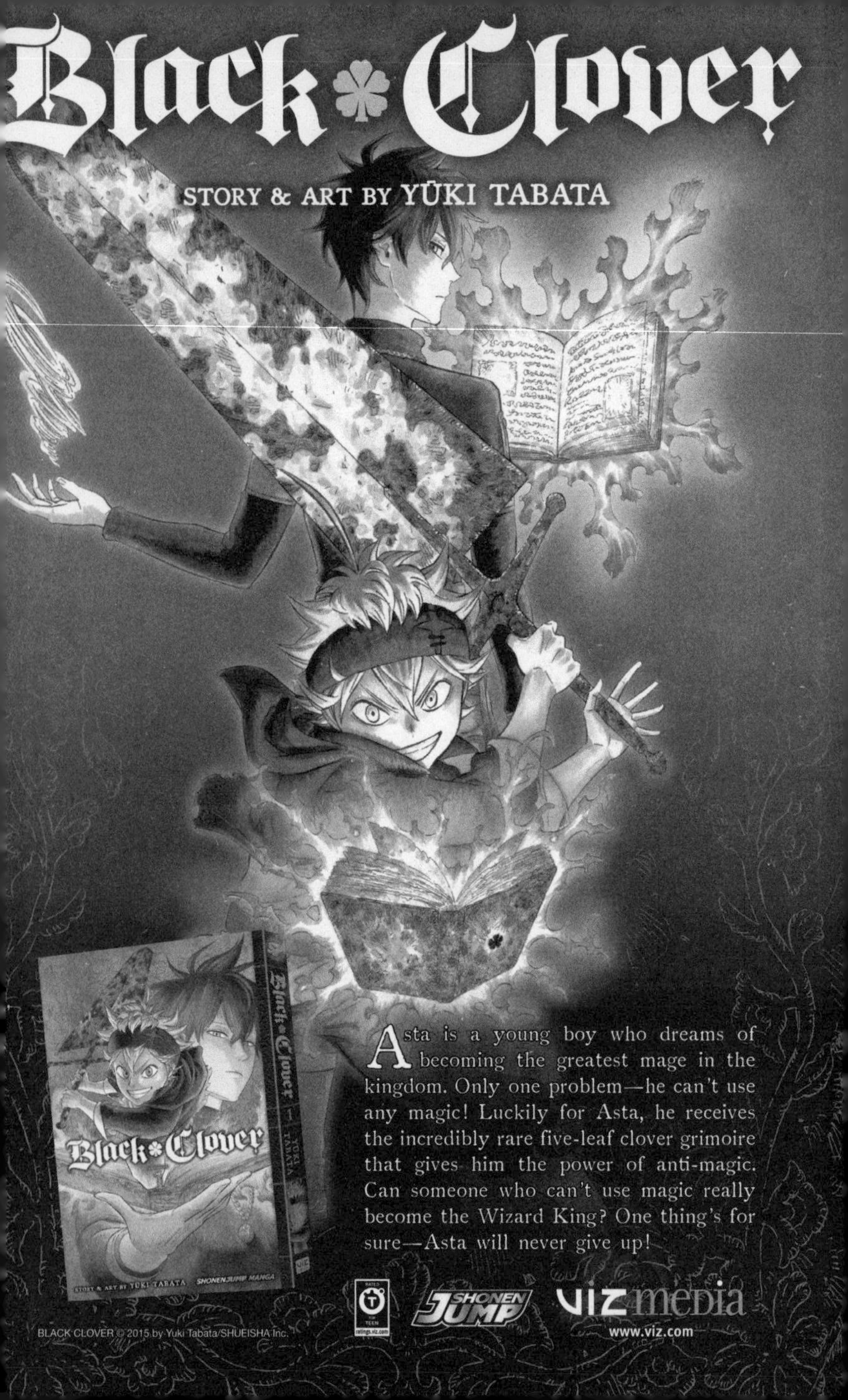
Black Clover
STORY & ART BY YŪKI TABATA
Asta is a young boy who dreams of becoming the greatest mage in the kingdom. Only one problem—he can't use any magic! Luckily for Asta, he receives the incredibly rare five-leaf clover grimoire that gives him the power of anti-magic. Can someone who can't use magic really become the Wizard King? One thing's for sure—Asta will never give up!
Black Clover
YUKI TABATA
STORY & ART BY YUKI TABATA
SHONEN JUMP MANGA
RATED T FOR TEEN
ratings.viz.com
SHONEN JUMP
VIZ media
www.viz.com
BLACK CLOVER © 2015 by Yuki Tabata/SHUEISHA Inc.

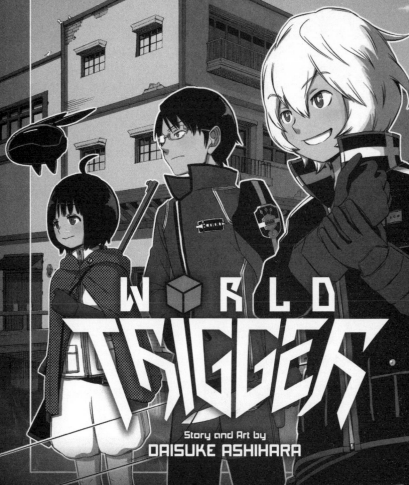

Story and Art by
DAISUKE ASHIHARA

DESTROY THY NEIGHBOR!

A gate to another dimension has burst open, and invincible monsters called Neighbors invade Earth. Osamu Mikumo may not be the best among the elite warriors who co-opt other-dimensional technology to fight back, but along with his Neighbor friend Yuma, he'll do whatever it takes to defend life on Earth as we know it.

YOU'RE READING THE WRONG WAY!

Astra Lost in Space reads from right to left, starting in the upper-right corner. Japanese is read from right to left, meaning that action, sound effects and word-balloon order are completely reversed from English order.

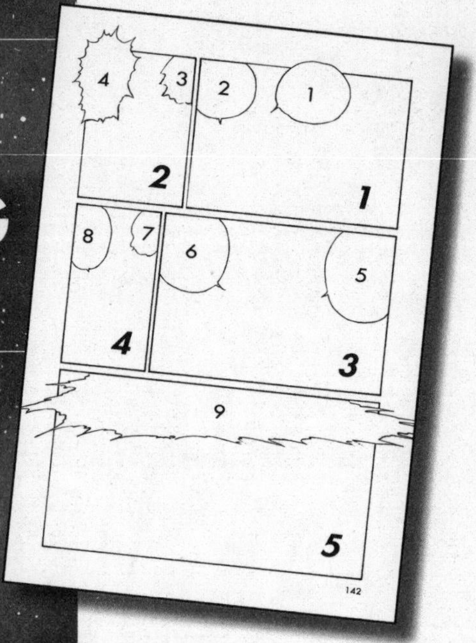
1
2
3
4
1
2
5
6
7
8
3
4
9
5
142

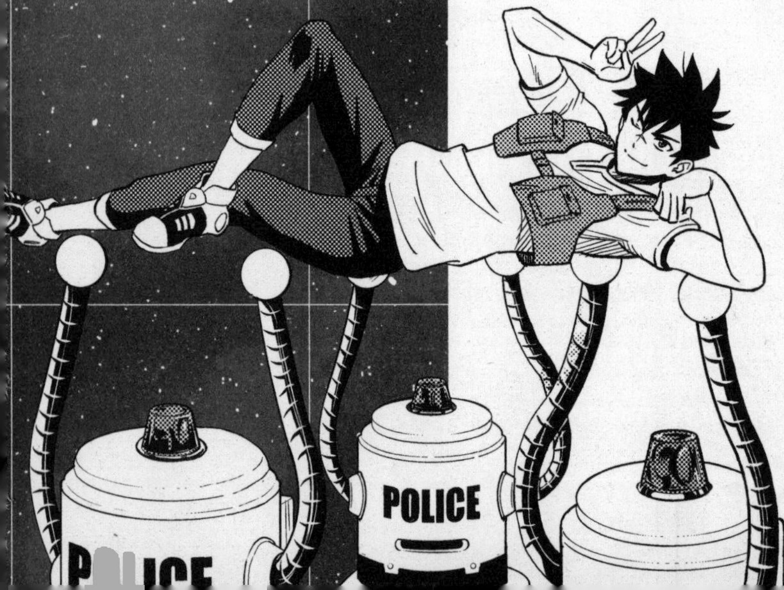
POLICE